They Went That-A-Way

101 Forgotten Westerns to Remember by
Douglas Brode

They Went That-A-Way
Copyright ©2022 Douglas Brode. All Rights Reserved.

No part of this book may be reproduced in any form or by any means, electronic, mechanical, digital, photocopying or recording, except for the inclusion in a review, without permission in writing from the publisher.

This book is an independent work of research and commentary and is not sponsored, authorized or endorsed by, or otherwise affiliated with, any motion picture studio or production company affiliated with the films discussed herein. All uses of the name, image, and likeness of any individuals, and all copyrights and trademarks referenced in this book, are for editorial purposes and are pursuant of the Fair Use Doctrine.

The views and opinions of individuals quoted in this book do not necessarily reflect those of the author.

The promotional photographs and publicity materials reproduced herein are in the author's private collection (unless noted otherwise). These images date from the original release of the films and were released to media outlets for publicity purposes.

Published in the USA by
BearManor Media
1317 Edgewater Dr. #110
Orlando, FL 32804
www.BearManorMedia.com

Softcover Edition
ISBN-10:
ISBN-13: 978-1-62933-918-4

Printed in the United States of America

for my son
Shane Johnson Brode
who grew as strong and straight
as his namesake

FROM HISTORY THROUGH LEGEND TO MYTH: The exploits of William F. Cody were romanticized initially for the live Wild West show, then further glorified in what might well be considered the first epic-sized Oater.

Introduction:

Lost And Found ...

The names of classic Westerns, from way long ago or more recently, bring back warm/strong memories for fans of the genre: *Shane, Hondo, High Noon, Unforgiven, Red River, Gunfight at the O.K. Corral, Fort Apache, True Grit, No Country for Old Men, Rio Bravo, The Searchers, Once Upon a Time in the West, Open Range, Tombstone ...*

FROM MARGINAL SIDESHOW TO MAINSTREAM ENTERTAINMENT:
The humble Nickelodeons that offered primitive flickers, Westerns included, at the turn of the century swiftly gave way to the golden age of motion picture palaces, where Oaters remained popular.

Though created by individual artists at various junctures in the history of motion pictures, they merge together into a single concept, once known by a wonderfully humble term: The Oater. Referring to the grains fed to a remuda (and on occasion cattle) in a form of narrative that came to be perceived as The Origination Fable for the United States of America. Tall tales and true, as Walt Disney once proclaimed about his own "Frontierland" sequences on television and theatrical Westerns, from our collective past. Once upon a time at the movies, such works united us as no other sort of film could. Featuring all-American heroes who were counted on to ride to the rescue, if at the last possible moment, then act decisively, boldly, fairly, and (most characteristically of all for our nation) *conclusively*. Now, and for those very same reasons that this genre once brought us together, The Western is as likely as to divide a populace as shattered, fragmented, and polarized as our 21st century politics have become.

"I don't believe in heroes anymore," actor/director Dennis Hopper (himself a veteran of some of those aforementioned classics) claimed on the release of his contemporary biker-Western, *Easy Rider* (1969). His own character offered a variation on the outlaw 'Billy the Kid' (whom Hopper had portrayed several times) while co-star Peter Fonda went by the name of 'Wyatt.' That can hardly help but bring back memories of an actual lawman (Earp) whom this young star's father had played as a tall, decent, iconic Man of the West in John Ford's *My Darling Clementine* (1946). In the context of Hopper's New Youth Film, Wyatt is not a hero to the community but an enemy of the people. *Easy Rider* was, of course, a huge hit during that year when all old American values came to be questioned.

And, in truth, things have never been the same since.

Today, a Western is as likely to reveal our wide, broad, deep social and cultural divisions as the old films such as *Drums Along the Mohawk* (1939) revealed our once characteristic ability to, at times of extreme duress, momentarily set aside any essential belief in rugged individualism and come together as a tight-knit community, if only for purposes of survival. Then go our own separate ways again, as the early settlers of upstate New York do. Does any

TOUGH GUYS: What Robert Warshow once defined as 'The Westerner' (part historic, part myth) has been defined by diverse male actors; Top row: Rory Calhoun, Royal Dano, Bill Williams; Middle Row; Jim Brown, Chief Thundercloud, Joseph Calleia; Bottom line: Tom Mix, Bob Steele, Sterling Hayden.

THE OFT-TOLD TALE ... ARGONAUTICA AMERICANA: Recurring images from the Hollywood studio era through to the later 'indies' allows the Western to offer a ritualistic continuum; the long ride across a hostile wilderness leads not only to a geographical destination but a symbolic reckoning with the antihero's difficult, confused sense of self in *Along the Great Divide* and *Ride (in) the Whirlwind.*

single movie so encapsulate that ideology as this Ford classic, with its epilogue about our then-new flag: A circle of stars for the union; evenly divided stripes for states' rights.

No genre, though, can be fully understood by the agreed upon milestones that even today remain with us thanks to cable TV channels, DVDs

They Went That-A-Way

'WESTWARD HO, THE WOMEN!' The female characters in Western films are as diverse in terms of personality and ethnicity as are the men: Top Row: Joanne Dru, Marjorie Main, Beulah Archeletta; Middle Row: Karen Steele, Loretta Young, Margaret O'Brien; Bottom Row: Gene Tierney, Jean Arthur, Katy Jurado.

(which may be around for a while longer), and ultra-modern forms such as STREAMING. But what of other pictures, many enjoyed and admired on initial release, which still exist . . . but for reasons sometimes easy, in other occurrences difficult, to explain no longer blink like shining stars in our memories of the genre?

"Say," and old friend and fellow Cowboy Movie Buff might whisper to a pal over a beer at the local watering place, "what was the name of that picture where Burt Lancaster and his kid set out in search of new horizons in the far west?"

"Why," comes the reply, "I haven't thought of that in years. It's . . . it's . . ."

"*The Kentuckian*," a third voice insists. Then there's a discussion of the most memorable sequences which once again burn brightly in the mind's eye; The star vs. villain Walter Matthau in what may be the most memorable whipping/fighting sequence in film history; the precise loading of an old one-shot rifle by a desperate man knowing that his nemesis is coming toward him fast, and for the kill, if he doesn't complete the process in time . . .

Once recalled, that dimly remembered 1955 gem is difficult to stop thinking about. Worth seeking as it is indeed still 'out there.' Like so many other 'forgotten' though not in truth 'gone' movies, waiting to be rediscovered. The purpose of this book? To set cineastes off on lonesome trails in hopes of locating one or more. Bringin' 'em back for a last roundup, so to speak.

Note, though: At some point during the late 1960s and early 1970s the Western altered, shifted, evolved, or de-evolved depending on any observer's point-of-view. The distinction between the classic Oater and its contemporary manifestation can be illustrated by lines of dialogue from films that define the one or other. "Ah, for the good old days that's gone," 'Sgt. Quincannon' (Victor McLaglen) sighs to a younger companion in Ford's *She Wore a Yellow Ribbon* (1949). The old timer's voice rings with Irish sentiment and American nostalgia while observing the last of the buffalo pass out of sight, and almost out of history. "There never were any good ol' days," Jack Beauregard' (Henry Fonda) explains to a young friend in producer Sergio Leone's *My Name is Nobody* (1973). A sense of profound pessimism underlines that comment.

THE OFT TOLD TALE ... THE HANGIN' TREE: Few issues pertaining to the West as it really existed are as controversial as the concept of Lynch Law, defended in *The Virginian* by Owen Wister, later criticized in *The Ox Bow Incident* by Walter Van Tilburg Clarke: Hollywood examples include *Along the Great Divide* and *Ride (in) The Whirlwind*.

Cynicism vs. sentimentality. Those ideologies define the movies that contain them and speak directly to the audience on any film's initial release. Westerns (all 'moving pictures,' in fact) both comment on and create the Zeitgeist in the era during which they were/are created, much as old novels or paintings and statues in a museum immortalize some bygone vision for the future.

SMALL SCREEN STARS: With the advent of television, the "B" Western gradually diminished in popularity as companies such as Warner Bros. set their second unit teams to work filling the great appetite for product of this new medium: left to right, Clint Walker (*Cheyenne*), Wayde Preston (*Colt. 45*), Ty Hardin (*Bronco*); Jack Kelly (*Maverick*) John Russell *(Lawman)*; James Garner (*Maverick*), Peter Brown (*Lawman*), Will Hutchins (*Sugarfoot*).

Of course, any book on a film genre must be prefaced by a definition of the essential term---here, The Western---at least in context of the volume and its ambitions, according to the author. That's not such an easy task, for there are far-ranging interpretations that not only contradict one another but bring out the fightin' side of aficionados. Serious 'fans' have their own strong opinions as to what constitutes a *true* example of what simultaneously exists as popular mass entertainment and an original American art form.

For conservative followers of such films, literary critic Mark Malatesta in 2018 offered a simple but effective statement:

stories that take place in the American Old West (and which) commonly include bounty hunters, gunfighters, outlaws, cowboys, settlers, brothels, whores, card games, horses, Native Americans (Indians), Civil War elements, and saloons. The settings in the western genre are often small out of the way towns with few people . . .Most are commonly set in some sort of wild, natural landscape that's hard to survive in: cold mountains with dangerous animals or dry deserts with poisonous snakes, constant sun, and possible dehydration.

Yet with Malatesta's definition in mind, would *Hud* (1963) qualify as a Western? After all, its cowboys are situated on a 20th century (rather than "Old West") stretch of Texas. Eliminate that adjective *Old* and that film 'works.' Adhere to the term and *Hud* does not. On the far side of this discussion, liberal voices recall that when aspiring TV avatar Gene Rodenberry first pitched *Star Trek* to NBC in the mid-1960s, he did so thusly: "*Wagon Train* in space." Explaining why each episode of that original series took place on what was postulated in "Space: The Final Frontier." Likewise, George Lucas included a shoot-out between 'Han Solo' and 'Boba Fett' in his first *Star Wars* that draws on *The Gunfighter* (1950) and so many other ritualized re-enactments.

Finally, there is a middle ground that insists *Hud* and *The Last Picture Show* (1971; both inspired by Larry McMurtry novels) constitute reasonable extensions of the genre. As to *Trek* and *Wars?* They represent "Space" rather than "Horse" Operas, a different genre that partakes of and for many replaces the traditional Oater, at least for a generation that has apparently lost interest in history.

This book will take such a middle position, including films set in the post-1900 American West if not outright science fiction or epic fantasy, per se. Nor will, say, Samurai epics---often considered, and rightly so, 'Eastern Westerns' owing to their derivation from the American form—be included. Yet a different sort of 'Eastern Western' *will* apper. If Owen Wister's *The Virginian* is often considered the first 'serious' narrative about the trans-Mississippi West (Dime Novels by sub-literary types such as Ned Buntline proliferating long before that), James Fenimore Cooper's Leatherstocking Quintet--*The Last of the Mohicans* best-remembered among them----still stands as the most accessible tale from a time when our geographical 'East' qualified as our symbolic 'West': The unexplored frontiers of upstate New York, Kentucky and Tennessee, and western territories in Pennsylvania still constituting 'the forest primeval,' to borrow from Longfellow.

HOW THE WEST WAS FUN: The action-filled Saturday Morning Cliffhanger brought the Oater to a 'popcorn, soda, and candy crowd' on a weekly basis during the 1930s and 1940s; during the following decade, such giddy entertainment would be revived for weekday after-school television programming.

But to end where we began . . . what about those fascinating films that don't make the cut? A decade ago, I was asked to help pick the 101 greatest Westerns, in collaboration with the editors of *American Cowboy* magazine, for a book published by Two-Dot Press. All those films mentioned at the start of this introduction were of course included. Every inch of the way, though, I . . . *we* . . . experienced frustration as to the many others that ought to at least receive honorable mention. That helps explain why the phrase "and a few you've never heard of" to the title. Well, here are a whole lot more (from early silent days to recent though unappreciated projects) deserving of your attention.

Like any antiquities from the past, Oaters (still my favorite term for such work, however forgotten today) must be evaluated in the context of the era during which they were made. Without such a critical frame, they and most other populist entertainments from the past will be subjected to Cancel Culture. In my analysis of each, I intend to provide just such points of reference. Hoping to lend these movies a new lease on life, if through a critical lens.

Douglas Brode
San Antonio, TX

1. ADVENTURES OF BUFFALO BILL, THE, aka LIFE OF BUFFALO BILL, THE (1917) Rating (Historical and Genre Significance): *****

CREDITS:

William Frederic Cody, numerous others, dir. (uncredited); Charles A. King, scr.; Cody, pro.; B&W; numerous running times; Essanay Film Manufacturing Company.

CAST:

'Buffalo Bill,' Louisa Frederici Cody, Frank D. Baldwin, Short Bull, Sitting Bull, Charles A. King, Jesse M. Lee, Marion P. Maus, Gen. Nelson Appleton Miles, H.G. Sickles, Chief Tall Bull (*selves*).

The Wild West, as we experience it within the realm of popular culture, properly begins with the man known as 'Buffalo Bill': William Frederic Cody (1846-1917). As a teenager, he rode for the Pony Express (1860-61), then became a buffalo hunter for the railroads and a scout for Gen. George Crook's frontier army during the Lakota war of 1876. In time, Cody became a popular 'star'/celebrity owing to dime novels that spread (and grossly exaggerated) his exploits. Eventually, Buffalo Bill starred as himself in a grand Wild West show that "brought the West to the East." And, shortly thereafter, to the world, during his successful European tours during the early 20th century.

ROUGH RIDERS OF THE WORLD: Those people of numerous races and varied countries who made up Buffalo Bill's large cast pose for a group picture, then enter the arena to entertain spectators while the cameras roll, Cody himself (far right) in the lead.

Coincidentally or by destiny, this was the same period during which motion pictures came into their own. In France, the Lumiere Brothers (Louis and Auguste) had begun shooting in the streets. 'Actualities,' these brief flickers were called. In all truth, the brothers directed their makeshift performers. Beginning with *Workers Leaving the Factory* (1895), real people playing themselves at the end of a day's work were coached to "be natural" as if this were an ordinary shift's end. Utterly impossible, as this was no normal day.

People either gazed directly at the camera or shied away from it. At any rate, in America, this notion was seized upon by Thomas A. Edison, who filmed belly dancers and acrobats, body builders and political speakers. Over at Essanay, Thomas Ince (1880-1924) followed suit, capturing special events for the public of that time who could not personally attend, also immortalizing the events on celluloid.

Not surprisingly, the camera was turned on acts present in Buffalo Bill's Wild West show, with its rodeos and Native American dancers. Also, carefully staged stunt performances of stagecoach pursuits by Indians and gunfighters shooting it out at high noon. Originally, short films of less than a minute were screened in the era's Nickelodeons, lining the thoroughfares of big cities. Meanwhile, the 'story film' had been created, early examples including *The Great Train Robbery* (1902/3) at Edison's Black Maria in New Jersey. By the time D.W. Griffith created his historical epic *The Birth of a Nation* (1915), feature films had become popular, particularly with the burgeoning immigrants who didn't understand English ... and, while attending this venue of entertainment, didn't need to.

A long-time friend of Cody's, Charles A. King, had an inspiration. The grand old man of the West was, by now, on his last legs. How fitting to take bits and pieces of earlier flickers, which included the now deceased Sitting Bull (1831-1890) during the time that he travelled with the show, also re-staging events from Cody's life. In some shots, the national hero would play himself. In others, a younger performer enacted 'Buffalo Bill.' There would also be images of Cody at home with his wife, the former Louisa Frederici (1844-1921), relaxing in their Wyoming home. One problem here: Bill and Louisa had experienced a turbulent marriage. As Cody had become an alcoholic owing to this and other personal (mostly financial) issues, the seemingly realistic portrait offered a great lie. At that moment, we might claim, the Hollywood sensibility was born. Never let real life get in the way of a great story.

Simultaneously, any distinction between history and myth met in a halfway point called 'legend.' In this case, the legend of America. Which shortly

AND STARRING AS THEMSELVES: Clockwise, from top left: Col. William F. Cody, Annie Oakley, Chief Sitting Bull, and Ned Buntline;.

became synonymous with the legend of The West. Indeed, all icons of frontier life depicted might be considered more mythic than realistic, even those that were accurately staged. Pitched battles between cavalrymen and Native People, even when offered up in the manner that such things did occasionally occur, had in fact been rare. Most people on the prairie were farmers, business people, townspersons, and miners. Only one percent ever witnessed anything so thrilling as a gunfight. One reason the O.K. Corral confrontation still looms large in the American consciousness is that on the afternoon of 10/26/1881, an incident in which two groups faced each other at close range and shot it out did indeed occur in Tombstone. Memorable, as a result of being so *a*-typical. As Evan S. Connell, author of *Son of the Morning Star* (1985) noted, the most appropriate term to describe everyday life on the frontier would be "boring"; except on those incalculable moments when all hell broke loose, such as at the Little Big Horn (6/25/1876).

Why did the Wild West shows and cowboy movies to follow *not* depict jobs: blacksmithing, nursing, school-teaching, management of general stores, or secretarial and legal work? As Alfred Hitchcock would state, movies are "life with the dull spots left out." Which included 99 per cent of what historically happened. So it was that one percent of what did occur came to represent for the masses the whole experience of 'westing.' Onstage in Cody's show between 1880-1915, then in a feature film shortly thereafter.

This, the first truly 'epic' Western (appearing six years before the better known *The Covered Wagon*), would set the pace for all to follow. In truth, if the Wild West show had been a recreation, then the filming of it offered a facsimile of that artifice; in today's terms, a simulacrum. At the time, few if any questioned the moral validity of what emerged as our great origination legend. Such terms as 'Anglo imperialism' or 'White Supremacy' in our own time cause the once (seemingly) glorious Manifest Destiny notion to be questioned and criticized. Even today, though, the remaining shards of this remarkable film, part documentary but also including fabrication, offer up celluloid bits and pieces of popular culture that enshrine a now hotly contested vision of what "the winning' of our frontiers had been all about.

2. ALL THE PRETTY HORSES (2000) RATING: ****

CREDITS:

Billy Bob Thornton, dir.; Ted Tally, scr.; Thornton, Robert Salerno, Bruce Heller, Sally Menke, many others, pro.; Larry Paxton, Marta Stuart, Kristen Williamson, mus.; Barry Markowitz, cin.; Menke, ed.; 2.39:1; C; 116 min. (theatrical release); 220 min. (director's cut); Columbia/ Miramax.

CAST:

Matt Damon *(John Grady Cole)*; Henry Thomas *(Lacey Rawlins)*; Penelope Cruz *(Alejandra Villarrarreal)*; Angelina (C.) Torres *(Luisa)*; J.D. Young *(Grandfather);* Laura Poe *(Mother);* Sam Shepard *(J.C. Franklin)*; Robert Patrick *(Cole)*; Lucas Back *(Jimmy Blevins)*; Yvette Diaz *(Girl)*; Ruben Blades *(Don Hector de la Rocha)*; Miriam Colon *(Doria Alfonso)*; Lonnie Rodriguez *(Esteban);* Augustin Solis *(Manuel)*; Bruce Dern *(Judge)*.

This film deserves acknowledgment as the first major attempt to revive the then-floundering Western genre for a new century. Not particularly well-received by critics, who largely found this a work full of "unrealized potential," *Horses* ikewise was not embraced by audiences. This, despite Matt Damon (1970-) and Penelope Cruz (1974-) having recently emerged as superstars. Director Billy Bob Thornton (1955-) had achieved a cult following with Western fans, largely owing to his brief but notable performance as a tin-horn gambler in *Tombstone* (1933). Like *No Country for Old Men* (2008) yet to come, *Horses* is based on a novel by Cormac McCarthy (1933-). Rhode Island born and Tennessee bred, that author has emerged as one of the most

"WHEN YOU RIDE WITH A MAN, YOU STICK WITH HIM!" A young cowboy (Matt Damon, center) rides South of the Border with two companions, one trustworthy, the other less so.

noteworthy 'serious' writers about Texas (the place, the people, the sensibility, and the 'way') since the golden age of Larry McMurtry.

One key element (this would *not* hold true for *No Country*) is that both book and movie fall into a unique subgenre which might be referred to as 'The Horse/Horseman Western,' films that consider the relationship of a rider to the animal that separates the American cowboy from a farmer. Examples include *Smoky* (1933, 1946, 1966), *The Wonderful Country* (1958), *Tonka* (1958), *Lonely Are the Brave* (1962), *The Appaloosa* (1966), and more recently *Mustang* (2015) and *The Rider* (2017). The concept is not limited to Westerns. Non-genre films that also explore the issue include *National Velvet* (1944) and numerous movies based on Anna Sewell's' 1877 novel *Black Beauty*. Still, the Oater has always been particularly appropriate for such an exploration of the special bond between a human and that magnificent creature. Lest we forget, the code of chivalry that defined knights of old derived from the French term for horse, *cheval*.

ROMANCE, WESTERN (BY WAY OF HOLLYWOOD) STYLE: Americano (Matt Dillon) and Latina (Penelope Cruz) meet on horseback in the wilds and, in civilization, take to the dance floor.

The film's young heroes, 'John Grady Cole' and 'Lacey Rawlins,' are often seen riding, traveling, or working at their chosen profession. That's not the case, though, in the opening sequence. Following a hard day's work, the two camp on the prairie, gazing at a big sky with countless shimmering stars. Rural, uneducated philosophers, they discuss everything from the unavoidable phenomenon of death to the possible existence of an invisible if almighty Trail Boss high above. Recent observers have suggested a patina of homoeroticism exists in the conception of two men, bunked side by side, as in *Ride the High Country* (1962). In a way, *Brokeback Mountain* (2005) might be seen less as "the first gay cowboy film," rather the first to directly address a heretofore implied issue that reappears here.

Eventually, *Pretty Horses* ends where it began: John and Lacey together in Texas. No matter that their long, eventful odyssey into Mexico, in search of a final frontier that recalls their beloved (if largely mythic) Texas before big business usurped the Lone Star state, led Cole into an intense love affair with the Spanish beauty 'Alejandra.' Lacey (his very name suggesting the feminine element Montgomery Clift embodied in Howard Hawks' *Red River*, 1948) appears threatened. He considers abandoning their life together when Cole seriously thinks about marriage. In addition to her obvious loveliness, John is drawn to Alejandra in large part as she too is a 'horse-person.' Like John or Lacey, the audience first sees her as the young men do: in the saddle, the sexual connotations of that phrase intentional. Cole is accepted by his inamorata as 'worthy' of her only after he rides down a mighty horse, which becomes his own, forever, as to emotional ties if not legal ownership. While Cole and Alejandra may be doomed as a couple, under no circumstances will he leave his beloved mount.

The film intriguingly plays with issues of race and class. Though John and Lacey are Anglo, they are perceived south of the border as hapless saddle tramps. Alejandro, a Latin lady, is apparently pureblood Spanish, as such an Old World style aristocrat. Thus, she must remain loyal to a code as strict as that of the American cowboy, this conflict in values and visions sealing their eventual fate despite lyrical lovemaking that includes a conventional

THE LAST SHOOT-OUT; Even in the 20th Century, the Cowboy Hero is often called upon to whip out a hand-gun and make a desperate stand.

moonlight swim in a deep, dark pond. A cliché, to be sure, though it works well in context. Another key element: The relationship of the amiable duo to a wild kid, 'Jimmy Blevins,' who by accident or destiny crosses the Rio Grande with them, proves indelible. That he has stolen a horse, an act they are later unfairly blamed of participating in, reinforces the significance of the cheval theme. Jimmy's thievery sets in motion the drama that envelops the two innocent cowboys during the film's second half. As for Jimmy, he is an amoral predecessor for the cold-blooded killing machine 'Anton Chgurh' (Javier Bardem) in *No Country*.

Fascinatingly, the genial heroes hardly know Jimmy. Nor do they like or respect him. Why then do these goodguys not simply ride off into the sunset and let Jimmy face the consequences he, and he alone, set into motion? The answer has to do with the essence of what it means to be a Cowboy. From the moment they reluctantly allow Jimmy to join their company, the boys are his saddle pals. Here we encounter a sort of unconditional love between men who wear Stetsons and ride, ride, ride. Nowhere has this been so well articulated as by 'Pike' (William Holden) in Sam Peckinpah's *The Wild Bunch* (1969): "When you ride with a man, you *stick* with him." For better or worse.

Now and forever.

That's The Cowboy Way. Also known as The Code of the West.

ANOTHER HARD-RIDING WOMAN OF THE WEST: Like such stars as Jean Arthur, Barbara Stanwyck, and Katy Jurado before her, Penelope Cruz here proves that a horsewoman can traverse the prairies with the same level of skill as any man.

3. ALONG CAME JONES (1945)
Rating: ****

CREDITS:

Stuart Heisler, dir.; Nunnally Johnson, scr.; Gary Cooper, Walter Thompson, William Goetz, pro.; Arthur Lange, Hugo Friedhofer, Charles Maxwell, mus.; Milton R. Krasner, cin; Thomas Neff, ed.; 1.37:1; B&W; 90 mi.; International Pictures.

CAST:

Gary Cooper *(Melody Jones)*; Loretta Young *(Cherry de Longpre)*; William Demarest *(George Fury)*; Dan Duryea *(Monte Jarrod)*; Frank Sully *(Avery)*; Don Costello *(Gledhill)*; Walter Sande *(Waggoner)*; Russell Simpson *(Pop de Longpre)*; Arthur Loft *(The Sheriff)*; Ray Teal *(Kriendler)*; Lane Chandler *(Boone)*; Willard Robertson *(Luke Packard)*; Erville Alderson *(The Bartender)*.

Discussions of the emergent post-war Western ordinarily focus on *(The) Treasure of the Sierra Madre, Red River,* and *Blood on the Moon,* all 1948. Here though we discover a precursor to the noirish photography, psychologically disturbed characters, and sense of a darkening world that would reach fruition in *The Gunfighter* (1950), *High Noon* (1952), *The Searchers* (1956) and other 'adult' Oaters. Rarely do historians mention this light-hearted feature, writing it off as a charming, innocuous sagebrush comedy in the manner of *Destry Rides Again* (1939). In fact, there is more to this once popular (a rock 'n' roll song paid tribute to it in the 1950s), now forgotten work than immediately meets the eye, beginning with Gary Cooper's (1901-1961) credit as producer. For here we encounter an early example of major stars forming

THE GOOD GUY AND THE BAD GUY... OBVIOUSLY: Beginning with the early Soundie *The Virginian* and on through *Along Came Jones* to his Oscar-winning role in *High Noon*, Gary Cooper embodied onscreen the man of few words and much action; having already established himself as an unforgettable snivelling villain in film noirs, Dan Duryea brought his icon of hissable cynicism to the Western genre with his appearance here.

production companies to control the quality of material as well as vividly define their screen personas. Coop's 'International' films would not long survive, absorbed only a few years later into Universal-International. Still, the company set the pace for things to come in the industry.

With the success of *The Virginian* (1929), Coop had become a representative figure for the man of the west, that the title of a 1958 film he would appear in. Though sagebrush sagas came Coop's way--*The Texan* (1930), *Fighting Caravans* (1931)---he insisted on doing comedies, melodramas, and period pictures to avoid typecasting. Still, the public most loved him in cowboy roles, from Cecil B. DeMille's *The Plainsman* (1936) to William Wyler's *The Westerner* (1940). Wisely, Coop combined the best of both worlds here, playing a mild-mannered Montana native (the state in which G.C. had been born), a naive cowpoke who wanders into

THE COWBOY AND THE LADY: Loretta Young's rough and all too willing frontier gal classes up her act under the guidance of softspoken hero Gary Cooper.

a ridiculously named town (Paynesville) where he's mistaken for a deadly gunslinger.

Coop had already played in such a piece, *The Cowboy and the Lady* (1938), opposite aristocratic Merle Oberon. Here he rescues a lowborn female from the trashy environs she was born into, helping her overcome a taste for 'bad boys.' Screenwriter Nunnally Johnson (1897-1977), best known for penning the John Ford version (1940) of John Steinbeck's *The Grapes of Wrath* (1939), managed to slip the girl's name ('Cherry') past the censors. Borden Chase would prove more daring still by allowing Montgomery Clift's cowboy companion (John Ireland) to go by that name ('Cherry' Valance) in *Red River*. As to Coop's control over *Jones*., note that he chose director Heisler (1896-1979), who guided the star through that earlier gentle (and genteel) Western *The Cowboy and the Lady*.

But the enjoyment-aspect of *Jones* ought not cause us to overlook more serious elements. That bleak sensibility, appearing one year later in *My*

Darling Clementine, is hinted at here. Stark blacks and whites provide a striking contrast to the film's fun elements. These include the striking opening, in which two saddle tramps, 'Melody' and an elderly sidekick 'George,' slowly ride toward the camera. This would introduce a convention of Westerns yet to come; note though that it had only been employed once before, in *The Ox Bow Incident* (1943) featuring Henry Fonda and Harry Morgan. The next time such a duo would be so portrayed: *Winchester '73* (1950; with James Stewart and Millard Mitchell); the vision would remain in place through *The Cheyenne Social Club* (1970) starring Stewart and Fonda, playing Western 'pards' for the first time though they previously shot it out as goodguy and badguy in *Firecreek* (1968).

A NEW TWIST TO THE OLD CLICHÉ: In movies like *The Virginian* or *Stagecoach*, the goodguy shot and killed the badguy at the end, then returned to the woman patiently waiting; in an era when contemporary feminism first blossomed, the self-empowered heroine (make that female hero) gets the job done when her man proves incapable of resolving the situation!

Another key connection between this film and *W.73*: Dan Duryea (1909-1968), heretofore a big city badguy in contemporary crime films including *The Woman in the Window* (1944) and *Criss Cross* (1949). As Young's dominating male 'friend,' he brings his half-crazed, utterly cynical delivery to *Jones*, his first Western. By the mid-1950s, Duryea would rate as a genre staple, his wild-eyed maverick often cast opposite Audie Murphy's silent hero in such Oaters as *Ride Clear of Diablo* (1954). It might not be too much of a stretch to suggest that Duryea hinted at the ultimate Western villain still far off on the Hollywood horizon: 'Chigurh' (Javier Barden), the nihilistic killing machine in *No Country for Old Men* (2007) by the Coen Bros.

Finally, there is Loretta Young (1913-2000). The glamour girl was no stranger to Westerns, having embodied the tragic heroine in *Romana*, included in this volume. Here, she introduces The New Woman to appear in post-war movies, reflecting a female's changing reality in society. Like her role in *Rachel and the Stranger* (1948) still on the horizon, she is portrayed at this film's opening as a recessive girl, victim of supposedly strong men. As in that upcoming film about an earlier Eastern frontier, she here experiences an arc. Cherry not only frees herself from Duryea's villain as to their 'romance' (if that term fits) but, by the end, halts that monster's reign of terror in a blaze of gunfire while the supposed male hero helplessly stands by. Such strong women would prove to be the New Norm, embodied by Joan Crawford in *Johnny Guitar* (1954) and Barbara Stanwyck in *Forty Guns* (1958). In its own small (perhaps) way, *Jones* advanced the feminist cause with a new role model for American women.

4. ALONG THE GREAT DIVIDE (1951) Rating: **** ½

CREDITS:

Raoul Walsh, dir.; Walter Doniger, Lewis Meltzer, scr.; Anthony Veiller, pro.; David Buttolph, mus.; Sidney Hickox, cin.; Thomas Reilly, ed.; 1.37:1; B&W; 88 min.; Warner Bros.

CAST:

Kirk Douglas (*U.S. Marshal Len Merrick*); Virginia Mayo (*Ann Keith*); John Agar (*Billy Shear*); Walter Brennan (*Timothy 'Pop' Keith*); Ray Teal (*Deputy Lou Gray*); Hugh Sanders (*Frank Newcombe*); Morris Ankrum (*Ed Roden*); James Anderson *(Dan Roden)*; Charles Meredith (*Judge Marlowe*); Lane Chandler (*Sheriff*).

At first glance, *Along the Great Divide* appears one more example of those 'program pictures' each studio churned out in the days before television; following that entertainment innovation, Warners concentrated on "A" theatrical features, their B units re-directed to small screen product: *Cheyenne, Maverick,* etc. *Great Divide*'s plot is traditional, at least initially: Marshal 'Len Merrick' and his deputies, young 'Billy Shear' and older, cynical 'Lou Gray,' interrupt a lynching in progress. Elderly 'Tim Keith' is about to face a necktie party for killing a cattleman, that fellow's wrathful father 'Ed Roden' and brother 'Dan' heading up the angry riders. Insisting that this man must have a fair trial, Merrick and his men seize Roden, heading across a nasty stretch of wasteland toward a distant outpost. On their way, they are saddled with Keith's feisty

GOOD GUYS SOMETIMES WEAR BLACK: Though Kirk Douglas's postwar Western character hardly recalls the stalwart figures of Hollywood's past, he is at the least an anti-hero who does the right thing at the end; to his left, John Agar; far left, Ray Teal.

daughter 'Ann' while relentlessly tracked by the vengeful cowboys, demanding their pound of flesh.

Many production elements elevate what might have been an effective time-killer into a uniquely powerful piece. First, there is the presence of action-oriented director Raoul Walsh (1887-1980), instrumental in creating the post-war 'noir Western' with *Colorado Territory* two years earlier. Expressing by implication the complexities of the Cold War Era, the piece insists on a backstory for each character rather than accepting them as stock figures. The smart script introduces Merrick as an upstanding arbiter of law and order that can be traced back at least to Walter Huston in the 1932 film of that title. Notable, though, is that, like William Boyd in the Hopalong Cassidy kiddie features, here is a 'good-guy' who wears black. Shortly, Merrick reveals small signs that he has more in common with villains in previous

Oaters than their ostensible heroes. Merrick can be simple-minded, so dedicated to 'the law' that he forgets about the equally (perhaps more) important issue of 'justice.' Also, he's notably aggressive toward the young woman, from their first encounter snarling with sexual suggestion in mind.

More fascinating still: His essential character flaw, which opens up this movie to dramatic possibilities on the order of such serious literature as Russian novelist Ivan Turgenev's *Fathers and Sons* (1866) and classic Greek tragedies by Sophocles. Earlier in life, Merrick failed to help his lawman father on a mission, leading to that man's lynching. Merrick's desire to prevent such an occurrence at all costs now may have less to do with honest feelings for this victimized bum (he initially could care less whether Old Man

HERO OR HEEL? The near-psychopathic lead played by Kirk Douglas proves as menacing to the heroine, Virginia Mayo, as many of the badmen were during the earlier, simpler days of Oaters.

Keith is legally hung following a jury's decision) than a burning desire to reclaim his sense of value by 'getting it right' this time around. Complicating this further: 'Pop' Keith calls Merrick 'son' in the casual, non-biological sense. Merrick, however, takes this on a familial level, causing him to wonder if his seemingly normal attraction to Ann may represent a desire to sleep with his substitute sister. Likewise, Roden's surviving son hungers to kill his father out of an Oedipal jealousy for that man's devotion to the preferred lost son. All of this suggests an affinity for the psychological film tradition that overtook Hollywood during the early 1950s, culminating with the fact-based Oscar-winner *The Three Faces of Eve* (1957).

Great Divide's emotionally disturbing visuals were achieved by cinematographer Hickox (1895-1982), who contributed to the emergent aesthetics

FRONTIER JUSTICE: If *The Ox Bow Incident* remains the most famous Hollywood film ever made about lynch mob mentality, many others include this hard aspect of the Western experience; here, Walter Brennan sits tall in the saddle while the self-appointed administers of justice make ready to send him "swingin'" from a sturdy tree.

of noir with *The Big Sleep* (1946) and *White Heat* (1949), the latter for Walsh. The team also took a cue from Alfred Hitchcock's notion of a MacGuffin, an object (tangible or not) that contains the key to a mystery which must be unlocked for the salvation (physical and spiritual) of all. Hitch preferred to employ a double MacGuffin: One a piece of jewelry, the other a song. Here, we have "Down in the Valley," a folk tune that cements that tragedy within a single family; and a watch, which in time (pun intended) unlocks the dark, disturbing father/son element.

This was among a pair of action Oaters that Douglas (1916-2020) made for Warner's (the other a lumberjack adventure, *The Big Trees*, two years later) to get free his long-term studio contract and become an independent star/producer. Yet however many Tinseltown genres Kirk would participate in, he always experienced an affinity to the Western. Douglas's first year of independent work, 1955, includes a pair of genre pieces, *The Indian Fighter* and *Man Without a Star*. In each, his anti-hero would be all but torn apart by his fellow man and natural forces, a syndrome suggested in *Great Divide*. This would continue to be the case in future Westerns such as *Gunfight at the O.K. Corral* (1957) and *The Last Sunset* (1961), Douglas's masterpiece *Lonely Are the Brave* (1962), also his embarrassing big-budget disaster *The Way West* (1967). In *Great Divide*, co-star Virginia Mayo (1920-2005) continued her association with the genre that began with Walsh's *Colorado Territory*. and would be furthered in *The Big Land* (1957), *Fort Dobbs* (1958), and *Westbound* (1959) opposite (respectively) Alan Ladd, Clint Walker, and Randolph Scott. As for Walter Brennan (1894-1974), who had already won one of his three best supporting Actor Oscars for a Western (*The Westerner*, 1940, as 'Judge Roy Bean'), his work here as the victimized sodbuster could well have won him another nomination.

5. ARIZONA (1940) Rating: **** ½

CREDITS:

Wesley Ruggles, dir.; Claude Binyon, scr.; Ruggles, Harry Cohn, pro.; Victor Young, mus.; Fayte M. Browne, Harry Hallenberger, Joseph Waller, cin.; William A. Lyon, Otto Meyer, mus.; 1.37:1; B&W; 125 min.; Columbia.

CAST:

Jean Arthur (*Phoebe Titus*); William Holden (*Peter Muncle*); Warren William (*Jefferson Carteret*); Porter Hall (*Lazarus Ward*); Edgar Buchanan (*Judge Bogardus*); Paul Harvey (*Solomon Warner*); George Chandler (*Haley*); Byron Foulger (*Pete Kitchen*); Regis Toomey (*Grant Oury*); Paul Lopez (*Estevan Ochoa*); Colin Tapley (*Bart Massey*); Roberto (*Uvaldo*); Varela (*Hilario Callego*); Earl Crawford (*Briggs*); Griff Barrett (*Sam Hughes*); Ludwig Hardt (*Meyer*); Iron Eyes Cody *(Native American)*.

The success of Cecil B. DeMille's *The Plainsman* (1936) and John Ford's *Stagecoach* (1939) convinced Hollywood's studio executives that the 'big' Western might be ready for a comeback. Such films were considered box-office poison since the failure of Raoul Walsh's *The Big Trail* (1930). At Columbia, head honcho Harry Cohn (1891-1958) decided to go all-out, investing more than $2 million on the then-risky concept of a sprawling epic in the tradition of *Cimarron* (1931). Not surprisingly, he tapped Wesley Ruggles (1889-1972), who had directed that Oscar-winning Best Picture, to helm the project. As it happened, Ruggles had recently read a novel by Clarence Buddington Kelland which, though set in the West, avoided most cliches associated with more formulaic variations. Focusing less on the usual issues of cattlemen and cowboys or law and order, the piece instead dealt with the impact of capitalism---the

IT'S A WOMAN'S WORLD: As the poster for *Arizona* makes vividly clear, it was (in the words of Western writer Edna Ferber) The Sunbonnet, more than the Sombrero, that civilized a wilderness; Jean Arthur early-on embodied the Woman with a Whip who will ride the range in many feature films to come.

national idea that anyone could rise to the top of the heap through luck and pluck---on a virtually untamed land. Here, the (female) hero's investment will be in a restaurant that in time leads to a great ranch.

The resultant script by Clyde Binyon offered a paradigm for 'good' and 'bad' forms of entrepreneurship. The varied inhabitants of Tucson live, talk, almost religiously believe in business. The enlightened form of capitalism is here represented by 'Phoebe Titus,' an American Dreamer fascinated by the moneymaking potential of bringing in needed goods from the east, and her equally honest partner 'Solomon,' a dull dry goods dealer, he inspired by Phoebe's dazzling vision of making lots of money honestly. Their foil:

A STAR IN EMBRYO: William Holden displays the easygoing aura that allowed him to become a top Hollywood performer, in Westerns and non-genre films as well.

Fancy-pants 'Carteret,' an interloping man in an Eastern tailored suit. He and his partner, store owner 'Ward,' are distrustful of one another yet drawn together by a desire to exploit the local economy. The film's 'happy ending' (in part a marriage between Phoebe and her rugged top hand, 'Peter') occurs once the honest capitalists win. Here was precisely the message: most Americans wanted/needed to hear at a juncture when the stock market crash and geographical Dust Bowl finally gave way to the initial signs of financial recovery.

Arizona takes an idealistic/sentimental approach to ethnicity, portraying a fair-minded past in which people of differing colors co-exist without conflict. Though the point is never stated openly, Solomon may be Jewish; like the protestant female-hero, he is as honest as the day is long, and so accepted by the film's decent citizenry. The Anglo male hero Pete arrives before the outbreak of Civil War, at the head of a herd; we view the swiftly growing city from his point of view. The subjective camera glances over indigenous people (for the most part portrayed by authentic Indians) as they go about their way of life, unmolested by more recent arrivals. The Spanish, high-born aristocrats and, socially speaking, lower-level mestizos, happily exist separate but equal under the law. As to the Apache people in the nearby mountains, they remain relatively mellow until incited (and are provided with rifles) by wicked Anglo manipulators as a means of eliminating competition. Importantly, the cliché of thieving Mexicans from south of the border is challenged. When such a group supposedly raids Phoebe's home, these turn out to be evil Whites employed by the key villain, the blame unfairly situated with the good-hearted vaqueros.

Post-feminist audiences will appreciate the portrayal here of a strong, at times 'butch,' female as the city and state's financial, communal, and moral center. Four years earlier, in De Mille's *Plainsman,* Jean Arthur (1900-1991) created a seemingly similar character, the fact-based 'Calamity Jane/Martha Jane Canary.' She there also carried a bullwhip and knew how to use a gun when this proved necessary. There, though, the situation offered a reactionary vision of the woman of the West. True to her name, Calamity precipitated one disaster after another, leading to the Male Rescue Myth. 'Wild Bill/James Butler

RECREATING THE PAST: To allow for ever greater realism, artisans built an accurate reproduction of Old Tucson on location in Arizona; then, the filmmaking crew filled the streets with a wide verisimilitude of historically costumed people and their animals to bring a long gone period to life again.

Hickok' (Gary Cooper) often hurried to save the endangered woman from a fate worse than death. Though at one point Holden's (1918-1981) likeable cowpoke does here arrive in time to prevent Phoebe's death at the hands of scoundrels, more often than not Phoebe extricates herself from difficult situations. Like other women as diverse as Claudette Colbert in *Drums Along the Mohawk* (1939) and Joan Crawford in *Johnny Guitar* (1954), the character challenges the questionable notion that women merely followed their men west. As Edna Ferber wrote in the novel *Cimarron*, if the truth is ever told about the frontier, it was The Sunbonnet, not the Stetson, that tamed the wilderness.

Perhaps the most long-lasting impact of this film would be the decision *not* to shoot in California's longstanding mock-ups of old-time Western towns, rather create the greatest permanent set in the genre's history. A faithful, historical replica of 'Old Tucson' was built in Arizona east of the contemporary city, adjacent to the Saguaro National Park, in the shadows of the area's towering mountains. This became one of the most popular locations for 'shooting' shoot-em-ups, employed for nearly 500 films (A, B, C in cost and/or quality), hundreds of TV episodes, also commercial advertisements. Owing to the explosion of Covid in the country in 2019-2021, Old Tucson (which survived a horrific fire twenty years earlier) at last closed down in March, 2021. Yet it will live forever in celluloid visions of the frontier captured there.

NO NEED FOR RESCUE BY THE MALE HERO: Jean Arthur proves herself totally able to deal with the bad=guys, symbolizing the strong, self-empowered women of the real West.

6. BACKLASH (1956)
Rating: ****

CREDITS:

John Sturges, dir.; Borden Chase, scr.; Aaron Rosenberg, pro.; Herman Stein, mus.; Irving Glassberg, cin.; Sherman Todd, ed.; 2.00:1; C 84 min.; Universal-International.

CAST:

Richard Widmark (*Jim Slater*); Donna Reed (*Karyl Orton*); William Campbell (*Johnny Cool*); John McIntire (*Jim Bonniwell/William Slater*); Barton MacLane (*Sgt. George Lake*); Henry Morgan (*Tony Welker*); Robert J. Wilke (*Jeff Welker*); Jack Lambert (*Mike Benton*); Roy Roberts (*Carson*); Edward (C.) Platt (*J.C. Marson*); Robert Foulk (*John F. Olson*); Phil Chambers *(Dobbs)*; Gregg Barton (*Sleepy)*; Frank Chase (*Cassidy*); Glenn Strange (*Stage Driver*); Chris Alcaide (*Lawrence*); William Phillips *(Rebel)*.

Despite the unique style of each classic Western's director, an unmistakable narrative line and thematic approach runs through films written by Borden Chase (1900-1971): Howard Hawks' *Red River* (1948; John Wayne and Montgomery Clift) and Henry Levin's *The Man from Colorado* (Glenn Ford, William Holden, both 1948), Anthony Mann's *Bend of the River* (1952; James Stewart, Arthur Kennedy), Robert Aldrich's *Vera Cruz* (Gary Cooper, Burt Lancaster, 1954); John Sturges' *Bad Day at Black Rock* (Spencer Tracy, Lee Marvin; 1955), and King Vidor's *Man Without a Star* (Kirk Douglas, Richard Boone; 1955) included. In each, roles played by the lead characters, however seemingly heroic on first sight, turn out to be what might be termed 'damaged

KING OF THE SNARLERS: During the late 1940s, Richard Widmark made his first great impact as a crazed villain in film noirs including *Kiss of Death*; as the tide turned for Westerns during the next decade and simple goodguys and badguys became a thing of the past, the cynical tough guy would become a perfect anti-hero for 'adult' Oaters.

goods.' Initially seeming to be conventional variations on the traditional Man of the West, such anti-heroes are scarred by earlier experiences, leading to classic examples of the psychological Western. Uncontrollable fears of everything from barbed wire to a hangman's rope paralyze deeply-troubled frontiersmen at the precise moment when they most need to act decisively, often leading to tragedy of a classical order.

In *Backlash*, adapted from a Frank Gruber novel, that concept is stretched considerably further. 'Jim Slater' initially seems one more man with a personal . . . make that *familial* . . . mission. Like James Stewart in *The Man from Laramie* (1955), he rides toward an isolated outpost to explore the remains of a massacre. In the former film, it's the lead's brother who died at the hands of Native warriors; here, the young man's father. Similarly, he is determined, even obsessed, with learning who among varied white settlers is responsible, holding no grudge against the Indians themselves. As Sophocles wrote 2,500 years ago, 'The end of man is to *know* . . .' though *never* knowing for certain if the truth will free or destroy him. Perhaps both. Here, a horrific possibility arises, one that all but freezes the central character. Possibly, he has been wrong in believing that his father died bravely in this battle. Could Pa have been the despicable sixth man who rode away with a cache of gold in his saddlebags and personal survival in mind? If so, will Slater be able to bring himself to kill his own flesh and blood? Here is Chase's recurring theme of conflict for a hero (like Montgomery Clift as 'Matthew Garth' in *Red River)* forced to decide between family loyalty and the good of the community at large. There, the resolution would surprisingly prove comical; here it takes on implications that reach back to the tragic situation of Oedipus at Thebes.

For the first time, a last minute redemption for the transgressor (as with Audie Murphy's character in *Night Passage*, 1957) is withheld, the ending less bittersweet than pessimistic. The father (John McIntyre) would be happy to embrace his son as a future conspirator in illegal, even devilish doings, this the result of the raw capitalism that motivates him. Yet the bitter man . . . an abject narcissist . . .will shoot down the boy if necessary to protect himself. The attitude present in *Backlash* recalls the occurrences in *Bend of the River*

A RETRO VISION OF WOMEN IN SOCIETY: As in so many film noirs (notably *Too Late for Tears* starring Dan Duryea and Lizabeth Scott), the female lead here becomes so attracted to the mean-spirited male by his physical abuse that she becomes a virtual slave to him afterwards.

four years earlier. When earnest pioneers set out to farm virgin land, businessmen gleefully sell them needed supplies at a fair price. But when gold is discovered in them thar hills, everything changes. With get-rich-quick prospectors pouring in, those goods (not yet delivered) will bring a higher price, even if it means leaving salt of the earth types starving during a long, harsh winter. Importantly, Chase does not dismiss capitalism per se. His true heroes hope to make money slowly, through hard, honest work. The villains are those who hope for huge profits to arrive swiftly, at the price of destroying innocent bystanders.

Slater is played by the ever-snarling Richard Widmark (1914-2008), a surly actor who brought a strange sort of sympathetic quality to his Western villains (*The Law and Jake Wade*, 1958) and a threatening aspect to his

AN ALL-PURPOSE CHARACTER ACTOR: Few performers proved as comfortable switching back and forth between good and bad men as John McIntyre; a charismatic villain here, he would play Elvis Presley's sweet though strong father in *Flaming Star* (1960) and as well as a trustworthy trail boss on TV's *Wagon Train*, replacing Ward Bond.

anti-heroes (*The Last Wagon;* Delmer Daves, 1956). Also notable: Donna Reed (1921-1986) as a frontier woman likewise eager to learn the truth as to what happened on that dark day. 'Karyl' serves as a striking predecessor to Barbara Stanwyck in Sam Fuller's *40 Guns* a year later. When the situation calls for it, she's a dominatrix-like woman in black leather, waving a fierce whip; at other moments, when Karyl deems it appropriate, she will slip into elegant gowns and turn seductively kittenish. She is all things to all men, if always her own woman. Finally, there's 'Johnny Cool,' a variation on the punk kid out to make his reputation by taking on a top gun as played by Richard Jaeckel and Skip Homier in *The Gunfighter* (1950). Here, though, such a character assumes attributes of the juvenile delinquents on view in *Rebel Without a Cause* (1955). John Sturges (1910-1992) directs with the self-assurance he would further display in *Gunfight at the O.K. Corral* (1957) and *The Magnificent Seven* (1960). Not to forget *The Great Escape* (1963), a WWII prison break epic that often plays like an Oater and features two of TV's top guns, James Garner (*Maverick*) and Steve McQueen (*Wanted, Dead or Alive*) as members of the ensemble.

OLD AND NEW: Barton MacLane brought his tough if compassionate image to the film, even as he would to TV's *The Outlaws* in the early 1960s; William Campbell here portrays a variation on the quick-tempered kid he had incarnated a year earlier in *Man Without a Star*.

7. BAD BASCOMB (1948)
Rating: ****

CREDITS:

S. Sylvan Simon, dir.; D.A. Loxley, William R. Lipman, Grant Garett, scr.; Orville L. Dull, pro.; David Snell, mus.; Charles (Edgar) Schoenbaum, cin.; Ben Lewis, ed.; 1.37:1; B&W; 112 min.; Metro-Goldwyn-Mayer.

CAST:

Wallace Beery *(Zeb Bascomb)*; Margaret O'Brien *(Emmy)*; Marjorie Main *(Abbey Hanks)*; J. Carrol Naish *(Bart Yancy)*; Frances Rafferty *(Dora McCabe)*; Marshall Thompson *(Johnny Holden)*; Russell Simpson *(Elijah Walker)*; Warner Anderson *(Luther Mason)*; Donald Curtis *(John Fulton)*; Connie Gilchrist *(Annie Freemont)*; Sara Haden *(Tillie Lovejoy)*; Renie Riano *(Lucy)*; Jane Green *(Hannah)*; Frank Darien *(Moab McCabe)*; Eddie Acuff *(Corporal Finch)*; Stanley Andrews *(Col. Cartright)*; Ralph and Roy Bucko *(Outlaw Brothers)*; Wally Cassell *(Curley)*; Arthur Space *(Sheriff)*; Joseph Crehan *(Gov. Ames)*.

One unique subgenre of the Western is 'The Wagon Train epic,' a paeon to early pioneers. The form began with *The Covered Wagon* (1923), an early, important, dramatically uneven epic. *The Big Trail* carried that tradition into the early sound era, though the public had temporarily lost interest in grand, optimistic spectacles. More preferred during the Depression were outlaw Oaters such as *Jesse James* (1939), period-piece equivalents of the rural-gangster films about rugged individualists who struck back at The System including *You Only Live Once* (1936). As World War II revived a sense of optimism in the American community, *Bascomb* represents MGM's stab at such

A KISS IS STILL A KISS... OR MAYBE NOT? The bizarre 'romance' between old timer Wallace Berry and female child Margaret O'Brien was considered charming upon the film's release; contemporary viewers may well find it ... discomfiting.

a retro-film. The hackneyed, corny, overly sentimental script aside, *Bascomb* comes closer to visually representing the historical reality than almost any other film of this type, excepting only John Ford's *Wagon Master* (1950).

Notably, horses for once do not pull Conestoga wagons, rather full teams of Oxen and mules. Picturesque though inaccurate images of a long line of 'white tops' are avoided. As in actuality, wagons push west alongside one another, huge herds of horses and mules on one side, cattle on the other. People are less often seen riding in wagons than walking alongside them, to keep down the weight their beasts must pull. At night, the Conestogas are not circled but laid out in parallel lines, more often the case with large caravans. For the sake of box-office appeal, *Bascomb* contains an enormous settlers-vs.-Indians battle at its conclusion, though such confrontations rarely if ever occurred. Recall, though, that the only "A" budget film to abandon this cliché, *The Way West* (1967), would rate as one of the genre's biggest bombs. The public may know little of history, but it does know precisely what it wants from a Western: High-style action!

Released the same year that *Red River* and *Blood on the Moon* literally reinvented the genre, *Bascomb* displays no trace of the character complexity, moral confusion, or social disorder found in them. This film might be thought of as a throwback to an earlier form, the old Good-Bad Man morality plays

THE BIG TRAIL: Despite its fictional narrative, *Bad Bascomb* presents one of the most accurate depictions of a carvan's movement west in Hollywood film history.

of the silent era. The key difference between this and previous pictures such as *Straight Shooting* (1917) is the comedic tone (despite bloodthirsty action). Director S. Sylvan Simon (1910-1951), a dependable studio journeyman, was mostly associated with that genre including Red Skelton in *Whistling in Dixie* (1942). Yet Simon shortly helmed one of the darkest post-war Oaters, *Lust for Gold* (1949), a bleak version of the Old Dutchman's Lost Mine legend.

From day one, however, this was conceived as a dual vehicle for two of MGM's most beloved stars. The eponymous role went to Wallace Beery (1885-1949), an embodiment of a beer-stained Bowery bum with the proverbial heart of gold. In his most memorable (and Oscar-winning) vehicle, *The*

RACISM IN THE WESTERN GENRE: As critic Philip French pointed out in 1970, many of the old Hollywood Westerns treated Native Americans with at least a modicum of respect; not so "the half breed," as embodied here by J. Carroll Naish, with the mixing of the races providing a handy if, in retrospect, offensive figure of villainy.

Champ (1931), pugilist Beery's rehabilitation was facilitated by an innocent kid (Jackie Coogan). Here, that role goes to a girl. If largely forgotten today, Margaret O'Brien (1931-) reigned throughout the 1940s as the sort of cloyingly charming precious little girl with big, pure eyes, tempered by an adult manner of delivering dialogue that Shirley Temple had been to the 1930s. In her two most memorable movies, the World War II tear-jerker *Journey for Margaret* (1942) and heartland Americana musical *Meet Me in St. Louis* (1944), little Margaret amazed her directors, then audiences, with an uncanny ability to sob on cue, never missing a beat. Here, that serves her well as the child cuddles with the deadly outlaw, he hiding among peaceful members of a Mormon community.

From today's perspective, their intensely physical relationship may cause a viewer to cringe. The eight-year-old orphan does not seek Bascomb out as a father figure, rather a fiancé. They even exchange rings and become engaged! Once, viewers may have found the images of a wretched old man and an underage girl cuddling . . . and *kissing!* . . . under the moonlight 'adorable.' In our era of intense awareness as to child abuse, such sequences prove both discomfiting and unsettling.

So too does one of the supporting characters. Irish actor J. Carroll Naish (1996-1973) often portrayed Native Americans, including a famous Lakota chief in the musical extravaganza *Annie Get Your Gun* (1950), repeating that role for the low-budget *Sitting Bull* (1954). Here he is cast as 'The Renegade,' a White Man raised by Indians and, in the film's context, atavistic: Drawn back into a primordial world, unable like Bascomb (who, wickedness aside, is all white) to reform. Such an abiding prejudice haunted old-fashioned Westerns. In *Daniel Boone* (1936), the title character (George O'Brien) is presented as a virtual saint; Simon Girty (John Carradine), an Anglo loyal to Indians, an evil force from the dark forest. In such Westerns to come as *Run of the Arrow* (1957), *A Man Called Horse* (1970), and *Dances with Wolves* (1990), a more modern view would prevail: Here, though, Bascomb will redeem himself by killing this former mixed-race companion, then go to the gallows with his head held high.

8. BAD COMPANY (1972)
Rating: *****

CREDITS:

Robert Benton, dir.; Benton, David Newman, scr.; Stanley R. Jaffe, pro.; Harvey Schmidt, mus.; Gordon Willis, cin.; Ron Kalish, Ralph Rosenblum, ed.; 1.85:1; C; 93 min.; Paramount.

CAST:

Jeff Bridges (*Jake Rumsey*); Barry Brown (*Drew Dixon*); Jim Davis (*The Marshal*); David Huddleston (*Big Joe*); John Savage *(Loney)*; Jerry Houser (*Arthur Simms*); Damon Douglas (*Jim Bob Logan*); Joshua Hill Lewis (*Boog Bookin*); Geoffrey Lewis (*Hobbs*); Raymond Guth (*Jackson*); Ed Lauter *(Orin)*; John Quade *(Nolan)*; Jean Allison (*Mrs. Dixon*); Ned Wertimer *(Dixon)*.

"Stick 'em up!"

Dozens of old Hollywood Western movies and TV shows feature that legendary line, which became something of a cornball cliché as a result of overuse in genre pictures. Only one movie *concludes* with it; fittingly, this rates among the nouveau Westerns that appeared once the studio system collapsed. The Youth Movement of the late 1960s and early 1970s radically altered our popular culture, and the two powerhouse Oaters of 1969---*Butch Cassidy and the Sundance Kid* and *The Wild Bunch*----set a future paradigm for films about the frontier as either ultra-violent cynicism or tongue in cheek sentimentality. *Bad Company* contains a bit of both. Here is an origination fable of sorts, detailing in episodic fashion the manner in which two very different boys might mature (if that is indeed the correct term) into the kinds of teams Paul Newman and Robert Redford, or William Holden and Ernest

LIKE FATHER, LIKE SON: Lloyd Bridges appeared in key Western films including *High Noon;* son Beau, here taking his first shot (pun intended) at the genre, would go on to win an Oscar as 'Rooster Cogburn' in the second version of *True Grit*.

Borgnine, portrayed in those then-recent classics. The tale involves two teenagers born and raised in the East; one ('Drew Dixon'), a properly brought-up middle-American farm boy; the other '(Jake Rumsey'), a fugitive from some big city slum, the case with the historic William H. Bonney (SEE: *Dirty Little Billy*). As they wander ever further west, initially in the company of five other runaways, the process of survival transforms both without their ever fully realizing what's happening from the kids they once were into rugged Westerners. The film's final line asserts that the transition is complete. As Glenn Ford confided to Jack Lemmon in *Cowboy* (Delmer Daves, 1958): The West doesn't toughen you up; it only makes you mean.

"GO WEST, YOUNG MEN!" Following the Cultural Revolution of the late 1960s and early 1970s, Westerns found in our past history tales that would comment on the current times; Jeff Bridges and Barry Brown play draft dodgers from the Civil War who, costumes aside, recall many of society's young dropouts during the Vietnam Era.

The story is set in 1863, as Drew's loving Ohio family attempts to hide their surviving son (the older boy died at Chickamauga) from a squad of Yankee soldiers sent to pick up draft dodgers. Though the period is effectively suggested in a simple, convincing, non-romanticized manner, the rare moviegoer of that time who sought out this marvellous 'little' picture sensed that, as so often happens, the past is here selectively revisited to comment on the present time. Though the Vietnam War appeared to be at last winding down, memories not only of our involvement but the American home-front remained vivid in the country's collective consciousness. Numerous young men, convinced that our involvement in Southeast Asia constituted an illegal and immoral endeavor, ran off rather than join up. *Bad Company* is, then, relevant from its opening. The 'good boy' hopes to join a wagon train and begin his 'westing' in the proper manner: Heading off to recreate himself, living out the American Dream of financial success through hard, honest work somewhere 'out there.' But nothing turns out as it's supposed to, in this movie as (more often than not) life. Robbed and beaten, Drew is forced to take up with the title characters, a scruffy group of misfits hiding in back alleys and stealing from whomever passes by.

As portrayed, they have less in common with anything previously seen in a Western than the London street gang portrayed by Charles Dickens in *Oliver Twist* (1837). With his jaunty hat and cocky manner, Bridges (1949-) plays the natural leader as an American variation on The Artful Dodger, assuming control of a sad little squad that has no adult 'Fagin' to direct their dishonest activities. As Jake, Drew, and others make their way west, there is nothing about their manner or dress to suggest this is a Western. Other

RETURN OF AN OLD TIMER: Jim Davis, who had played lawmen and outlaws in numerous films and TV shows (including *Stories of the Century*) during the 1950s and would go on to star on TV' *Dallas* here brings his living legend status to the role of a no nonesense marshal.

than the tired horses and sad mule they share, along with pistols collected from Civil War surplus, they have seemingly nothing in common with the Western outlaws they (the survivors, that is) will eventually become. Yet every wild bunch must start somewhere. Here is a possible scenario revealing step by step how the world-at-large turns them into a James-Younger/Doolin-Dalton type bunch that would, when solidified as a gang, step into a bank, calmly draw their guns, and say to those Establishment types standing there: "Stick ... 'em .. *up*."

Following hard upon the late Peter Bogdanovich's far more popular *The Last Picture Show* (1971), *Bad Company*. forwarded Bridges' career as a Western movie icon which would lead to the ultimate proof of that status, *True Grit* (2010). The writing team of Texas's Robert Benton (1932-) and New York City's David Newman (1937-2003) had all but created The New American Cinema with their script for *Bonnie and Clyde* (1967), a quasi-Western that set in place many themes developed here. Gordon Willis (1931-2014) wisely chose to abandon the process of referencing such well-known painters of the west as Frederic Remington and Charles Russell, with their gloriously colorful tributes, in favor of an approach that more resembles Andrew Wyeth with his stark, stern point-of-view of a land that withholds more than it gives.

Notes on two of the actors. This film serves as a worthy tribute to Jim Davis (1909-1981), who looked and sounded the part of an authentic cowboy from his early TV starring role on *Stories of the Century* (1954-55) to his final appearance on *Dallas* (1978-81). He literally embodied the American cowboy, as did Ben Johnson. If the latter actor had won his role as 'Sam the Lion' in *Last Picture Show* as much owing to iconography as acting ability, that was true too of Davis here that same year. Tragically, co-star Brown (1951-1978) was only able to win one other notable lead, opposite Cybill Shepherd in *Daisy Miller* (1974), thereafter taking his own life in despair.

9. BALLAD OF CABLE HOGUE, THE (1970)
Rating: *****

CREDITS:

Sam Peckinpah, dir.; John Crawford, Edward Penney, scr.; Peckinpah, Phil Feldman, Gordon (T.) Dawson, William D. Faralla, pro.; Jerry Goldsmith, mus..; Lucien Ballard, cin.; Lou Lombardo, Frank Santillo, ed.; 1.85:1; C; 121 min.; Warner Bros.

CAST:

Jason Robards (*Cable Hogue*); Stella Stevens (*Hildy*); David Warner (*Rev. Joshua Douglas Sloan*); Strother Martin (*Bowen*); Slim Pickens (*Ben Fairchild*); L.Q. Jones (*Taggart*): Peter Whitney (*Cushing*); R.G. Armstrong (*Quittner*); Gene Evans (*Clete*); William Mims (*Jensen*); Kathleen Freeman (*Mrs. Jensen*); Susan O'Connell (*Claudia*); Vaughn Taylor (*Powell*); Max Evans (*Webb Seely*); James Anderson (*Preacher*); Felix Nelson (*William*); Darwin Lamb (*The Stranger*); Mary Munday (*Dot*); William D. Faralla (*Lucius*); Victor Izay (*Clerk*); Easy Pickens (*Easy*).

To claim that Sam Peckinpah (1925-1987) offered a contradiction in terms is to understate the obvious. That had been the case too with John Ford, whom he succeeded as our essential avatar of the Western genre. Peckinpah's second film, *Ride the High Country*, was released in 1962, the same year as Ford's penultimate Oater, *The Man Who Shot Liberty Valance*. Each employed a pair of legendary stars (John Wayne and James Stewart, Joel McCrea and Randolph Scott) in elegiac visions of a fading frontier; sweet, sad farewells to the Hollywood genre in its conventional form. Both are filled with nostalgia,

MAKING THE AMERICAN DREAM COME TRUE: Forsaking gunfighters, cattle drives, and all other aspects of the generic Western, Sam Peckinpah told a simple and in truth typical to history tale of a dedicated small business entrepreneur, starring Jason Robards in the title role.

sentiment, and a melancholic sense that a Golden Age was coming to an end. In *Major Dundee* (1965) and more forcefully still, *The Wild Bunch* (1969), 'Old Sam' (while still relatively young) drew upward the violence inherent in Westerns from its beneath-the-surface status, visualizing blood, guts, and fury with a maniacal intensity that struck audiences as appropriately in-tune with then-current broadcasts of the war in Southeast Asia on our TV news.

If Ford's sensibility had been undeniably optimistic, a reflection in art of the times in which he lived and worked, Peckinpah's tended toward nihilism. In part this can be explained as a reaction to the darkening world around him. The sense of community and moral righteousness present in our society during the World War II years . . . the Ford years . . . contrasted with the bitterness, aura of mistrust, and drop-out mentality following the 1963 assassination of President Kennedy. And yet, if a filmmaker of his time, Peckinpah

NEXT TO GODLINESS: Cable washes down his inamorata in their little Eden, happy together until snakes... human as well as reptile... arrive.

like Ford also rates as an American storyteller for *all* time; as such, a singular individual with a prickly disposition that would not allow for compromise. As with Ford, it's impossible to tag him as a political conservative or liberal, his viewpoint combining elements of each. The irony inherent in Peckinpah's work: A filmmaker who made his first impact with the sweet-spirited *High Country* (*Guns in the Afternoon* in the U.K.) would become renowned for his two most brutal films, *Wild Bunch* and the contemporary-set *Straw Dogs* (1971).

How fascinating, then, that in-between those brutal classics, Peckinpah helmed an even kinder, gentler film than *High Country. Ballad*, written by two characters actors with little experience as cinematic scribes, is set in the same period as *Wild Bunch*... those transitional years as the 19th century drew to a close. Horse-drawn stagecoaches and motorcars pass one another on prairie trails. Some of the citizenry manages to adjust ('Cable,' here, for a while at least) while those who cannot ('Pike' and his companions) are doomed as prisoners of the past. If they represented frontier libertarianism, Cable is the even-headed, single minded capitalist... importantly, though, an enlightened one.

Abandoned by two fellow desert rats, he symbolically turns lemons into lemonade. Discovering water and setting up a profitable stage stop, Cable can be considered a frontier equivalent to Horatio Alger's American Dreamer of Eastern cities a few years later: the go- getter who succeeds while neighbors fail. King of his little castle, Hogue shares the business with his woman, 'Hildy.' No matter that she is a former prostitute or plans to someday leave their other-Eden to marry a millionaire. The two exist in the present tense. Each recreates him/herself in relationship to the other. But like the romantic couple in Ernest Hemingway's novel *A Farewell to Arms* (1929), such an idyll cannot long exist owing to an ever-encroaching and utterly merciless reality surrounding them. Try as you might, a separate peace cannot long flourish.

For as Jean-Paul Sartre once noted, "Hell is other people." And, sooner than later, such a threat appears on the horizon. This film only turns violent when the old 'partners'—L.Q. Jones (1927-) and Strother Martin (1919-1980) in roles all but identical to the ones they played in *Wild Bunch*-- return. Raw capitalists, they plan to steal what Cable honestly built. Here, Peckinpah projects a theme that expresses his philosophical identity, causing Pauline Kael to a year later hail and condemn *Straw Dogs* as "a fascist masterpiece." Each movie illustrates "territorial imperatives," as conceived in 1966 by Robert Ardrey. Even as humankind strives to achieve civilization, we carry in our DNA an element of ancient animal origins. In the Wild West or rural Cornwall, the anti-heroic figure can tolerate only so much from atavistic forces. "You will *not* do violence to this house," 'David Sumner' (Dustin Hoffman) screams as the quiet intellectual turns deadly when his small bastion is under siege. Ardrey argued that individual ownership brings out not the best but the beast in Everyman. Cable will fight and kill to defend what is 'his'... less as to legal papers, more a male sense of himself: Peckinpah's tragic figures embrace what Eugene O'Neill suggested early in the century can best

DÉJÀ VU: Fans of Sam Peckinpah's *The Wild Bunch* recalled, while watching *The Ballad...*, Strother Martin and L.Q. Jones in almost identical roles to the slimy, self-serving characters they played in that bloodthirsty classic.

be described as a hairy ape, still lurking in some invisible inner cave, deep within the cavern of every person. Or, at least, every male.

As in such diverse Westerns as *Shane*, *The Unforgiven*, and *High Noon*, 'The Westerner' as Robert Warshow long ago defined him stands tallest when under the most extreme pressure, even as Jason Robards does here. An individualistic person and the place he established are inseparable, even unto death. A theme worthy of a ballad. Perhaps even an epic. Peckinpah like Ford can be considered an American Homer, if adjusted for an entirely different generation.

10. BARON OF ARIZONA, THE (1950)
Rating: **** ½

CREDITS:

Samuel Fuller, dir.; Fuller, Homer Croy, scr.; Fuller, Carl K. Hittleman, Robert L. Lippert, pro; Paul Dunlap, mus.; James Wong Howe, cin.; Arthur Hilton, ed.; 1.37:1; B&W; 97 min.; Deputy Corp.; Lippert Prods.

CAST:

Vincent Price *(James Addison Reavis)*; Ellen Drew *(Sofia de Peralta-Reavis)*; Vladimir Sokoloff *(Pepito)*; Beulah Bondi *(Lorna)*; Reed Hadley *(Griff)*; Robert (H.) Barrat *(Judge)*; Robin Short *(Lansing)*; Tina Pine/Rome *(Rita)*; Karen Kester *(Sofia as a Child)*; Margia Dean *(Marquesa)*; Jonathan Hale *(Governor)*; Edward Keane *(General Miller)*; Barbara Wood(d)ell *(Carrie Lansing)*; J. Stanford Jolley *(Mr. Richardson)*; Fred Kohler Jr. *(Demmings)*; Gene Roth *(Father Guardian)*; Angelo Rossitto *('Angie the Gypsy')*; Tristram Coffin *(McClearly)*; Ed East *(Hank)*; Wheaton Chambers *(Brother Gregory)*; Russell Custer, Tex Driscoll *(Townspeople)*.

Midway through *The Big Red One* (1980), a cocky soldier (Robert Carradine) notices that a young replacement reads a pulp paperback novel during a lull in the fighting. The former asks the kid how he likes it; the latter casually responds; 'Why do you want to know?' The seasoned warrior quips, 'Because I wrote it.' The Carradine character is referred to as 'Sam,' a representation of the person who wrote, directed, and produced this long-planned masterwork about his companions in World War II. *Big* . . . . marked one of the only times that Fuller (1912-1997) worked with a major studio and a large budget. More often during his career, a rugged filmmaker--nicknamed 'Old Sam' long before Peckinpah arrived on the scene---turned out ultra-low-budget quickies made so swiftly and inexpensively that producers rarely interfered, since there was so little money . . . thus, risk . . . at stake.

Bring it in on budget, and we'll accept whatever you want to do . . .

A yellow journalist and sometimes screenwriter before the war, Fuller made the move to Hollywood shortly after his return. He approached Robert Lippert (1909-1976), an entrepreneur who during the 1940s acquired a chain of second-rate theatres in California. Fuller convinced the canny businessman that, by turning out their own pictures, the collaborators could increase profits. Lippert gave Fuller the freedom to make any movie he wished, just so long as he cut corners at every turn. The result: *I Shot Jesse James* (1949), a shoestring Western that told the tale of the famed outlaw's assassin, Robert Ford (John Ireland), from his side of the gun barrel. Critics noted the edgy imagery and several suggestions of a homoerotic obsession by 'that dirty little coward' for the famed bandit. Next up: A Western so *anti-*generic that, aside from its shot-on-location Arizona locales, this had little if anything in common with any previous Oater.

Fuller became fascinated with James Addison Reaves (1843-1914), a former Confederate volunteer who achieved some success as a real-estate agent in his hometown of St. Louis MO. While negotiating questionable deals, Reaves discovered his previously unknown abilities at forgery. Simultaneously, regarding one of his cases, J.A.R. studied the Treaty of Gaudalupe-Hidalgo, which concluded the Mexican American war of some two decades earlier by stating that all Spanish land grants would be honored, so long as full/proper documentation could be provided. A fantasy formed in Reaves' fertile mind: Find a poor Spanish girl, educate her to the manner of an aristocrat, and create a series of seemingly authentic papers. Then, marry the lady and present his wife as the legal owner of more than 20,000 square miles of land in Arizona and New Mexico, qualifying him as Baron: A European style dictator within the boundaries of our democratic nation. The scam

HE ALMOST GOT AWAY WITH IT: James Addison Reavis attempts to convince the powers-that-be in Arizona that he is, by marriage, entitled to rule over the territory as a virtual tyrant.

almost worked. If it had, the history not only of the southwest but America itself would have unfolded differently.

With a strong script, Fuller dared approach lofty two-time Oscar-winner Frederic March (*Dr. Jekyll and Mr. Hyde*, *The Best Years of Our Lives*) to play the role. When that actor's financial demands could not be met, Fuller hired Vincent Price (1911-1993). During the past decade Price had proven himself effective as pretentious, shady characters in such lofty "A" productions as *The Song of Bernadette* (1943), *Laura* (1944), *Dragonwyck* (1946), and *The Three Musketeers* (.1948), now anxious for his first 'character-lead.' Fuller sensed he had his man upon learning that Price, like Reaves, was born in St. Louis. The icing on this celluloid cake would be provided when an old acquaintance of Fuller's, James Wong Howe (1899-1976), offered to provide his considerable skills for a fraction of his usual fee. Howe's genius at creating black-and-white, deep-focus shadow-worlds onscreen would in time win him Oscars for *The Rose Tattoo* (1955) and *Hud* (1963). Howe's work brought *The Baron*. to

AN INTRIGUING INDIE: No major studio was interested in Sam Fuller's treatment about Reavis and his wife (Ellen Drew) owing to the lack of generic action, so the writer-director-producer instead worked with one of Hollywood's so-called 'minor' companies and, on a shoestring budget, had the opportunity to make precisely the movie he had dreamed about creating.

heights neither Fuller nor Lippert could have imagined as stark black-and-white visuals meld with diverse shades of grey for a unique chiaroscuro effect onscreen.

Fuller would return to the genre with a pair of memorable classics, *Run of the Arrow* and *40 Guns*, both 1957. Though Price would soon become associated with campy horror roles, he did revisit the Western in a pair of minor entries, *The Jackals* (1967) and *More Dead Than Alive* (1969). The Madonna-like *(not* the pop singer!) beauty Ellen Drew (1914-2003) would also play the female lead that same year in an undistinguished Lippert Oater, *Davy Crockett, Indian Scout*. The part of "Pedro,' Reaves' trustful Mexican co-collaborator, is played by Vladimir Sokoloff (1889-1962), known to Western buffs as the elderly peasant who recruits the title group in *The Magnificent Seven* (1960). Intriguingly, Tris(tram) Coffin (1909-1990), cast here as a doubter of Reaves' claim, would return to the history of Arizona as the historical Capt. Thomas Rynning, leader of the Arizona Rangers, in the popular syndicated TV series *26 Men* (1957-1959).

ONCE AN ARIZONIAN, ALWAYS AN ARIZONIAN: Tris(tram) Coffin, who plays a supporting role in Fuller's impressive indie as a state official, would return to Arizona on TV playing the real-life Capt. Thomas Rynning (right) on 26 *Men* with Kelo Henderson (left); this series would be produced by Russell Hayden, onetime sidekick ("Lucky") of Hopalong Cassidy.

11. BIG COUNTRY, THE (1958)
Rating: *****

CREDITS:

William Wyler, dir.; James R. Webb, Sy Bartlett, Robert Wilder, Jessamyn West, scr.; Wyler, Gregory Peck, Robert Wyler, Jerome Moross, mus.; Franz (F.) Planer, cin.; Robert Belcher, John Faure, ed; C; 166 min. United Artists.

CAST:

Gregory Peck (*James McKay*); Jean Simmons (*Julie Maragon*); Carroll Baker *(Patricia Terrill)*; Charlton Heston (*Steve Leech*); Burl Ives (*Rufus Hannassey*); Charles Bickford (*Major Henry Terrill*); Alfonso Bedoya (*Ramon Gutierrez*); Chuck Connors (*Buck*); Chuck Hayward *(Rafe)*; Buff Brady (*Dude*); Jim Burk (*Blackie/'Cracker'*); Dorothy Adams (*Mrs. Hannassey*); Chuck Roberson, Bob Morgan, John McKee, Slim Talbot, George Huggins, Chuck Hamilton (*Cowboys*); Rudy Bowman, Richard Alexander, Ralph Sanford, Harry Cheshire (*Party Guests*).

Though *The Big Country* was a box-office hit in its time, also well-received by critics, here is a major movie that disappeared from the public consciousness once this all-star production concluded its initial run. In hindsight, perhaps the movie was too 'big' for its own good. A top of the line cast, spectacular widescreen process, thundering musical score, and considerable running time caused some to perceive that this Oater that took itself *too* seriously: The director, European émigré William Wyler (1902-1981), had earlier earned a reputation for studied sophistication: *Jezebel* (1936), *Wuthering Heights* (1939), *The Best Years of Our Lives* (1946), *Roman Holiday* (1953); and shortly thereafter *Ben-Hur* (1959), all designed with multiple Oscar nominations in mind. Wyler did have several Westerns to his credit: *Hell's Heroes* (1929), an early variation on 'Three Godfathers,' and *The Westerner* (1940). Notably, these impressive genre entries lacked the Ford/Walsh/Hawks sense of rough-edged spontaneity, offering a studied sensibility which some felt was a bit too sophisticated for this genre.

In retrospect, though, *Big Country*'s combination of genre conventions and fresh approaches appears seminal. The movie goes against the grain of cliché early on. The first image . . . a stagecoach tearing across an open plain

TENDER YET TOUGH: Building on the Donna Reed role in *Backlash*, Jean Simmons here plays a highly educated and potentially sensual old-fashioned woman who can, when push comes to shove, grab a gun and take on all comers.

. . . recalls dozens of roadshow attractions from the past. A powerful music theme enhances the sense of a traditional Western done bigger, and perhaps better, than ever. But when the stage reaches town, we are in for a reversal of expectations. As star Gregory Peck (1916-2003) steps down into an isolated town, he bears no resemblance to the rugged Westerner Peck so capably embodied in *The Gunfighter* (1950). Wearing an expensive suit and bowler hat, 'James McKay' hails from the East, arriving to marry a woman he met and fell in love with back in Baltimore. Meeting him shortly, 'Patricia' wears the very sort of cowboy-ish clothing we identify with the genre's tomboy heroines. In

REVISIONISM FOR 'THE FIST FIGHT': In earlier Westerns including the classic *Red River*, a fistfight between the two stars provided glorious, even in a manner of speaking romantic, entertainment; William Wyler banished that Howard Hawks aesthetic from *The Big Country*, offering what may have been the nastiest, unsentimentalized, and realistic brawl (between Charlton Heston and Gregory Peck) up to that time, as part of this spectacular film's virtual re-invention of 'The Western.'

comparison to Ford's *My Darling Clementine* (1946), the civilizing element from the East, in this variation of a continuing theme, is a man; the harshness of the West represented by a woman.

Also in town are two typical cowboys: 'Steve Leech,' who works for Patricia's father 'Terill' on their upscale ranch; and 'Buck,' a lazy redneck. The latter and his brothers labor (only when forced to) for their trashy father 'Rufus.' These focal brutes are at odds because their bosses/father figures feud over water rights. Otherwise, they might well ally together against McKay, whose gentlemanly manner both despise at first sight. The wild card here is a local schoolmarm, Julie. She owns the rights to Big Muddy, a river that passes through the grasslands. Like her deceased father, Julie allows equal access to this all-important source of survival. Though also born a Westerner, she takes a civilized attitude to the situation. The others, true machismo Westerners, would prefer to kill one another off, winner take all, rugged individualism in full sway.

However breathtakingly Wyler and his collaborators capture the look, the feel, the wideness and of course 'bigness' of the West, the director intended his movie as an oblique commentary on the moment in time when he created

LIKE FATHER, LIKE (ADOPTED) SON: Charlton Heston and Charles Bickford play the last of the old-time rugged individualists, open range cattlemen who resist change and the supposed progress this will bring to the very end; in particular, Bickford's character might be thought of a variation on Emile Meyer's rancher 'Ryker' in *Shane*, here developed as a more three-dimensional character.

the work. Here is a metaphor for the Cold War between the U.S. and Russia. Indeed, Burl Ives (1909-1995; Oscar winner, Best Supporting Actor) purposefully resembles a big angry bear. The final confrontation between Rufus and the typical American Dreamer portrayed by Charles Bickford (1891-1967) stands in for a potential atomic war between then-reigning superpowers. The absurdity of total annihilation from such a conflict offers a clear cautionary fable, if in disguised terms, for its audience.

Wyler does present a variation on one of the Western's ongoing themes--What it means to be a man--offering a unique answer. The rowdy cowboys question McKay's masculinity when he refuses to 'prove himself' by attempting to ride a dangerous mustang. When alone, he secretly asks top vaquero 'Ramon' to bring that horse around. With no witnesses, he rides the bucking bronc down. Likewise, when Leech openly challenges McKay to a fistfight in front of all, the latter refuses. Later, though, while everyone else is asleep, McKay visits Leech. They head out to the prairie and have it out. And, like the iconic fistfight between John Wayne and Montgomery Clift in *Red River*, the result is (significantly) a draw.

All similarity to the Hawks film ends there. In *R.R.*, the duel is presented as a series of swiftly-edited closeups, allowing (in truth, encouraging!) a viewer to be at one with the fight, portrayed as a 'fun experience,' machismo accepted at face value. *T.B.C.* offers the opposite. The fight is communicated in long shot. Wyler (working closely with his cinematographer beforehand and editor afterwards) chose to convey the brutality from a distance, with no exciting cuts to close-ups, only a few dissolves suggesting the passage of time. There is no laughter to be had here when the two find themselves unable to continue; they are devastated, clearly in too much pain to fight on, or they would. McKay proves his manhood to himself.

Machismo in *Red River*? A public show. True masculinity, as displayed here, must be a private affair.

Both women are complex. As onetime friends find themselves in competition for McKay, each reveals an obsession with her father, living or deceased. The Electra Complex is at work; the females try to live up to idealized images of her their dads, one a peacemaker, the other a brawler Ultimately, *The Big Country* (despite its devastating scenery) plays less as 'a Western' in any generic sense than a serious drama of human nature, set on the last frontier.

"BADGES? WE DON'T NEED NO STINKIN' BADGES!" Alfonso Bedoya's role as a Mexican bandido in John Huston's *Treasure of the Sierra Madre* led to more Hollywood work including a positive portrait of a vaquero in *The Big Country*.

12. BIG GUNDOWN, THE (1966)
Rating: **** ½

CREDITS:

Sergio Solima, dir.; Solima, Sergio Donati, Franco Solinas, Fernando Morandi, scr.; Tulio Demicheli, Alberto Grimaldo, pro.; Ennio Morricone, mus.; Carlo Carlini, cin.; Gaby Penalba, ed.; 2.35:1; 110 min. (director's cut), 89 min. (U.S. theatrical); Produzion Europee Associate; Columbia.

CAST:

Lee Van Cleef (*Jonathan 'Colorado' Corbett*); Thomas Milian (*Manuel 'Cuchillo' Sanchez*); Walter Barnes (*Brokston*); Nieves Navarrow *(The Widow)*; Gerard Herter *(Baron von Schulberg)*; Maria Granada (*Rosita Sanchez*); Roberto Camardiel (*Sheriff Jellicol*); Angel del Pozo (*Chet Miller*); Luisa Rivelli *(Prostitute)*; Tom Fellaghy (*Chet's Father*); Galisto Calisti (*Mr. Lynch*); Benito Stefanelli (*Jess*); Nello Pazzafini (*Hondo*); Antonio Casas (*Brother Smith & Wesson*); Jose Torres (*Paco*); Fernando Sancho (*Captain Segura*); Spartaco Conversi (*Mitchell*).

The Spaghetti Western came into being in 1961 with the nondescript *Savage Guns*. Reason for its inception: During the 1950s, Hollywood turned out ever fewer B Westerns, the stateside market diminishing as a result of TV's Oaters. In Italy, televisions were still too expensive for most members of the citizenry, yet pretty much everyone adored low-budget cowboy films. So began the production of Spaghetti (Italian) and Paella (Spain) Westerns to satisfy the market. No one knew at the time that director Sergio Leone would elevate such a *declasse* product into a cinematic art form. With the critical as well

THE MAN IN BLACK: If Johnny Cash owned that title in the world of Country Western music, Lee Van Cleef came to embody the Dark Visage in spaghetti Westerns.

as commercial success of *For a Fistful of Dollars* (1964) internationally, U.S. distributors rushed to pick up such items for the Drive-In and second tier indoor theatres.

Second-billed to Clint Eastwood in *For a Few Dollars More* (1965) and *The Good, The Bad, and the Ugly* (1966), Lee Van Cleef. (1925-1989) was promoted to full star for *Gundown*. Born and bred in New Jersey, he had following WWII service going into accounting. The firm's clients hesitated to meet with this particular employee as he appeared too menacing. Van Cleef's boss quipped that Clarence (his given first name; Lee 'the middle') ought to head for Hollywood and play villains in movies. Inspired, Van Cleef auditioned for the role of silent 'Jack Colby' in *High Noon* (1952). His crowning glory came with a performance in *The Man Who Shot Liberty Valance* (1962), as one of two gunmen (the other played by Strother Martin) who back-up eponymous villain Lee Marvin. When that actor turned down 'The Man in Black' role, Leone hired the 'other' Lee.

Gundown's co-writer/director, Sergio Solima (1921-2015), had been a staple of Rome's film industry in many capacities. As screenwriter, he

RETURN OF THE BOUNTY HUNTER: A hunter of men, the lone American wanders South of the Border in track down and then capture fugitives from the law up Texas-way.

provided scripts for such sword and sandal mini-epics ('Peplums') as *Goliath Against the Giants* (1961), in time directing rip-offs of the suddenly popular James Bond spy movies (*Requiem for a Secret Agent*, 1966). Shot on a larger budget than most such fare, *Gundown* proved to be his make-or-break movie. When released in the U.S., the 89 min. print received stronger than usual reviews. Eventually, the full 110 min. cut surfaced. Observers as diverse as critic Leonard Maltin and filmmaker Quentin Tarantino hailed this extended version as the best single Spaghetti Western ever, excepting only Leone's.

The script----in part written by Sergio Donati (1933-), who would play a key role in constructing the complicated plot for Leone's *Once Upon a Time in the West* (1968)--looks forward to that masterwork with implications of radical (some claim Marxist) politics. 'Colorado' is a bounty killer with a conscience. However ruthless, he is not the sort of man who would shoot down an unarmed enemy. Nor can he grasp, much less tolerate, the omnipresent mindless cruelty around him. A Mexican, living in Texas and known as 'Cuchillo,' apparently raped and murdered a twelve-year-old girl. Now, he's heading for the Rio Grande, certain no U.S. lawman will follow. Outraged, Colorado vows to journey to hell and back if necessary to bring this fugitive to justice. A game of cat and mouse follows, the deadly duo encountering everything from humorous Mormons to a sadistic dominatrix female ranch owner. But as the chase continues, Colorado wonders if he might be pursuing the wrong man. A powerful group of San Antonio politicians and businesspeople, highborn Spanish and Anglo aristocrats, sent Colorado on his mission with the promise of a political career should he succeed. Yet Cuchillo is a scapegoat, the peon picked out to pay for a crime committed by a member of the social/economic elite.

In this film, and in sharp contrast to *Once Upon a Time . . .* , a railroad is never seen. However, talk about the coming of the Iron Horse, as well as vast amounts of capital it will provide, remains constant. Both films appear to take their cue(s) from *The Octopus* (1901), a muckraking novel by self-confessed communist author Frank Norris. In that book, as in these films, the railroad is depicted as a monstrous beast, its invisible tentacles stretching out in

FROM BIT PLAYER TO B MOVIE STARDOM: Beginning with a non-speaking role in *High Noon,* Lee Van Cleef worked his way up through the ranks to top-billed tough guy after Lee Marvin turned down the 'Bad' role in Sergio Leone's Spaghetti Westerns; here, he embodies the sort of pugilistic figure John Wayne earlier portrayed in such films as *Red River* and the sound remake of *The Spoilers.*

every direction, crushing the common man (farmers, small landowners, etc.) as fat cats monopolize this industry for stupendous profit. As in the Leone film, however, the tone never turns archly didactic: Here is a work of rugged entertainment, full of excitingly staged gunfights, these underlined by droll comedy. The Ennio Morricone (1928-2020) score is as fine as anything that composer provided for The Dollars Trilogy.

Unfortunately, Solima was not able to successfully follow up on this, his single important film. A sequel, *Run Man Run* featuring *Gundown*'s Thomas

Milian (1933-2017) repeating his scruffy bandido role, failed to make a mark with either mainstream moviegoers or Spaghetti Western aficionados. Though something of a one-shot wonder, Solima's reputation remains intact thanks to the cult forming in deference to this pre-eminent Spaghetti Western.

COMPANY OF KILLERS: Sheb Wooley, Ian MacDonald, Lee Van Cleef, and Robert J. Wilke stalk the streets of 'Hadleyburg' in search of Gary Cooper in *High Noon* (1952), Lee making his film debut.

13. BIG SHOW, THE (1936)
Rating: ****

CREDITS:

Mark V. Wright, Joseph (Joe) Kane, dir.; Dorrell & Stuart E. McGowan, scr.; Nat Levine, Armand Schaefer, pro.; Edgar Lyons, William Nobles, cin.; Robert Jahns, ed.; 1.37:1; B&W; 71 min.; Republic.

CAST:

Gene Autry ('*Gene Autry*'/*Tom Ford*); Smiley Burnette (*Frog Millhouse*); Kay Hughes *(Marion Hill)*; Sally Payne *(Toodles Brown)*; William Newell (*Lee Wilson*); Max Terhune (*Ventriloquist*); Charles Judels (*Swartz*); Sons of the Pioneers, The Jones Boys, The Beverly Hill Billies, The Light Crust Dough Boys *(Musicians)*; Rex King *(Fred Collins)*; Champion *(Himself)*; Harry Worth (*Tony Rico*); Mary Russell (*Mary*); Christine Maple (*Elizabeth Van Every*); Jerry Larkin *(Blackie)*; Jack O'Shea *(Joe)*; Sally Rand *(Exotic Dancer)*; Leonard Pack *(Texas Ranger Captain)*; Yakima Canutt *(Truck Driver)*; Bob Nolan, Roy Rogers (*Singin' Cowboys*).

'The Singing Cowboy' was not a myth but essential to Western history. Early Anglo cowboys learned from the Vaqueros who preceded them that music calmed steers and kept them from stampeding. During the early 20th Century, such born and bred ranch-hands as Carl T. Sprague, John I. White, and Montana Slim performed authentic pieces on southern and Western regional radio stations. As national networks developed, the once folksy/country numbers were enhanced with elements of jazz, ragtime, and eventually Big Band to better appeal to mainstream northeastern audiences as Western Swing came

BACK IN THE SADDLE AGAIN: Already the veteran of several Republic "Singin' Cowboy Musicals," Gene Autry solidified his reputation as the pre-Roy Rogers "King" of that genre by playing a variation of his own self in this uniquely appealing oddity.

into being. Eventually, listeners found it difficult to tell the difference between a pop star like Bing Crosby and Singing Cowboy Gene Autry (1907-1998).

With the addition of recorded sound to motion pictures during the late 1920s, musicals including (but not limited to) Singing Cowboys appeared. Most film historians agree that the first such picture was *Son(s) of the Saddle* (1930) starring Ken Maynard, for Universal. The subgenre's first superstar would be Autry, a few years later equalled by Roy Rogers (1911-1998). Already a radio star, Autry played a version of himself and sang in the campy Mascot serial *The Phantom Empire* (1935), a combination of "B" Western and science fiction. Certain the tightly budgeted Singing Cowboy product was the way to go, Republic Pictures scooped up Autry, who appeared in their films for more than two decades, before switching over to television with his own Flying 'A' Productions. The authentic Texas rodeo rider (who performed all but his most dangerous 'gags') had filmed a baker's dozen such pictures when cast in *The Big Show*, his most fascinating feature. For this is not, in truth, a

A WESTERN-SET MUSICAL ABOUT MAKING WESTERN MUSICALS:
Republic was endowed with a (temporary) fake name so that some of the early sequences could literally be shot on location.

Singing Cowboy film, rather an edgy musical-comedy about the *making* of a Singing Cowboy film.

And a faux origination fable for Autry's rise to stardom. The Premise: Mammoth Productions in Hollywood churns out Westerns with a self-important star, 'Tom Ford.' His genial stuntman 'Gene Autry' performs all the rough riding. When the latest shoot concludes, Ford heads off for a vacation, unaware he's supposed to appear at the Texas Centennial in Dallas. Desperate, P.R. people convince Autry to again double for Ford, this time passing himself off as the lookalike in person. This was one of the rare Republican pictures to be shot mostly on location in the Lone Star State, so all the pageantry, shows, parades, and radio broadcasts at the event could be incorporated, thereby allowing a shoestring budget product to appear extravagantly costly.

One sure-fire sign that this is something other than a typical Singing Cowboy musical, despite the onscreen presence of Roy Rogers and the Sons of the Pioneers, is the introduction of such non-Western performers as The Jones Boys, a gifted African American group that performs in a style which combines Harlem nocturnes with New Orleans jazz. For once, Autry sings more Crosby-esque romantic ballads than he does trail tunes, though they too are present. While there is, as always, cowboy comedy performed by the sidekick figure---in this case, Smiley Burnette (1911-1967) as ambiguously gay 'Frog Millhouse'---such shenanigans take a backseat to the sort of screwball humor popular in less generic Hollywood offerings. Ditzy blonde 'Toodles,' a giddy flapper, apparently sleeps with any male who offers to make her 'a star.' The film proceeds as a Vaudeville movie, with one fine band or comic making room for the next.

Also, as one of the zany absurdist pictures that all but defy definition: *Million Dollar Legs* (1932; W.C. Fields), *Duck Soup* (1933; The Marx Bros.); *The Big Broadcast* (1938; Bob Hope), *Hellzapoppin'* (1941; Olsen and Johnson), and what may be the greatest serio-comedy ever made, Preston Sturges' *Sullivan's Travels* (1941) . . . which, when re-watched after seeing *The Big Show*, appears to have been influenced (unconsciously or otherwise) by

SCENE STEALERS: Max Terhune introduced the concept of the ventriloquist as sidekick, which would become a staple of low-budget 'B' Westerns; Roy Rogers (who would shortly give Gene Autry strong competition as the King of the Singin' Cowboys) joins The Sons of the Pioneers to perform a commercialized version of cowboy music.

this remarkably madcap piece, particularly the sudden intrusion of talking animals into a relatively realistic onscreen 'world.'

Another noteworthy performer: Max Tehune (1891-1973), appearing here as an unofficial secondary sidekick to pleasingly plump Burnette, appears to be a flesh and blood combination of Porky Pig and Elmer Fudd. A gifted Vaudeville performer hailed for his comedy pranks and magical tricks, Max made a name for himself as one of the era's best Ventriloquists. His 'dummy': Skulky Nulk. The same year Max here played a scene-stealing cameo, he joined Robert Livingston and Ray 'Crash' Corrigan as one of 'The Three Mesquiteers,' a Poverty Row series. Kids were delighted by the sidekick's own wooden 'sidekick.' Appearing too is Roy Rogers, as one of the Sons of the Pioneers. In time, head of Republic Herbert J. Yates realized that Roy had as much charisma and charm, as well as an excellent voice, as Gene, and began top-billing him. From then on, matinee audiences would have to choose between their two favorite Singing Cowboy stars.

14. BONE TOMAHAWK (2015)
Rating: *****

CREDITS:

S. Craig Zahler, dir.; Zahler, scr.; Dallas Sonnier, Jack Heller, many others, pro.; Zahler, Jeff Herriott, mus.; Benji Bakshi, cin.; Greg D'Auria, Fred Raskin, ed; 2.35:1; C; 132 min.; Caliber/Platinum Platypus/RLJ Ent.

CAST:

Kurt Russell *(Sheriff Hunt)*; Patrick Wilson *(Arthur)*; Matthew Fox *(Brooder)*; Richard Jenkins *(Chicory)*; Lili Simmons *(Samantha)*; Evan Jongkeit *(Deputy Nick)*; David Arquette (Purvis); Fred Melamed *(Clarence)*; Sid Haig *(Buddy)*; Maestro Harrell *(Gizzard)*; James Tolkan *(Pianist)*; Kathryn Morris *(Lorna)*; Zahn MClarnon (The Professor); Michael Emery *(Redhead)*; Jeremy Tardy *(Buford)*; Michael Pare *(Mr. Wallington)*; Sean Young *(Mrs. Porter)*; Jamison Newlander *(Mayor)*; Eric Chavarria *(Ramiro)*; Omar Leyva *(Guapp)*; David Midthunder, Jay Tavare *(Troglodytes)*; Raw Leiba *(Wolf Skull)*; Geno Segers *(Boar Tusks)*.

In the seminal Mountain Man epic *Jeremiah Johnson* (Sydney Pollack, 1972), the title character (Robert Redford) ignites a brutal feud with Native Americans by crossing over a sacred burial ground. This, despite his knowledge that to do so, whatever the reason, is an insult. Shortly, the Crow raid the cabin and kill his family. Similarly, In *Bone Tomahawk,* the first film to be directed as well as written by S. Craig Zahler (1973-), a pair of hapless thieves stomp across such holy ground. One, 'Buddy,' is quickly dispatched. The other, 'Purvis,' makes his way to an isolated settlement. But the Native

THE LAST POSSE: Jeff Bridges (second from left) plays one more throwback to those old-fashioned value-driven lawmen of yore, a cinematic second cousin to Ben Johnson in *The Sugarland Express* and Tommy Lee Jones in *No Country for Old Men*, here riding out on his final mission of mercy.

People follow, taking their wrath out on innocent villagers as well as the guilty man, also kidnapping several people including the town's doctor, 'Samantha.' Shortly, her husband (a cowboy), the local sheriff, his aged deputy, and an oddly remote fellow with a superior attitude and particular grudge against Indians in the tradition of 'Ethan Edwards' in *The Searchers*, set out to find the abducted woman and return her, if necessary at the cost of their lives.

In the past, the Western has been crossed with some unlikely genres, sometimes successfully, more often leading to failure. Ranging from traditional horror (*Billy the Kid Versus Dracula* and *Jesse James Meets Frankenstein's Daughter*, both 1966) to the sci-fi invasion story *Cowboys and Aliens* (2011), filmmakers have collapsed the thriller into the Oater. As to the latter, it's important to note that in the later Steven Spielberg produced feature, Native Americans were treated with a respect that reflects contemporary thinking. Though not mentioned in the title, Indians on view are in *Cowboys and Aliens* are not posited as 'The Other'; that status goes to the Martians, or whatever planet the deadly creatures hail from. Likewise, here it is not the Crow (as in *J.J.*) or Comanche *(T.S.)* who murder . . . and worse. (*Much* worse!)

RETURN OF THE RESCUE MYTH: Even as rugged frontiersmen rode long and hard to retrieve an abducted Anglo woman from indigenous people, so here does Samantha (Lilli Simmons) find herself a helpless captive until several Riders in the Sky arrive to bring her back home at any cost.

Though in *Bone Tomahawk* Indians do not (as in *Cowboys and Aliens*) choose to stand alongside Anglos against the agents of chaos, neither are they identified as anything but peaceful citizens. One, asked to serve as scout for the daring quartet, flatly refuses. His own people (this takes place on the Texas/New Mexico border, circa 1900) are as terrified by unknown forces as are the Whites.

Here, the agents of darkness are Troglodytes, final survivors of a race that precedes both Anglos and Indians . . . figures from pre-history that come crawling out of their caves when convinced human beings (of any and all ethnicities) threaten their existence. More disturbing still, they are cannibals, who abduct human beings not to rape and torture and kill, rather to eat their prey. Here, then, the Western (or aspects of it) are crossed with what may be the most controversial of horror films, the Cannibal Holocaust flick. Though there are antecedents, in relatively modern times such a narrative form began with Ruggero Deodato's 1980 'found footage' movie of that very title. That film sharply divided critics and the public as to whether they had witnessed the ultimate piece of despicable exploitation or a valid work of art in the manner of absurdist stage productions including 'the Theatre of Cruelty.'

A DIFFERENT SORT OF 'OTHER': In 21st century Westerns, it's no longer considered politically correct to cast Indians as 'the menacing other'; here, that role is filled by ancient cave dwellers who frighten both the local Anglos and Native Americans.

Devised by Antonin Artaud in early 20th Century France, such avant-garde artists set out to disturb their audiences in hopes that such an approach might force middle-class patrons to reconsider their own existence as a result of dramatic 'shock therapy.' Certainly, the sophistication of Zahler's technique offers evidence that this is, stylistically speaking, a work of art . . . even if the subject matter may seem more appropriate for a junk/exploitation flick.

Essential to the film's viability is the presence of Kurt Russell (1951-) as the relentless hero. Though he has appeared in everything from light comedy to 'serious' contemporary drama, Russell's affinity for this genre is obvious from the inception of his career as a child star. In the 1960s, he had the title role in *The Travels of Jamie McPheeters* (1963-1964), then played five different characters on Fess Parker's titular *Daniel Boone* (1964-1970) TV series. Young Russell starred in the TV version (1974) of Jan Troell's *The New Land* as well as a small-screen variation on *The Searchers*: *The Quest* (1975). He and writer-director John Carpenter were well aware that their theatrical collaborations, *Escape from New York* (1981) and *Big Trouble in Little China*

(1986), were dystopian fantasy variations on the Cowboy Way. Appearing as Wyatt Earp in *Tombstone* (1990) cinched Russell's Western identification. Not unlike Jeff Bridges, he has returned to the genre enough times to gradually become an icon of the West on the order of Clint Eastwood. Appearing in Quentin Tarantino's *The Hateful Eight* the same year as this considerably less known but no less formidable update cinches Russell's status as a true Western icon.

CANNIBAL HOLOCAUST: For many viewers, *Bone Tomahawk* was less a Nouveau Wester than an extreme horror flick set on our final frontier.

15. BRONCO BILLY (1980)
Rating: ****

CREDITS:

Clint Eastwood, dir.; Dennis Hackin, scr.; Dennis Hackin, Robert Daley, Neal H. Dobrofsky, Fritz Manes, pro.; David Worth, cin.; Joel Cox, Ferris Webster, ed.; 1.85:1; C; 116 min.; Warner Bros.

CAST:

Clint Eastwood *(Bronco Billy)*; Sondra Locke *(Antoinette Lily)*; Geoffrey Lewis *(John Arlington)*; Scatman Crothers *(Doc Lynch)*; Bill McKinney *(Lefty LeBow)*; Sam Bottoms *(Leonard James)*; Dan Vadis *(Chief Big Eagle)*; Sierra Pecheur *(Lorraine Running Water)*; Walter Barnes *(Sheriff Dix)*; Woodrow Parfrey *(Dr. Canterbury)*; Beverlee McKinsey *(Irene Lily)*; Doug(las) McGrath *(Wiecker)*; Hank Worden *(Mechanic)*; William Prince *(Edgar)*; Pam Abbas (Mother Superior); Douglas Copsey *(Reporter)*: Merle Haggard *(Himself)*; Alison Eastwood *(Orphan)*; George Wendt *(Bartender)*.

If Steve McQueen and Paul Newman had reigned as the unquestioned kings of the box office during the 1960s, Clint Eastwood (1930-) ruled as our Numero Uno hero-figure between 1970-1980. His contemporary crime films (*Dirty Harry*, 1971), country comedies (*Every Which Way but Loose*, 1978), and of course Westerns (*The Outlaw Josey Wales*, 1976) were blockbusters. The exception: *Bronco Billy*, the least seen among his starring vehicles. Fans hunger to watch Clint as a rough-hewn winner, whether a particular vehicle calls for laughs, violence, or both. While this movie did contain comedy bits and a modicum of action (family style), the narrative offers up a sentimental melodrama in a self-consciously corny manner. The star here recalls James Stewart and Gary Cooper, not in their rugged Westerns for Anthony Mann (*Winchester '73*, 1950; *Man of the West*, 1959); rather the gentle, whimsical, emotionally resonant films each appeared in for Frank Capra: *Mr. Smith Goes to Washington*, 1939; *Mister Deeds Goes to Town*, 1936. In most of his movies, Eastwood plays the man who gets the job done. Here, he's Everyman; or, more correctly, an *American* Everyman of a sort that has passed out of favor, with the exception of Tom Hanks' warm, winning alter-egos. 'Bronco Billy' (we never learn the character's birth name) struggles to maintain a lofty set of standards that few, in our cynical age, still believe in. A Western version of Walter Mitty, he's a dreamer/idealist who cannot stand the current state of our world and so invents a preferred alternative-fantasy one. Even if he cannot keep the nostalgic dream alive, Bronco Billy rates as a hero for being the last man to continue making the effort.

THE SOFTER SIDE OF A SPAGHETTI WESTERN STAR: In his films for Sergio Leone, Don Siegel, and in time himself, Clint Eastwood played one of meanest 'heroes' in movie history; here, in what may be the director/star's most deeply 'personal' work, he waxes sentimental both in performance and filmmaking style.

B.B. runs a small, sad little Wild West show. Not on the order of Buffalo Bill's famous one, this more akin to the small traveling circuses that played medium-sized cities throughout the first half of the 20th century. Drawing from such bygone traditions as the Medicine Show, Vaudeville, and Country Fair exhibitions of sharpshooting, Billy's troupe boldly faces one crisis after another. Most pressing: People don't care anymore about the legends of the West. If they want to catch a Western, more likely it will be something brutal on the order of *The Wild Bunch* (or Clint's own upcoming

INEXPLICABLE INAMORATA: Lacking the charisma and charm of a legitimate light comedienne such as Jane Fonda, Goldie Hawn, or Jill Clayburgh, leading lady Sondra Locke failed to live up to the bittersweet though good-hearted aesthetic of this unique Nouveau Western.

THE LAST ROUND-UP: Billy (Clint Eastwood) fights to keep the tradition of The Wild West show alive if not well; that's the beloved scene steal (and musician) Scatman Crothers (best known for Stanley Kubrick's *The Shining*) to his immediate right.

masterpiece, *Unforgiven*, 1992) than one of those charming mini-musicals about good vs. evil that starred Roy Rogers or Gene Autry. Yet Bronco Billy, or the man who tries to keep that image (which reaches back at least to the earliest silent-era Oaters) alive, if no longer well, is a man on a mission. Making money is the least of his interests. As long as Bill can eke out meagre profits that allow his show to continually move on in search of ever smaller audiences, he will stick with it. In a way, Bronco's the opposite of the honest to goodness 'career cowboy' played by Lee Marvin in *Monte Walsh*. When decent jobs disappeared as the ranches failed one by one, Monte was offered the opportunity to dress up in a Rhinestone Cowboy outfit for a two-bit show. Though devoid of any other means of making a living, Monte declines, whispering; "I'm not spittin' on my whole life." Contrarily, B.B. is not the authentic cowboy he poses as. Only a well-intentioned, in truth ordinary fellow who deeply admires such figures, real and/or mythic. And hopes that if he can convince even one ticket-buyer he's the real deal, then his life has meaning. "It ain't over," he might (to paraphrase Marvin's Monte Walsh) say, "As long as there's still one Wild West showman, performing on a horse with blazing guns that pretend to protect the righteous and doom the wicked, it ain't over."

But, of course, it is. Still, as was the case with Cervantes' Don Quixote, there is a nobility to this impossible dreamer's sweet-spirited naivete and an aura of tragedy regarding his necessary end.

Sadly, the film is burdened by the awesomely inadequate presence of Sondra Locke (1944-2018), whom Eastwood first hired for *Josey Wales*, then insisted on as his co-star in film after film. Here, she plays a part akin to the wonderful runaway heiresses of the 1930s, incarnated during Hollywood's golden age by the likes of Claudette Colbert and Carole Lombard. At the time of *B.B.*'s filming, several actresses might have dazzled in such a part: Goldie Hawn, Jane Fonda, and Jill Clayburgh come to mind. But even a great filmmaker has his blind spots. Despite Locke's mindless mugging in what ought to have been a low-key performance, *Bronco Billy* exerts a genial charm that appears in none of Clint's other films. Indeed, there are Eastwood fans who believe that with this film, Clint most openly unlocked his mind, heart, and soul.

SCENE STEALER: Jazz musician and actor Scatman Cruthers added his appealing screen presence to the mix; he can also be seen with friend Jack Nicholson in two non-Westerns, *One Flew Over the Cuckoo's Nest* and *The Shining*.

16. BRONZE BUCKAROO, THE (1939)
Singin' Cowboy Movie Rating: * ½
Historical Importance Rating: *****

CREDITS:

Richard C. Kahn, dir.; Kahn, scr.; Kahn, pro.; Lew Porter, mus.; Roland Price, Clark Ramsey, cin.; 1.371: B&W; 58 min.; Hollywood Pictures.

CAST:

Herb Jeffries (*Bob Blake*); Lucius Brooks (*Dusty*); Artie Young (*Betty Jackson*); F.E. Miller (*Slim Perkins*); Clarence Brooks (*Buck Thorne*); Lee Calmes *(Lee)*; The Four Tones (*Quartet*); Rollie Hardin (*Joe Jackson*); Earle (J.) Morris (*Bartender*); Rollie Hardin (*Joe Jackson*); Tom Southern (*Poker Player*); John Thomas (*Man in Bar*).

Here is one of those unique films that ought to be revived (in a contemporary context of carefully framed viewership) for reasons other than aesthetic appreciation. On the surface, this is nothing other than one more ultra-low-budget Singin' Cowboy movie of the type so popular with child-audiences at matinees before disappearing from sight, revived during the early days of television when local channels aired virtually anything to fill time. This picture (shot on a dude ranch near Victorville CA) featured such limited resources as to production that appear lavish in comparison to many Poverty Row Oaters from Mascot, Monogram, and P.R.C. Not to mention the considerably

REVISITING 'THE RACE WESTERN': In a segregated America, theatres in black neighborhoods satisfied their communities with motion pictures that featured all African American casts, with Westerns an essential part of that half-forgotten paradigm.

more expensive/expansive versions of the Western subgenre coming out of Universal and Republic. What sets this one apart: An all-black cast, with most of the behind-the-camera team African American as well. For *Bronze Buckaroo* belongs to a type of film that many casual movie fans do not today know once existed: The Race Movie.

This form derived as a result of two pressing issues. First, following the release of D.W. Griffith's *The Birth of a Nation* (1915), set in South Carolina before, during, and after the Civil War, many black artists, academics, and intellectuals railed at the racist/exaggerated portrayal of black characters, along with that film's depiction of the Ku Klux Klan as an American variation on the Knights of the Round Table. As a result, black businessmen were encouraged to create their own films, with African American characters portrayed in a less caricatured light. During the late 1910s, Chicago based entrepreneur

"GENE AUTRY, MOVE OVER!" Musician turned actor Herb(ert) Jeffries embodied the popular vision of a righteous hero who rides out of Harlem (rather than, say, Dodge City) to right the wrongs perpetrated by villains on honest settlers.

William Foster (aka (Juli Jones) turned out ethno-centric films, specifically for an audience comprised of people of color. Here was the other great motive that explains the need for such product: In many American cities, particularly in the South, blacks were either restricted from attending movie theatres that catered to Anglo audiences or forced to take seats in restricted areas such as the balcony. In some cases, this held true in the northeast. Rightly offended, many African Americans chose to attend movie houses owned by people of their own race, these catering to the black community. Yet such ticket buyers were less than interested in seeing Hollywood's films featuring black actors in menial, often degrading roles. The so-called 'race movies,' highlighting black performers, were welcomed here.

They ran the gamut from melodramas through romances to musicals and crime stories. And Westerns. Louisiana-born Richard C. Kahn (1897-1960) turned out a trio of Singin' Cowboy Pictures, this middle offering sandwiched between *Two-Gun Man from Harlem* (1938) and *Harlem Rides the Range* (1939). All starred Herb(ert) Jeffries (1913-2014; born in Detroit), a popular jazz baritone who performed at clubs owned by Al Capone during the infamous gangster era. In addition to his considerable gifts as a singer, Jeffries stood tall and appeared extraordinarily handsome. In a later era, he might have like Harry Belafonte and Sidney Poitier been accepted by all audiences, ethnicity aside. But such color blindness, at least in theory, was yet to come. So Jeffries (who bore a notable resemblance to Spanish star Cesar Romero) took what roles open to him in the race films.

Quality-wise, *Bronze Buckaroo* is considered a step above the other two faatures, though the plot is ordinary. Our N.Y.C. hero heads to Arizona where an old pal has been kidnapped. Searching for the bad-guys, he also falls in love with the victim's pretty sister. On hand too is a ventriloquist not unlike Max Terhune in more mainstream Oaters of that time. Indeed, *Bronze Buckaroo* typifies a race film in a unique and fascinating way. We do not encounter a proud black hero standing up to bad white men as so often would be the case with the Urban Crime Dramas and Westerns churned out in the early 1970s, more often than not starring James Brown and/or

Fred Williamson. Here we encounter a fantasy West that is *entirely* black: The good, the bad, the ugly and beautiful characters on view are all African American. This created an entire 'world' for the viewers, an alternative to the almost all-white films featuring Roy Rogers.

As for Jeffries, he chose an outfit almost identical to that of "B" movie superstar Tom Mix, with black shirt and pants. Also, a high, wide white sombrero to cap off his impressive appearance. Though untrained as to acting, Jeffries turned out to be a natural, whether it was wooing the girls or punching out, and in some cases shooting, villains. Such race films disappeared beginning in the late 1940s, when the Civil Rights Movement finally had its great, full impact following the integration of our armed forces during World War II. At this time, Hollywood belatedly began making mainstream movies for all audiences about black characters; *Lost Boundaries* (1949) a formidable early example. With ever more theatres nationwide becoming integrated, the need for special movie houses and films to play there dissipated. Jeffries then

THE SLOW-WITTED SIDEKICK: As with Slim Pickens, Gabby Hayes, and 'Fuzzy' Knight in Anglo Oaters, this B Cowboy Movie featured a gullible, guileless pal to the handsome hero; Lucius Brooks embodies 'Dusty,' no smarter or dumber than any of the other companions to goodguys in more mainstream movies of the time: Gabby Hayes, Smiley Burnette, Fuzzy Knight, and so many others.

starred in *Calypso Joe* (1957), a modest entertainment that brought the brief craze for 'exotic' musical and dance styles to an adult public even then turning to such records, while the teenagers opted for rock 'n' roll. Though Jeffries had top billing, many cast members were white, allowing for onscreen integration. The attitude of that film: The times are changing; don't position yourself on the wrong side of history. Though largely unknown today, Jeffries was among the first performers of color to break racial barriers. And an African American Western-town-tamer a quarter of a century before Cleavon Little incarnated "Black Bart" in *Blazing Saddles*.

THE SHAPE OF THINGS TO COME: A generation later, Woody Strode would play a more realistically portrayed African American Westerner in John Ford's *Sergeant Rutledge* (1960).

17. BUTCH AND SUNDANCE: THE EARLY DAYS (1979)
Rating: *** ½

CREDITS:

Richard Lester, dir.; Allan Burns, scr.; Steven Bach, Jack B. Bernstein, Gabriel Katzka, William Goldman, pro.; Patrick Williams, mus.; Laszlo Kovacs, cin.; George Trirogoff, ed.; 2.35;1; C; 115 min.; 20th Century-Fox.

CAST:

William Katt (*Harry A. Longabaugh/The Sundance Kid*); Tom Berenger (*Leroi Parker/Butch Cassidy*); Jeff Corey (*Ray Bledsoe*); John Schuck (*Harvey Logan*); Michael C. Gwynne (*Mike Cassidy*): Peter Weller (*Joe Le Fors*); Brian Dennehy (*O.C. Hanks*); Chris(topher) Lloyd (*Bill Carver*); Jill Eikenberry (*Mary*); Joel Fluellen (*Jack the Bartender*); Regina Baff (*Ruby*); Peter Brocco (*Old Outlaw*); Vincent Schiavelli (*Bank Guard*); Hugh Gillin (Cyrus Antoon); Jack Riley (Messenger); Sherril Lynn Rettino *(Annie)*; Charles Knapp (Telegrapher); Noble Willingham (*Capt. Prewitt*); Patrick Stewart (*Sam*); Walt Stevens *(Grissom)*; Arthur Hill *(Governor)*.

Even as 'Now!' movies like *The Graduate* (1967) and *Midnight Cowboy* (1969) were catching the public's attention, some observers of the cinema scene again announced that the period-Western was dead. Wrong! When Hollywood's Big Movies were released in December, they included *Butch Cassidy and the Sundance Kid*. Any box-office attraction demands a follow up, not so easy in this case considering the finality of that classic's concluding shot. When Fox proposed a prequel, Paul Newman and Robert Redford made clear they had no interest in portraying younger versions of their characters. Original screenwriter William Goldman (1931-2018) would only become peripherally involved in the script. That task fell to Allan Burns (1935-2021), a gifted writer and producer of 'smart' TV sitcoms: *The Mary Tyler Moore Show*, *Lou Grant*, etc. When George Roy Hill passed on the opportunity to direct, another "A"-list filmmaker signed on. Pennsylvania born, British trained Richard Lester (1932-) displayed a quirky way of telling diverse tales (*A Hard Day's Night*, 1964; *The Three Musketeers*, 1973; the underappreciated *Petulia* (1968) and, a year following *B&S: The Early Days.*, *Superman II*.

TOGETHER AGAIN FOR THE FIRST TIME: Paul Newman and Robert Redford as Butch and Sundance in the 1969 classic; Tom Berenger and William Katt in the underrated prequel.

In this version of the initial meeting of good-natured Butch and intense Sundance, the tone and pacing are entirely different from what viewers experienced a decade earlier. Largely, this was on release perceived as a failure to recapture the original's glory days. The situation might better be perceived, though, as a different artist telling the tale in his own special manner. As in all Lester films, this unique storyteller prefers to set up a sequence in which his lead characters stand precariously close to the camera, engaging in dialogue that strikes us as ever less interesting. Meanwhile, behind them or on the sides, diverse bits of business vie for our attention. Here then is a more demanding sort of direction, if hardly what fans of the first film expected, causing a generalized sense of disappointment.

For the viewer willing to accept this movie on its own terms, *The Early Days* offers many rewards. Happily, stars William Katt (1950-) and Tom Berenger (1949-), however influenced by their legendary predecessor stars, never slip into mimicry. The genius-level cinematographer Laszlo Kovacs (1933-2007;

"STICK 'EM UP ... AGAIN!" One of the most popular conventions in Western films occurs when a pair of appealing bandits defy the laws of the land and allow an audience a vicarious moment of outlaw-adventure.

Easy Rider, 1969; *Five Easy Pieces*, 1970; *Shampoo*, 1970) received Lester's go-ahead to shoot various sequences in vivid southwestern locations (New Mexico, Arizona, Southern Colorado), most of which had not been previously employed for Westerns. Particularly memorable: Butch and Sundance getting to know one another amid bizarre natural structures of Toadstool Park, as striking in its own humbler way as John Ford's beloved Monument Valley. Appears as to majestic grandeur Likewise, the story's middle section takes place during a ferocious blizzard, rare in Westerns.

Best of all are two set-pieces. The elaborate railroad robbery that concludes the film outdoes similar sequences in the original. Most significant, though, is a gunfight between the Kid and a crazed gunman, 'O.C. Hanks.' Other than a routine fist fight, no convention of the genre is more over-used than the traditional shootout. The test of a film, then, and filmmakers who choose to include one, has to do with how unique and fresh they are able to make the cliché appear in a new context. Rather than a spectacular (and expected) fast draw match between two cold-blooded characters, here are two believable people — uncertain why or how they worked their way into a terrible but irreversible situation — who hesitate not out of fear but concern for the implications of their actions. Why am I here, what does all of this *mean* ... if anything?

The sequence is staged in springtime; the streets of this sad little city are flooded. The wary opponents barely manage to remain standing as dirty water soaks their paints. Here Lester and his company found a way to make something very old appear new again with their inspired approach to what had long since come to be considered mundane material.

Not that the film is without flaws. Once Butch's family has been introduced as a surprisingly normal wife and sons for such a notorious figure, 'Mary' ought to have been better developed ... allowing us to grasp why such a clean-cut lady would spend her life waiting around for such a ne'er do well husband to perhaps someday show up. The same holds true for lawman 'Joe Lefors,' effectively portrayed as a distant, menacing figure in the first film. Once he has been particularized, with a notably gifted actor (Jeff Corey, a

WHEN HISTORY MEETS HOLLYWOOD: The actual Hole in the Wall gang sat down for this authentic picture; Richard Lester's cast offers a striking replica of that moment.

holdover from the original film), something more ought to have been done with him. The same holds true for 'Kid Curry' and other gang members who gather together towrd the end. These characters were present near the first film's opening sequence, each revealing a distinct personality. Here, they are so many 'extras,' none allowed anything distinctive to do. And, despite the desire to present a perfect prequel to a movie everyone loved, there are details which contradict the mythology already in place. We witness Butch and Sundance revealing their real names to one another shortly after meeting; in the 1969 film, the older incarnations finally did so shortly before their joint demise. Previous to a shoot-out with bandidos, Redford's Sundance admitted to Newman's Butch that he had never before killed a man. Here, though, he guns down at least one. Minor quibbles, these, in an appealing and unique genre entry that is better appreciated for its own qualities than as a companion piece to a classic.

BLACKLIST SURVIVOR: Despite being condemned by HUAC during the postwar Red Scare, Jeff Corey (1914-2002) staged a triumphant comeback that included playing Ray Bledsoe in both Butch and Sundance films as well as Wild Bill Hickok in *Little Big Man* (1970).

18. CANYON PASSAGE (1946)
Rating: **** ½

CREDITS:

Jacques Tourneur, dir.; Ernest Pascal, scr.; Walter Wanger, Alexander Golitzen, pro.; Frank Skinner, mus.; Edward Cronjager, cin.; Milton Caruth, ed.; 1.37:1; C; 92 min.; Universal.

CAST:

Dana Andrews (*Logan Stuart*); Brian Donlevy (*George Camrose*); Susan Hayward (*Lucy Overmire*); Patricia Roc *(Caroline Marsh)*; Ward Bond (*Honey Bragg*); Fay Holden (*Mrs. Overmire*); Hoagy Carmichael (*Hi Linnet*); Stanley Ridges (*Jonas Overmire*); Lloyd Bridges (*Johnny Steele*); Andy Devine *(Ben Dance)*; Victor Cutler (*Vane Blazier*); Rose Hobart (Marta *Lestrade*); Halliwell Hobbes (*Clenchfield*); James Cardwell (*Gray Bartlett*); Onslow Stevens *(Jack Lestrade)*; Ted and Danny Devine (Dance Children); Erville Alderson (*Judge*).

During the mid-20th century, a mythic vision of 'two Americas' became firmly set in our national consciousness: The East represented an overcrowded cesspool of capitalism where people care about nothing except profits; the West offered an alternative land of idealistic simple folk who cared little (if at all) about making money, anxious to create a New Eden and assert basic Christian values of Western Civilization. East is east, according to popular culture, and West is west. Innocent, honest Red States; corrupt and cynical Blue ones.

That, at least, was the legend. And nowhere did this admittedly skewed vision exist so significantly as in generic Westerns.

A SECOND EDEN: Pioneers (Dana Andrews, Susan Hayward) attempt to live out The American Dream of achieving happiness and success through entrepreneurship in the far west.

One of the rare/notable exceptions is *Canyon Passage*. The lead character, 'Logan Stuart,' defines himself less as a Westerner than a Businessman. He travels from Portland, OR to the in- embryo community of Jacksonville for a single reason: As people pour in, there's an opportunity for him to get rich. Not 'quick,' like the hordes of miners eager to discover gold. Rather, slowly, building a series of businesses (from a stagecoach line to a network of general stores) that result in an American Empire all his own. As always, though, there are no guarantees. Forces beyond anyone's control can wreak havoc on the proverbial best laid plans of mice and men.

For Logan remains so focused on investing whatever profits he makes in the next venture that, Ebenezer Scrooge-like, he loses the love of a demure fiancée, 'Caroline.' No question, though, that Logan is an enlightened (honest) capitalist. That's not the case with friend 'George Camrose,' who runs the local bank. Secretly addicted to gambling, George siphons off dust kept in

EVERYDAY LIFE ON THE FRONTIER: Though this unique film does include an Indian raid (bottom right) lifted directly from Fox's earlier Eastern-Western Drums *Along the Mohawk* (1939), the film focuses primarily on the everyday lives of diverse Americans attempting to achieve their ambitions in a non-generic sense.

his safe from decent clients like 'Johnny Steele.' George recalls the corrupt banker in *Stagecoach* (1939), absconding with the town's funds. This should not come as a surprise, as *Canyon Passage*, like Ford's film, was based on a *Saturday Evening Post* story by Ernest Haycox.

As to this film's director, Paris-born Jacques Tourneur (1904-1971) had a long history of making movies in which the characters' working-lives are

"HEY, WILD BILL! WAIT FER *ME*!": Andy Devine, once a Shakespearean clown on the 'legitimate' stage, would earn the adoration of children as sidekick to Guy Madison on a beloved 1950s TV show about famed marshal Hickock; here, he enjoyed an early opportunity (following John Ford's *Stagecoach*, 1939) to reveal How the West Was Fun.

notably on display, rather than merely hinted at as boring off camera activities, the case in most commercial films. In such R.K.O. thrillers as *Cat People* (1942), *I Walked with a Zombie* (1943), and *The Leopard Man* (1943), characters are often depicted in their offices and, by implication, judged by their level of professionalism. This uniquely qualified Tourneur for the directorial position here. Though there is indeed a brutal fist fight, a street shootout, and a climactic battle with Indians, such generic conventions (though well-handled in context) are the least significant aspects. As in a tale of ordinary, everyday folk that might have been set in any time or place, we watch what we believe to be 'people' rather than 'characters' form and break relations with others. Happily, this never descends into soap opera but is as fully and richly developed as in such intellectually rendered 'realistic' plays as Henrik Ibsen's *An Enemy of the People* (1888) or Arthur Miller's *Death of a Salesman*. (1949).

Understandably, then, the piece largely excludes the Western convention of 'good guys' and 'bad guys.' With the exception only of the bully 'Honey Bragg,' a narcissistic drunkard played by Ward Bond in a manner that recalls his role in Ford's *Young Mr. Lincoln* (1939). Only when he rapes an innocent Indian girl does the tribe go on the warpath; otherwise, local indigenous people only ask to be treated with a modicum of respect from separate but (so far as we can see, at least) equal Anglo neighbors. Even the banker, though dishonest, is never reduced to a mere cliché, as with the corresponding character in *Stagecoach*. 'George' is a complex, well-intentioned, essentially weak fellow who cannot overcome his addiction.

NEXT STOP, SEA HUNT': In a strong supporting role, Lloyd Bridges embodies a fair-minded capitalist who hopes to achieve fame and fortune without stepping on anyone else to do so: though Bridges' famous TV series would feature him as a contemporary diver, he would indeed play the lead in a Western, *The Loner*, created during the mid-1960s by Rod Serling.

Dana Andrews (1909-1992) occasionally worked in Westerns: *Kit Carson* (1940), *Belle Starr* (1941), and a towering classic, *The Ox-Bow Incident* (1943). Yet he has always been most associated with contemporary Everyman types: the world-weary G.I. in *A Walk in the Sun* (1945), a jaded returning vet in *The Best Years of Our Lives* (1946), and the typical Man in a Gray Flannel Suit in *Madison Avenue* (1961). Here, his 'regular guy' owns (and when absolutely necessary carries) a handgun. Yet he rarely employs the weapon. Likewise, none of the other townspeople ever do, even as in the real West the carrying of pistols was prohibited within almost all city limits.

Like Andrews, Susan Hayward (1917-1975) as Lane's eventual *inamorata* did on occasion gravitate to Westerns (virtually everyone in Tinseltown did in those days) but defined her screen image as The Modern Woman incarnate in *House of Strangers* (1949). Last but hardly least, the lean, learned Hoagy Carmichael (1899-1981; he the original choice for 'Sam' in *Casablanca*, 1943) brings an aura of chorus-like detachment to his role of 'The Balladeer.' Carmichael composed the film's theme song, "Old Buttermilk Sky," which became a popular hit for decades to come--well remembered in a way that, sadly, this striking film is not. Western buffs may note that in the first season of NBC's *Laramie* (1959-60), Hoagy played an identical role ('Jonesy') to his memorable one here.

THE SECOND TIME AROUND: Hoagy Carmichael would recycle his character from *Canyon Passage* (while slightly changing the name) for the first season of NBC's *Laramie*: from Left to Right: John Smith (previously featured on *Cimarron City*), Robert Crawford Jr. (brother of *The Rifleman's* Johnny Crawford), Hoagy, and Robert Fuller (later to replace Robert Horton on *Wagon Train*).

19. CATTLE ANNIE AND LITTLE BRITCHES (1980)
Rating: ****

CREDITS:

Lamont Johnson, dir.; Robert Ward, David Eyre, scr.; Alan King, Robert Hitzig, many others, pro.; Sahn Berti, tom Slocum, mus.; Larry Pizer, cin.; William Haugse, ed.; C; 97 min.; Hemdale/Universal.

CAST:

Amanda Plummer (*Annie*); Diane Lane *(Jenny)*; Burt Lancaster (*Bill Doolin*); John Savage (*Bittercreek Newcomb*); Rod Steiger (*William H. Tilghman*); Scott Glenn (*Bill Dalton*); Redmond Gleeson (*Red Buck)*; William Russ (*Dick Raidler*); Ken(ny) Call (*Weightman*); Buck Taylor *(Dynamite Dick)*; Michael Conrad *(Engineer)*; Perry Lang (*Elrod)*; John Quade *(Morgan)*; Yvette Sweetman (*Mrs. Sweetman*); Jerry Gatlin (*Law Officer)*; Russ Hoverson *(Prison Guard*); Nicole Massie (*Girl at the Festival*).

Why is it that some lawmen (Bat Masterson, Wyatt Earp) achieve ongoing legendary status while other worthies, including those luminaries' friends Charles Bassett and Bill Tilghman, have been mostly overlooked? The same holds true for outlaw gangs. More than two dozen theatrical films and TV shows have portrayed the James/Younger boys from Missouri. On the other hand, the equally fascinating Doolin-Dalton bunch appear in only several features and are all but unknown to the modern mainstream film fan. The single modern movie that focuses on their activities, *Cattle Annie* . . . received

REAL AND 'REEL': The actual outlaw girls; Hollywood's rendering of them.

such a lousy reception when introduced in major cities that the piece was pulled from distribution and sold directly to pay cable.

As for earlier Oaters, onetime legend-in-his-own-lifetime Bill Doolin (1858-1896) has been the subject of only three "B" Westerns: *Return of the Bad Men* (1948; starring Robert Armstrong), *The Doolins of Oklahoma* (1949; Randolph Scott), and *The Cimarron Kid*, 1951; Audie Murphy). One year previous to the release of *Cattle Annie . . . .*, Bo Hopkins played Doolin in a TV movie, *The Last Ride of the Dalton Gang*, which depicted several events (ending with the disastrous Coffeyville KS. Raid) that precede (and provide an unconscious prelude to) this film. The intrepid federal marshal who rounded up the gang, William H. Tilghman (1854-1924), only appeared fleetingly in several episodes of TV's *The Life and Legend of Wyatt Earp* and a single *Death Valley Days* instalment. Sam Elliott would play the character in the made-for-TV movie *You Know My Name!* (1999). During his final days of celebrity, Tilghman had portrayed himself (and also directed) the self-glorifying homage to his onetime heroism, *Passing of the Oklahoma Outlaws* (1915). Here, Rod Steiger (1925-2002), an unlikely candidate for Westerns, does the honors.

As in Ward's novel, on which the film is based, one liberty taken had to do with elderly actors (Steiger; Lancaster; 1913-1994) portraying the respectful combatants as grand old men of a fast-fading frontier. In fact, each was middle-aged at the time when these events unfolded. But for the post-*Wild Bunch/Monte Walsh/Cable Hogue* era, most movies about the West's good men and bad romanticize them as relics from a golden age. Since most post-1970 Hollywood films played directly to a youth audience, and as this was also the feminist era, here the focus is not on The Boys but historical Anna Emmaline McDoulet (1882-1978) and Jennie Stevenson (1879-1978). Great attention went to the picking of actresses Plummer (1957-) and Lane (1965-), focusing not only on their considerable talent(s) but physical resemblance to the actual girls. The two are portrayed as running away from homes in the East to seek adventure in a glamorous world of handsome anti-heroes, only to discover that the Dime Novels created by the likes of Ned Buntline present

THE LAWMAN AND THE OUTLAW: A pair of Oscar winners were hired to portray Big Bill Tilghman (Rod Steiger), the man with a star, and Big Bill Doolin (Burt Lancaster), the marshal's prey . . . and alter-ego.

a glorified legend of what turns out to be a difficult reality. In this piece of historical fiction, Doolin, handsome young Bitter Creek Newcomb, and other members of 'the bunch' find themselves attempting to live up to the girls' idealized images of them.

Something more than a mere journeyman, Lamont Johnson (1922-2010) cut his teeth on high quality filmed episodic TV in the late-1950s and 1960s (*The Defenders*, *Twilight Zone*, and the memorable Richard Boone Western *Have Gun, Will Travel*). He here shifted his talents to the big screen. While the film's disastrous box office returns (little more than $500,000 on a more than six million investment) dimmed any such hopes, he had previously

REVISIONISM HITS THE WESTERN: Traditional cowboy movies presented only those continuing cliches inherent in genre films while leaving out other historical details; nouveau Westerns such as this expanded the Western's horizons by depicting baseball, enjoyed by women (here, Diane Lane) as well as men, for a more accurate depiction of the frontier.

helmed the little-seen Kirk Douglas/Johnny Cash Western *A Gunfight* (1971) and would return to such frontier sagas a single time, with *The Broken Chain* (1993), concerning Native American involvement in the Revolutionary War. Johnson's ability to "make rooms appear lived in" rather than (as is too often the case in quickly lensed works) thrown together swiftly for a shoot would characterize the director's high-quality TV work on his contemporary cop shows, *Hill Street Blues* and *Miami Vice*.

The 'world' in which the Dalton/Doolin gang once inhabited was painstakingly recreated, so as not to bear too much resemblance to other (more conventional) Hollywood versions of the fading frontier. Likewise, gang members (even those with small and in some cases non-speaking roles) are fleshed out, hinting at strong back stories. As with a fine film from more than a decade earlier, *Will Penny* (1967), we might guess that here much fascinating material dropped down to the cutting room floor. With the cowboys there, the outlaws here, every actor appears to have been totally committed to what each sensed to be a special project, adding to a rich verisimilitude of people and places, these reconsidered and interpreted with loving attention. While all the expected visual details necessary for any genre film (lariats to Stetsons) are on view, the script by Ward and direction via Johnson also draw attention to actual elements of Western life that have been ignored in favor of more mythic elements. Other than *Ulzana's Raid* (Robert Aldrich, 1972) and *The Great Northfield Minnesota Raid (Philip Kaufman, 1972)*, this stands as the only major film to focus on the popularity of baseball on our final frontier. The Westerners have organized teams, complete with uniforms; the spirited playing of their sport of choice adds one more delightful if unexpected surprise to this underappreciated gem.

20. CHINA 9, LIBERTY 37 (1978)
Rating: ****

CREDITS:

Monte Hellman, dir.; Jerry Harvey, Douglas Venturelli, Ennio De Concini, many others, scr.; Hellman, Gianni Bozzacchi, Valerio De Paolis, many others, pro.; Pino Donaggio, John Rubinstein, mus.; Giuseppe Rotunno, cin.; Hellman, Cesare D'Amico, ed.; 2.35:1; C; 102 min.; Aspa Prods./Allied Artists.

CAST:

Warren Oates (*Matthew*); Fabio Testi (*Clayton*); Jenny Agutter (*Catherine*); Sam Peckinpah *(Wilbur Olsen*); Isabel Mestres *(Barbara)*; Gianrico Tondinelli *(Johnny)*; Franco Interlenghi *(Hank)*; Carlos (Charly) Bravo (*Duke*); Paco Benlloch (*Virgil)*; Sydney Lassick (*Citizen*); Richard C. Adams (*Sheriff*); Natalia Kim (*Cassie*); Ivonne Sentis (*Prostitute*); Romano Puppo (*Zeb*); Luis Prendes (*Williams*); Helga Line (*Cottrell's Wife*); Mattieu Ettori (*Cottrell*); David Thompson (*Jack*); Tony Brandt *(Jefferson)*; Piero Fondi *(Tanner)*; Luciano Spadoni (Hangman).

Allied Artists morphed out of the lowly Monogram company which, between 1931-1953, had turned out ultra-low-budget series including The East Side Kids and modest Westerns starring Bob Steele, Tex Ritter, Tom Keene, and a pre-*Stagecoach* (1939) John Wayne. After Walter Mirisch assumed control, any hopes of upscaling the product quickly dissipated following the box-office disaster of *Friendly Persuasion* (1956) with Gary Cooper; solid full-color Oaters became their stock in trade or, as such were referred to then, bread and

TWO OF A KIND: Actor Warren Oates and filmmaker Sam Peckinpah appeared in Monte Hellman's salute to both these bold men of the West; Oates, would eventually star in one of Old Sam's most bizarre films, *Bring Me the Head of Alfredo Garcia*.

butter pictures . . . unambitious Oaters that put food on the table for those who collaborated on such works. When the Hollywood "B" Western became all but extinct during the transitional 1960s, A.A. executives wondered if perhaps they might yet survive by plugging into the Spaghetti/Paella phenomenon. In truth, even then, that form likewise wobbled on its last legs. This intriguingly titled film turned out to be the last for the once successful U.S.-based company, as well as one of the final medium-budget Westerns shot in Spain: Almeria/Audalucia, to be specific. The director, however, would here (as in his earlier collaborations with Jack Nicholson) proffer a special style that would soon earn him cult status, if not the hoped-for mainstream success.

Born in Brooklyn, raised in L.A., Monte Hellman (1929-2021) studied at Stanford and UCLA before entering the film business as one of Roger Corman's golden boys. He and Nicholson, sharing a love of the Western genre and Existential drama, collaborated on *The Shooting* and *Ride (In) the Whirlwind*. Following the cultural revolution of the late 1960s/early 1970s, Hellman appeared to belatedly be about to come into his own with *Two-Lane Blacktop* (1971). That post-*Easy Rider* 'road movie' focused on a pair of hippies (musicians James Taylor and Dennis Wilson) menaced by a middle-aged cheaply-suited redneck (Warren Oates) while driving across a desolate if starkly beautiful section of the southwest. Another box office flop, its failure shut down any Hollywood insider dreams. Hellman continued to work with Oates, with whom he felt kinship as a scroungy outsider existing on the edges of big time Tinseltown. They collaborated on the highly controversial *Cockfighter* (1974), a dazzling in-your-face film (and predecessor to the works of Roberto Rodriguez, including *El Mariachi*, 1992). Like that later work, Hellman's film offended and fascinated equal numbers of people (Middlebrow vs. The Edge). No surprise then that when Hellman won the directorial position on *China 9 . . .* , he coaxed Oates to take on one of the male leads.

Long a character actor for Sam Peckinpah (*Ride the High Country*, 1962; *Major Dundee*, 1965; *The Wild Bunch*, 1969), Oates (1928-1982) had recently become something of a top-billed star in such films as John Milius' *Dillinger* (1973). Together, Oates and Hellman (who held Peckinpah in virtual reverence) convinced Old Sam to make a rare appearance in this unique Western as 'The Mythmaker,' essentially playing himself had he existed on the wild frontier, a land almost as dangerous for decent, honest men as the modern Hollywood that all but devoured Sam and Monte whole. Here, Oates is cast as 'Matthew,' a desert rat who, with a beautiful young wife named 'Catherine,' lives in a pathetic shanty out in the middle of nowhere. Shades of Sam Peckinpah's 'Cable Hogue,' for which Oates had been considered before Jason Robards was cast. Matthew is not as crazy as he seems. Soon, the railroad will arrive and his hideous stretch of bleak wilderness will be worth a fortune. (Shades of *Johnny Guitar* and *Once Upon a Time in the West*!) Rather than buy

Matthew off, the Establishment businessmen and politicians (raw capitalists, as compared to Matthew's enlightened one) assign 'Clayton'---a gunfighter about to the be executed---to purchase his freedom and a wad of money if he will head out to the distant hell hole and murder the old-timer.

One problem in fulfilling his mission: While staying at the place under the pretense of 'just passing through' (the unwritten Laws of Hospitality as applicable in the badlands as they were in the ancient world), he learns to like and respect Matthew. The other issue: Catherine. From the moment the two lay eyes on one another (he astride his horse, she horizontal and naked in a natural hot water pool), passions flicker, then blaze. No matter what the consequences, the attractive people will inevitably become lovers, with tragic consequences for all.

Though it's tempting to employ the term 'romantic triangle' to describe what occurs, this is a truly intricate piece about the conflicting demands of loyalty and passion. For the first time in her life (and not unlike D.H. Lawrence's 'Constance Chatterley'), Catherine surrenders to abject lust after deserting the shabby outpost of civilization that is her family home, deep in the romantic realm of nature. One of the few 'serious' actresses of this era who was comfortable appearing in the nude, Jenny Agutter (1952-) conveys the full sense of

LADY CHATTERLEY'S LOVER GOES WEST: In a narrative line that recalls D.H. Lawrence's famous if controversial 1928 novel, this film's heroine---frustrated in her limiting marriage---dares to take as a lover a 'natural man' (Fabio Testi), surrendering to abject sexuality while far from the madding crowd.

release that her heroine experiences. Always, though, the ferocity of her feelings must be tempered by Catherine's difficult sense of duty to her erratic husband.

Never before has any mainstream Western so completely laid bare the all-encompassing experience of human sexuality (not even *Duel in the Sun* or *The Outlaw*) and done so largely from a woman's point of view. Further proof this may be viewed as something of a feminist film: When Warren slaps his wife, Catherine responds by stabbing him with a butcher knife. Here, in a period setting, we discover a prototype for the modern woman who refuses to accept abuse and will respond not only with equal but mightier force.

WELCOME TO THE NIHILISTIC WESTERN: Goodbye to the happy ending in any conventional sense as Warren Oates and Jenny Agutter burn there farmhouse to the ground, then ride off to try and survive together, despite their common knowledge that she not only committed adultery with a handsome stranger but attempted to kill her husband.

21. CONNAGHER (1991)
Rating: **** ½

CREDITS:

Reynaldo Villalobos, dir.; Jeffrey M. Meyer, Sam Elliott, Kathryn Ross, scr.; Elliott, John A. Kuri, pro.; J.A.C. Redford, mus.; James R. Bagdonas, cin.; Zach Staenberg, ed.; 1.33:1; C; 94 min.; Imagine Ent./TNT/Turner.

CAST:

Sam Elliott *(Conagher)*; Katharine Ross *(Eilie Teale)*; Barry Corbin *(Charlie McCloud)*; Billy Green-Bush *(Jacob Teale)*; Ken Curtis *(Seaborn Jay)*; Paul Koslo *(Kiowa Staples)*; Gavan O'Herlihy *(Chris Mahler)*; James Parks *(Curly)*; Daniel Quinn *(Johnny McGivern)*; Pepe Serna *(Casuse)*; Buck Taylor *(Tile Coker)*; Dub Taylor *(Station Agent)*; Cody Braun *(Laban Teale)*; James Gammon *(Smoke Parnell)*; Richard Jury *(Webb)*; Jeffrey M. Meyer *(Beaver Sampson)*; Peter P. Oliver *(Apache)*; Craig Pinkard *(Marshal)*; Archie Smith *(Storekeeper)*: Kate Hall, Angelique L'Amour *(Stage Passengers)*.

During Hollywood's Golden Age in general, The Western genre in particular, larger than life actors dominated the screen in heroic roles: Gary Cooper, John Wayne, James Stewart, Henry Fonda, and Burt Lancaster, to name but a few. As each retired from the screen and/or passed into that Great Corral in the sky, only a few bold stars refused to allow a great tradition to end. In theatrical releases, no one has done more for 'the cause' than Clint Eastwood. As to the small screen, his equivalent---as an iconic actor and a behind-the-scenes avatar (in this case, producer)—there is Sam Elliott (1944-).

Douglas Brode

KEEPING THE TRADITIONS ALIVE: Tall, dark, and handsome Sam Elliott came to represent onscreen the man of few words who always acts with integrity that, in an earlier era, had been embodied by the likes of James Stewart, Henry Fonda, and Randolph Scott.

The California-born performer won his first 'bit' parts in Westerns: one awful (*The Way West*, 1967), the other classic (*Butch Cassidy and the Sundance Kid*, 1969). Varied TV movies and mini-series led in time to a pair of star-making vehicles: *The Sacketts* (1979) and *The Shadow Riders* (1982), both co-starring Tom Selleck, another bright light of the contemporary Western. Each also derived from novels by Louis L'Amour (1908-1988); the most popular genre novelist following Zane Grey. Elliott's wife Kathryn Ross (1940-), had been regularly associated with Westerns since her role as 'Etta Place' in *Butch...*; she and Elliott involved themselves in picking projects and the development process of high-quality Oaters for an era when fans of that genre (mostly older, estranged from modern movies) preferred to stay home and watch television. Elliott would play historic figures in *The Legend of Texas* (1986; Sam Houston), *You Know My Name* (1999, Bill Tilghman), *Buffalo*

OLD AND NEW: One continuing element of the nouveau Western has been a tendency to include performers whose very presence serves as an homage to earlier Oaters; here, Sam Elliott (right) faces off with Ken Curtis, known for his film *The Alamo*, (1960) and television ('Festus' on CBS' *Gunsmoke*) appearances.

Gals (1995; James B. Hickock), and the theatrical feature *Tombstone* (1990, Virgil Earp). He (re)-incarnated the original Marlboro Man, David McLean, in *Thank You for Smoking* (2005). And forever after came to symbolize the modern man of the West in the Coen Bros. dark comedy *The Big Lebowski* (*1998*) , embodying a ghost-like Lonesome Stranger who . . . well . . . keeps the legends alive, as the saying goes.

Of all the small-screen projects Elliott has associated himself with, *Connagher* rates as the best in its purity, simplicity, and refreshing lack of pretension. The appealingly old-fashioned piece enshrines the style and values of Western narratives harkening back to the earliest Oaters while drawing realistic elements into play too often overlooked in the coded mythology of past movies. Though set on an isolated stretch of cow country, here is an intimate chamber drama about two believable people separated as to place by the proverbial wide-open spaces. On one edge of this frontier, widow woman

'Ellie Teale' lives in a small cabin. With the help of her children, she ekes out a living as a farmer and runs a stage stop. Elsewhere, a 'man-with-one-name' hero in the tradition of Grey's 'Lassiter' or Jack Schaefer's 'Shane,' (L'Amour's own 'Hondo' actually had one, 'Lane') labors on a failing ranch for a decent old-timer, 'Jay.' Every once in a while, fate throws the strong rider and even stronger pioneer woman together. In time, their common destiny becomes clear to each, even as it has been to us all along.

The plot closely follows a much-admired novel by L'Amour, the North Dakota resident who, like Grey, wrote Westerns that mostly fall into the pulp

'MISS ETTA PLACE' RIDES AGAIN!: Though Katharine Ross made her first great impression in the contemporary comedy drama *The Graduate* (1967), she became a woman of the wide open spaces in *Butch Cassidy and the Sundance Kid* two years later; here, as in other films starring and/or produced by husband Sam Elliott, Ross continues to forward an iconic cowgirl image.

fiction/generic category. Rugged action is favored over dialogue or prose. But if Grey's great gift was mostly inherent in his poignant descriptions of settings, L'Amour's special contribution drew on his inclusion of realistic detail within conventional stories. Initially, when a small family heads West by covered wagon, the children do not ride but step ahead of the team, removing potentially dangerous rocks. Ellie's husband is not killed by outlaws or Indians but a seemingly minor mistake he makes while in the saddle, causing an abrupt fall off a ridge. Later, the loneliness of a prairie existence almost drives Ellie as mad as Lillian Gish's character in *The Wind*, though in the post-feminist era, our heroine (make that female-hero) empowers herself by writing poetry. Not only do the bad guys drink rotgut; likewise, positive male figures, alcoholism a more pressing problem in the historical West than most Hollywood classics reveal. Though there is an attack by Apaches on the stage in which native people are, as in the past, portrayed as the menacing 'Other,' Elliott includes this historical fact while adding often overlooked elements on frontier life. Perhaps the most significant detail on view, as it was in *Will Penny* and *Monte Walsh*: A cowboy wanders across the range not out of love for freedom but because jobs were scarce. Despite the fantasy that a body could live off the land, the West contained endless stretches of dirt, ungiving as to any supposed natural 'largesse.' Connagher alone among the cowboys is worthy of heroic stature because he is the rare Westerner who still lives by a code. When others desert their boss owing to pressure from an unscrupulous cattle baron, he 'sticks.' "I take a man's money," Connagher stoically insists, "I ride for the brand." If, necessary, to his death, as an end that has value. If luckier, should he survive the conflict, stepping into the arms of a woman whose own female/feminist code is every bit as unbreakable as his own.

22. CRIPPLE CREEK BAR-ROOM SCENE (1898)
RATING, Present Day Standards: *
RATING, Cinema History Value: *****

CREDITS:

James H. White, dir.; Thomas Edison, pro.; 1.33:1; B&W; 43-47 secs., varied running times; The Edison Manufacturing Company/Black Maria Studios.

CAST:

None available; Edison Company Extras.

A long-standing myth about early movies holds that the first Western ever was *The Great Train Robbery* (1902/1903). Based on the final Wyoming raid of The Wild Bunch in 1899, this incident would be recreated in the wilds of New Jersey by members of Thomas A. Edison's recently formed filmmaking crew. Like so many difficult-to-dispel falsehoods, this is not true. A full four years earlier, Edison (1847-1931) had one of his most trusted assistants/co-workers, James H. White (1872-1944), shoot a fleeting vignette set in a rough frontier saloon and liquor store. Accomplished in one continuous take (creative editing as we know it would not evolve for nearly ten years), a skeleton crew shot the brief flicker within the confines of a makeshift studio. Here we encounter an irony: The first pre-Hollywood Oater set somewhere in Big Sky country had been an interior (rather than on-location) production.

Originally built in 1892, The Black Maria consisted of a simple/crude/ large barn-like building, covered in tar paper (hence its nickname). T.B.M.

WHERE EAST MEETS WEST: The authentic appearance of a late 19th century frontier saloon was recreated during the early 20th in a makeshift New Jersey studio, setting the pace for endless Oaters yet to come.

featured an adjustable roof that could be raised high or rotated to make use of existing light for the modest flickers shot within. Edison had been inspired by news that England's William Friese-Greene had (drawing on other diverse experiments previous even to that Brit's own experimentation) devised 'a magic box'; filming a succession of individual pictures which, when viewed in swift succession, allowed the impression of watching a single picture 'move.' At once, the Genius of Menlo Park determined that America must create its own Movie Industry, overseen by none other than himself. Dozens of ten-second mini-movies were created, including *The Kiss* (1896), a close-up of two people (John Rice and May Irwin) doing precisely that.

Audience reaction proved ecstatic and, indeed, controversial; public smooching was then illegal in New York, though the film's popularity would

HOLLYWOOD EAST: More than twenty years before the foundation of Hollywood, America's earliest filmmaking pioneers shot their humble films in upstate New York, Long Island, and (here) nearby New Jersey, where stood the legendary Black Maria.

soon cause that to change. Offering an early example of the impact that mass media could have on everyday life.

In search of a filmmaking identity all his own, Edison not only provided more of the same but experimented with further possibilities, including an early if unsuccessful attempt to include sound. The next step was to stage, as authentically as possible, people and places in intriguing 'stories.' As Buffalo Bill's Wild West show enjoyed spectacular success on tour, and the public ate up pulp novels by such sub-literary scribes as Ned Buntline, Edison decided on (among many topics) a Western ... indeed, the first ever to be immortalized on film.

The idea of 'construction' in motion pictures (allowing an audience to believe they witness the real deal though the image presented is a convincing if faux approximation) essentially begins here. How many viewers of that era comprehended that this was not the "real" Cripple Creek but a mock-up? Studying the Lumiere 'actualities' filmed in Paris, Edison noticed something significant: Though a single shot flicker fascinated audiences for a short while, viewers absorbed each setting swiftly . . . and, just as rapidly, grew bored. To counter this, the Lumieres had begun their presentation of a light-hearted snowball fight as a 'straight' documentary. Then, a bicycle rider arrives from the street's far end. The two teams turn on him, pummelling the poor fellow. It's a hilarious bit; if not scripted per se, then conceived, rehearsed, and performed on the spot. Impressed, Edison instructed his Canadian-born director to do something of the sort with his recreation of a bar's interior.

First, there are the people in this place. Which in and of itself is intriguing enough to hold us for about twelve seconds, owing to the setting's unfamiliarity. Shortly, we have observed all of what 'the shot' has to offer. The movie then reaches what film aestheticians refer to as its 'content curve'; If something doesn't happen to pick up the pace, observers will lose interest. At that point, a drunk stumbles in and orders a whiskey shot, picking up the pace by his very presence. The barmaid (it is indeterminate if the actor is a woman or a female impersonator; most decent ladies of the fin-de-siecle Manhattan theatre wanted nothing to do with the doggerel film industry) sizes him up, considers the situation, then decides to serve the rough-neck despite the sad fellow's inability to maintain his balance. Character development, however crude, has been introduced, as well as the slightest hint of what might be called 'narrative.' Yet the story does not end here. Having downed his drink, the out-of-control stumblebum picks a fight with some card players. Following several seconds of rough and tumble action, he's tossed out by the owner, setting a future for Western films in which women will be portrayed as strong and decisive.

Notably, the fellows on view are not cowboys but miners, the dominant male icon of the West evolving only after the publication of Owen Wister's novel *The Virginian* (1901). Finally, the roughness of the setting and costumes make clear that early Westerns were not influenced by the romanticized paintings of Frederic Remington, rather by the first (and notably bleak) images of the actual West then available in the East thanks to photographs by Edward Curtis and others. However much the incident depicted here is

"I'M READY FOR MY CLOSE-UP NOW, MR. EDISON!" The Genius of Menlo Park was among the earliest avatars of motion pictures as a commercial entity for the emergent modern audience.

something of a creative invention, the piece was designed to convey a sense of authenticity. This would be the case with all of the earliest Westerns, including Porter's better-known film for the Edison studio several years later. Note, though, that, when this now all-but-forgotten flicker proved a great success with East Coast audiences, the wide acceptance of projected motion pictures emerged as a new venue of popular entertainment, swiftly replacing the peek-inside-a-machine Nickelodeons. This film, then, led not only to the Western tradition but movies, in general, as we know them today.

23. DAYS OF HEAVEN (1978)
Rating: *****

CREDITS:

Terrence Malick, dir.; Malick, scr.; Jacob Brackman, Bert & Harold Schneider, pro.; Ennio Morricone, mus; Nestor Almendros, cin.; Billy Weber, ed.; 1.85:1; C; 94 min.; Paramount.

CAST:

Richard Gere *(Bill)*; Brooke Adams *(Abby)*; Sam Shepard *(The Farmer)*; Linda Manz *(Linda)*; Robert (J.) Wilke *(The Foreman)*; Jackie Shultis *(Linda's Friend)*; Stuart Margolin *(Mill Foreman)*; Timothy Scott *(Harvest Hand)*; Gene Ball *(Dancer)*; Doug Kershaw *(Fiddler)*; Richard Libertini *(A Wrestler)*; Sahbra Markus *(Vaudeville Performer)*; Bob Wilson *(An Accountant)*; Muriel Jolliffe *(Headmistress)*; John Wilkinson *(Preacher)*; King Cole *(A Worker)*; Terrence Malick *(Man in Mill)*.

"Nobody's perfect," little 'Linda' intones. "You're a half angel and half devil inside." From the mouths of babes ... Linda, a fictional if all-too-real character, is one of the slum denizens who survives on the mean streets of overcrowded big cities following the great wave of immigrants during the first two decades of the 20th century. In Chicago, men pour heaping shovelfuls of raw coal into factory fires that resemble gateways to hell. Women scrub other people's clothes or find diverse forms of menial work in order to continue eating. And, perhaps, afford a flop-house bunk for the night, where lice embed worn, unclean sheets. Occasionally, such "hollow men" (to borrow from T.S. Eliot) and women meet up in an asphalt jungle which F. Scott

WESTWARD, THE COURSE OF HISTORY: The conventional Western focused on wagon trains headed to California during the mid-19th century; Nouveau Westerns such as Days of Heaven remind us that in the early 20th, the next generation headed west to make their dreams come true by way of the Iron Horse.

Fitzgerald described as "the valley of ashes" in *The Great Gatsby*. That's the case with 'Bill' and 'Abby,' occasionally finding time between long terms of hard labor to lay down together in an approximation of lovemaking. Linda, a ragamuffin whose inner monologue pastes the film's loose narrative's episodes together, attaches herself to the couple as they search for a way out. Which, at that juncture in our national history, still meant heading West.

As they hop a dangerously overcrowded train and roar through ever changing landscapes to the vast wheat fields awaiting, Linda offers her sometimes naïve, occasionally philosophic views on all that occurs. The odd trio become humble sackers on an isolated farm owned by a young, seriously ill American aristocrat, such status assigned less often in the U.S. by birthright than money. Hardly a raw capitalist, this intriguingly unnamed entrepreneur sincerely cares about the welfare of his dayworkers, though involvement in their betterment consists more of mental concern than positive action. In what might be considered a romantic triangle (though here is yet another case in which that cliched concept seems reductive in the context of a soaring

IT'S A WOMAN'S WORLD: Abby (Brooke Adams) searches the locust ridden landscape in hope that one of the two disparate men she has come to love may still be alive.

masterpiece), the Farmer becomes enamoured of the enigmatic beauty Amy, who (for safety's sake) passes herself off as Bill's unmarried sister. Then, a dark plan hatches: If Amy were indeed to marry the Farmer, expected to pass within the year, wouldn't Bill then be able to live out The Dream: Going from rock-bottom blue collar worker to handsomely dressed king of the hill once Amy inherits the kingdom? As was the case in Victorian literature (a notable influence here), there's a dangerous needle in the seemingly lush haystack: What violence may erupt if the lady falls in love with her intended mark?

And so we have Linda's observation, quoted above. There are no good guys/girls or bad here, only flawed, desperate, hungry, confused, ambitious, unsatisfied people, each with his/her own agenda and a fierce determination to realize that narcissistic dream. This holds true for the characters that populate other works in the sparse but noteworthy cinema of Terrence

Malick (1943-): the Illinois born, Oklahoma raised, Texas-educated (previous to Harvard) writer-director offers oblique/objective portraits of people less likely to be thought of as moral or immoral than amoral. Beyond good and evil, as Nietzsche put it ... the strangely sympathetic young cold-blooded killers in *Badlands* (1973), the threatened World War II warriors in *The Thin Red Line* (1998), the varied 1950s family members in *The Tree of Life* (2011). So: how best to describe Malick's style in words, though that in fact is (as with any great filmmaker) virtually impossible? In our pantheon of 21st century greats, T.M. might be thought of as the opposite pole from Steven Spielberg. That artist's theatrical films, beginning with *The Sugarland Express* (included in this book), are designed to make an audience *feel*. As to that, he exists in a tradition that includes John Ford, Frank Capra, Charles Chaplin

WHEN DREAMS DIE: Rather than focus on threats from hostile Native People or rampaging outlaws, as was the case in traditional Westerns, the Nouveaux order concentrates on the more widespread war waged between farmers and nature, which unleashed plagues of a Biblical proportion.

and Walt Disney. More on the order of Eric von Stroheim, Orson Welles, Buster Keaton, Japan's Yosujiro Ozu, Germany's Werner Herzog, or France's Robert Bresson, Malick creates self-consciously artistic works that aim for the mind rather than the heart. If Spielberg rates as his generation's greatest mass entertainer (that is not intended as a slight), Malick is a master of cult cinema, turning out movies which only a miniscule portion of the public would ever choose to see. His team is a once-in-a-lifetime collection of talents: Almendros (1930-1992) surpasses his nuanced visualizations in *Sophie's Choice* (1982) and *Places in the Heart* (1984) with a sense of America's east and west as connected by that symbolic Octopus, the railroad; Morricone stretches forward from the elegiac sounds of the open ranges in Leone's *Once Upon a Time in the West* to in this film also include the harsh wall of noise

THE LAST HARD MAN GOES SOFT: Robert J. Wilke, seen here in the most memorable of his early badguy roles (*High Noon*) at last won an entirely sympathetic part as an aged manager who wishes not only to keep the farm safe but also its vulnerable young owner.

of crowded big city alleyways in his forthcoming collaboration with Leone, *Once Upon a Time in America*. For one of the most remarkable and unforgettable conclusions in movie history, a vast team of F/X geniuses were brought onboard to simulate a devastating plague of locusts.

Finally, there is Robert J. Wilke (1914-1989) as the old time Foreman. He of the sneaky-mean eyes, the broad but weary shoulders, the snide and angry voice, Wilke's villains were shot in the back by Grace Kelly in *High Noon* (1952), beaten to a pulp by Montgomery Clift in *From Here to Eternity* (1954), and knifed by James Coburn in *The Magnificent Seven* (1960). A bully and braggart in several hundred films and TV shows, here he finally reveals the tender underbelly of his tough as leather exterior playing an old timer who gives up the bygone ways and makes room for this still-new century with all its own values . . . or lack thereof.

THE GENTLEMAN FARMER: Playwright and filmmaker Sam Shepard here performs the role of an aristocratic and liberal minded landowner who is despised by his day workers owing to their hatred of his class, no matter how decent, honest, and fair such a man who lives in that house high on the hill may be.

24. DEAD MAN (1995)
Rating: *****

CREDITS:

Jim Jarmusch, dir.; Jarmusch, scr.; Demetra J. McBride, Karen Koch, pro.; Neil Young, mus.; Robby Muller, cin.; Jay Rabinowitz, ed.; 1.85:1; B&W; 121 min.; Pandora/JVC Ent./Newmarket.

CAST:

Johnny Depp (*William Blake*); Gary Farmer *('Nobody')*; Crispin Glover (*Train Fireman*); Eugene Byrd *(Johnny 'The Kid' Pickett)*; John Hurt (*John Schofield*); Robert Mitchum (*John Dickinson*); Iggy Pop *('Sally' Jenko)*; Gabriel Byrne (*Charlie Dickinson*); Jared Harris (*Benmont Tench*); Mili Avital (*Thel Russell*); Jimmie Ray Weeks (*Marshal Marvin*); Mark Bringelson (*Marshal Lee*); John North (*Olafson*); Peter Schrum (*Drunk)*; Billy Bob Thornton (*'Big' George Drakoulious*) ; Alfred Molina (*Missionary*): Steve Buscemi (*Bartender*).

To date, Johnny Depp (1963-) has appeared only sparingly in Westerns. Aside from the charming animated-spoof *Rango* (2011) and Robert Rodriguez' contemporary variation on the theme, *Once Upon a Time in Mexico* (2003), there have been only two. One, the regrettable *The Lone Ranger* (Gore Vabrinsky, 2013); the other, an odd mini-masterpiece. Little seen (other than by those who seek out the most challenging/disturbing alternative movies), *Dead Man* re-considers the narrative tropes of generic Westerns in the same manner that James Joyce's *Ulysses* (1922) approached the epic scope of Homer's *Odyssey*: i.e., ironically, by including every key element while removing the romance and adventure, as well as the strong (make that overpowering) sense of story.

Douglas Brode

AN EXISTENTIAL (MAKE THAT NIHILIST?) WESTERN HERO: Johnny Depp enacts the character of William Blake (who may or may not be a reincarnation of the pre-Romantic Movement poet) in what is best described as a Minimalist Western.

Born in the rural Midwest (Ohio), educated in the heart and soul of intellectual cinema sensibility (New York: Columbia University; Tisch School of the Arts), J.J. (1953-) prefers to craft tightly budgeted indie films, thereby avoiding any threat of commercial/corporate interference. His work (often but not always in black and white, as if to purposefully turn away conventional ticket-buyers) heavily relies on minimalist employment of camera (mostly static); stark representations of middle America as portrayed in the paintings of Grant Wood or the music of David Byrne and Talking Heads; and a focus on male loners as soul-searchers unable to adjust to wherever fate takes them. This had been the case in the films of Nicholas Ray, one of Jarmusch's professors, perhaps most notably in the rodeo western *The Lusty Men* (1952). Like the anti-heroic character played by Sterling Hayden in Ray's *Johnny Guitar* (1954), any Jarmusch leading figure could claim: "I'm a stranger here, myself."

In this case,' the stranger' embodies that traditional element of earlier generic Westerns, a man from the East who heads west not on an idealistic

"THIS IS THE WAY IT HAPPENED ... MOVIN' WEST!" That memorable line, spoken by narrator Walter Coy at the end of every episode of the TV Western *Frontier* (1955-1956), also serves as a signifier of most theatrical films as well, including Jim Jarmusch's intellectual take on the genre.

quest for glory or profit, rather as a runaway. Something horrible occurred back where he once lived. Rather than deal with it, the loner hopes to recreate himself and achieve a happy Second Act to his thus-far disastrous life. This Stranger calls himself William Blake, though we are never certain whether this is his given name or one he assumed. In a Jarmusch context, this ought to be taken as a reference to the English poet of that name (1757-1827). His work (including "Tyger Tyger Burning Bright") earlier inspired Jim Morrison and The Doors to create such intellectualized/transcendental rock set-pieces as "Break on Through to the Other Side." The film's Blake initially hopes to do so as well. But a town called Machine turns out to be--true to its title--industrialized. This is 1888, so the worst aspects of Eastern cities precedes Blake. Demoralized, he strikes out for the primeval wilderness in the company of a Native American, Nobody. This figure partakes a parallel role to that of 'Chingachgook' with 'Leatherstocking' in James Fenimore Cooper's novels of the early frontier. Here, the Native's name references popular culture (the eponymous Westerner in *My Name is Nobody*) as well as classical literature.

After all, 'Odysseus' presents himself to the Cyclops not by his Ithacan title but as 'No-man.'

As to Blake, he may (the title hints at this) have died before the film begins. A trio of bounty hunters pursue him, and he appears to be sorely wounded. As such, Blake recalls Charles Bronson as 'Harmonica' in Sergio Leone's masterwork *Once Upon a Time in the West* (1968), shot down in the opening sequence by killers waiting for him at a *High Noon*-like train station. Dispensing with them, he too falls, only to rise again. We cannot be sure if this is intended to indicate that Harmonica was 'only wounded' or has Lazarus-like been born again. Likewise, this film's Blake may well have, to borrow from Morrison, *already* broken on through to the other side. 'Nobody' guides the Anglo not only on a physical journey to some vague destiny awaiting him but a spiritual one as well. Jarmusch---like Morrison and the original Blake---implies that nature- oriented religions of seemingly 'unsophisticated' people are more pure and valid than our own.

LAST OF THE OLD-TIMERS: A veteran of numerous Westerns as well as film noirs, Robert Mitchum's presence serves as both a loving homage and a fond farewell to the old Hollywood Oaters that he once upon a time starred in.

Though a serious artist with an original vision entirely his own, Jarmusch nonetheless sought full collaboration from his co-creators. Folk-rocker Neil Young, grasping the need to merge 'old and new' elements of the Western into a single vision honoring 'the traditional' while acknowledging a pressing need for revision, balanced his organic score with contemporary electric guitar *and* old-fashioned acoustics. Cinematographer Robby Muller (1940-2018), best known for *Breaking the Waves* (1996), sensed that Ansel Adams' vivid but never idealized landscapes ought to provide this film's visual paradigm. That delicate balance is achieved too in the casting; old time Western star Robert Mitchum (in his final role) as well as Iggy Pop. With *Dead Man*, the once populist concept of the Western Film finally shifts over to what might be called an arthouse approach. Fittingly, since the old-fashioned version of the genre had, like this strangely seductive movie's main character, long since reached the end of its Studio Era trail.

"THE MAN WHO KNOWS INDIANS": *Dead Man* continues a longstanding tradition of righteous Anglos who feel more at home with their Native American blood-brothers than in the confines of civilization that can be traced back at least to James Fenimore Cooper's Leatherstocking novels.

25. DIRTY LITTLE BILLY (1972)
Rating: ****

CREDITS:

Stan Dragoti, dir.; Dragoti, Charles Moss, scr.; Jack L. Warner, pro.; Sascha Burland, mus.; Ralph Woolsey, cin.; David Wages, ed.; 1.85:1; 93 min.; WRG Prods./Warner Bros.

CAST:

Michael J. Pollard (*Henry Antrill/William Bonney*); Lee Purcell (*Berle*); Richard Evans (*Goldie*); Charles Aidman (*Ben Antrim*); Dran Hamilton (*Catherine Bonney McCarty*); Willard Sage (*Henry McCarty*); Alex Wilson (*Len*); Ronny Graham (*Charlie Nile*); Josip Elic (*Jawbone*); Richard Stahl (*Earl Lovitt*); Gary Busey (*Basil Crabtree*); Dick Van Patten (*A John*); Scott Walker (*Stormy*); Rosary Nix (*Louisiana*); Dan Lesser (*Slits*); Henry Proach (*Lloyd*); Severn Darden (*Big Jim McDaniel*); Craig Bovia (*Buffalo Hunter*); Ed Lauter (*Tyler*); Doug Dirken (*Orville*).

"Billy the Kid was a punk!"

So announced the one-sheet advertising poster for this effectively nasty 'little' Nouveau Western, featuring an image of a grinning, moronic looking Michael J. Pollard (1939-2019) as an historic character (1859-1881) previously portrayed by handsome Hollywood stars: John Mack Brown, Robert Taylor, Paul Newman, and Audie Murphy, among many others. The latter's version was titled *The Kid from Texas* (1950) to rationalize that performer's Lone Star drawl. *Dirty Little Billy* for once gets it right: Bonney was born and raised in the lower depths of New York City's Hell's Kitchen. Compared to

A NEW APPROACH TO AN OLD ICON: Any previous romanticization of Henry Antrill/Billy Bonney was put to rest by this early 1970s exercise in revisionism.

the tall, dark, handsome presence of Kris Kristofferson in the role that same year in Sam Peckinpah's larger-scale (though equally disastrous at the box-office) *Pat Garrett and Billy the Kid*, the youth born Henry Antrill (McCarthy was the name of his mother's second husband) had been relatively short and unattractive, at least conventionally speaking. Perhaps this film came too close to the truth for those who longed to hang on to the legend. For here we encounter the most authentic presentation of 'the Kid' up until Emilio Estevez in *Young Guns* (1988). Indeed, the two might make a striking double bill, as *Dirty . . .* concludes where the first *Y.G.* begins: Billy initiating his career as an outlaw, having shed big city values in favor of a life more appropriate for the west.

The film opens with the arrival of the family from the East; historically, they had moved from N.Y.C. to Indianapolis for a spell before reaching Kansas. Billy's mother, a consumptive, accompanies her abusive male companion from one failed business to another, with 15-year-old Billy in tow. This movie concerns the previously unexplored (by Hollywood, at least) period following their arrival by train in Wichita and Billy's subsequent

REAL AND 'REEL': The actual William Henry Bonney; Michael J. Pollard, scene-stealer from *Bonnie* and *Clyde*, as a remarkably close approximation of 'the bandit prince.'

runaway to Coffeyville. *D.L.B.* concludes as he heads off to New Mexico where his 'reputation' as a gunslinger, bandit, and 'regulator' would turn him into a mythic figure. This was the first feature for Stan Dragoti (1932-2018), a creator of clever television commercials; owing to their success, these mini-movies allowed him entrance into the feature film business at a time when the Old Hollywood had collapsed. Mature producers like Jack L. Warner desperately searched for young talent to keep their studios afloat. Dragoti designed a piece that would follow a recently established approach: The debasing of figures from our past who had previously achieved heroic status. This paradigm worked well in *Little Big Man* (1970), which included a vicious caricature of George Armstrong Custer, less so in *Doc* (1971), an incompetent put-down of John Holliday and Wyatt Earp. While *Dirty Little Billy* never achieves the classic status of Arthur Penn's mighty epic, this tightly-budgeted piece does offer a convincing, believable reconsideration of a dubious frontier legend.

Though shot in color, virtually everything we see onscreen is presented in sepia tones to suggest a faded daguerreotype from the era in which this anecdotal piece takes place. As such, the film's visual sensibility recalls a still existent icon featuring the historic Billy leaning on his rifle, grinning idiotically, wearing a cheap top hat rather than a Stetson. In *D.L.B.*, there are no traditional cowboy 'ten gallon' headpieces on view, rather the derbies and bowlers which authentic Irish immigrants who headed west brought along with them from Manhattan. The only exception as to such self-conscious use of diminished color: A bright red, white, and blue flag that majestically flies over the brown cesspool of a town below, offering an ironic contrast between the American Dream and its often disappointing reality. There are no cowboys on view in this anti-Western, only farmers. Ugly stretches of open flat land lead to unpleasant outposts of civilization, muddy trails connecting the two. No one is threatened by Indians or outlaw gangs, though all fear that an epidemic sweeping through a nearby village may reach their shambles of a town. Billy is not some romantic dandy but a lazy sleep-aholic who, when awake, rarely talks, far too occupied with trying to consume any morsel of food in sight. Unlike classic Westerns, there are no pure women from the

A BEVY OF BILLIES: Various incarnations of 'the Kid' include: (top row) Dennis Hopper (TV's *Sugarfoot*, 1957*)*, Audie Murphy (*The Kid from Texas*, 1950), Robert Taylor *Billy the Kid*, 1941); (middle row) Clu Gulagher (TV's *The Tall Man*, 1960-1962); Don(ald) "Red" Barry (*I Shot Billy the Kid*, 1950); Emilio Estevez (*Young Guns*, 1988); (bottom row): Johnny Mack Brown (*Billy the Kid*, 1930); Jack Beutel (*The Outlaw*, 1943), and Paul Newman (*The Left Handed Gun, 1958*).

East as opposed to whores with hearts of gold, only strained and challenged females who, like the men, struggle to survive from one day to the next.

'Berle,' a jaded, cynical young female, turns hooker whenever that becomes an economic necessity for survival, while trying to maintain something of a normal relationship with crazy (and abusive, first verbally, then physically) local bad boy 'Goldie.' In a prelude to *Brokeback Mountain*, this ambiguous night rider maintains a relationship with her that includes unenthusiastic sexual activity, though clearly it is newcomer Billy he truly loves. In yet another concluding image of homoerotic behaviour, the two eventually head off for greener pastures in what is clearly the most important coupling for each, Berle now gone and forgotten. Earlier, though, the three formed a *menage-a-trois*, which producer Warren Beatty had originally hoped for in *Bonnie and Clyde* (1967) with girlfriend Fay Dunaway and sidekick 'C.W. Moss.' Here, Billy is more or less a redux of Pollard's character from that film, now cast in the central role. Five years after *B&C*, what producer Jack Warner had been too timid to allow 'way back then' seemed the natural way to go for a New Movie in which a supposedly impossible three-way (*Butch Cassidy and the Sundance Kid* was originally to have included one as well) now seemed the only way to go.

REVISIONISM OF A ONCE GLAMORIZED GANG: In *Dirty Little Billy*, the Bonney gang is for the first time portrayed not as romantic outlaws but common criminals.

26. FLAMING FEATHER (1952)
Rating: ****

CREDITS:

Ray Enright, dir.; Gerald Drayson, Frank Gruber, scr.; Nat Holt, pro.; Paul Sawtell, mus; Ray Rennahan, cin; Elmo Billings, ed.; 1.37:1; C; 77 min.; Paramount.

CAST:

Sterling Hayden (*Tex McCloud*); Forrest Tucker *(Lt. Tom Blaine)*; Arleen Whelan (*Carolina*); Victor Jory *(Lucky Lee,* aka '*The Sidewinder*'); Barbara Rush *(Nora Logan)*; Richard Arlen (*Showdown Calhoun*); Edgar Buchanan (*Sgt. O'Rourke*); Carol Thurston (*Turquoise*); Ian MacDonald (*Tombstone Jack*); George Cleveland (*Doc Fallon*); Carl Andre (*Jubal*); Victor Adamson (*Barfly*); Heini Conklin (*Townsperson*); Paul E. Burns (*Prospector*); Nacho Galindo (*Jose*); Bryan 'Slim' Hightower (*Chief Black Cloud*); Frank Lackteen (*Hopi Joe*).

"So tell me, now," Sterling Hayden (1916-1986) famously (and only half-jokingly) asked of every producer once their current project reached completion, "who did you *really* want?" More often than not, the answer (at least for those willing to respond): John Wayne. In retrospect, we might note that if the Duke had leaned Red rather than a Right-Wing Commie Basher, he would have been S.H. Career-wise; think of Sterling as the "Road Company" Wayne. That proved true in 1955, when The Duke (still under contract with Republic) was turned down by movie mogul Herbert J. Yates after requesting a considerably larger than usual budget (at least for that second-string

SPECTACLE ON A BUDGET: Even as the B (or C through Z) Western bit the dust in the early fifties owing to competition from the popular TV cowboy shows, a new form took shape: The B+ Oater, less mind-blowing perhaps than John Wayne's big pictures yet in color, and sometimes widescreen, to lure viewers back to the thetres.

studio) for a major movie about the Alamo. When Big John 'walked' to initiate work on his own indie epic, Yates developed a less extravagant (though 'big' by Republic standards) version starring Hayden. If Wayne was by then well on his way to equalling Gary Cooper as the top-of-the-"A"-list cowboy star, Hayden (mostly stuck in "B"s) became a cult sensation, in large part for playing the title role in Nicholas Ray's *Johnny Guitar* (1954) opposite Joan Crawford. And, years later, a crazed military officer who hopes to begin World War Three in Stanley Kubrick's *Dr. Strangelove* (1964), one more role that had been written with Wayne in mind.

Hayden's reputation would be enhanced by his participation in *The Killing* (1956; a classic "B" budget noir, also for Kubrick). He ties Lee Marvin as favorite noir actor of Quentin Tarantino, who would have cast one or the other as the old-timer in *Reservoir Dogs* (1992) had those stars still been alive. As for Hayden, he refused to take Tinseltown seriously, employing his

"I SEE TV IN YOUR FUTURE!" Two of Hayden's co-stars would in time have TV Westerns of their own; Edgar Buchanan (left) would be featured in *Judge Roy Bean*, Forrest Tucker (middle) in *F Troop*.

earnings to set out to sea, in time writing about such exploits in his autobiography, *Wanderer* (1962). As much a maverick in real life as any of the characters he portrayed, one might argue that if Ernest 'Papa' Hemingway had chosen movie acting over writing, he would have been Sterling Hayden. In this film the latter plays a misplaced Texan now ranching in Arizona. (The fictional character may have been inspired by historical John Slaughter, who did indeed make such a move.) When Ute Indians, led by a mysterious masked Anglo outlaw known as 'The Sidewinder,' burn the small homestead, Tex embarks on the vengeance trail, setting all else aside to catch the bandit.

For reasons not easy to explain, this has become the least accessible of all Hayden's films. That, and the mystique surrounding its star, has elevated *Flaming Feather* to cult status among Oaters of the 1950s. Worth noting: Here is an early example of what would come to be called 'The B+ Western.' With TV providing cheaply produced black and white cowboy entertainments on a daily basis, each studio set aside production of such theatrical fare in favor of color (and, after 1954, widescreen) movies. These cost close to a million per, anything over that falling into the "A" category As to *Flaming Feather*, absolutely everything about this conventionally written, strikingly handsome film strikes the viewer as generic: The tall hero, polar good and bad girls, the good guy's friendly-enemy cavalry companion, that officer's comic relief sergeant, the snarling/hissing villain, and a pair of deadly gunfighters. Though that avatar of pulp Westerns, Zane Grey, had nothing to do with this project, the broadly drawn caricatures might lead one to believe this to have been based on one of his books. Director Enright (1896-1965) plays his characters and plot at face value rather than attempting to flesh out the roles or narrative developments. Cliché-ridden in almost all regards, here is a true paradox: A movie that rates as 'ordinary' in almost every aspect, yet its traditional elements so perfectly realized that *F.F.* rates as 'definitive' of its type. As, such, well worth seeking out.

There is, however, one regard in which *F.F.* must be considered exceptional. Rather than shoot on Hollywood sets, the Paramount team headed for northeastern Arizona to allow their film a special look. This includes an

THE MAN IN THE SUIT: As film historian William K. Everson pointed out nearly a half century ago, the badguy (here, Victor Jory) was less likely to be identified by a black costume (many heroes, Hopalong Cassidy included, wore them) than fine-tailored duds that signified corrupting elements from the East pushing into "God's Country."

outstanding shootout between the good, the bad, and the ugly staged high up on the Montezuma National Monument in Camp Verde, not far from John Ford's better known Monument Valley. The distinction: As to M.V., all its vivid grandeur is of a natural/organic nature. What qualifies Montezuma (the title is a misnomer; the area was never inhabited by Aztecs) as a national treasure is the cliff-dwellings. Here, a pre-Columbian people inhabited clay apartment buildings, these constructed over a 300-year period. Though the natives ('Sinagua') virtually disappeared in the mid-1400s, Hopi Indians who have long resided in the area are thought to be descendants of that lost tribe. Somehow, some way, producer Nathan Juran (1907-2002) talked local authorities into letting him shoot the film's grand finale on this iconic site, though laws did restrict Anglos from entering at that time. Hopi hired for the 'shoot' were so disturbed at the thought of walking among ghosts of their past that they declined to participate in this sequence. Juran had to import hundreds of Navajo for the spectacular battle set high in the sky. Regarding the film's claim to fame: Though several other Westerns feature Montezuma in the background, *Flaming Feather* rates as the only Oater actually filmed on location there.

WHERE GHOSTS OF THE PAST STILL CONGREGATE: The remarkable Montezuma National Monument in all its historic glory.

27. FOUR FACES WEST (1948)
Rating: **** ½

CREDITS:

Alfred E. Green, dir.; C. Graham Baker, Teddi Sherman, William and Milarde Brent, scr.; Harry Sherman, Vernon E. Clark, pro.; Paul Sawtell, mus.; Russell Harlan, cin.; Edward Mann, ed.; 1.37:1; B&W; 89 min.; Enterprise Productions.

CAST:

Joel McCrea *(Ross McEwen)*; Frances Dee *(Fay Hollister)*; Charles Bickford *(Pat Garrett)*; Joseph Calleia *(Monte Marquez)*; William Conrad *(Sheriff Egan)*; Martin Garralaga *(Florencio)*; Raymond Largay *(Dr. Eldredge)*; John Parrish *(Bank Manager Frenger)*; Dan White *(Clint Waters)*; Davison Clark *(Burnett)*; House(ley) Stevenson *(Anderson)*; Glenn Strange *(Deputy)*; George McDonald (The Winston Child); Eva Novak *(Mrs. Winston)*; William Haade, Gene Roth *(Poker Players)*; Jack Tornak *(Train Passenger)*.

Should you ever choose to drive southwest on New Mexico's barren old Highway 53, likely you're either a local going about your private business or a tourist hoping to take in some of those still standing vestiges of our half-forgotten frontier heritage. Most of the latter turn north to take in the old Pueblo of Zuni and, perhaps further down this dusty road, veer southward to see the reservation where descendants of that ancient race live today. There's one other attraction you ought to also partake of. Not far from the town of Morro, where life continues today not all that differently than it did a century and a half ago, a sweeping sandstone bluff reaches high into the powder blue,

ONCE IN A LIFETIME: Most cowboy heroes dare to ride the range on a bucking broncho, but Joel McCrea was the maverick who dared to do so on a brahma bull.

white clouded sky. Though not as known (or, in truth, visually impressive) as Monument Valley over at the Four Corners or the spectacular Grand Canyon, here's a place that deserves attention for its stark, craggy, profound beauty.

People call it Inscription Rock. In the old days, pioneers halted here on their way west by wagon, horseback, mule train, or in some cases (though this is largely forgotten now) bicycles. Or on foot, with pushcarts. The reason for a stop-over? The only one that mattered for those suffering the winds of the wasteland: *Water!* Here, a deep, dependable hole provides the nourishment for those people .... Navajo, the Spanish, Anglos .... who passed this way.

Many among them, 2,000 more or less, chose to create a legacy, chipping their names and the dates of arrival into the soft surface of a natural tower that also provided much-appreciated shade. Such crude if memorable imposition of encroaching civilization, imposed on what appears a piece of paradise in an otherwise Godforsaken territory, was not lost on one Eugene Manlove Rhodes

ONE MORE COWBOY, ONE MORE LADY: Frances Dee joins husband Joel McCrea for one of his outdoor epics; nothing can come between them but his horse!

(1869-1931). A Nevada-born cowboy, he found his own special garden in N.M., the place and its people inspiring him to capture the aura of this particular corner of the American west, and its unique history, in words, even as Charles M. Russell had in vivid paintings. Most of Rhodes' stories and novels failed to catch on with the public in the manner that those of Zane Grey did. Still, he stuck to it, earning himself a following that appreciated the authenticity of his observations. Also, the quaint, curious prose in which he immortalized the past, somewhere between a sentimentality that hinted at spirituality of the sort Native people perceived in the ragged landscape and a harsh honesty revealing the essential loneliness and isolation of this way of life. One of his works did reach a somewhat larger audience: *Pasa Por Aqui* (1926), based on a story (halfway between history and myth, something of a local legend), about a young cowboy turned outlaw who redeemed himself in the eyes of the law (and some say God) by risking capture by sheriff Pat Garrett (1850-1908) to stop and save the lives of a humble Mexican family suffering from diphtheria. Born again by this selfless act, the youth offered something of an alternative to Billy the Kid: Here was an outlaw who saw the light and chose the 'right' path, saving him from being shot down in the manner that Billy Bonney had.

The book was not lost on Harry Sherman. Though Massachusetts born, he dedicated himself to producing top quality if low budget Westerns, including the Hopalong Cassidy series starring William Boyd. Enamored with 'He Passed this Way,' Sherman set out to raise over a million dollars to properly bring this personally beloved project to the screen while shooting in the actual locations. Though a bit long in the tooth for the 'kid' role, Joel McCrea (1905-1990) continued to identify himself with the Western genre, offering a minimalist form of acting (some refer to his style as 'stoic') that proved effective for genre pieces. Can anyone who has watched this film ever forget the sight of McCrea riding (that's him, not a stuntman!) a brahma bull across the plains? The female lead, a nurse who becomes enamored of the fugitive from justice and impulsively throws her conventional way of life aside to join him on the outlaw trail (might she be inspired by real-life Etta Place, girlfriend of

"HE PASSED THIS WAY": Shooting on the actual southwestern locations allowed for a haunting sense of the actual journeys west immortalized in this natural tower.

the Sundance Kid?), is portrayed by elegant Frances Dee (1909-2004), long-time wife of the star. Previously, they had appeared in a Western epic about the founding of a stagecoach company, *Wells Fargo* (1937). The acting honors, though, go to Charles Bickford (1889-1967), convincingly world-weary as a man sometimes praised as the saviour of the southwest, damned by others as a killer with a badge; and Joseph Calleia (1897-1975), an enigmatic Spanish actor who here appears as a combination guardian angel for the young lovers and Greek chorus, filling us in on the background. Alfred E. Green (1889-1960) had entered the film industry as an actor for the old Polyscope Co. before turning director for such diverse projects a *Disraeli* (1929) and *The Jolson Story* (1946), as well as such "B" Oaters.

Like the endless screen variations of Peter B. Kyne's *3 Godfathers*, here's a slow-moving story of redemption, Western style, that seduces, then at the end overpowers even the most jaded viewer. There's yet another claim to fame: this is the only Hollywood Western ever made in which guns, though drawn, are never fired. We sit on the edges of our seats, waiting for the 'release' of a loud crack, only to accept at the conclusion that this was not to be.

REAL AND REEL: The historical Sheriff Pat Garrett; character actor Charles Bickford playing that famed lawman.

28. FRISCO KID, THE (1979)
Rating: ****

CREDITS:

Robert Aldrich, dir.; Michael Elias, Frank Shaw, scr.; Mel Dellar, Hawk Kochi, pro.; Frank De Vol, mus.; Robert B. Hauser, cin; Jack Horger, Irving Rosenblum, May Weintraub, ed.; 1.85:1 C; 119 min.; Warner Bros.

CAST:

Gene Wilder *(Avram)*; Harrison Ford *(Tommy)*; Ramon Bieri *(Mr. Jones)*; Val Bisoglio *(Chief Gray Cloud)*; George DiCenzo *(Darryl Diggs)*; Leo Fuchs *(Head Rabbi)*; Penny Peyser *(Rosalie)*; William Smith (Matt Diggs); Jack Somack *(Samuel Bender)*; Beege Barkette *(Sarah Mindl)*; Shay Duffin *(O'Leary)*; Walter Janovitz *(Elderly Amish Man)*; Joe Kapp *(Monterano)*; Clyde Kusatsu *(Mr. Ping)*; Allan Rich *(Bialik)*; Vincent Schiavelli *(Brother Bruno)*; Ian Wolf *(Father Joseph)*; Kenny Selko, Warren Selko *(Little Boys)*; Ben Kahlon, Michael Elias, Rolfe Sedan, Rusty Blitz *(Rabbis)*.

In 1974, Warner Bros. released two films simultaneously: the huge, garish, highly budgeted musical *Mame* starring Lucille Ball in her return to the big screen; and *Blazing Saddles*, a modest burlesque of Westerns by Mel Brooks. As to the latter, studio executives hoped that they might make their money back, the case with such New York City/Jewish Brook-sian work as *The Producers* (1967). As for *Mame*, Warner's top brass waited for the profits to pour in. And waited. And . . . To their (and everyone else's) surprise, the opposite occurred. Despite the big publicity build-for a 'surefire hit,' virtually no one showed up. If a musical were to succeed in this brave new world of the

PARDNERS: The buddy-buddy Western that premiered in 1968 with *Butch Cassidy and the Sundance Kid* continued to dominate a decade later, this time with Gene Wilder as a Jewish immigrant and Harrison Ford as his Anglo companion; in truth, Ford is himself half-Jewish.

youth-oriented box-office, it had better be cutting edge style, *a la* Bob Fosse's *Cabaret* (1972). On the other hand, edgy/off-the-wall humor was in the process of going mainstream, moving beyond its onetime Manhattan boundaries to a hipper New Normal.

The fate of those two films caused each of the surviving Hollywood companies to reassess how they did business. Over at Warner's, everyone hoped to find another comedy-Western vehicle for *B.S.*'s standout star, Gene Wilder (1933-2016). Wisely, he chose to forego a quickly thrown together sequel, knowing such a movie could end his career as a serious comedic actor as surely as it would bringing in large profits. Instead, Wilder re-joined his

They Went That-A-Way

Producers co-star Zero Mostel for a film based on Eugene Ionesco's classic play *Rhinoceros* the same year that *B.S.* hit, worked for Brooks again in yet another movie spoof, *Young Frankenstein* (1974), and headlined a slick commercial comedy-romance-adventure *Silver Streak* (1976). Wilder did agree to return to a Western comedy (albeit of a non-burlesque order) with this critically acclaimed if only modestly successful piece. Here, the wild breakneck pace of Brooks' 'living cartoon' was replaced by a leisurely paced, character driven, low-key style of comedy. Despite the movie's high quality, those hoping for a farce headlining Wilder were in for a disappointment, which may explain why this one-of-a-kind 'dramedy' set on the 1850 frontier barely returned its $9 million budget.

Wilder plays 'Avram,' the least distinguished of a group of rabbinical students at a Yeshiva in Poland. Not knowing what to do with him, the rabbis

NOW, *THAT'S* A HIGH RIDIN' RABBI!: Though Gene Wilder flatly refused to do a Blazing Saddles 2 project, he did return to the genre in this notably different, and far more 'serious' comedy.

decide to send Avram off to a position no one else wants: Gold Rush-era San Francisco, where the Jewish community must survive in an entirely other world than the one they knew back in The Old Country. Crossing the ocean, Avram embarks on a 3,000 mile journey. A Candide figure, he's the blissful innocent who maintains an optimistic smile no matter how terrible things become. Avram's spirit will not be broken, even when Matt Diggs and his troublemakers steal the cherished Torah Avram faithfully carried across the sea. Fortunately, the hapless hero has a guardian angel:'Tommy,' an erstwhile train-robber who finds himself saddled with this greenhorn and, inspired by the rabbi's essential goodness, takes on the task of helping Avram reach his destination, no matter how huge the obstacles (including the highest cliff ever seen in a film) in their way.

Here is one of those buddy-buddy films so popular during this decade when feminism called out for more authentic and well-rounded portraits of women on film. Tinseltown's mostly male filmmakers were so fearful of writing female-oriented scripts that might then be found wanting that they instead focused on men dealing with other men, precisely the opposite of what the Women's Movement wished for.

Film historians have commented that there exists in such mano-e-mano movies an element of homoeroticism. This is present in *Frisco Kid*. Though Avram has an arranged fiancée waiting for him (eventually, he will fall in love with and marry her younger sister), and Tommy always reveals his interest in attractive women whether the two are in a frontier town or an Indian encampment, the film recalls Howard Hawks' famous words about his own Westerns (*Red River*, *The Big Sky*, etc.): "All my films have been love stories between men." Physical attraction does flash onscreen between Montgomery Clift and John Ireland or Kirk Douglas and Dewey Martin in *The Big Sky*, Hawks' early black and white Ford-like frontier epic. In *The Frisco Kid*, anything other than friendship and respect does not present itself until midmovie, when the buddies curl up close together to survive a blizzard. Near the end, when they have reached the West Coast, the two men swim together in the ocean. As they run back to the beach, Avram tackles Tommy in what

"LOVE STORIES BETWEEN MEN...": Long before *Brokeback Mountain* brought that continuing motif out of the cinematic closet, hints of physical attraction between seemingly macho heroes were suggested in Howard Hawks' *The Big Sky* (Kirk Douglas, Dewey Martin) and *Red River* (John Ireland, Montgomery Clift), also Robert Aldrich's *The Frisco Kid.*

appears to be a half-joking, half-serious manner that suggests an upcoming erotic encounter. Before this can transform into a predecessor of *Brokeback Mountain*, their roll in the sand is interrupted by the deadly outlaw gang. It would be interesting to know, though, how things might have progressed had violence with the bad guys not ended their idyllic oceanfront tryst.

TIE ME UP! TIE ME DOWN! The image of Harrison Ford's cowboy undergoing torture by Native Americans may hone to the realities of history, but today no self-respecting filmmaker would dare to include it for fear of being labelled politically incorrect

29. GIRL OF THE GOLDEN WEST, THE (1938)
Rating: ****

CREDITS:

Robert Z. Leonard, dir.; Isabel Dawn, Boyce Debaw, scr.; Leonard, William Anthony McGuire, pro.; Herbert Stothart, mus.; Oliver T. Marsh, cin; W. Donn Hayes, ed.; 1.37:1; B&W; 121 min.; Metro-Goldwyn Mayer.

CAST:

Jeanette MacDonald (*Mary Robbins*); Nelson Eddy (*Ramirez/Lt. Johnson*); Walter Pidgeon (*Jack Rance*); Leo Carrillo ('*Mosquito*'); Buddy Ebsen ('*Alabama*'); Leonard Penn *(Pedro)*; Priscilla Lawson (*Nina Martinez*); Bob Murphy (*Sonora Slim*); Olin Howland *(Trinidad Joe)*; Cliff Edwards (*Minstrel*); Billy Bevan (*Nick*); Brandon Tynan (*The Professor*); H.B. Warner (*Father Sienna*); Monty Woolley (*The Governor*); Charley Grapewin (*Uncle Davy*); Noah Beery Sr. (*The General*); Bill Cody Jr. (*Gringo*); Ynez Seabury (*Wowkle*); Francis Ford (*Elderly Miner*); Russsell Simpson (*Pioneer*); Jeanne Ellis *(Mary as a Girl)*.

Barely recalled today, the vehicle (in fact franchise, long before that concept came into being) which was 'The Girl of the Golden West' owned a prominent place in American (and, in truth, international) popular culture during the 20th century's first half. Much like Owen Wister's *The Virginian*—a 1901 novel that would become a stage play, numerous movies, and in the 1960s a popular TV series—this softer piece exerted a major impact on people's perception of The West. *Girl* originated as a big, splashy Broadway spectacle

THE FIRST FRANCHISE: Or, at least, one of the first... *The Girl of the Golden West* (though more or less forgotten today) enthralled an international public with touring stage versions and this definitive vehicle for the 'classy' musical team of Janette McDonald and Nelson Eddy.

in 1915, at that juncture when The Great White Way emerged as the centerpiece of American theatre. Intellectual works by the likes of Eugene O'Neill, America's answer to such European realists as Anton Chekov, appealed mainly to an elite/intellectual audience. In mid-town New York, Florence Ziegfeld introduced sexy but sophisticated extravaganzas in which glamour girls sensuously performed to the new popular music. Simultaneously, David Belasco (1853-1931) presented Victorian melodramas: Soap-operas (before that term existed) that enshrined traditional values shortly to be challenged during The Roaring Twenties. Members of the emergent middleclass flocked to see anything presented by the latter two.

As for Belasco, no single piece proved more popular than *Girl*. The premise: An ambitious though highly moral young woman (like other post-Victorian, pre-Roaring 20s idealized girls of the era's theatre and fiction, she insistently remains a virgin until marriage) owns a raunchy saloon but also sings in church on Sundays. Mary must choose between two would-be husbands: black-suited, corrupt sheriff Jack and a handsome young army officer, Johnson. Though each supposedly pursues Ramirez, a Mexican bandido, the townsfolk gradually realize the bold soldier and charming bandit who terrorizes the area near Monterey are one and the same. Written, produced, and directed by Belasco (with "incidental" music by William Furst), the show sold out nightly. Touring companies brought this 'popular' (rather than 'literary') classic to the far reaches of America where an isolated citizenry hungered for such sentimental entertainment. The first of four eventual films appeared in 1915, even as brief flickers made way for full length features. Already, Italy's Giacomo Puccini had turned *Girl* into an opera that fascinated European audiences with its heightened vision of the 'real' Wild West. Yet another entertainment venue had come into being in Rome and Paris: The operetta, or 'light opera': A dramatic play in which character's conversations were primarily sung, with shards of spoken dialogue included as well. Also: crowd-pleasingly happy endings, with silly comedy and social satire relieving the intensity. Johann Strauss and Jacques Offenbach were among Europe's most appreciated creators, their work soon popular in the U.S. as well.

TORN BETWEEN TWO LOVERS: Jeanette McDonald is wooed by the super-suave Nelson Eddy and serenaded by roughewn Buddy Ebsen, later to play the sidekick role to Fess Parker and Keith Larsen on two of TV's Eastern-Westerns, *Davy Crockett* and *Northwest Passage*.

If the Barrymores emerged as the most applauded 'serious' actors in live theatre and film, then the team of Jeanette McDonald (1903-1965) and Nelson Eddy (1901-1967) rated as box-office attractions within this predecessor to the modern American musical theatre, which would emerge after World War II. Not surprisingly, MGM . . . which prided itself on being a step above all other Hollywood studios as to presenting 'classy' photo plays . . . embraced the concept.

Re-imagining the piece for their version, Louis B. Mayer's (1884-1957) team adapted the basic plot, scuttling all incidental or operatic (*La Fanciulla de West*) music previously associated with *Girl*. To add a sense of upscale popular culture, Hungarian émigré Sigmund Romberg (1887-1951), busily creating theatrical operettas for the Schubert Bros. in New York, was persuaded to do the honors here. His contributions would be expanded via inclusion of earlier Americana tunes by Stephen Foster and modern jazz-influenced lyrics by Gus Kahn. Of all eight McDonald/Eddy projects, this stands as the most iconic, a transitional piece that serves as a key example of a motion picture that draws on varied earlier popular forms for its identity.

AN UNSAVORY STEREOTYPE: All ethnic groups were subjected to caricaturing during the Golden Age of Hollywood; here, Leo Carrillo (in actuality, a Spanish aristocrat) embodies the cliché of a slow-witted, ever hungry, half drunken, but always smiling Mexican-American;. During the early fifties, Carrillo would revive such a role as 'Pancho' to Duncan Renaldo's hero on *The Cisco Kid*.

Today, the broad caricature of Leo Carrillo (1881-1961) as a none-too-bright Mexican strikes most moviegoers as embarrassing and angering. Importantly, though, Buddy Ebsen (1908-2003) portrays an Anglo in an equally exaggerated manner. White southerners as well as South of the Border Americans are employed here for goofy comedy. Likewise, there is an elaborate Mariachi sequence which features mostly Anglo performers as Latinos, in an artificial Hollywood rendering of a folk form from another country. This can be written off as one more example of 'cultural appropriation.' Still, the dance is portrayed in an elegant manner that contrasts with the more vulgar goings on at the Americano saloon. Clearly, the filmmakers wished to portray Latin dancing and music in a positive light, encouraging the middlebrow audience to admire those people here represented. This marks a notable change from the despised 'Greaser' cliché that permeated Anglo society, and Western movies, a quarter century earlier. If this film rates more as a musical set in the west than a generic Western per se, *Girl* remains a landmark portrayal of America's last frontier, setting the pace for a 'modern' musical such as *Oklahoma!* or *Paint Your Wagon* yet to come.

"ALL SINGING! ALL DANCING! ALL WESTERN!": One of the great stage musicals of the early 20th century was effectively brought to the screen in this lavish Hollywood production.

30. GREAT K & A TRAIN ROBBERY, THE (1926) (Silent Western) Rating: **** 1/2

CREDITS:

Lewis Seiler, dir.; Paul Leicester, John Stone, scr.; Seiler, pro.; William (P.) Perry, mus.; 1.33:1; B&W; 53/54 min.; Seiler Productions/Fox Film.

CAST:

Tom Mix (*Tom Gordon*); Tony the Horse (*Tony*); Dorothy Dwan (*Madge Cullen*); Will Walling (*Eugene Cullen*); Harry Gripp(e) (*DeLuxe Harry*); Carl Milton Pell (Sr.) (*Burton Holt*); Edward Pell (Sr.) (*Bill Tolfree*); Curtis McHenry *(Snowball)*; Sammy Cohen (*Train Passenger*); Duke K. Lee *(Outlaw)*; Marion (John Wayne) Morrison *(Bit Player)*.

"Like a Rhinestone Cowboy ... " The title of a classic Glen Campbell song describes the sort of self-conscious Drugstore variety of Westerner, duded up with fancy, expensive costumes of the sort no actual cowboy would be caught dead in. The first such figure to appear in films would be played by Tom Mix (1880-1940), who strutted about in a tall, wide white Stetson, wearing an all-black outfit and fancily crafted boots, silver pistols by his side. During the sound era, such an approach would become a standard of the mini-musical vehicles for Gene Autry, Roy Rogers, and a dozen other B movie entertainers. Of course, serious moviemakers of the John Ford (*The Searchers*, 1956) or Howard Hawks *(Red River*, 1948) variety would have no truck with such nonsensical stuff.

IN THE TRADITION OF THE GREAT TRAIN ROBBERY: Building on the popularity of that early Thomas Edison/Edwin S. Porter Western, Mix's production company set out to produce the biggest and best entry in this unique subgenre of the Western film.

"WHO WAS THAT MASK(ED) MAN?": Could this sequence, in which hero Mix romances pretty flapper-era girl Madge Cullen while in the guise of an outlaw, possibly have inspired "The Lone Ranger" franchise?

Mix came to movies in a roundabout way: formerly working as everything from a bartender to a drum corps major, this son of an Oklahoma lumberjack found employment with several of the minor-league Wild West shows. Proving to be a natural at rodeo, Mix swiftly honed his skills; when filmmaker Lewis Seiler (1890-1964) contacted Will A. Dickey of the Circle D. Ranch in hopes of recruiting hard riders to perform stunts for moving pictures, Mix received a hearty recommendation. While on the set, he made a strong impression as a tall, handsome, wide-shouldered specimen of masculinity. Seiler promoted the unknown to 'star.' That factual narrative would in time supply the basis for the Autry musical *The Big Show*.

Meanwhile, the halting and robbing of Iron Horses had become a popular trope beginning with *The Great Train Robbery* (1902-1903). Actual robbers, including Al Jennings, made a good living by playing themselves in re-enactments of their earlier 'activities.' When the government frowned on such romanticisation of criminals, Hollywood reversed the situations. Here, a railroad owner, 'Cullen,' hires a straight-shooter to eliminate the gang. 'Tom' does this by pretending to be an outlaw himself, eventually getting the job done while winning the heart of 'Madge,' Cullen's impetuous daughter.

If the scenario is simple enough that it might have been scribbled down on the inside of a matchbook cover, the film itself is rich and rewarding as a definitive example of what became the standard for Westerns during the final years of the Silent Era. If Broncho Billy Anderson rates as the first Western star, William S. Hart the first 'great' one, Mix holds the status of the best-loved entertainer working within the genre. A lowbrow pulp fiction hero come to life, he played all his roles in the over-the-top manner of a pantomime artist, also performing his own stunts. Mix's hopping up and down on the train recalls Buster Keaton's similar acrobatics in the seminal comedy *The General*, released that same year. Likewise, Mix could swing on ropes as effectively as Douglas Fairbanks (Sr.) playing 'Zorro.' Many believe Mix to be the originator of the cowboy cliché in which the hero kisses his beloved wonder-horse: Tony, a predecessor of Champion, Trigger, and so many others. In this film Mix also introduced the notion of a comic sidekick in the guise of 'De Luxe' Harry,' a clownish tramp. Also, this is one of the first (if not *the* first) Western to anachronistically have cowboys casually carrying Colt .45s, 19th century-style, even though the movie seemingly takes place the year during which it was produced.

The film proved a box-office bonanza owing to its Cliffhanger-style reliance on action, action, and more action. The brief mid-section in which characters actually speak to one another is performed in the wild manner of a Keystone Cops comedy so the dialogue (which we read) doesn't drag down the spellbinding shooting, riding, and fighting appeal. There's a dazzling combination of long shots of wide-open spaces in and around Glenwood Springs, CO, these juxtaposed with closer shots of the ever-grinning hero and sneer of the villains. Highly effective parallel editing constantly shifts us from one area of interest to another with every shot held the least amount of time possible

"TONY? TAKE A BREAK . . . " As most early Westerns were set at fin-de-siecle or shortly thereafter, cowboy heroes on the silver screen could shift from horses to the most (then)-modern devices.

for maximum impact, this *Train Robbery* leaves an audience in a state of literal exhaustion, then or now.

Do note, the film is burdened with those outdated, embarrassing stereotypes present in virtually all movies of the time. The character of 'Snowball,' a combination cook and valet to the railroad owner, is so archly played as a coward and fool that he makes the work of a better known black performer, Stepin Fetchit, appear almost enlightened. Also, the film is fervently homophobic. The suited secretary (who turns out to be in league with the robbers) is identified by this introductory title card: "If he went to college, it must have been Vassar." Later, he is laughed at even by his own outlaw colleagues and forced to wear a woman's dress. There is no defense to this, other than to state: William Shakespeare included nasty anti-Semitic 'gags' in plays like

Much Ado About Nothing. To expect artisans and entertainers from the past to live up to our currents standards is, in a word, unrealistic. They were as much products of their time as we are of ours. This is not meant to justify such stereotypes, only to help explain them. Movies, enjoying a sort of immortality thanks to their preservation and accessibility not accorded to many other forms including live-theatre, serve as a history of what was best and worst about us in the past.

A COWBOY'S BEST FRIEND IS HIS HORSE: Whether Tom Mix ever actually kissed Tony is debatable; no question they were pals of the saddle.

31. GREAT NORTHFIELD MINNESOTA RAID, THE (1972)
Rating: ****

CREDITS:

Philip Kaufman, dir.; Kaufman, scr.; Jennings Lang, Cliff Robertson, Bruce Graham, pro.; David Grusin, mus.; Bruce Surtees, cin.; 1.85:1; C; 91 min.; Universal.

CAST:

Cliff Robertson (*Cole Younger*); Robert Duvall (*Jesse James*); Luke Askew (*Jim Younger*); R.G. Armstrong (*Clell Miller*); Dana Elcar (*Allan Pinkerton*); Donald Moffat (*Manning*); John Pearce (*Frank James*); Matt Clark (*Bob Younger*); Wayne Sutherlin (*Charley Pitts*); Robert H. Harris (*Wilcox*); Jack Manning (*Heywood*); Elisha Cook (Jr.) *(Bunker)*; Royal Dano (*Gustayson*); Mary-Robin Redd (*Kate*); William Callaway (*Calliopist*); Arthur Peterson (*Jefferson Jones*); Barry Brown (*Henry Wheeler*); Nellie Burt (*The Doll Woman*); Liam Dunn (*Drummer*); Valda Hansen (*The Nude Girl*); Madeleine Taylor Holmes *(Granny)*; Herbert Nelson (*Detective*).

The Western won acceptance during the 20th century's first half as America's origination, story, however historically questionable that notion may be. According to the Marxist dialectic, every force must produce its equal counter-force. As the 1900s wore on, the participants of once idealized events were 're-considered' by youthful avatars of The New Hollywood. George Custer and 'Wild Bill' Hickock (*Little Big Man*, 1970), Wyatt Earp and Doc

RIDE A CROOKED TRAIL: Any romantic approach to the last raid of the James/Younger gang that appeared in earlier film versions was set aside for this grim portrait of worn, wane men making their way down an unappealingly muddy street.

Holliday (*Doc, 1971*), and William H. Bonney (*Dirty Little Billy* and *Pat Garrett and Billy the Kid*, both 1972) were reassessed and found wanting. It hardly came as a surprise that the supposed 'noble outlaw' of the Old South, Jesse James (1847-1882) and his partner-in-crime Cole Younger (1844-1916), came under closer scrutiny.

The younger James brother had long been depicted as a righteous Robin Hood figure (Tyrone Power *in Jesse James*, 1939; Roy Rogers in *Jesse James at Bay*, 1941), and George "Superman-to-be" Reeves (*The Kansan*, 1943). Such incarnations proved particularly powerful during the post-Black Tuesday Depression era. Then, bank robbers (like then-current John Dillinger or Bonnie and Clyde) were widely perceived as guerrilla warriors in the good fight against failed capitalism by citizens whose life savings had gone down the drain. In another era entirely, Jesse (as played by Robert Wagner in a role originally intended by filmmaker Nicholas Ray for his *Rebel Without a Cause* star James Dean) would be re-envisioned as a confused teenager

(*The True Story of Jesse James*, 1957). But in the early 1970s, such hippie *outlaws* of the Arthur Penn Warren Beatty/Fay Dunaway opus of five years earlier came to instead be perceived as horrific *criminals*; i.e., Robert De Niro as 'Travis Bickle' in Martin Scorsese's upcoming *Taxi Driver*, 1976). Here, then, Jesse emerged as a self-possessed narcissist, cold blooded killer

REAL AND 'REAL': The historic Jesse James; Robert Duvall, in time to win a Best Actor Oscar for *Tender Mercies*, as a notably psychotic and narcissistic portrait of the outlaw.

of ordinary people, a sentimentalist as to animals, and a whacked out self-anointed messiah.

At last, Robert Duvall (1931-) found a role that propelled him from the sidelines of Western films to a more central position. Three years earlier, the long-time character actor had made his first great impact as the fictional 'Ned Pepper' in *True Grit* (1969). There, he played a crazed if notably charismatic desperado (opposite John Wayne's heroic 'Rooster Cogburn', no less) not all that different from the historical one he essays here. That same year, the craggy, countrified actor supported Clint Eastwood in *Joe Kidd*. Though the versatile Duvall would appear as varied figures during his career, always he would be drawn to the Western, be it 'Gus' in the monumental mini-series *Lonesome Dove* (1989) or 'Boss' in Kevin Costner's 21st century classic Oater, *Open Range* (2003). His co-star here, Cliff Robertson (1923-2011), was more often associated with modern projects, including *Charly* (1968), for which he won a Best Actor Oscar. Westerns were something of a sidelight, though Robertson did write, direct, co-produce and star in *J.W. Coop* (1971), a contemporary rodeo tale; and spoofed the genre as the cowboy villain "Shame" on ABC's *Batman* in 1967.

This distinction between radical screen personas helps to create a perfect balance between Robertson's Cole Younger and Duvall's Jesse. If the latter comes across as a prisoner of the past, doomed to continue fighting the Civil War until his eventual assassination by a trusted gang member, then this film's Cole has an eye on the future: fascinated by everything from baseball to the time-lock on a modern bank's safe. Also, with the steam-powered tractors that now pass along through the streets of a farming community (though set in MN, the film was shot in Oregon) to a complicated calliope he simply can't resist tinkering with.

Filmmaker Philip Kaufman (1936-) approaches the material (this his only Western) in the same obscure, oblique manner that he did Science Fiction (*Invasion of the Body Snatchers*, 1978), 1950s teenage gangs (*The Wanderers*, 1979), and would in time our post-war space program (*The Right Stuff*, 1983) and European politics (*The Unbearable Lightness of Being*, 1988).

At one moment, the style is unrelentingly realistic: the famed bank robbery (9/7/1876) takes place not in broad daylight but on a grey, drizzly, depressing day; the shootout between mounted outlaws and enraged townspeople is swift and unglamorous, as compared to the onscreen spectacle that Walter

A BUNGLED ROBBERY, A DEMEANING GETAWAY: In Northfield, Jesse's old "Stick 'em up!" approach failed to click as the gang came to an ignoble end; rather than riding away from a posse on their magnificent steeds, Frank and Jesse sneak away in a buckboard with the latter lamely disguised as a woman.

The essential through line: Is Cole a coward owing to his desire to avoid violence whenever possible in favor of a chess match approach to banditry, or is Jesse an outrageous fool for considering his wiser fellow Missourian an inferior 'man'? Kaufman presents us with the question but leaves the answer up to each viewer. In retrospect, *Northfield Raid.* was indeed precisely the 'right' Jesse James film for the juncture in time during which it was made.

Hill would offer in *The Long Riders* (1980). A moment later, Kaufman twists his tale into an outrageous black comedy. If Monty Python's Terry Gilliam ever opted for an Oater, the result might have been this.

32. HANGING TREE, THE (1959) Rating: ****

CREDITS:

Delmer Daves, Karl Malden, dir.; Wendell Mayes, Halsted Wells, scr.; Martin Jurow, Richard Shepherd, pro.; Max Steiner, mus.; Ted McCord, cin.; Owen Marks, ed.; C; 107 min.; Baroda/Warner Bros.

CAST:

Gary Cooper (*Dr. Joseph Frail*); Maria Schell (*Elizabeth Mahler*); Karl Malden (*Frenchy Plante*); Ben Piazza (*Rune*); George C. Scott (*Grubb*); Karl Swenson (*Tom Flaunce*); Virginia Gregg (*Edna Flaunce*); John Dierkes (*Society Red*); King Donovan (*Wonder*); Emile Avery, Oscar Blank, Ted Driscoll, frank Hagney, Dick Hudkins, Cactus Mack (*Townsmen*); Fern Barry (*A Mother*); William Benedict *(A Trapper)*; Danny Borzage (*Dan*); Annette Claudier (*Dance Hall Girl*); Martin Eric (*A Father*).; Dorothy Klewer (*Duck Girl*).

Early in *The Hanging Tree*, inhabitants of an 1873 Montana mining town attempt to shoot down a young sluice robber. A rough and tumble fistfight occurs, followed by a stagecoach robbery. Near film's end, a shootout takes place. All the while, a ballad of the type that became essential to the genre following *High Noon* appears, here sung by Western performer Marty Robbins. Like that earlier seminal film, the lead is played by Gary Cooper, grand old man of the West, here appearing in his final genre piece. Those details, taken together, might seem likely to qualify *Hanging Tree* as a Western in the classic tradition. And, appearing at this decade's end, one of the final examples

A DIFFERENT IMAGE FOR AN OLD-TIME HERO: As in *High Noon* with Grace Kelly during the decade's early years, Gary Cooper her defends another blonde goddess, Maria Schell; all similarities end there, for in this odd Western opus Coop plays not another straight-forward man of the law but an emotionally scarred manipulator of a town's citizenry.

of such filmmaking before *The Magnificent Seven* turned the genre in a new, youth-oriented, notably internationalized direction.

But that is not the case. Despite genre trappings and vivid outdoor locations, *Hanging Tree* strikes viewers less as one of the big "A" budget Westerns of its period than a deeply disturbing contemporary social drama. Turgid in tone, quietly terrifying as to implications about the dark sides of seemingly normal people, *T.H.T.* has more in common with Eugene O'Neill's stark American tragedies (*Desire Under the Elms*, 1924; *Strange Interlude*, 1925) than one of John Ford's colorful 1950s Westerns. Drawn from a fascinating novella by Dorothy M. Johnson (1905-1984), author of "The Man Who Shot Liberty Valance," here is an unsettling character study of one of the most unique figures to dominate a Golden Age studio film.

In the opening sequence, a stern-faced, darkly attired man (he might be a religious leader or professional killer) solemnly rides into one of those dirty, makeshift camps swiftly assembled wherever precious metals were found. He

FACE OF FURY: A little more than a decade later, George C. Scott would win an Oscar for playing the lead role in *Patton;* here, he offers a chilling portrait of one those religious maniacs who did haunt the west, a similar character to the one played by Donald Pleasence in Will Penny (1967) opposite another Western icon, Charlton Heston.

calls himself 'Frail,' though rumors preceding the hard, unsmiling man hint that this is not his birth name. However tall and strong, Frail--true to his moniker--is a collection of neuroses, the result of something horrible in his past. From the moment Frail sets himself up in a cabin high on a hill, considering all down below from a self-sustained God-like perspective, the mistrusted newcomer leads a double life. As the only doctor in this territory, he offers his skills at the profession to any who need it. Payment for his services are unnecessary; a kiss on the cheek from a child is all it takes to bring a satisfied smile to this seemingly messianic man's face.

On the other hand, Frail runs his own sluice in a more despicable manner than any of the other gold-hungry men. He magnanimously saves young Rune's life following a bullet wound, nursing the youth with warm soup and gentle care. No sooner is the lad able to move than do Frail's eyes and manner turn threatening. He announces that, in exchange for a hiding place from the

THE DARK SIDE OF OUR OLD WEST: Karl Malden embodies a get-rich-quick miner whose lust for gold transforms into a desire for the enclave's golden goddess (Maria Schell)

law, Rune must become the older fellows 'Manservant': a virtual slave and, more likely than not, sexual victim.

No such physicality occurs with 'Elizabeth,' an immigrant woman. Though everyone in town (as tents gradually give way to buildings) assumes she is Frail's bed-mate, he will not (indeed, *cannot*) touch her other than as a surgeon. Memories of a wife he apparently slew owing to her adultery has caused Frail to be as repelled by a beautiful young female as he is drawn to the equally beautiful boy. A smoldering citizenry, whipped to a mania by their lust for gold, proves easy prey for a religious maniac (and character foil to Frail) called 'Grubb.' Here is George C. Scott (1927-1999) in an early role, one that may remind viewers of Joseph Wiseman playing a similar part that same year in John Huston's *The Unforgiven*.

As a result of an accident during the stagecoach robbery, Elizabeth is blind, if not necessarily permanently. As it turns out, her ability to 'see' again has less to do with physical recuperation than emotional distress. Elizabeth cannot see because, however unknowingly, she does not want to. The world around her has become an ugly, merciless pit following the death of her father. Symbolically speaking, such a situation holds true for Frail, Rune, the animal-like 'Frenchy' (Karl Malden), and 'the Flaunces,' a middle-aged couple who hope to bring mainstream values to this nasty outpost.

The Hanging Tree not only contains blindness on a narrative level but is *about* blindness, in the tragic sense of an ancient Greek play. Here is a story that addresses the issue of setting everyday 'sight' aside to gain greater insight into oneself and the universe we all inhabit. Like all of Delmer Daves' (1904-1977) Westerns, the classic *Broken Arrow* most notable, this strange, yet strangely satisfying, piece concludes with a glimmer of hope for the future. Only by accepting that each of us must cease to be a prisoner of the past, and however painfully come to grips with who we are in the present, will we achieve a modicum of freedom from the invisible prisons in which we unwittingly place ourselves.

WHAT A CHARACTER!: Seen here in the classic *Shane*, John Dierkes added considerable grit to such Westerns as *The Hanging Tree* and John Wayne's *The Alamo* (1960).

33. HANNAH LEE: AN AMERICAN PRIMITIVE (1954)
Rating; Generic 'B' Western: **
Rating, One of a Kind Western Experiment: **** ½

CREDITS:

John Ireland, Lee Garmes, dir.; MacKinlay Kantor, Alford Van Ronkel, scr.; Ireland, Garmes, Jack Broder, Jerry Thomas, pro.; Paul Dunlap, Stan Jones, mus.; Garmes, cin.; Edward Sampson, Chester W. Schaeffer, ed.; C/3-D; 75 min.; Realart.

CAST:

Joanne Dru *('Hannah Lee'/Hallie McLaird)*; Macdonald Carey (*Bus Crow*); John Ireland (*Marshal Sam Rochelle*); Tom Powers (*Pearl City Sheriff*); Ralph Dumke (*Alesworth)*; Stuart Randall (*Jeff Montgomery*); Frank Ferguson (*John Britton*); Don Haggerty (*Bill Crenshaw*); Peter Ireland *(Willie Stiver)*; Tristram Coffin (*Paulson the Bartender)*; Alex Pope *(Gare Striver)*; Ruth Whitney (*Mrs. Striver)*; Kay Riehl (*Mrs. Bainbridge*); Dean Cromer (*Charlie Bevan)*; Alan Frazier (*Bart the Desk Clerk*); Harold J. Kennedy (*Banbridge*); James Bell (*Carousel Rider*): Mort Mills (*The Doctor*); 'Snub' Pollard *(Jailbird)*; Chuck Roberson (*A Cowboy*).

During the on-location filming of *Red River* (1948), every man on the set (from star John Wayne down through the 'gaffers') knew the essential rule

A WARMLY REMEMBERED 'CRAZE': To attract audiences away from their TV sets, the briefly lived 3-D phenomenon included several B Westerns, *Hannah Lee* perhaps best remembered among them.

of this game: Keep your distance from the female star, Joanne Dru (West Virginia-born belle Joanna Letitia LaCock, 1922-1996). Though married to singer Dick Haymes, she was reported to be "Howard Hawks' 'Girl'"; this had as much to do with her winning that prime role as her striking beauty and at best minimal acting skills. Apparently, no one shared this important information with Canadian-born John Ireland (1914-1992), who interrupted his relationship with co-star Montgomery Clift to pursue a 'friendship' with the striking brunette. Hawks had his revenge: 'Cherry Valance' (a role once earmarked for Cary Grant) was whittled down during production, and later

A FAMILY AFFAIR: Director John Ireland shares his vision of the production with wife Joanne Dru; Ireland's young son Peter also plays a role.

in the editing room, from the third lead to a virtual bit. No sooner was the film completed than Dru and Ireland were married, a relationship that would last until his infamous affair with Joan Crawford. While the couple did win terrific roles in the Oscar-winning classic *All the King's Men* (1949), mostly they appeared in Westerns, sometimes together, as in the A budget *Vengeance Valley* (1951) headlined by Burt Lancaster and Robert Walker, also *Southwest Passage* (1954) for the house where "B" Westerns thrived: Republic.

For an even less prestigious company, Realart, they also co-starred that year in *Hannah Lee: American Primitive*, which, as the title suggests, is in many ways most oddball Oater turned out during this rich decade of experimental Westerns. The piece is based on the novel "Wicked Water" (1949). Author McKinley Kantor (1904-1977), a virtual unknown at the time, was then on the verge of proverbial fame and fortune, his Civil War bestseller/Pulitzer-prize winner *Andersonville* appearing shortly after this colorful (to say the least) film premiered and swiftly disappeared. Surprisingly, *Hannah* was rarely shown on television even as most other "B" Westerns constantly popped up to fill local late-afternoon movie slots.

The narrative drew on the life of controversial Tom Horn (1860-1903), who during his lifetime transformed from Indian scout and Pinkerton detective to hired killer or Regulator. While paid by big-time cattlemen in and around Iron Mountain WY to chase away or kill off small-time ranchers, Horn apparently shot down a fourteen-year-old-boy. Whether guilty or not (Horn buffs argue the subject to this day), he was subsequently hung for murder. That shooting appears in *Hannah Lee*. Here, 'Bus Crow' employs a heavy-duty rifle with an early telescopic sight, always leaving the empty shell (as Horn reputedly did) near a victim's body as his bizarre signature of the shooting. In the film, the child (played by co-producer/co-director/co-star Ireland's son Peter) is (apparently) seen falling down dead after Horn/Crow fires (suggesting the incident was an unfortunate accident), then miraculously survives.

During its troubled production, the script was rewritten nightly, for no one quite knew what to do with such brutal material. Originally, Ireland (who plays a marshal tracking down the gun for hire, a former lover of the title

SINGIN' COWBOY, THE REAL DEAL: The gifted Stan Jones, whose best remembered trail tune is "(Ghost) Riders in the Sky," was hired to create a sufficiently stark ballad for this oddball Oater.

saloon-girl, she now involved in a sado-masochistic affair with the bad guy), hoped to close *Hannah Lee* with his leading lady swinging on a rope. The excellent theme song, written by Stan Jones (1914-1963) of "Riders in the Sky" fame, insists in the manner of a Greek chorus that such a sequence will occur. This would have been the ultimate example of the anti-lynching Westerns so prominent during the 1950s. Instead, we witness a faux happy ending in which 'reformed' Hannah and the lawman ride off into the sunset, side by side.

The shoot was plagued by problems during production, including the use of a 3-D technique that slowed down the schedule. In fact, the inclusion of this process turned out to be non-essential: Other than a single close-up of a pistol pointed at the audience, there appears no reason to have featured this. (For a "B" Western that more effectively employs 3-D to the limit, see

The Charge at Feather River.) By the time *Hannah* was ready for release, the notably brief 3-D craze had ended; theatres preferred to show a 'flat' print. As for Ireland, one of the most effective villains in films of that era, he is wasted in the heroic role. He would have been much more effective as the snarling amoral bad man than Carey (1913-1994), better cast as quiet gentlemen as he would be in the later TV soap opera *Days of our Lives*. In a 1967 "B" picture, *Fort Utah*, Ireland would play a character called 'Tom Horn,' though that figure bears little resemblance to the historic personage.

Evidence suggests that Ireland hoped to work behind the cameras again, becoming a 'total filmmaker' (as Clint Eastwood would later do) until driven to distraction while shooting this film. His drinking, already infamous, increased. As a result, he never became involved in 'production' again, playing out his roles in rare "A" (*Gunfight at the OK. Corral*, 1957, as Johnny Ringo) and numerous "B" pictures including *Gunslinger* (1956) for a then up and coming youngster named Roger Corman. During the final season of TV's *Rawhide* (1965), Ireland joined Clint Eastwood as a drover modelled on . . . *Red River*'s 'Cherry Valance.'

REAL AND REEL: Regulator Tom Horn (1860-1903); Actor MacDonald Carey (1913-1994).

34. HELL OR HIGH WATER, aka COMANCHERIA (2016)
Rating: *****

CREDITS:

David Mackenzie, dir.; Taylor Sheridan, scr.; Peter Berg, Carla Hacken, Julie Yorn, many others, pro.; Nick Cave, Warren Ellis, mus.; Giles Nuttgens, cin.; Jake Roberts, ed.; 2.35:1; C; 102 min.

CAST:

Jeff Bridges (*Marcus Hamilton*); Gil Birmangham (*Alberto Parker*); Chris Pine (*Toby Howard*); Ben Foster (*Tanner Howard*); Dale Dickey (*Elsie*); Joe Berryman (*Bank Manager*); Buck Taylor *(Old Timer)*; Kristin K. Berg (*Olney Bank Teller*); William Sterchi (*Mr. Clauson*); Keith Merriweather *(Rancher)*; Jackamoe Buzzell (*Archer City Deputy*); Katy Mixon (*Jenny Ann*); Travis Sheridan (*A Cowboy*); Debrianna Mansini (Waitress); Ariel Holmes (*Thug*); Marie A.K. McMaster (*Casino Teller*); Gregory Cruz (*Bear*); Melanie Papalia *(Hooker)*. Nicole Brady *(Reporter)*; Heidi Sulzman (*Margare*t); Christopher W. Garcia (*Randy*).

If, as old-timers insist, Texas exists a world unto itself--part western, part southern, part southwestern, yet not truly belonging to any one of those specific possibilities---then West Texas ought to be considered a separate kingdom within that immense realm. And hardly a hospitable one. Don't look for the plentiful waters of San Antonio in South Central. Vast, arid, unrewarding prairies north of El Paso, stretching westerly from the 98th Meridian as far as

They Went That-A-Way

THE GOOD GUYS...MORE OR LESS: A tough old Anglo Texas Ranger (Jeff Bridges) and his multi-ethnic partner (Alberto Parker) walk a mean stretch of the West that doesn't appear to have altered at all during the past century and a half since the supposed 'wild days' ended.

the eye can see, appear as hard as those folks who live there. Once, this was called *Comancheria*: A territory so mean in spirit that, before the coming of the White Man, no Indian nation chose to inhabit this hell on earth other than those deadly Cossacks of the Plains from which the nation within a nation within a country takes its name. Punctuated by misshapen mountains (the Guadalupe and Chiso), its ungiving land surface rises high if flat as a pancake. Here, baking under what seems an eternal sun, the place and people merge in a manner never fully captured on film until this remarkable Western. If *Hell and...* were reduced to a simple message, it'd signal us that West Texas has not altered since those days when grizzled, embittered men on both sides of the law shot it out on parched, unpaved streets.

And those who fell down dead were considered the lucky ones.

"I've been poor my whole life," hopeless cowboy 'Toby Howard' mumbles as to the lousy poker hand life dealt him. "It's like a disease that passes from generation to generation." Now, though, he's reached the breaking point. Owing to small print technicalities in a loan the area's dominant banking chain extended to Toby's late mother, the sad little shack he and his brother 'Ben' share is due for repossession. But this modern man of the West is mad as hell and he's not going to take it any longer. So it is that Toby devises a bizarre but fathomable plan to rob from the rich and give to the poor ... namely themselves, he and his brother ... in the tradition of Robin Hood or, in America, Frank and Jesse James. The duo will hit one after another of the banks in wasted towns like Odessa, Wichita Falls, and Del Rio, seizing small amounts of cash until they have enough to pay off the required amount to save the only home they've ever known for future generations. These include Toby's kids by an estranged wife, 'Elsie.'

For if there remains alive a single element of the American Dream here, it's that maybe ... just *maybe* ... tomorrow will shine a little brighter for the Next Generation. But, as Texans like to put it, the fly in the buttermilk is: A clause insists they must complete negotiations (legal or otherwise) before the all-important note becomes due. Come hell or high water, at least one

AND THE BAD GUYS ... PERHAPS: Contemporary outlaws or retro criminals? Chris Pine and Ben Foster play modern bank robbers who, like Jesse James and Cole Younger in the bad old days, took up their 'trade' owing to the impossible pressures of an insensitive society.

Howard must meet the man in a suit, not arriving a split second late. Here, then, we encounter the greatest Western ticking-clock since *High Noon*.

Where there are outlaws, there must also be lawmen. Texas Rangers in the tradition of such iconic figures as Big Foot Wallace and John R. Hughes still wander the wastelands. 'Marcus Hamilton' may be on the verge of retirement, but his wits remain as keen as ever. Like similar characters played by Ben Johnson in *The Sugarland Express* and Tommy Lee Jones in *No Country for Old Men*, Marcus would rather out-think than out-shoot contemporary desperadoes. A man of deep, profound meditation if few words, he out-foxes the human coyotes, casually sitting back to observe them slip into his invisible trap. Accompanying him is a far younger man, 'Gil Birmingham'; part Latino, part Native American. If Marcus appears to be all head, no heart, Gil provides a necessary foil/compliment, even as each of the bandit brothers does for one another. Here are balanced pairs of obsessed men, traveling on a collision course toward one another.

Among other weighty issues, race is essential to this film's sensibility. Marcus cannot speak to his deputy without degrading the forlorn fellow. Every remark, concerning their pursuit or more private matters, contains a racial slur, delivered in a sarcastic manner. As the junior member of this team, Gil can do little but grin and bear it. Then, fate intervenes . . . . and we see in

"STICK 'EM UP" . . . ONE FINAL TIME: The traditional bank robbery takes on a contemporary semblance as the wild west suddenly explodes again in modern times.

Marcus's eyes a sentiment that contradicts his foul words. Seemingly, Marcus is West Texas' White Meanie, pure, simple, and nasty. That hardly precludes a deep sense of humanity which men from this part of the Lone Star State are loathe to openly reveal. The same holds true for the siblings. A remarkable moment occurs in a rural saloon. Ben notices an Indian sitting nearby at a bar. Apparently out to pick a fight, Ben hoarsely addresses the man, who of course takes umbrage. But before the first punch can be thrown, everything becomes crystal clear. "*I'm* a Comanch," Ben insists. This pickup-truck rider of the quasi-purple sage identifies, rather than perceives a conflict with, the Native American.

In West Texas, you see, every redneck considers himself a Comanch in status if not blood.

For this—more even than outer space--is the final frontier A dead-end trail street with no name. Accurately portrayed on film at long last for those who know that country first-hand. And educational for audiences living elsewhere who appreciate of those rare contemporary movies that offer something beyond two hours of mindless escapist entertainment.

AN AMERICAN UNDERCLASS: The plight of the poor is realistically depicted in this exceptional modern Western in which beloved genre conventions are refreshingly absent.

35. HELL'S HINGES (1916)
Rating: ****

CREDITS:

William S. Hart, Charles Swickard, dir.; C. Gardner Sullivan, scr.; Thomas H. Ince, pro.; Victor Schertzinger, mus.; Joseph H. August, cin.; 1.33:1; B&W; 64-66 min, running time (varied); Kay-Bee Pictures/Thomas Ince Prods.

CAST:

William S. Hart (*Blaze Tracy*); Clara Williams (*Faith Henley*); Jack Standing (*Rev. Robert Henley*); Alfred Hollingsworth (*Silk Miller*); Robert McKim (*Clergyman*); J. Frank Burke (*Zeb Taylor*); Louise Glaum (*Dolly*); John Gilbert *Redneck*); Jean Hersholt (*Bartender*); Tracy's Loyal Horse ('*Fritz*') Bob Kortman (*Lout*); Wheeler Oakman, Leo Willis (*Hell's Hinges 'Citizens'*).

In his heyday, William S. Hart (1864-1946) majestically embodied the cowboy icon which the less-talented 'Broncho Billy' Anderson had initiated. Co-directing and overseeing the writing as well as playing a singular hero with a different folksy name in each project, Hart painted a dark vision of a frontier which, in the 1893 'thesis' of historian Frederick Jackson Turner, had recently 'closed.' In Hart's vision, good folks ... simple settlers, honest ranchers, decent business-people ... were few and far between. Here and in other films from this ruggedly individualist Victorian-era moralist, most 'citizens' were trash. Their town must not only be 'reformed' but destroyed in an Old Testament fire. Hart's villain-turned-hero will Lot-like exit this American Sodom to begin civilization again somewhere else. Happily, his bride-to-be does not make the mistake of glancing back.

THAT MAN WAS CLINT EASTWOOD LONG BEFORE CLINT WAS EVEN BORN!: As 'Blaze Tracy' in *Hell's Hinges* as well as a dozen and a half other influential Oaters, William S. Hart forsook the sentimentalism of John Ford's historical pageants to portray a West in need of Biblical cleansing by a hard-edged man of action.

Though filmed on location in California's lovely Lake Arrowhead area and San Bernardino National Forest, Hart and co-director Clifford Smith (1894-1937) created an onscreen vision of unadulterated ugliness rather than any mythic New Eden. Importantly (and in Hart's scheme of things necessarily), the story opens in the East. A well-intentioned but unfit weakling of a preacher, 'Henley,' is assigned by elders to 'go west, young man.' Ironically, they make this decision owing to a belief that big cities—filled with political corruption, widespread gambling, and undisguised/open prostitution—would prove too much for such a sorry soul. They, like many Easterners, have bought into the Romantic myth (forwarded by among others Eastern-born Theodore Roosevelt) of the west as a rich, virgin land; indeed, God's country. Such naiveté of a romantic order leads to disaster; shortly after arriving, Henley is sucked in by crooked gamblers and wanton women who populate 'the territories.' Not even the strength of his

VEIN OF IRON: As in the writings of such female Western novelists as Edith Wharton, the strong female (Clara Williams, center) and not her whimsical brother (Jack Standing, left) who can stand up to such notorious gunslingers as Blaze Tracy (Hart, right).

formidable sister (aptly named 'Faith'; her middle name might be Courage or Conviction) can save him.

The two polar figures in this forlorn outpost are 'Blaze'--a no-nonsense shootist who at the very least lives by his own code of personal integrity--and his dark(er) doppelganger, 'Silk.' Like Clint Eastwood compared to Lee Van Cleef in Sergio Leone's Spaghetti Westerns, one is 'the good' only in comparison to the 'worse other.' They face off in a cow town where no one ever appears to do any cowboying, rather hangin' 'round town, lazy louts all. Only Blaze (who will enact fire and brimstone much like the lead in Eastwood's *High Plains Drifter*, 1973) is capable of redemption. Faith's physical beauty and inner purity enrapture him at first sight. "I reckon God ain't watchin' me, Ma'am," Blaze admits when Faith insists the Lord is observant of even the humblest folk, "but when I look at you, I feel I've been ridin' the wrong trail."

He then sides with the 'pilgrims' (Faith and her brother, joining the precious few 'good folk') as, at mid-movie, they build a church. Hart's vision is diametrically opposed to that of sentimentalist John Ford, notably in *My Darling Clementine* (1946). There, our first vision of Tombstone does not appear any different from Hell's Hinges. Wild rednecks roam the streets, recklessly firing pistols in the air. But if this initially seems the devil's domain, hero Henry Fonda as Wyatt Earp discovers otherwise. The good people (in Ford, always in the majority) likewise build a church. The marshal's progressive sense of law and order combines with solid if liberalized religion, and the other key element of true civilization, education, which the eponymous new schoolmarm (Cathy Downs) will shortly establish. Only the small group of hardcore trash--the Clantons--cannot be cleansed, and are killed off before an American Utopia can be established. In *Hell's Hinges*, the most horrific

BORN AGAIN: What separates the ostensible 'hero' among the town's miserable lot is the capacity to reform and become a rigid fundamentalist himself.

affront to the church (eventually burned down, as just such a building will be in the aforementioned Eastwood film), occurs when rednecks arrive on Sunday. Rather than content to pray with the devout few, they dare to dance! For Ford, dancing would be what good people do after praying. For the reactionary Hart, it is the devil's worst temptation. If Ford's view of religion (like his later portrayal of education in the schoolroom sequence from *The Man Who Shot Liberty Valance*, 1962), is easygoing and freewheeling. For Hart, such things must be ultra-reactionary if they are to have impact.

Hart's vision is archly puritanical: any such gleeful diversions are posited as a Satanic influence, precisely the opposite of Pappy's allegorical 'West.' In Ford's microcosm of the U.S.A. (a flag proudly flies beside the half-completed church), solid citizens who work hard during the week have a right to enjoy themselves on their single day off with a picnic and party. Indeed, in Ford films, drinking and gambling are in no way portrayed as evil. The Marshal spends evenings in the saloon and will even take up a hand at cards. Just so long as this is kept honest and upright, with a common-sense aura of balance. Excess leads to chaos. Think of Ford's sensibility as arising from his inherent Irish Catholicism: Each of us exists as a combination of the good and the bad, and heaven help them who embrace the latter.

In Hart, a touch of alcohol and/or sex dooms (or for that matter a simple bit of fun) a person from here to eternity. Nowhere is this so obvious as in the personage of Faith's pathetic brother, a cautionary figure as to the way of all flesh. Beware! In *Clementine.,* Wyatt rides away at the conclusion, temporarily owing to familial duties, assuring 'Miss Carter' he'll return. They will marry, live as marshal and teacher, and attend church (and dance afterwards, happily) on Sunday. Here, Blaze and Faith ride away from a doomed land. Without Hart's half-forgotten film, we cannot fully appreciate Ford's more 'forgiving' (anti-Victorian) view of the West as our country's origination myth. Serious minded Western scholars must experience the full range of possible interpretations to fully grasp that the West we witness in any film is only partially a recreation of history, moreso a portrait of a singular creative artist's personal vision of America.

36. HEROES OF THE ALAMO (1937) Rating: ***

CREDITS:

Henry L. Fraser, dir.; Roby Wentz, scr.; Anthony J. Xydias, pro.; Lee Zahler, mus.; Robert (E.) Cline, cin.; Arthur A. Brooks, ed.; 1.37:1; B&W; 75 min.; Columbia.

CAST:

Bruce Warren (*Capt. Almeron 'Al' Dickinson*); Ruth Findley (*Anne 'Susannah' Dickinson*); Earl Hodgins (*Stephen F. Austin*); Lane Chandler (*Col. David Crockett*); Roger Williams (*Col. James Bowie*); Rex Lease (*Lt. Col. William B. Travis*); Jack C. Smith *(William H. Wharton)*; Lee Valanios (*Lt. James Bonham*); Edward Peil Sr. (*Gen. Sam Houston*); Julian Rivero (*Gen. Santa Anna*); Willy Castello (*Gen. Cos*); Paul Ellis *(Gen. Castillion, aka 'Castrillion'*); Jim Corey, Steve Clark (*The Hunters*) Marilyn Haslett (*Angelina Dickinson*); Lafe McKee (*Storekeeper*) Frank Ellis (*The Messenger*); Tex Cooper (*Delegate to Washington-on-the-Brazos*).

Which Western offered the most expensive as well as expansive version of the Alamo myth? That (adjusted for inflation) would be a tie between John Wayne's 1960 epic and the modern Disney company's woe-begotten 2004 film. The cheapest? Though Walt Disney cut corners on his "Davy Crockett at the Alamo" (TV; 1955), that was shot in color with enough extras to make the battle sequence convincing enough in context. Less spectacular (and considerably less successful!) was this cut-rate (the term "B" movie is too kind), barely released celebration of the famed battle which raged for thirteen days

FROM TENNESSEE TO TEXAS: The tale of our American Thermopylae has been told many times on film and TV, though never perhaps with such unbridled enthusiasm (hampered by a woefully inadequate budget) as in *Heroes of the Alamo*.

in San Antonio TX before concluding with a brutal last stand on March 6, 1836.

That date is significant in terms of this movie's evolution. The motivation to do such a film derived from Anthony J. Xydias (1879-1952). The Greek émigré had, like so many other people who drifted into 'development,' began his career as a theatre owner. He scrapped up enough cash to purchase a small Rialto in Dallas, TX; strong response led to him buying more until his chain dominated the city. Aware that others were eliminating the middlemen by producing their own films, he (a Western buff) set out to do that with a string of cheaply made pictures. More interested in the actuality of our frontier than the romantic myth, his team set to work on little films about big figures in our chronicles: Kit Carson, General Custer, Buffalo Bill among them. His favorite was the most famous of the frontiersmen, featured in *With Davy Crockett at the Fall of the Alamo* (1926). At best, the films broke even. Then tragedy struck. Diagnosed with leukemia, Xydias found himself bedridden. While recovering, he wrote frequently to friends and family in Dallas. In their responses, these correspondents mentioned a huge event that would be featured in their city. In 1936, the state of Texas would celebrate a centennial with massive shows, rodeos, parties, and the like on the one hundredth anniversary of the Alamo's fall.

MAKE IT AGAIN, ANTHONY: Unable to round up a suitable budget for his desired epic, producer Xydias recycled stock footage from his own earlier silent film on the same subject.

Inspiration time! Guessing that no one else had thought to make a motion picture about the event, he set out to do so ... honoring that Texas Thermopylae (as a Texan of Greek descent, the concept fascinated Xydias) with a film to premiere in Dallas during the event, then be sent out all across Texas. And, with a little luck, the country. Sadly, nothing worked out as it was supposed to. Xydias' resources were so depleted that the now struggling producer could not afford to hire a lower-level professional writer. Instead, first (and last) time scribe Roby Wentz came on board. The nearest thing to a 'star' would be Lane Chandler (1899-1972), who rode the range as a bit player in numerous shoestring productions. Here, he plays the remarkable Davy Crockett. Hungry to get a Hollywood hand to direct, Xydias signed Harry L. Fraser (1889-1974), who directed bottom-of-the-barrel features with a pre-*Stagecoach* Wayne, including *Randy Rides Alone* (1934). (How intriguing it might have been had the then hungry-for-employment Duke been hired to play Crockett!) As the thought of restaging the spectacular battle was not feasible, Xydias would instead 'suggest' the fighting by cutting stock footage from his earlier silent version of the tale into the new film. In long shots, a sizable force of Texans appears to battle a Mexican army. For closer images, only a small handful of bit players could be afforded to represent soldiers on either side. Filmmaking dragged on to the point that *Heroes* was not ready for a screening at the big show. With this 'premiere' cancelled, Xydias tried to independently distribute his movie but there were few takers. A year later, Columbia did pick up the piece to pair as a second feature with their own modest potboilers.

So: What in *Heroes*... legitimizes its inclusion here? Note that this Alamo movie focuses not on Crockett, Bowie, and Travis, but Almeron Dickinson (1800-1836). He is portrayed as a simple man drawn to the cause of independence owing to harsh experiences with occupying forces in this Mexican province. Here then is an Everyman's Alamo. As Frank Thompson noted in *Alamo Movies*, 'Al' is a farmer in this version. At the time of this film's humble release, the country wept for the ruined heartlands during the disaster that came to be called The Dustbowl. This film's Dickinson has more in common

FROM BIT PLAYERS TO AMERICAN HEROES: Lane Chandler and Rex Lease survived in The Biz as character-cowboy players, though here they had the opportunity to embody legendary Texans Davy Crockett and William Travis.

with the actual Okies of John Steinbeck's *The Grapes of Wrath* than heroic figures in popular Oaters. Here then was precisely the right Alamo movie for The Great Depression.

The role of Dickinson's wife Susannah (1813-1883), here referred to as 'Anne,' is expanded beyond any previous depiction, allowing for the admission that the fort's defense was not merely 'a guy thing.' Though portrayed as cruel tyrant (which he was), the film's Santa Anna is also chivalrous (true, too). Not the Satanic madman who relishes crushing the heads of white children, the false impression given by D.W. Griffith's self-consciously racist *Martyrs of the Alamo* (1915). Often set on the sidelines owing to his role as politician rather than warrior like Sam Houston, Steven Austin is granted a strong moment in the spotlight. This is the only Alamo movie to depict William H. Wharton (1802-1839), whose fiery speeches had a great deal to do with convincing Texicans/Tejanos to revolt against the unconstitutional practices imposed upon them from the dictatorship in Mexico City. For those dedicated to keeping The Western alive, this all but unknown item (though hardly a lost gem) is indeed worth seeking out.

37. HOPALONG CASSIDY, aka HOPALONG CASSIDY ENTERS, aka HOP-A-LONG CASSIDY (1935) Rating: *** ½

CREDITS:

Harold Bretherton, dir.; Doris Schneider, Harrison Jacobs, scr.; Harry Sherman, George Green, pro.; Hugo Friedhofer, mus.; Archie Stout, cin.; Edward Schroeder, ed.; 1.37:1; B&W; Paramount.

CAST:

William Boyd (*William 'Hop-a-Long' Cassidy*); James Ellison (*Johnny Nelson*); Paula Stone (*Mary Meeker*); George Hayes (*Uncle Ben*); Kenneth Thomson (*Jack Anthony*); Frank McGlynn Jr. (*Red Connors*); Charles Middleton (*Buck Peters*); Robert Warwick (*Jim Meeker*); Willie Fung (*Salem the Chinese Cook*); Frank Campeau (*Frisco*); Jim Mason (*Tom Shaw*); Ted Adams (*Hall*); Franklyn Farnum (*Riley*); Sid Jordan (*The Wrangler*); John Merton (*Alcoholic*).

"There are no second acts," F. Scott Fitzgerald (1996-1940) claimed shortly before his death, "in American Lives." Speak for yourself, Francis! True, the creator of such definitive jazz-age novels as *The Great Gatsby* drifted out of our public consciousness during the Depression, when readers turned to such social-realism works as John Steinbeck's *The Grapes of Wrath*. But had F.S.F. held on a while longer, this descendant of Francis Scott Key (composer of "The

ENTER AN AMERICAN HERO: Tall in the saddle on his majestic white horse Topper, the man in black embodied old-fashioned American values . . . quite a changeover from Clarence Mulford's foul-mouthed and impudent ranch hand!

Star Spangled-Banner") would have witnessed a massive revival of his work. Anyone who truly grasps the American paradigm knows this is, in fact, the land of second chances, from cast-off Pilgrims who landed at Plymouth Rock in 1620 to pioneers pushing westward hoping to start over again. Helping explain why the Western remains our definitive American genre: Stories of people who fail to achieve what they went after, change locations, and try, try again.

That's the essence of this surprisingly realistic (considering the family-friendly 'Hoppies' yet to come) "B" Oater. 'William Cassidy' was once a cowhand on the Bar 20 Ranch who struck off to forge his own cattle empire. Such hopes busted, he returns to the old homestead where he's re-hired, reunited with reliable cowboy 'Red' and gritty old timer 'Uncle Ben.' Cassidy also enters into a friendly enmity with an arrogant young hand, 'Johnny Nelson.' They ride for the Bar 20 in honest competition with 'Meeker,' both sides desperate for all-precious water. And, in time, enter the good fight as the two cattlemen set their range war aside to join forces against a renegade outlaw band. Beneath the surface level of action, adventure, and romance, there is here a serious subtext that defends American democratic capitalism so long as it is played out fair and square, the theme of so many varied Oaters.

If Will Cassidy receives a second chance, that proved true also for William Boyd (1890-1972). Shortly after arriving in Hollywood, the prematurely silver-haired would-be star caught the eye of Cecil B. DeMille, winning roles in that director's super-productions including *The King of Kings* (1927). There was also a Western, *The Painted Desert* (1931), co-starring young Clark Gable. Then, the bottom fell out of a budding career. When New York actor 'Stage' Boyd was arrested on a morals charge, newspaper editors erroneously printed photographs of William, entirely innocent. At once, he found himself out of work.

At that time, Boston-based exhibitor Harry Sherman (1884-1952) decided to produce his own films. Aware that low-budget Westerns remained popular in rural markets even as "A" Oaters bombed nationwide, Sherman bought the rights to a popular series of books, initiated with *Bar 20* (1906). Saddened by Boyd's virtual banishment, Sherman offered him the supporting role of ranch foreman 'Buck.' Boyd convinced the initially wary producer to

THE MAN BEHIND THE GUN: A rare image of author Clarence Mulford, who created the pulp fiction character which would become a B movie, and in time TV, legend.

allow him to play the lead. Though Paramount executives held their breath in collective fear that Boyd's unfairly tarnished reputation might prove a problem, that did not occur. This film's unexpected success led to a series and franchise (books, toys, hats).

To the delight of everyone . . . except Illinois-born author Clarence E. Mulford (1883-1956). Inspired by Owen Wister's *The Virginian* (1901), the first book to set the record straight and depict The Cowboy Way as it had been in comparison to Ned Buntline's romanticized Dime Novels, C.E.M. set out to emphasize the rowdiness of hired ranch hands. Particularly his non-hero,

'Cassidy,' name derived from a famous Wyoming outlaw. An authentic campfire ballad described the sad fate of such buckaroos: "Cigarettes, rye whiskey, and wild, wild women, they'll drive you crazy, they'll drive you insane." That defined Cassidy, more a cautionary figure than role model for readers.

Boyd had other ideas, perceiving 'Hopalong' as a means of salvaging himself and his public image. He refused to include any of those temptations in the films he appeared in, outraging Mulford. The latter cried all the way to the bank, refusing to meet with Boyd for several decades. As to this, the first film, it's worth noting that Mulford's vision of what life amid the sagebrush had really been like does come across. Shot in the burning hills surrounding Lone Pine, CA, *Hopalong Cassidy* features a gritty, rugged look that the more fanciful Singin' Cowboy films already in emergence did not. There are singing cowboys on view, but they perform in an authentic off-key manner, not the more commercialized approach of the Sons of the Pioneers.

The myriad difficulties of making a ranch work, economically speaking, underline the piece. Mulford's plot--which combines a Romeo and Juliet-style

STRANGE HOMECOMING: Hoppy (William Boyd) returns to the Bar 20 after attempting to establish a ranch of his own: That's the greatest sidekick ever, George 'Gabby' Hayes, as 'Uncle Ben' on the far left, James Ellison as a younger pal (later to morph into the character called 'Lucky' during later instalments of the series.

love affair between Johnny and Meeker's daughter, accompanied by an element of *Othello* as an Iago-like manipulator plays the two honest enterprises against one another for personal profit--remains poignant. An origination fable for Cassidy's nickname (his leg wounded in an accident) has the hero stumbling about during the film's second half, though this disappeared as the series continued. Present here, though disappearing from future instalments: Hoppy's propensity (like that of The Virginian) to embrace lynching as a 'regrettable necessity' in bringing about law and order.

But back to Fitzgerald's pronouncement. Boyd would enjoy a profitable *Third* Act. As 'The Hoppies' lost steam during the post-war years, television came along with its insatiable hunger for product. Though no one knows why, when Boyd had signed his contract with Sherman, he included a clause insisting that the star owned all future TV rights to the series, despite that medium's commercial nonexistence in the Thirties. By 1950, his old movies were a staple of late-afternoon TV, making Boyd a millionaire. In comparison to F.'s assessment, we might better coin an alternative old phrase: 'He who laughs last . . . laughs best.'

THE LONG-TERM 'LUCKY': Fans of the series will recall Russell Hayden as the actor who most often played Bill Boyd's handsome young sidekick; he would in time produce such TV Westerns as *Cowboy G-Men, Judge Roy Bean,* and *26 Men.*

38. HOSTILES (2017)
Rating: **** ½

CREDITS:

Scott Cooper, dir.; Cooper, Donald E. Stewart, scr.; Cooper, Stewart, Ken Kao, Max Richter, Byron Allen, many others, pro.; Masanobu Takayanagi, cin.; Tom Cross, scr.; 2.35:1; C; 134 min.; Grisbi Prod./Waypoint Entertainment.

CAST:

Christian Bale (*Capt. Joseph J. Blocker*); Rosamund Pike *(Rosalee Quaid)*; Wes Studi (*Chief Yellow Hawk*); Rory Cochran (*Master Sgt. Thomas Metz*); Jonathan Majors (*Corp. Henry Woodson*); John Benjamin Hickey (*Capt. Royce Tolan*); Stafford Douglas (*Corp. Molinor*); Scott Shepherd (*Wesley Quaid*); Ava Cooper *(Lucy Quaid)*; Stela Cooper *(Sylvia)*; Stephen Lang (*Col. Abraham Biggs*); Bill Camp *(Jeremiah Wilks)*; Timothee Chalamet (*Pvt. Philippe DeJardin*); Adam Beach (*Black Hawk*); Xavier Horsechief *(Little Bear)*; O'orianka Kilcher (*Elk Woman*); Tanava Beatty (*Living Woman*); Peter Mullan (*Col. McCowan*); Robyn Malcolm (*Minnie McCowan*); Ryan Bingham (*Malloy*); Ben Foster (*Wills*); Scott Anderson (*Muny*). Scott Wilson (*Cyrus Lounde*).

As to earlier Hollywood movies that deal with the issue of Anglo-Indian relations, two stand out as seminal. First, *The Searchers* (1956), John Ford's monumental epic. The lead character (John Wayne as 'Ethan Edwards') flat-out hates Indians, owing to experiences in which friends and relatives were killed by Native Americans. Second, Kevin Costner's *Dances with Wolves* (1990), an Oscar winning Best Picture. Here, the more amenable (and anachronistically contemporary hero 'John Dunbar') heads west to discover that

THE LAST MISSION: Christian Bale revealed his rich acting gifts with this complex portrait of a cavalry officer who agrees to complete a job that he despises only to discover that his world-view has been changed in the process.

the indigenous people he encounters are non-violent, except when provoked. The oppositional approaches as to the iconic films' key Anglo character (and focus of each work) allow them to be perceived as polar possibilities by which other, more recent films can be properly understood in the historical context of The Western.

In this context, Scott Cooper's (1970-) *Hostiles* presents 'Blocker,' an army captain as jaded as to his position on Native Americans as Wayne's Ethan Edwards. In the film's underlying irony, Blocker is assigned to transport aging, ill Cheyenne chief 'Yellow Hawk' from a New Mexico cavalry outpost up to his homeland in Montana. Elected officials in Washington, D.C hope to address past unpleasantness by allowing the chief to die in the territory he loves. *Hostiles* does not offer a rewrite of history (as *D.W.W.* did) by suggesting Indians (for Costner, the Lakota) were not warlike. In truth, the northern Cheyenne---like the southwestern Comanch-- practiced torture as well as revelling in combat. Blocker witnessed the gutting of a close friend by the very man he must now protect on the journey. But as a soldier, he does his

THE FRONTIERSWOMAN: Rosamund Pike found a role worthy of her talent as a pioneer woman who learns to despise Native Americans owing to harsh experience, only to shed herself of such prejudices during a dangerous odyssey across the last frontier.

duty, following orders to the letter, no matter how disgusted the protagonist may be by this hand that destiny has dealt him.

During their long, often tedious, always contentious, occasionally violent journey, the two face many obstacles. At the conclusion, there are redneck whites who will fight and die rather than allow Native people to be buried on what is now legally their land. The military escort party includes a widow woman, 'Rosalee,' whose husband and three children were earlier killed in an unprovoked raid on their farm by Comanches. *Hostiles'* brutally effective opening recalls the massacre of the Edwards' ranch by members of this very tribe in the John Ford classic. The comparison allows us to note how films have changed during the intervening decades. While 'Pappy' necessarily (owing to censorship restrictions as well as artistic sensibility) left the bloodshed off screen, hinting at rather than depicting the horror, this contemporary project depicts everyday people as they are decimated, the husband scalped. In this film's context, these 'hostile Other' (Comanch) are as feared and hated by the Cheyenne as are the bluecoats and their lady companion. The two previously hostile factions---Anglo and Cheyenne---must come together or both groups will be exterminated by their current mutual enemy. Fighting

Douglas Brode

THE NOT-SO-'VANISHING' AMERICAN: Like the great Jay Silverheels in an earlier era, Wes Studi offered authentic portrayals of our indigenous people in such varied films as *The Last of the Mohicans*, *Geronimo: An American Legend*, and *Hostiles*.

alongside one another, they unwittingly become a community. And when the battle is done, they necessarily view each other with empathy and understanding that neither would have believed possible when they first set off on what seemed a God-forsaken mission. The old adage that the enemy of my enemy is my friend serves as this film's theme; Cooperation is most effectively achieved when mutual survival of all is at stake.

Like the captain, 'Mrs. Quaid' arcs from an Indian hater to more a enlightened human who, by the end, evaluates people as individuals, with no concern for race. Coming to grasp that Comanches and Cheyenne are two distinct American nations, even as say the Irish and the Russians are in Europe, each with its own culture and values allows her to arc. Likewise, Yellow Hawk is freed of generalized prejudices against Whites. *Hostiles*, then, rates as a curious and important film that avoids extremes of PC on the one hand or retro-thinking on the other. No question the Comanches on view are horrific in their brutality. But as the wife of an army officer at a post the group visits notes, they are hardly motiveless malignancies. The reservation where the Comanch were located was situated on filthy, uninhabitable land not fit for farming or any other human endeavor. The agents were corrupt, pocketing much of the money our government's Indian Bureau designated for proper blankets by purchasing cheaper supplies. Though we (through the eyes of this film's Anglo leads) may recoil at the dark, bloody deeds, a justification for the Comanches' anger and outrage is offered. All but comatose following her family's fate, the ever more understanding Mrs. Quaid eventually chooses to love and protect an Indian child in lieu of the children she has lost, in so doing regaining her own humanity.

In a fitting if melancholy closing, even the seemingly embittered former captain undergoes a transformation, joining the lady and her adopted child on a train to the East. In the upcoming century about to dawn, they will attempt to put the horror behind them. By accomplishing this, they will no longer be prisoners of their own, and our country's, dark past. In a film that refuses to take either extreme of a pro-Indian or pro-Anglo stance, *Hostiles* arrives at a difficult if profound truth: It's all up to the individual. Or, more correctly, those individuals who overcome prejudices that they believed 'true' but in fact are not, and setting long-standing hatred aside to become a makeshift American family.

39. IN OLD ARIZONA (1928/1929)
Rating: *** ½

CREDITS:

Irving Cummings, Raoul Walsh, dir.; Tom Barry, Paul Gerald Smith, scr.; William Fox, pro.; Arthur Edison, cin.; Louis (R.) Loeffler, ed.; 1.20:1; B&W; 95 min.; Fox Film Company.

CAST:

Warner Baxter (*The Cisco Kid*); Edmund Lowe (*Sgt. Mickey Dunn*); Dorothy Burgess (*Tonia Maria*); Henry Armetta *(Barber)*; James Bradbury Jr., John Webb Dillion (*Soldiers*); Joe Brown (*Bartender*); Frank Campeau (*Bounty Hunter*); Alphonse Ethier (*Sheriff*); Jim Farley (*Citizen*); Pat Hartigan, Duke Martin, Frank Nelson (*Cowpunchers*); Soledad Jimenez (*Tonita*); Ivan Linow (*Russian Immigrant)*; Tom London (*Man in Saloon)*; Helen Lynch, J. Farrell MacDonald (*Stagecoach Passengers*); James A. Marcus *('Pop' the Blacksmith)*; Tom Santschi (*Cowhand*).

One of many legends surrounding William Sydney Porter (1862-1910), better known by his pen name 'O. Henry,' concerns an incident that occurred when the North Carolina native travelled west when (not unlike Doc Holliday) a nagging cough caused him to seek a sunnier environment. During a brief layover in New Mexico, Porter raised the ire of local lawmen who tossed the budding author in a jail cell with an ornery cowboy, none other than Henry Antrill, aka Billy Bonney, i.e. 'Billy the Kid' (1859-1881). Porter

They Went That-A-Way

AN ETHNIC VARIATION ON BILLY BONNEY: O'Henry's incarnation of 'the Kid' was based on the actual person he had once shared a jail cell with; in Hollywood's version, the character would be portrayed as Latin, if initially with Anglo actor Warner Baxter (Oscar winner) in the role, when adapted by Hollywood.

tucked memories of this braggart away for future reference. It is possible, some historians suggest, that a third cell-mate was Elfego Baca (1865-1945), a Mexican-American who would soon become a famous lawman and, later still, attorney at law. His adventures would reach television in 1958 thanks to Walt Disney, starring Robert Loggia as the hero.

At any rate: When Porter eventually abandoned the West to become a writer in New York, "O. Henry" penned "The Caballero's Way," a 1907 yarn in which The Kid turns the tables of his cheating Latin Lover. Once the popular short story had been re-published in an anthology, *Hearts of the West*, a year later, 'The Cisco Kid' became a symbol of the romantic bandit. When the first film, *The Caballero's Way* (1914), remained in production, exhibitors grew concerned that the country's vast non-reading audience might become

THE BETRAYAL: Cisco's two-timing lover (Dorothy Burgess) cheats on 'her man' with the very soldier (Edmund Lowe) assigned to bring the Kid in, dead or alive. More often than not in the century's first half, women from South of the Border were portrayed as double-dealing scoundrels, though this would change in the 1950s beginning with such groundbreaking films as *High Noon* and *The Iron Mistress*.

confused by the terms 'Cisco,' often associated with Mexican vaqueros. As a result, 'the Kid' instead became a Spanish bandit, the case too in the second feature, another silent, *The Border Terror* (1919). Any association with the historic Billy the Kid swiftly ended.

By the time Fox's version (one of the earliest sound films, and certainly the first Western in which all exterior dialogue sequences were shot on location, with primitive microphones), popular if aging star Baxter (1888-1951) further eliminated the youthful element from the original story. He played 'Cisco' as a lovably if lazy lout who robs from the rich (Wells Fargo and other capitalist institutions) while giving to the poor, Spanish and Anglo alike. The populace of the small Arizona town is comprised of Irish, Italians, Russians, Asians, and other diverse immigrants. Surprisingly, Cisco is not portrayed as a native Mexican, rather from Portugal, perhaps owing to the horrific widespread prejudice against below-the-border people at that time in our often embarrassing social history. Like virtually everyone else in the scenario, Cisco views the West not as a second Eden/Virgin Land, rather a prison without walls. Wherever they may hail from, every onscreen character has but one dream: To get back home, bitter about being misled by faux romances of the range. Most hail from New York City, waxing idealistic about Broadway and the Bowery, Coney Island and Chinatown. This portrait comes closer to the reality of the civilizing process than the idealistic myth of 'just plain folks' enjoying their new existence, most notably incarnated in John Ford's *My Darling Clementine* (1946).

If Cisco does embody a cliché in the making---the jovial if none too bright Caballero---at the very least he represents a step up from the despicable negative portrayals in earlier films. These include *Broncho Billy and the Greaser* (1914), in which the Anglo hero put a Mexican in his place for merely glancing at a white woman. On the other hand, Dorothy Burgess portrays 'Tania' as a character utterly without redeeming virtues other than her superficial beauty. She reveals herself to be a flirtatious, promiscuous, amoral, vain, hypocritical, greedy, negative caricature of the Spanish woman as a menace to *all* men, Latin and Anglo alike, deserving of her ironic fate. Sad to say, this was

"STICK 'EM UP ... AGAIN!": Cisco robs a stage to steal from the rich and, as a Robin Hood of the old southwest, give to the poor ... including himself.

an all-too-common stereotype of 'the dark woman' as Devil in the Flesh in the era's popular culture. Th;ankfully, things would indeed change during the postwar years, in large part to President Roosevelt's Good Neighbor Policy.

Originally, co-director Raoul Walsh (1887-1980), a popular star at the time, was to have played the lead. But a bizarre automobile accident caused Walsh to lose an eye and forever after wear a black patch, adding to the filmmaker's growing 'maverick' mystique. As the idea of casting ethnic performers in appropriate roles or any sensitivity to such minorities did not then exist, Ohio-born Baxter portrayed Cisco in the broadest manner possible. Winning a Best Actor Oscar, he would return to the role for half a dozen follow-ups. The self-conscious nastiness with which he sets up his former lover for a virtual execution by the chief Anglo competition, a much-admired twist with viewers of the time, would come to seem ever less amusing as cultural and social changes led to more sympathetic portraits of the West's ethnic women, including the upcoming sound and color version of the oft-filmed *Ramona*. With each progressive potboiler, the Latina would be portrayed gentler and gentrified.

Baxter would eventually be replaced by (significantly, and at long last, with Latin stars) Cesar Romero, Gilbert Roland, and Duncan Renaldo. The latter carried the tradition through radio to the small screen in an early shot-in-color series that ran between 1950-1955. By that time, any trace of the rogue was long gone, the Kid as stalwart a hero as 'The Lone Ranger', Gene Autry, Roy Rogers, or 'Hopalong Cassidy.' While that led to a simplistic portrayal, this redux did prove positive for 1950s children, encouraged to perceive a Latin American as a heroic figure.

40. IRON MISTRESS, THE (1952) Rating: ****

CREDITS:

Gordon Douglas, dir.; James R. Webb, scr.; Henry Blanke, pro.; Max Steiner, mus.; John F. Seitz, cin.; Alan Crosland Jr., ed.; 1.37:1; C; 110 min.; Warner Bros.

CAST:

Alan Ladd *(James Bowie)*; Virginia Mayo *(Judalon de Bornay)*; Joseph Calleia *(Juan Murrow)*; Phyllis Kirk *(Ursula de Veramendi)*; Alf Kieljin *(Phillipe de Cabanal)*; Douglas Dick *(Narcisse de Bornay)*; Anthony Caruso *(Black Jack Sturdevant)*; Nedrick Young *(Henri Contrecourt)*; George Voskovec *(John James Audubon)*; Richard Carlyle *(Rezin Bowie)*; Robert Emhardt *(Gen. Cuny)*; Don Beddoe *(Dr. Cuny)*; Harold Gordon *(Andrew Marschalk)*; Jay Novello *(Judge Crain)*; Nick Dennis *(Nez Coupe)*; Sarah Selby *(Mrs. Bowie)*. Edward Colmans *(Don Juan de Varamendi)*; George J. Lewis *(Col. Wells)*; Gordon Nelson *(Dr. Maddox)*.

Western fans who arrived at this "A" feature biopic of frontiersman James Bowie (1786-1836) expecting a rip-roarin' rendering of the Alamo battle were in for a surprise. For here is the rarely told tale (partly fictionalized for a post-war audience demanding romance, action, and a happy Hollywood ending) of that historical character's early years. We first meet the Tennessee born Bowie (played here by Alan Ladd, 1913-1964) while living in the bayou country of Louisiana with his mother and brothers. They are (accurately) portrayed less as staunch pioneer types than rowdy, backwoods hillbillies. The

THE TEMPERED BLADE: Forsaking the oft-told Alamo story, here is the only film that concentrates on the early life of famed frontier fighter James Bowie (Alan Ladd).

boys challenge each other to a rough and tumble free-for-all to determine which will bring their lumber to glamorous New Orleans. Jim wins; whether the friendly fight happened or not, the sequence does accurately suggest the regional lifestyle of those times. On his first day in the big city, Bowie meets and befriends John Jacques Audubon (1785-1851), shortly to become a famous illustrator of American wildlife, particularly birds. In the film, it will be James who brings John into the wilds where he can paint. No hard evidence exists this occurred; then again, no one can prove it didn't. Their meeting opens the door for a fictional plot within the historical context of a city that appears sophisticated on its surface, if shallow as to human values. Audubon recently painted a gorgeous Southern belle, the fictional 'Judalon,' a 'bird' in the British double-meaning of that term. Here, Bowie takes one look at the glamorous lady and falls in love; not, significantly, with her (as a person) but that idealized/perfected image.

TOUGH AND TENDER: The film illustrates Bowie's legendary violent side in several brutal confrontations (here, with Anthony Caruso as 'Black Jack') but also his tenderness with his great love, 'Ursula' (Phyllis Kirk).

Her character was created by Paul Wellman, who several years previously had written an epic novel on which this film was based. If 'Judalon' is not as a distinct person true to fact, she *is* true to type: This is among the most accurate depictions of a Southern 'belle' in Hollywood movies, alongside those in *Jezebel* and *Gone with the Wind*. Wellman 'collapsed' several women from Bowie's New Orleans visits into a single person, such simplification necessary for historical fiction. Trained in the supposedly fine art of flirtation, Judalon's hobby is breaking hearts; her aim, to marry the most eligible (wealthy and prestigious) man in the South.

As to the star, Ladd had only recently left Paramount, where one of his final assignments had been *Shane*. That film's enormous success opened the door for more Westerns, though the short, elegant, gentle-mannered actor proved all wrong for the historic Bowie. A huge bear of a man with a fierce temper, Bowie would be better cast when Sterling Hayden played him in *The Last Command* (1955). John Wayne considered taking on the Bowie role during early preparation for *The Alamo* (1960) before settling on Davy Crockett. On the other hand, Ladd would prove perfect for the film's highly fictionalized vision of a character who goes by Bowie's name. Ladd played the eponymous hero of *The Great Gatsby* in the 1949 film version of F. Scott Fitzgerald's 1925 jazz age amorality play: The story of a poor boy who determines to become rich to win the hand of an aristocratic if elusive beauty. *Iron Mistress* might be thought of as a remake of that tale, only with Southern and Western settings and a happy ending that is (for once) indeed true to life.

In the film's closing image, Bowie weds 'Ursula de Veramendi' in San Antonio, even as he did in reality. Notably, *Iron Mistress* reverses a racist paradigm that haunted Westerns (and other, non-genre films) during the 20th century's first half. Beginning with the crude 'Broncho Billy' flickers, continuing on through the sound era, 'decent' Anglo men had been tempted by overly-sexualized Latin women, who seduce helpless, hapless fellows already engaged to pure white women. (A rare exception to this syndrome was provided by numerous film versions of *Ramona*, the most famous included in this volume). Why the changeover? During the war years, Pres. Roosevelt had

BIRTH OF THE BLADE: With the help of a historical blacksmith named Black, Jim Bowie designs the world's most famous knife; in actuality, it was like Jim's brother Rezin who worked with Black. Then again, as Mr. Hitchcock once said: "It's only a moooo-vie!" And, as John Ford added: "When the legend becomes a fact, print the legend."

requested that Hollywood filmmakers cease depicting Latinos in a negative light so as to firm up all Americas against the Axis. Here is one of the first major movies to reveal the fruits of that approach. *High Noon*, released the same year, is another.

Two sequences stand out in memory. First is 'the birth of the blade,' in which James Bowie and a true-to-life blacksmith, James Black, design, then create the famed knife. The concept for an exceptional weapon, to be used exclusively for killing rather than hunting, follows the line of actual events, if with one key difference. More likely, Rezin--Jim's older brother--worked with Black. Also, an invented 'bit' allows the fact-based tale to project an almost Arthurian quality of mythic adventure. Here, Black tosses into the boiling cauldron a piece of a falling star even as the blade tempers. What emerges from the black kettle can be considered an

American Excalibur, as an historical event morphs (thanks to Hollywood) into the realm of legend.

The other, even more spectacular sequence, features Bowie in a midnight duel with a Big Easy aristocrat. The latter wields a sword; the battle, actual or invented, takes place even as a storm rages outside, their deadly encounter in darkness lit only by occasional bursts of lightning. No attempt at description will be provided. As 'pure cinema,' this confrontation must be seen to be believed. And appreciated.

FROM THE OLD SOUTH TO THE NEW WEST: The film's version of James Bowie tires of an aristocratic Belle (Virginia Mayo) and her cynical, sophisticate game playing but finds a second Eden in Texas.

41. JACK McCALL, DESPERADO (1953)
Rating: *** 1/2

CREDITS:

Sidney Salkow, dir.; John O'Dea, David Chandler, scr.; Sam Katzman, pro.; Richard Milburn, Septimus Winner, mus.; Henry Freulich, cin.; Aaron Stell, ed.; 1.37:1; C; 76 min.; 1.31:1; Columbia Pictures.

CAST:

George Montgomery (*Jack MCall*); Angela Stevens (*Rose Griffith*); Douglas Kennedy *(James Butler 'Wild Bill' Hickok)*; James Seay *(Bat McCall)*; William Tannen (*Spargo*); Jay Silverheels (*Chief Red Cloud*); John Hamilton (*Col. Cornish*); Selmer Jackson (*Col. Brand*); Victor Adamson (*Barfly*); Emile Avery (*Juror*); Kenne Duncan (*Outlaw*); Alva Marie Lacy (*Hiega*).

Beginning in the autumn of 1951, children and young teens arriving home from school to enjoy middleclass families' new TV sets were treated to a succession of pluperfect heroes. George Reeves in *(The) Adventures of Superman* may have been the favorite, but a Western featuring handsome Guy Madison as 'Wild Bill Hickock' offered mighty competition: always clean-shaven, in *Shane*-like spotless buckskin clothing, dedicated to 'doing the right thing' for innocent folks in trouble. Though loosely based on a real person, television's James Butler H. (1837-1876), might be described as the 'Lone Ranger' minus his mask. Not that the real Wild Bill in any way, shape, or form resembled the heroic figure on display. Though Hickock's more

FROM BACK-SHOOTER TO PEACEMAKER: In an early example of revisionism, the man who shot Wild Bill Hickock in the back would be transformed into a hero who creates a worthy bridge between Anglo (Angela Stevens) and Native (Eugene Iglesias) Americans.

illustrious actions included stints as pony express rider, Union Civil War volunteer, Indian scout, and town marshal appointments in Abilene, Kansas and Deadwood, South Dakota, James B. was also known as an alcoholic, an inveterate and obsessive gambler, frequenter of whorehouses, charlatan stage actor (along with pal William F. Cody), and a cold-blooded gunslinger pursued by federal lawmen for the killing of two of Tom (older brother of the General) Custer's troopers. In truth, earlier films did (while lionizing W.B.) include some of his less savory activities, Cecil B. DeMille's *The Plainsman* (1936) starring Gary Cooper prominent among them. But even if American boys of the Fifties had caught that oldie on TV, they headed out to their local theatres in the spring of 1953 to catch the latest "B" Western without a clue of what might be coming.

As *Jack McCall* opens, viewers were treated to a ritualized beginning for a B Western: The tired desperado rides into town, a determined look in his eyes. Audiences sat still, awaiting a shoot-out. The rugged star (George Montgomery, 1916-2002), already familiar as a frontier hero thanks to such previous pictures as *The Texas Rangers* (1951), dismounts and shuffles into a saloon. That's when shock waves set in. For this was none other than Jack McCall (1852/3-1877); the 'bad man' he challenged, Wild Bill, incarnated here by Douglas Kennedy (1915-1973). Though the history of the West

A TRUE AMERICAN ICON: In addition to portraying the Lone Ranger's trusted sidekick 'Tonto,' Native American actor embodied such famous chiefs as 'Red Cloud.'

insists, thanks to witnesses, that McCall shot Hickok in the back without warning while Wild Bill played cards holding aces and eights (forever after known as the "Dead Man's Hand"), the filmmakers here take a huge liberty. The film's Hickock rises and goes for his gun first. Only then does 'heroic' Jack shoot him down in a fair fight.

The term Revisionism would not come into play so far as popular culture is concerned until the early 1970s. In time, unsavory depictions of Hickok would appear in *Little Big Man* (1970; Jeff Corey), *The White Buffalo* (1977; Charles Bronson); *Deadwood* (2004; Travis Pearson); and *Wild Bill* (2011; Jeff Bridges). But back in the Eisenhower era, when virtually every historic Westerner was transformed by television into a mythic figure? Not only 'questionable' figures such as Wyatt Earp and Pat Garrett, but abject low-lives including Johnny Ringo and Bill 'The Texan' Longley? Inconceivable! Spellbinding, too, as amazed kids witnessed a story told in flashback during Jack McCall's infamous murder trial. Here Wild Bill is not only a thief but a coward, like one of those wicked lawman that celluloid vigilantes take down for the good of the community. He's not above setting the frontier ablaze with yet another Indian war, manipulating the fine and decent chief Red Cloud into attacking peaceful Anglos so that a corrupt ring can reap great profits from the holocaust. Little matter that history informs us Red Cloud had abandoned the warrior's path following a conflict with the U.S. Army ten years earlier after signing the Fort Laramie Peace Treaty of 1867. When this film takes place (1876), the Lakota leaders were Sitting Bull, Gaul, Crazy Horse, and Rain-in-the-Face.

Intriguingly, producer Sam 'King of the Quickies' Katzman (1901-1973) and director Sidney Salkow (1909-2000), who together ran the B feature unit at Columbia Pictures, were far from finished. The following year, they offered up *Sitting Bull*, with J. Carroll Naish returning to a role he had previously played in the high-profile "A" musical *Annie Get Your Gun* (1951). In this new film, Dale Robertson portrayed an enlightened cavalry officer who hopes to create peace. Opposing him is another historical figure, here for the first (if hardly last) time in a film depicted as evil incarnate: George Armstrong

RETURN OF THE KILLER B's: McCall (George Montgomery) loses control and tries to kill one of the villains who framed him for murder in this, a typical example of the medium-budget color Oaters turned out during the 1950s from Columbia's B unit, such items forever known as "Katzman's Quickies."

Custer. Fascinatingly, the Lt. Colonel was played by Douglas Kennedy, whom kids recalled as 'the bad' Wild Bill from a year earlier.

There's nothing inherently wrong with revision, particularly when it sets a false record straight. But no matter how questionable the real Hickok may have been, the actual McCall was worse. At the film's conclusion, a jury finds McCall innocent on all counts and carries him into the street on their shoulders, a Frank Capra-like populist hero ("Mr. Smith," "Mr. Deeds," "John Doe") who saved the community from corruption. Not mentioned in the film's context: Six months later, the decision of that initial court was set aside as obviously fixed. Jack McCall was indeed tried twice for the same crime, found guilty, and shortly thereafter hanged by the neck until he was dead, dead . . . dead.

42. JOHNNY CONCHO (1956)
Rating: ****

CREDITS:

Don McGuire, dir.; McGuire, David P. Harmon, scr.; Frank Sinatra, Henry W. Sanicola, pro.; Nelson Riddle, mus.; William C. Mellor, cin.; 1.37:1; B&W; 84 min.; Kent/United Artists.

CAST:

Frank Sinatra (Johnny Concho/Johnny Collins); Phyllis Kirk (*Mary Dark*); Keenan Wynn (*Barney Clark*); William Conrad (*Tallman*); Wallace Ford (*Albert Dark*); Dorothy Adams *(Sarah Dark)*; Christopher Dark (*Walker*); Howard Petrie (*Joe Helguson, the Blacksmith*); Harry Bartell (*Sam Green*); Dan Riss *(Judge Earl Tyler*); Willis Bouchey (*Sheriff Henderson*); Robert Osterloh (*Duke Lang*); Leo (V.) Gordon (*Mason*); Claude Akins *(Lem)*; John Qualen (*Jake*); Budd Knapp (*Pearson*); Ben Wright (*Benson*); Joe Bassett (*Harry*); Malcolm Atterbury (*Milo*); Strother Martin (*Cripple Creek Townsman*); Russell Thorson (*A Lawman*).

Following his Oscar win for *From Here to Eternity* (1953) and the success of several melancholic saloon-singer albums (most notably, "In the Wee Small Hours of the Morning"), Frank Sinatra (1915-1998) made an overnight leap from has-been to superstar: An American icon of dapper modernity that continued into the 1960s and beyond. Shortly, he won leading roles in top-drawer studio dramas (*Man with the Golden Arm*, 1955), musicals (*High Society*, 1955), and spectacular costume films (*The Pride and the Passion*, 1957). Intriguingly, though, Sinatra also chose to appear in 'small' indie movies, shot

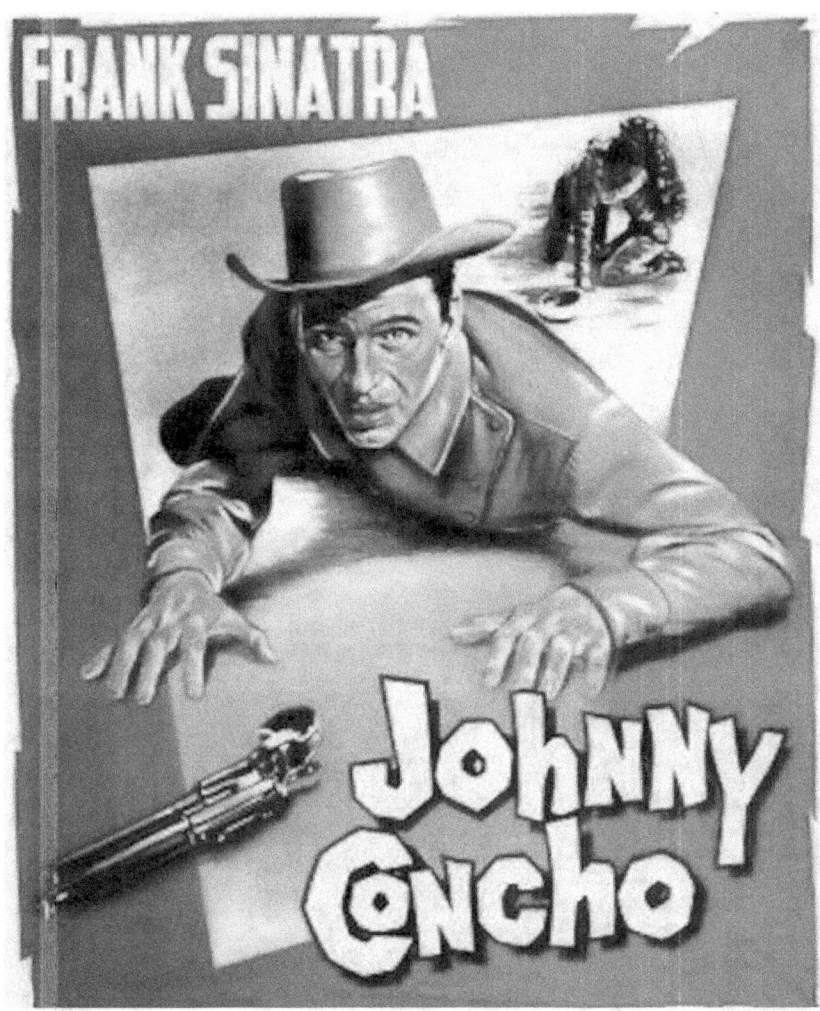

A 'DIRTY LITTLE COWARD' AS WILD WEST ANTI-HERO: Searching for challenging roles, Frank Sinatra chose to play a snivelling sidewinder who achieves redemption by film's end.

on a purposefully low budget, allowing him to perform in different guises than those Hollywood blockbusters allowed for. The First: *Suddenly* (1954), in which he played a maniacal would-be presidential assassin. Two years later, 'The Chairman of the Board' appeared in a post-*High Noon* Western, and the first of several films he would co-produce under his own Kent banner. The movie is derived from a TV play, "The Man Who Owned the Town" (*Studio One*, 11/1/1954) from the Golden Age of Live Television. Beginning in 1949 and continuing through to the late 1950s, most broadcasting originated in New York. The best among those original dramas---*Patterns, Requiem for a Heavyweight, 12 Angry Men, The Days of Wine and Roses, Judgment at Nuremberg*---were optioned by West Coast producers for feature films. This included Westerns: *The Fastest Gun Alive* and *The Left-Handed Gun*, revamped as star vehicles for Glenn Ford and Paul Newman, had originally been viewed by the relatively small number of citizens who early on could afford TV sets.

Sinatra happened to catch the piece (teleplay by David P. Harmon, 1918-2001) which told an out of the ordinary story of our last frontier. 'Johnny Devlin' (in the original) is the nasty, self-possessed, lazy, good for nothing younger brother of one of the West's fast guns. When he settles in Cripple

SWEET REDEMPTION: Johnny (Frank Sinatra) is reborn thanks to the love of a fine woman (Phyllis Kirk, who earlier played Alan Ladd's love interest in *The Iron Mistress*) and a hard-knuckled, no nonsense preacher (Keenan Wynn).

Creek (incorrectly positioned in Arizona, though an actual city in Colorado), the townsfolk treat this short, snotty punk as if he were their local wrathful god. All fear that if they cross him in any way, they'll pay dearly when Johnny's infamous brother shows up. He takes horses and saddles without paying, supposedly 'on credit.' And gambles in the saloon, always winning, he and he alone not required to reveal the hand he supposedly holds. Everyone loathes him except a remarkable young woman, 'Mary" (her name may be symbolic) who despises what Johnny is but adores what he might be if only the coward were to step out from under his brother's shadow.

One day, a seasoned gunfighter named 'Tallman' drifts into town and, observing the situation, announces that two days earlier he killed Johnny's brother. Immediately, the townspeople turn against the unpleasant runt, throwing him out. Shortly, it appears that the citizenry has collectively leaped out of the frying pan and into the fire. Realizing that in their collective fear these people resemble a herd of frightened sheep, Tallman decides to put down roots, taking over as king of this little hill. In an incredible irony, the only person who might rid the citizenry of this killing machine is their one-time faux-deity, suddenly returning as a hero willing to sacrifice himself in order to buy freedom for the crowd.

Sinatra is mesmerizingly despicable during the film's early sequences, believably terrified of what fate might await him once everything changes at mid-movie, and finally powerfully convincing as the born again figure who comes into his own, if necessary surrendering his life to clean up the mess he himself made. Never before (not even as doomed 'Angelo Maggio' in *Eternity*) had the performer allowed himself to appear so physically vulnerable. The opening title sequence focuses on a snake, slithering across a barren stretch of wilderness. Most viewers assumed this to be a signifier of Sinatra's character yet to come and, perhaps, as he in his darkest moments saw himself. Frank might well have been nominated for a Best Actor Oscar if only the film had scored better than it did at the box-office, playing second-string theatres (much as *Suddenly* had done) on a double bill with minor "B" fare. In the future, Westerns would not prove to be Sinatra's forte. Lavish, over-produced,

I GET BY WITH A LITTLE HELP FROM MY FRIEND: High Noon's Gary Cooper visited the Johnny Concho set to mentor first-time Western star Frank Sinatra on the art of gunfighting.

poorly scripted 'stunts' like *Sergeants Three* (1963) and *4 For Texas* (1964) less convincingly cast him in more traditionally heroic/romantic roles. *J.C.* (the character's name may be a Biblical reference to the returning figure's saviour-like quality) is considered the least accessible of all Sinatra films, yet it is the one that offers full proof of how incredible he could be when appropriately cast.

As for the inevitable final gunfight, here we witness an alternative to *High Noon*. In the earlier film, the hero (Gary Cooper) gave up hoping that the town might back him, killing off the rawhiders with only his wife to aid him. Here, our anti-hero cannot complete the mission. Instead, the townsfolk rally *en masse* and shoot the gunslingers down in cold blood. At the time of *Johnny Concho*'s release, these scenes caused audiences (however small) to applaud such an unexpected variation on what had become the theme of a cowardly American community, also present in such contemporary fare as *The Wild One* (1952) with Marlon Brando. Today, the ferocity more recalls the crazed citizenry in Shirley Jackson's short story "The Lottery": mob violence, as heralded in this film as it was decried in the earlier, better known Oater, *The Ox Bow Incident* (1943).

SOMETMES BADGUYS, BUT ALSO HEROES: William Conrad, cast in *Johnny Concho* as a killer, had originated the role of 'Mat Dillon' on radio's *Gunsmoke*; Claude Akins would in the mid-1960s replace Neville Brand as the titular Texas Ranger on NBC's *Laredo*.

43. JUNIOR BONNER (1972)
Rating: **** ½

CREDITS:

Sam Peckinpah, dir.; Jeb Rosebrook, scr.; Mickey Borofsky, Joe Wizan, pro.; Jerry Fielding, mus.; Lucien Ballard, cin.; Frank Santillo, Robert L. Wolfe, ed.; 2.35:1; C; 100 min.; Wizan/Booth/Gardner/Solar Prods..

CAST:

Steve McQueen (*Junior Bonner*); Robert Preston (*Ace Bonner*); Ida Lupino (*Elvira*); Ben Johnson (*Buck Roan*); Joe Don Baker *(Curly)*; Barbara Leigh (*Charmagne*); Mary Murphy (*Ruth Bonner*); Bill McKinney (*Red Terwiliger*); Dub Taylor *(Del)*; Sandra Deel (*Arlis*); Don 'Red' Barry (*Homer Rutledge*); Charles (H.) Gray (*Burt*); Matthew Peckinpah (*Tim Bonner*); Sundown Spencer *(Nick)*; Rita Garrison (*Flashie*); Casey Tibbs *(Himself)*; Roxanne Knight (*Merla*); Sandra Pew (*Janene*); Rod Hart (*Guitarist*).

Once upon a time (1955, to be precise) in the West that really was, a visitor from the East bumped into Casey Tibbs (1929-1990), the greatest all-around cowboy following a gruelling succession of rodeo wins. "*Why* do you put yourself through this?" the fascinated outsider asked about these brutal competitions, "though there other venues of your trade (wrangler, top ranch hand, etc.) that are less destructive than entering the arena?" Casey smiled, then related a story about a traveling circus which had once passed through a major city. A storeowner, watching the parade from his doorway, noted that at the tail end, a sad looking fellow followed behind, scooping up the animal dung. The man didn't simply perform his job; he gave it his all. Impressed, the

RETURN OF THE RODEO WESTERN: Sam Peckinpah's *Junior Bonner* starring Steve McQueen rated as the best among a flurry of such films in the early to mid 1970s.

local businessman approached the worker, told him how much he admired this fellow's gusto, and offered him ten times whatever he might be making if he would quit and take a high-paying executive position with him.

"What?" the circus fella asked in amazement. "And give up *show business*?"

Whether the Easterner understood Casey's drift remains unknown. The point: Certain professions are addictive. Like the sad would-be superstar who never made the big time but sings: "Rock 'n' roll, I gave you the best years of my life . . ." Even as cowboying itself was to Lee Marvin's character in *Monte Walsh*, so is the specific venue of 'rodeo' to this film's eponymous hero. Junior, pushing thirty, returns to Prescott AZ, his hometown, for another bout at the riskiest event, bull-riding. The fella in charge, wondrously named 'Buck Roan,' warns Junior that, considering the beating that this no-longer young man has recently taken, Junior would best stick to broncs. That only causes Junior to determine he must 'go the limit,' even at the risk of death. . . . there's always one more rodeo to enter, always a prize you haven't yet won somewhere, someplace . . . down the highway, over the next mountain. To paraphrase author Somerset Maugham, for Junior, rodeo is a fatal disease he doesn't want to be cured of.

The same holds true for his papa. Ace drinks, brawls, deserts his family when they need him most, then returns with pleading eyes, begging forgiveness. Always, he dreams of talking someone into a grubstake and heading for greener grasses, perhaps in Australia. Wife 'Elvira' hangs on as best she can, taking in boarders, selling 'cowboy antiques' (junk left over from their glory days), knowing she shouldn't take Ace back, though always she does. Their other son, Curly, has sold out, going into the real estate business. All Stetson, no steers! Curly offers Junior a steady job with good pay, but the

LIKE FATHER, LIKE SON: 'Junior' attempts to live up to the legend of his Pap (Robert Preston)

individualistic sibling won't take it. Not won't: Can't! Y'see, there's this big black bull just *beggin'* for a face-off. As rodeo aficionados claim: "There's never been a mount that can't be rode; there's never been a cowboy can't be throwed."

Junior Bonner may be the best fiction-film ever made about rodeo, capturing the heart and soul of this 'sport.' If there's a better one out there, it's *The Rider* (2017), a docu-drama that follows a season in the life of an actual participant. Among earlier Hollywood movies, the finest is *The Lusty Men* (1955), Nicholas Ray's grim study of just such a loner starring Robert Mitchum. The great impact of *Junior Bonner* has much to do with the presence of Steve McQueen (1930-1980), finally happening on a role worthy of his squint-eyed presence that's equal to 'Vin' in *The Magnificent Seven*. Though born and bred in New York City, screenwriter Jeb Rosebrook chose to live in Scottsdale AZ where he absorbed cowboy culture like the proverbial sponge. That's why every line of dialogue rings true. This is not some Tinseltown scribe's conception of how rural rednecks talk; for once, their idiom is accurate. Sam Peckinpah (1925-1984) employs his unique method of shooting (with master cinematographer Lucien Ballard, plus a highly creative team of editors) that allows us to feel a part of, rather than mere onlookers, at the gleeful, glorious, gory proceedings. His combination of slow-motion photography and cross-cuts from an uncertain present to a dark past allow for a stream-of-consciousness that accurately communicates such harsh machismo activities. It hardly hurts that a supporting cast includes Casey Tibbs himself. The only major flaw: beautiful beyond belief Barbara Leigh as a circuit princess, providing the film's conventional romantic interest. This character appears to be added for commercial appeal rather than integrity to the subject at hand. On the other hand, Lupino and Preston might well have received Best Supporting Actress and Actor nominations for their finely etched performances. And likely would have, if *Junior Bonner* had been a box-office hit.

But back to Casey himself. After politely nodding to the stranger, he headed into a nearby drugstore. There, he spent the last two dollars in his wallet on three objects A pack of cigarettes, a bottle of soda, and a lottery ticket. Some desperate, odds-against-tomorrow hope for an elusive cure-all, combined with precisely the worst elements a human being can draw into his lung and stomach. Self-destructive? To be sure. But that of course is the 'way' of a rodeo rider, a unique brand of Western contrarian, neatly revealed in this film's narrative.

THE ARENA: Unique among sports, Rodeo events are based on specific skills garnered from the actual work of a cowboy.

AMERICA'S ALL-AROUND COWBOY: Casey Tibbs managed to parlay his rodeo fame into a brief lived Hollywood career, appearing in such B movies as *Wild Heritage* (1968) and *Breakheart Pass* (1975).

44. KENTUCKIAN, THE (1955)
Rating: *****

CREDITS:

Burt Lancaster, dir. A.B. Guthrie, scr.; Lancaster, Harold Hecht, James Hill, pro.; Bernard Herrmann, Roy Webb, mus.; Ernest Laszlo, cin.; George E. Luckenbacher, ed.; 2.55:1; C; 104 min.; Hecht/(Hill)/Lancaster Prods., United Artists.

CAST:

Burt Lancaster (*Elias Wakefield, aka 'Big Eli'*); Dianne Foster *(Hannah Bolen)*; Diana Lynn (*Susie Spann*); Walter Matthau (*Stan Bodine*); Donald MacDonald *('Little Eli')*; John McInture (*Zack* Wakefield); Una Merkel (*Sophie*); John Carradine (*Ziby Fletcher*); John Litel *('Pleasant 'Tuesday' Babson)*; Rhys Williams (*The Constable*); Edward Norris (*Roulette Wheel Dealer*); Clem Bevans *('River Queen' Pilot)*; Lee Erickson *(Luke Lester)*; James Griffith (*Gamblin' Man*); Glenn Strange (*Drunken Whip Wielder*); Douglas Spencer, Paul Wexler (*Frome Bros.*).

From the moment actor/star Burt Lancaster (1913-1994) read the non/generic Western novel "The Gabriel Horn" by Felix Holt (1951), he knew that he'd found precisely what he had been looking for: A project which he could develop, produce, and star in for his own newly formed company, Hecht/Hill/Lancaster (the middle name was added after this project was released). Lancaster adored this tale of a rough widower who, circa 1825, makes the decision to head out with his ten-year-old son and their dog to newly opened territories in Texas. But Big Eli makes the mistake of stopping

A MERGING OF ART FORMS: Director Burt Lancaster not only hired one gifted American writer, A.B. Guthrie, to adapt a novel by another, Felix Holt, but also brought regionalist Thomas Hart Benton on board to create a masterful painting that crystalized the theme of 'Westing.'

by a typical frontier settlement to visit his older brother, a successful tobacco farmer Suddenly, his realistic plans threaten to dissolve into bygone fantasies. For Eli must now make a choice: Marry the formerly bonded girl Hannah and strike out for the unknown--The West--risking everything; or, tossing out that daring American Dream as mere wistful thinking. Remaining in town; trading in his buckskins for a suit, marry the refined schoolmarm Susie, making money in a way that only works if he abandons rugged individualism to 'grow up' at last, and conform to the strict rules of civilization.

So committed to the project was Lancaster that he shaped the piece step by step during pre-production. He wanted nobody but A.B. Guthrie (1901-1991) for his screenwriter. A Pulitzer-prize winning novelist (*The Big Sky*, 1947; *The Way West*, 1950), Guthrie had successfully transferred Jack Schaefer's classic novel of the West *Shane* (1949) into a perfect film. *The Gabriel Horn* like *Shane* is told from the point of view of a child who hero-worships a true frontiersman. Rather than rely on the time-worn and overdone convention of a voice-over, Guthrie with each of his film projects crafted the scripts so that this concept is visually implied. Lancaster then contacted the artist Thomas Hart Benton (1889-1975), convincing him to create an immense mural-like painting of the film's central premise: Man and boy (and dog) facing West. A member of the Regionalist School of U.S.A. painters, Benton idealized the common man, projecting his inherent potential for greatness in striking images of stalwart people who settle the land and, despite all odds, survive. Like mid-Western journalist-turned-novelist Ernest Hemingway, the acclaimed painter paid tribute to a notion of masculinity as the essence of American excellence.

If the philosophy behind painting and book may be dated as a retro-glorification of machismo/Anglo imperialism for some critical modern viewers,

WHAT A CHARACTER!: Lancaster brought on board two of the great movie villains of that era, John Carradine and Walter Matthau, to round out the impressive cast.

the film perfectly embodies the once-admired, now challenged concept of 'Westing.' Close attention was paid to the details of history as to everyday living: Business deals, entertainment, the creation of legal and binding contracts, courting rites. If some audiences were disappointed by the lack of action, *The Kentuckian* holds true to 'real' rather than 'reel' history. Here is a low-key fable about those women and men who must deal with emotions and ideas on a daily basis. How appropriate that the civilized 'lady' (like Lillian Gish in *The Unforgiven*, she reveals her civilized aura of sophistication by playing a piano, that harbinger of culture) does not embody a negative cliché. Susie is every bit as fine a person as Hannah. The idea of a simplistic morality drama—choosing between good and evil women—thankfully does not recur here. Big Eli's choice has to do with the creation of a new self as compared to accepting the quietude of conformity.

At mid-movie, there is an extended fight sequence between whip-wielding settler Bodine (Walter Matthau in one of his early roles) and a weaponless Big Eli. The unforgettable sequence features bloodletting on a level not

THE LURE OF THE WILDERNESS: Despite his half-hearted attempts to normalize himself and fit into an outpost of civilization, Big Eli yields to what Jack London referred to as the call of the wild where he, his dog and son, and a bonded girl feel truly at home.

seen in any Western, or Hollywood film, during the Eisenhower era. And, despite expectations, our hero does not somehow manage to magically win. This, followed by an equally rugged confrontation between Big Eli and a pair of trashy varmints (displaying the manner in which a single shot rifle would be readied for a shooting), are the rare action moments in a work otherwise filled with nuance.

Dianne Foster (1928-2019) played a similarly no-nonsense frontierswoman earlier that year in *The Violent Men* and would do so again in *Night Passage* (1957). A child prodigee as a musician (that's really her playing a piano in *Kentuckian*), Diana Lynn (1926-1971) was at her best as a pioneer woman blessed/cursed with a touch of class, the case a year earlier in *(The) Track of the Cat*. Veteran Western actor John McIntire (1907-1991), who had supported Lancaster in *Apache* (1954) as legendary frontier scout Al Seiber, would assume the roles of wagon-master on *Wagon Train* (from 1959-1965) and ranch owner on *The Virginian* (1967-1970) when actors playing those roles (Ward Bond, Charles Bickford) passed away. Shifty-eyed, subtly menacing James Griffith (1916-1993) earned his role as a professional gambler owing to his impressive playing of Doc Holliday the previous year in *Masterson of Kansas*. A drunken braggart at an authentically staged outdoor celebration is well played by Glenn Strange (1899-1973), whose hulking villains would include 'Butch Cavendish' on TV's *The Lone Ranger* (1955). Strange would conclude his career as bartender 'Sam' on TV's *Gunsmoke*. Horror fans recall his effective performance as The Monster in *Abbot and Costello meet Frankenstein* (1948).

45. LAST STAND AT SABER RIVER, THE (1997)
Rating: **** ½

CREDITS:

Dick Lowry, dir.; Ronald M. Cohen, scr.; Tom Selleck, Mary Ann Braubach, Thomas John Kane, Stephen (J.) Brandman, many others, pro.; David Shire, mus.; Rick Waite; cin.; William B. Stich, ed.; 1.33:1; C; 96 min.; TNT/Turner Television.

CAST:

Tom Selleck (*Paul Cable*); Suzy Amis (*Martha*); Rachel Duncan *(Clare)*; Haley Joel Osment *(Davis)*; Keith Carradine (*Vern Kidston*); David Carradine (*Duane Kidston*); Tracey Needham *(Lorraine)*; Chris Stacy (*Chris*); Harry Carey Jr. (*James Sanford*); Patrick Kilpatrick (*Austin*); Eugene Osment (*Wynn Dodd*); Denis Forest (*Cornet*); David Dukes *(Edward Janroe)*; Lumi Cavaznos (*Luz)*; Raymond Cruz (*Manuel*); Fredrick Lopez *(Paco)*; Rosalie De Aragon (*Carlita*); Raymond Frank (*Joe Bob*); Paul Blott (Royce); Rex Linn (*Bill)*; J.D. Garfield (*Luke*).

"Any enemy of my enemy is my friend," Koatilya stated in the ancient work *Arthashastra*. Another sage, Plato, had this to say: "Politics makes for strange bedfellows." If any Western were designed to convey both these ideas to viewers, it is *Last Stand* ... The reason for such a seriousness of intent can be traced to Louisiana-born, Detroit-raised Elmore Leonard (1925-2013), today best known for his grim, grisly neo-noir crime novels-turned-movies: *Get Shorty*

They Went That-A-Way

KEEPIN' THE LEGENDS ALIVE: Much like Sam Elliott, who might be Tom Selleck's nonidentical twin (the two have played brothers in TV Westerns), here is one of the rare performers who keeps the classic Oater alive, if more often than not on the small screen.

(1990), *Rum Punch* (1992), *Be Cool* (1999). Earlier, Leonard made his reputation with Argosy-type pulp Westerns that likewise became important films, in this case high-level Oaters: *Hombre, Valdez is Coming, 3:10 to Yuma, The Tall T,* and *Joe Kidd* among them. *Last Stand* (his fifth book in print) did not receive the traditional Hollywood treatment. Ted Turner, the avatar of modern cable broadcasting, had always been a huge fan of overlooked classics. Turner Television proved to be precisely the right medium for bringing back the best of generic Westerns at a time when Hollywood, like the mainstream moviegoing audience, had lost interest.

Like Sam Elliott, who played his brother in L'Amour's *The Sacketts* (1979) and *The Shadow Riders* (1982), Tom Selleck (1945-) grasped that if he were to wait around for appropriate cowboy roles, this born-to-the-saddle-star might be out of work for a long time. In addition to appearing, Selleck helped guide this through to completion. 'Paul Cable' wanders back to Texas. A world-weary Confederate vet approaching the home he shared with his small family. Initially, he recalls John Wayne as Ethan Edwards in

THE WHOLE KIT AND KABOODLE!: *Last Stand* features all the traditional elements; clockwise, from top left: a strong frontierswoman (Suzy Amis), a hissable villain (David Carradine), a deeply torn individual (Keith Carradine), and even an old fashioned stageacoh pursuit.

The Searchers, a prisoner of the desert who seeks solace amid blood relatives. But if Edwards intruded on a homestead (and wife) that truly belongs to his brother, Cable returns to a seemingly more hospitable situation. Though believing her spouse to have been killed in combat, this film's Martha (is it mere coincidence that she and the lady in *The Searchers* share the same name?) has been holding down (barely) their spread with the help of her elderly father, Sanford, and two surviving children. Cable would be happy to set such wartime action aside, however embittered he is to learn their youngest child has died of a plague. Had he remained home, as Martha begged him to, might poor little Mary still be with them? Bitter, Mary nonetheless agrees to travel with him by covered wagon to Arizona, where they in less oppressive times owned a ranch.

Previously, director Lowry (1944-) had helmed several made-for-TV Oaters starring Kenny Rogers, *The Gambler* (1980) and *Wild Horses* (1985). Though each had proven popular, both were simplistically generic. Likewise, writer Cohen (1939-1998) had cut his teeth on such warmly remembered TV shows as *Shane* and *The Legend of Jesse James*, both 1966. Their work here reached higher levels thanks to Leonard's ability to tell a familiar tale in such a manner that the characters remind us more of 'the people next door' than those mythological figures who ride the range in a Zane Grey potboiler. Anything

AN HOMAGE TO AN OLD-TIMER: Harry Carey Jr., who worked alongside John Wayne in several top John Wayne/John Ford films (*Three Godfathers, Rio Grande, The Searchers*, etc.) adds a special quality of old-school traditionalism thanks to his humble/charming presence here.

but a gentle flower of the prairie, Mary is a modern woman, though this is never so exaggerated that she appears anachronistic for the mid-19th century period. Quicksilver as to moods, she chastises her tall, handsome husband for his failures one moment (Selleck appears like 'Dagwood Bumstead' from the 1950s *Blondie*, avoiding her angry glances while muttering a half-hearted self-defense). But when the shooting starts owing to Yankee carpetbaggers who have confiscated their old house, she's as quick to grab a gun and fight back as Cable. Indeed, she 'takes out' more of them than he does. We don't need to be told that she's Cable's equal in all regards. We see it for ourselves.

Most fascinating is the ever-changing loyalties between the Cables and those who inhabit their secluded *Shane*-like valley. If we assume their fellow southern sympathizers, who agree to help battle the brutal bluecoats led by land baron 'Duane Kidston' will provide a set of allies in the conflict, we are in for a surprise. A succession of reversals more resembles real life than typical Western narratives. Perhaps most fascinating is the treatment of a Confederate legend, Gen. Bedford Forrest. Cable, we learn, went off to fight at the general's suggestion, doing so for a sense of honor even though Cable did not approve of the institution of slavery. Then came the horrific incident at Fort Pillow in which that historic officer (later to form the Klan) ordered his troops to shoot down more than 300 unarmed captives. At that moment, Cable turned. He came to accept the terrible absurdity of war itself, rejecting that such an undertaking could in any way partake of anything 'honorable.' Like the WWI hero of Ernest Hemingway's *A Farewell to Arms* (1929), which might well have been the subtitle here, he only wants to make a separate peace, apart from the world at large, with the woman he loves. As compared to Papa's bleak, nihilistic view on doing so, here we do experience a bittersweet if less than simplistically happy ending.

46. LAW AND ORDER (1932)
Rating: *****

CREDITS:

Edward L. Cahn, dir.; John Huston, Tom Reed, scr.; Carl Laemmle Jr., pro.; David Braekman, David Klatkin, mus.; Jackson Rose, cin.; Philip Cahn, ed.; 1.37:1; B&W; 75 min.; Universal.

CAST:

Walter Huston (*Frame 'Saint' Johnson*); Harry Carey (*Ed Brandt*); Russell Hopton (*Luther Johnson*); Raymond Hatton (*Deadwood*); Ralph Ince (*Poe Northrup*); Harry Woods (*Walt Northrup*); Richard Alexander (*Kurt Northrup*); Russell Simpson (*Judge R.W. Williams*); Andy Devine (*Johnny Kinsman*); Walter Brennan (*Lanky Smith*); Barney Beaseley, Hank Bell, Frank Brownlee (*Barflies*); Stanley Blystone (*Mob Leader*); D'Arcy Corrigan (*Undertaker Parker*); Richard Cramer (*Cheating Gambler*); William Dyer (*Ben Burley*); Alphonse Ethier *(Sheriff Fin Elder)*.

Tragically overlooked (and largely forgotten, even by many Western buffs), *Law and Order* rates as one of the most significant, as well as artistically innovative, films of this genre. The project went into production early in 1929, a sea change year for motion pictures in two major ways. First, Sound (always desired, not mastered until 1927) was accepted by Hollywood as the shape of things to come rather than a temporal craze. Second, the German émigré Carl Laemmle (1867-1939)—who worked as a distributor of films in Chicago, then founded Universal Pictures in 1906—initiated the process of turning over that company to his son, Carl Jr. (1908-1979). At the time,

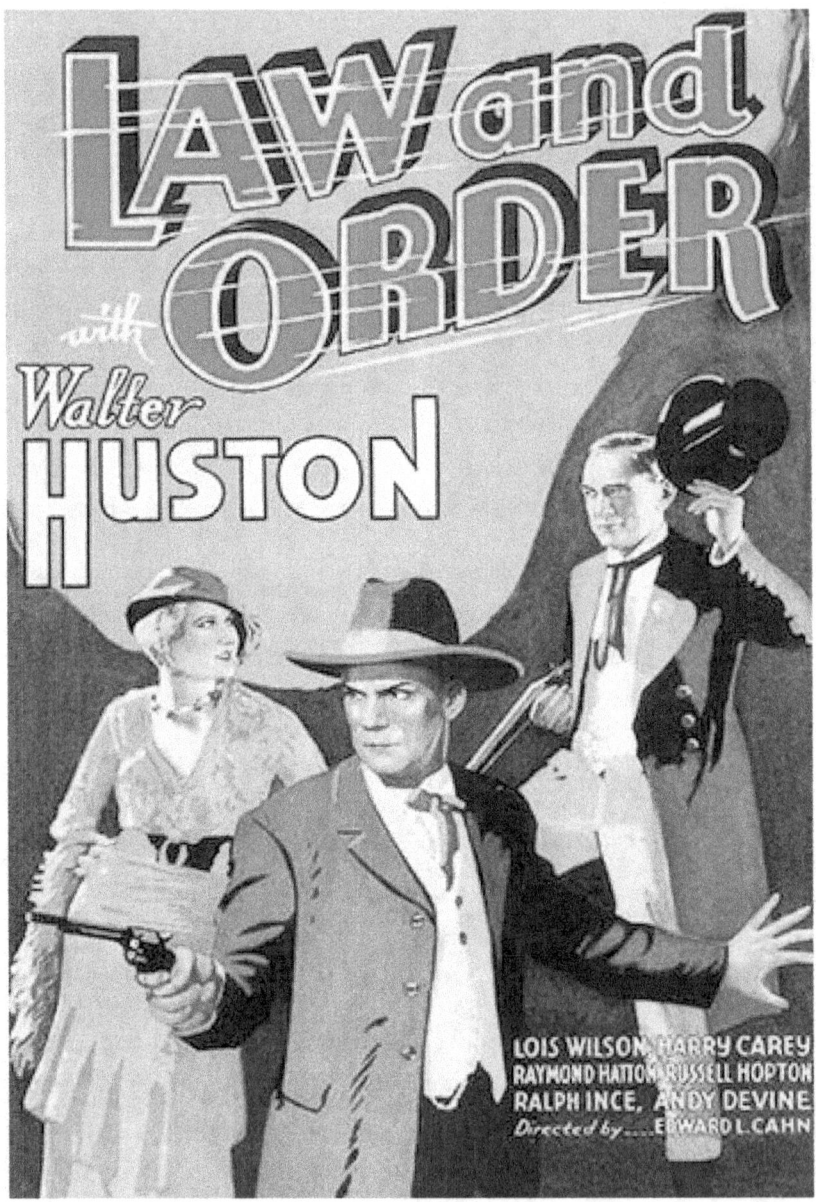

HOW THE WEST WAS WON: Despite fictional names being designated to key characters, *Law and Order* offered one of the earliest portrayals of Wyatt Earp.

the studio verged on bankruptcy. Then Junior's *Dracula* (1931) achieved such success that Universal leaped from also-ran to one of the Majors. Noting that *The Virginian* (1929) had proven popular, Jr. decided that Universal would balance arch thrillers with roughewn Westerns. Cinematographer Jackson Rose immediately set out on a search for the proper location, happening on the Vasquez Rock Formation in Aqua Dulce, CA. Inspired by his and director Cahn's ethusiasm, David Braekman and David Klatkin created a musical score which contains elements of symphony, tinged with a hint of folk ballads, setting the pace for the future of Western soundtracks.

Now, however, they needed a story. Happily, Jr. sensed the enormous gifts of then-young John Huston (1906-1987), son of one of the era's greatest actor-stars (more on that later). Before the team could progress, they required a specific subject. And, once again, the timing proved perfect. In 1927, Walter Noble Burns' *Tombstone: An Iliad of the Southwest* had been published to critical acclaim and impressive sales. Laemmle (Jr.) perceived this as an initial attempt to create an historical Western boasting the self-conscious importance of a Greek epic. Stuart N. Lake's subsequent *Wyatt Earp, Frontier Marshal* (1931) offered instead the (dubious) biography of the lawman's adventures in Tombstone and elsewhere, turning that figure into a household name. Meanwhile a major problem arose, which confounded anyone interested in making the first Wyatt film. Josephine Marcus (1861-1944), who may have worked as a prostitute before becoming Earp's (1848-1929) wife (legal or common-law), threatened to sue anyone who included the dubious lady's name or personage in a movie about her recently deceased husband. Without a love story, how could commercial filmmakers proceed?

As if Laemmle's project were meant to be, destiny provided an alternative approach. W.R. Burnett, a pulp fiction writer who helped pave the way for hardboiled noirs even then about to emerge, had penned a book based on the developing legend. However, he changed the lead character's name to 'Frame Johnson,' eliminating Josie entirely, thereby evading any lawsuit. Laemmle optioned the book and picked a well-regarded studio hand, Edwin L. Cahn (1899-1953), to direct. Cahn's later genre films are undistinguished—*The*

TRANSFORMING MEN INTO ICONS: The real-life Wyatt Earp and Doc Holliday entered into the realm of legend thanks to stellar performances by Walter Huston and Harry Carey (Sr.); some observers did believe that the roles ought to have been reversed.

Outlaw Trail (1942); (The) *Gunfighters of Abilene* (1959)—rating as minor fare at best. Here, he outdid himself, though there are those who insist the stark integrity we see onscreen derived from his many gifted collaborators, particularly John Huston.

Now, a star---one recently associated with a hit Western---was necessary. Acclaimed Broadway actor Walter (father of John) Huston (1883-1950) had arrived in Hollywood and made a huge impression as the killer Trampas opposite Gary Cooper in *The Virginian*. Some at the studio wondered if the sly, devil-eyed Huston might have been a better choice for the Doc Holliday role, here called 'Ed Brandt.' But Huston offered up a saint-like lawman with the dignity and dedication to the film's title concept worthy of his performance in *Abraham Lincoln* for D.W. Griffith two years earlier. Huston did eventually play Doc in the Howard Hughes/Howard Hawks 'sex Western' *The Outlaw* (1943). For Brandt, the team chose Harry Carey (Sr.) (1878-1947), largely as a result of his 'good-badman' image from such earlier Westerns as *The Three Godfathers* (1916), *The Outcasts of Poker Flat* (1919), and perhaps

LIKE FATHER, LIKE SON: A then-young John Huston collaborates with his already legendary father Walter in this rare, never before published shot; more than fifteen years later, the two would again collaborate for the towering epic *The Treasure of (the) Sierra Madre*.

most memorably, John Ford's *Straight Shooting* (1917). The grand old man of the West long before Gary Cooper assumed that position, Carey would appear in Oaters up until his last, *Red River* (1948), in which he passed the torch as Ford's favorite to John Wayne, even then maturing from 'kid' roles to tough older men.

For what may have been the first time, spoken dialogue was not merely recorded along with the images (both augmented by music) but combined in a creative manner, allowing for what in time would be acknowledged as the Yin/Yang of movies: Sight and Sound. During the O.K. Corral gunfight sequence (the first version ever filmed), the cracks of pistols are artistically heightened to intensify the experience, also the first in a Western. As to the Wyatt Earp myth in movies, the icon would come a little closer to full realization with 'Michael Wyatt' (George O'Brien) in the first screen adaptation of

Lake's book, called *Frontier Marshal* (1934; now considered a lost film though diehard Western buffs continue to search. Five years after that, Randolph Scott would be the first actor to assume onscreen the lawman's name in the *Frontier Marshal* remake. Josie, though, remained out of sight, everyone in Hollywood still fearful of litigation. Finally, she would be portrayed in *Tombstone* (1993) and *Wyatt Earp* (1994) long after the petulant lady moved on to that great ranch house in the sky.

THE CARETAKER OF WYATT EARP'S LEGACY: Whether a common law wife or officially married to the former marshal, Josephine Marcus dedicated her later years to protecting his ... and her own ... reputation from filmmakers.

47. LIGHT IN THE FOREST, THE (1958)
Rating: **** ½

CREDITS:

Herschel Daugherty, dir.; Edward Watkin, scr.; Walt Disney, pro.; Ellsworth Fredericks, cin; Stanley E. Johnson, ed.; 1.75:1; C; 83 min.; Buena Vista Releasing.

CAST:

Fess Parker (*Del Hardy*); Wendell Corey (*Wilse Owens*); Joanne Dru (*Milly Elder*); James MacArthur (*Johnny Butler/True Son*); Jessica Tandy (*Myra Butler)*; John McIntire (*John Elder*); Joseph Calleia (*Chief Cuvloga*); Carol Lynley (*Shenandoe*); Rafael Campos *(Half Arrow)*; Dean Fredericks, aka Norman Frederic (*Niskitoon*); Marian Seldes (*Kate Owens*); Stephen Bekassy (*Col. Henry Bouquet*); Sam Buffington (*George Owens*); Pat Brady (*Musician*); Tex Brodus (*Party Guest*); Iron Eyes Cody *(Native Counsellor)*; Myrna Fahey *(Hannah)*; Eddie Little Sky (*Little Crane*).

Yet another key sub-genre of the Western is 'the Eastern,' featuring stories set in Colonial or early 18th century America when upstate New York and southern Pennsylvania still constituted our wild frontier. If never as popular as trans-Mississippi stories about cowboys and Indians, tales of the East-as-West come closer to offering our nation's *true* origination fable. None are more famous than the Leatherstocking stories of James Fenimore Cooper, whose *The Last of the Mohicans* (1826) has been filmed countless times. Other movies

'SPLENDOR IN THE GRASS': Despite Walt Disney's reputation as a vanilla/whitebread producer who avoided the dark edges of life in his family entertainments, in truth such films as this vividly portray the angst of teenagers attempting to discover where lust leaves off and love begins.

range from melodramas about farmers, pioneers, and settlers such as *Drums Along the Mohawk* (1939) and *Rachel and the Stranger* (1948) to historical epics concerning the French and Indian War (*Northwest Passage* (1940) and its immediate aftermath (*Alleghany Uprising*, 1939). One of the best, if least known, 'Easterns' is Walt Disney's (1901-1966) production *The Light in the*

"THERE'S GOOD AND BAD ON BOTH SIDES!" Walt Disney's Westerns do not simplify issues regarding ethnicity: this film's confused young hero can rely on a rugged frontier scout (Fess Parker) and an equally sincere Native American (Joseph Calleia) for advice laced with wisdom.

Forest, adapted from an acclaimed novel for young readers by Pulitzer Prize winner Conrad Richter (1890-1968). The scribe's carefully researched study of race relations in his birth-state led to this low-key, authentic portrayal of Anglo-Indian relations, depicted in a more complex manner than many films supposedly intended for adult audiences. As is the case with most Disney Westerns of the 1950s, *Light*... comes closer in its attitude to contemporary political approaches to race than almost any other Hollywood product of that now-long ago time.

Set in 1704, the premise derives from an actual occurrence in which well-intentioned attempts to 'normalize' relations between pioneers and Natives caused confusion and pain rather than the hoped-for healing process. Representatives of Great Britain struck a treaty with local Delaware people that called for a return of prisoners taken on either side during bloody days of conflict. Among the hapless victims: A teenage boy, called 'True Son' by the people of the great forest, born 'Johnny Butler' in a nearby village. His Anglo parents are delighted to have him back, though Johnny turns bitter about this arrangement. Color and/or ethnicity aside, he considers himself a Delaware and wants to escape what he considers to be the true imprisonment . . . living in civilization . . . and return to what he feels are his true roots. The issue, rarely explored in Hollywood films (John Ford's *Two Rode Together* 1962, is one of the rare Big Westerns to do so), is related here with an even hand. "There's good and bad on both sides," scout Del Hardy articulates the issue at mid-movie. If the nasty adult' Wilsie' is an outright racist, 'Niksitoon' among the Delaware is likewise consumed by hatred for Anglos. Most other characters in each encampment are decent folks who hope to live and let live, perhaps in time with peaceful interaction between the two American 'peoples.' While Ford chose to emphasize the horrors inherent in white imprisonment at the hands of Indians, Disney focuses instead on the great love many captives came to feel for their non-biological families.

In our own time, the issue of personal self-identification as opposed to genetic identity has become a focal and much debated issue. Heated controversies have arisen (and duly reported by the media) as to people who identify themselves, and officially register, as African American though their antecedents were Anglo. Should our society as a whole resolve such a prickly situation, might this be left up to the minority faction involved, or does a person have a right to do so for him/herself? Though posited here within a period piece, aimed at a teenage audience, such significant concerns are nowhere more intelligently analyzed than in this 'Disney version' of a previous time, however many observers wrong-headedly consider that a derisive term. *Light in the Forest* appears daring in its willingness to approach other delicate issues which a youthful viewer, to become acquainted with and prepared for the dark side of life, must at this point in their development comprehend. A sweet young love blossoms between Johnny and 'Shenandoe,' a withdrawn bond girl. Their innocent romance is threatened when the man who virtually owns this child-woman, dominating and insensitive male Wilsie, comes to believe he has the right to claim the virginity of his white slave. Those who believe Disney's live action films and/or animated releases offer nothing more than escapist froth for families will be shocked to encounter the attempted rape sequence here. Yet Del, a minor figure in Richter's novel, emerges as

"IT TAKES A VILLAGE TO RAISE A CHILD!" Hilary Clinton's pronouncement well describes the communal values on view in a Walt Disney Western, as Joanne Dru and Fess Parker rally their fellow frontiersmen in support of a young man with an identity crisis.

the Disney hero. He intrudes to assure that, if not a simplistic happy ending, the film concludes on a bittersweet note: insisting on hope for the future as the Plato-like Good on both side, come together in worthwhile if less than perfect harmony.

Del is played by Fess Parker (1924-2010), discovered by Disney while searching for precisely the right presence in the "Davy Crockett, King of the Wild Frontier" TV mini-series and movies. In these and other projects such as *Westward Ho, the Wagons* (1956) and *Old Yeller* (1957), as well as the *Daniel Boone* NBC-TV series (1964-1970) co-produced by Parker himself, Fess emerged as a latter-day equivalent to such formidable film stars as Gary Cooper, Gregory Peck, and James Stewart: figures of masculine strength to be sure, but also of (in most roles) gentle emotions and wise thought.

48. LITTLE BIG HORN (1951)
Rating: **** ½

CREDITS:

Charles Marquis Warren, dir.; Warren, Harold Shumate, scr.; Warren, Carl K. Hittelman, Murray Lerner, pro.; Paul Dunlap, Ralph Flanagan, mus.; Ernest (W.) Miller, cin.; Carl Pierson, ed.; 1.37:1; B&W; 96 min.; Lippert Pictures.

CAST:

Llloyd Bridges (*Capt. Philip Donlin*); John Ireland *(Lt. John Haywood)*; Marie Windsor (*Celie Donin*); Reed Hadley (*Sgt. Maj. Peter Grierson*); Jim Davis (*Cpl. Doan Moylan*); Wally Cassell (*Pvt. Danny Zekka*); Hugh O'Brian (*Pvt. Al DeWalt*); King Donovan (*Corbo)*; Richard Emory (*Mitch*); John Pickard (*Vet McCloud*); Robert Sherwood *(Dave Mason)*; Sheb Wooley *(Quince)*; Larry Stewart (*Stevie Williams*); Rodd Redwing (*Cpl. Arika*). Dick Paxton (*Hall*); Gordon Wynn (*Hofstette*r); Red Avery (*Harvey*); Anne Warren (*Anne*); Barbara Wooddell (*Margaret*).

When Western buffs get together to down beer, devour wings and ribs, and reminisce about their favorite films and filmmakers, the gathered multitude mostly agree on the most significant pre-Eastwood directors of successful "A" Oaters: John Ford, Howard Hawks, and Raoul Walsh. Then, the subject turns to those mavericks who offered hard-bitten, occasionally mean-spirited (and often tightly-budgeted) projects which offered an alternative perspective via harsh depictions of a less romanticized frontier. Aficionados of cowboy cinema likewise settle on a trio of talents: Joseph Kane (*The Maverick Queen*), Samuel Fuller **(***Run of the Arrow*), and Charles Marquis Warren (1912-1990).

They Went That-A-Way

"WELL, NOW YOU KNOW!" That infamous line, most often associated with soap operas, appears here as officer Lloyd Bridges realizes that his wife, Marie Windsor, has been 'spending time' with predator John Ireland. :

The latter is less known today than his compatriots, though Warren's career deserves a belated revival and closer study--despite several disturbing elements that cause his harsh philosophy to fall into today's politically incorrect category. With *Little Big Horn*, Warren turned out one of the final pro-Custer films, though the brevet-general/lieutenant colonel never appears.

If Ford's *Fort Apache* (1948) offered a complex rather than heroic (if slightly-disguised vision) of that controversial officer, *Sitting Bull* (1954; Sidney Salkow) would initiate a long succession of anti-Long Hair cinematic tirades. As to Warren's in-between film, that distant figure is treated with great respect by the characters . . . . more, perhaps, than he in fact deserved. As there wasn't enough money at Poverty Row 'Lippert Pictures' to restage the famed battle of what the Sioux and Cheyenne refer to as The Fight at Greasy Grass, Warren devised an affordable alternative. We witness a romantic triangle as a captain (stolid Lloyd Bridges, 1913-1998) and his slimy lieutenant (snarling John Ireland, 1914-1992) all but come to blows over the former's less-than-faithful wife. The naughty lady is played by cult favorite Marie Windsor (1919-2000), a staple of Westerns during her career, also portraying Joan Crawford-like femme fatales in modest film noirs. Notable among

CUSTER'S LAST STAND ... ON A BUDGET: Unable to mount a full-fledged version of the Little Big Horn battle, Charles Marquis Warren had to make do with a fictional (though highly convincing) tale of a squad that attempts to head Custer off from disaster and, unable to arrive in time to save him, likewise goes down fighting to the last man.

them: Stanley Kubrick's *The Killing* (1956), in which she has one of the most memorably ironic lines in movie history. Shot by erstwhile husband Elisha Cook Jr. (no stranger to Westerns himself thanks to the doomed little farmer in *Shane*), she manages to cynically gasp before falling down dead: "This is like a bad joke without a punch line!"

But back to *Little Big Horn*. The premise: When top ranking officers at Fort Abraham Lincoln learn that the number of Lakota gathered at the title river is ten times larger than originally estimated, they assign a squad to fight its way through hostile territory and warn Custer before he can attack the great camp and be wiped out. In Warren's bizarre combination of pessimism and idealism, the men arrive too late; then decide to follow the general on his trail to glory by making a splendid *beau geste* by attacking the 10,000 Native Americans (presented here via stock footage) to go out in a small but similar blaze of glory as to what Custer himself achieved. To say that the final impact is powerful is to put it mildly, viewers then and now riveted by the confrontation and events leading up to it. These incidents play like a redux of the classic *A Walk in the Sun* (1945) as a Western rather than WWII film. At the conclusion, a title card informs us that a few miles from the Custer battlefield stand the unmarked graves of these unheralded heroes.

That, in fact, is Warren's little joke on a gullible audience: The story he tells is entirely fictional. In truth, Custer didn't require such a warning. His own scouts attempted to convince the onetime 'boy general' not to attack the immense Indian village their arrogant commander disregarding all such frantic insistences. Yet how convincing all of this appears onscreen. As for Warren, he turned again to the Indian Wars several years later with *Arrowhead* (1953), featuring Charlton Heston as an Al Sieber-like tough-as-nails scout and Jack Palance as a Geronimo-type 'take no prisoners' warrior. That film might be seen as Warren's response to (and corrective of) *Broken Arrow* (1950), as well as other movies which projected an image of the Apache nation as a less violent nation than had previously been offered. Considering that assessment to be both absurd and historically incorrect, Warren offered an even nastier portrayal of the Mescalero there than he did the Lakota here in *Little Big Horn*.

NEXT STOP, SMALL SCREEN STARDOM: Hugh O'Brian and Rod(d) Redwing play a cavalryman and a Native American here; shortly, they would co-star on ABC-TV's *The Life and Legend of Wyatt Earp* (1955-1961), with Hugh in the title role and Rod as his deputy, 'Mr. Brother.'

Warren viewed the new medium of TV as a rich possibility for presenting his vision to a large audience, as a result developing the *Gunsmoke* (1955-1975) series. His concept for the show: A mini-*High Noon* in every installment. That lasted for about four years. When CBS decided they wanted this to become a kinder, gentler series about just plain folks, Warren pulled out and set to work creating *Rawhide* (1959-1965), which he hoped would offer a more authentic vision of the cowboy's (drover's) daily work than any film or series had done. That would be the case during the cattle drive show's initial years, when the majority of its 'hell bent for leather' scripts were penned by Warren. His third and final involvement would be with *The Virginian* (1962-1971), NBC's experiment with a 90 min. color show or, as star James Drury has stated, "a B+ 71 min. theatrical Western once a week!"

49. LONE RANGER AND THE LOST CITY OF GOLD, THE (1958) Rating: *** ½

CREDITS:

Lesley Selander, dir. Robert Schaefer, Eric Freiwald scr.; Sherman A. Harris, pro.; Les Baxter, mus.; Kenneth Peac, cin.; Robert Golden, ed.; 1.37:1; C; 81 min.; Jack Wrather Prods.

CAST:

Clayton Moore *('The Lone Ranger'/John Reid)*; Jay Silverheels *(Tonto)*; Douglas Kennedy *(Ross Brady)*; Charles Watts *(Sheriff Oscar Matthison)*; Noreen Nash *(Frances Henderson)*; Lisa Montell *(Paviva)*; Ralph Moody *(Padre Vincente Esteban)*; Dean Fredericks, aka 'Norman Fredric' *(Dr. James Rolfe)*; John Miljan *(Chief Tomache)*; Maurice Jara *(Redbird)*; William Henry *(Travers)*; Lane Bradford *(Wilson)*; Belle Mitchell (Caulama); Bob Woodward *(Badguy)*.

Like Superman or Captain Marvel, The Lone Ranger is a fictional character, something of a superhero (though like Batman without special powers) of the old West. He may well have been inspired, however unconsciously, by Zorro, here re-imagined as an Anglo version of that Latin avenger. There is reason too to believe this mythic hero's inception may have been inspired by a pair of historic frontier fighters. A freed slave, Bass Reeves (1838-1910), became the first African American Federal Deputy Marshal. John R. Hughes (1955-1947) did indeed survive the massacre of his Ranger squad, dedicating the

"HI, YO, SILVER---AWAY!" The franchise . . . which had already proven popular on radio and TV, as well as comic books, Sunday color comics, and cliffhanger films, enjoyed further success thanks to several B+ color Westerns in the late 1950s.

rest of his life to bringing the perpetrators to justice. Precisely how aware the co-creators of 'The Lone Ranger Legend' were of these precedents has been debated for decades. No question, though, that writer Fran Striker (1903-1962) devoured Western pulp fiction and its historical counterparts while growing up in Buffalo, New York during the 1920s. When Striker accepted a job as staff writer at Detroit radio station WXYZ, the owner, former lawyer George W. Trendle (1884-1972), suggested in 1932 that they follow the example of other media outlets by creating family entertainment for late-afternoon/early evening broadcasts.

"COWBOYS AND INDIANS---REVERSING THE STEREOTYPE!: Here, as in many more ambitious films, old racial cliches were challenged: Lisa Montell portrays a wonderful Native American woman who is dedicated to helping the larger community composed of her own people and Anglos too; Douglas Kennedy (star of TV's *Steven Donovan, Western Sheriff*) is a cowboy eager to exploit not only the indigenous people but his fellow whites as well.

Their Western, which would run for nearly 3,000 instalments, was shortly picked up for syndication, then broadcast on the ABC radio network. When that mega-corporation entered the new TV medium in 1946, executives set to work on an inexpensively produced kiddie Western version. With Jack Wrather (1918-1984) assigned to produce, the series became that struggling network's only Top Ten Show (Thursday evenings at 7:30 P.M. Eastern time) for their first five years of ABC's existence. A total of 221 episodes were filmed, mostly on old studio sets, the final season's entries in color. By then, 'The Lone Ranger' had already become a franchise with daily and Sunday comic strips, comic books, novels for children, and various merchandising items including masks, guns, and hats.

Before TV, there had been two successful serial versions from Republic studios in 1938 and 1939 but (perhaps surprisingly) never a single feature film. Wrather wondered if The Ranger's built-in popularity (by mid-decade, the series had been 'stripped,' reruns appearing daily Monday through Friday afternoons) might serve as a basis for a theatrical series. He persuaded executives at Warner Bros. that the way to go was with upscale B+ Oaters of the type which even then starred Joel McCrea, Randolph Scott, and Audie Murphy, mostly shot on location in photogenic Old Tucson, Arizona. The bet paid off: *The Lone Ranger* (Stuart Heisler, 1956) did solid enough business that a follow up beacme inevitable. In fact, *City of Gold* would not reach Rialtos until the series left the air. Here then was an exercise in nostalgia, a bringing down of the curtain (temporarily!) on a sagebrush saga that had come to seem curiously quaint in the age of such 'adult' TV Westerns as *Cheyenne* and *Gunsmoke*. Fittingly, Clayton Moore (1914-1999) and Jay Silverheels (1912-1980) embodied the Ranger and noble Apache Tonto for the final time.

Part of the film's ongoing appeal has to do with that aura of familiarity, which extends beyond the basic concept for the franchise itself. A number of immediately recognizable character people brought their ongoing appeal to the piece. The villain 'Ross Brady,' leader of a Ku Klux Klan sort of hooded terrorist organization, is portrayed by Douglas Kennedy (1924-1999), star of TV's *Steve Donovan, Western Marshal* (1955-56). A noble Native American

FRIENDS, PARTNERS, AND EQUALS IN ALL WAYS: In addition to the entertainment value, this film (like all other renderings of The Lone Ranger) illustrated the need for acceptance of racial equality in the United States, 'Tonto' achieving the same heroic status as 'The Ranger' owing to his qualities as a person and actions in the world, with no concern for his color.

who travelled east to win a medical degree, 'James Rolfe,' is played as a figure of decency and dignity by Dean Fredericks (1924-1999), a non-Indian who brought a new, refreshing respectability to such indigenous roles in TV's *The Adventures of Rin Tin Tin* (1954-1957). As 'Paviva,' the Native American woman who aids Rolfe in the difficult process of 'coming out' as an Indian even if that ruins his practice with local Anglos, Polish émigré Lisa Montell (1933-) portrays the same sort of courageous person that she did in *The Wild Dakotas* (1956) and *Tomahawk Trail* (1957). Director Selander (1900-1979) was an old hand at B+ Westerns starring Rory Calhoun (*The Yellow Tomahawk*, 1954), Sterling Hayden (*Arrow in the Dust*, 1954), and Randolph Scott (*Tall Man Riding*, 1955).

Such long beloved elements were balanced with several innovations. The screenwriters concocted an effective mystery in which well-behaved Indians are tormented by evil Anglos eager to locate the title object, a spiritual place to the Native people if an inspiration for raw capitalism to worst of the Whites. The film though never falls into the trap of Anglo bashing; as in Walt Disney's *Light in the Forest*, released at about the same time, there are good and bad people on both sides. Les Baxter co-composed a new song ('Hi Yo Silver, Hi-Yo') which is alternated with the traditional public domain 'The William Tell Overture,' included in the radio and TV versions. The villain and his henchwoman Mrs. Henderson clearly have an intense (and rather ugly) sexual involvement. Most incredible: For the first time, The Lone Ranger shoots to kill when attacked. In the past, he had been an idealist who would never fire a fatal bullet. Lone Ranger aficionados debated whether this added a realistic touch missing from the franchise up to that point or violated the very premise that had made the show and comics so popular with anti-violence parents as well as their children.

A NOBLE *NON-SAVAGE*: Here and in Disney's The *Light in the Forest* (pictured), elegant actor Dean Fredericks played Native Americans as wise and good as Jeff Chandler's 'Cochise' in the classic *Broken Arrow*.

50. LONE STAR (1991)
Rating: *****

CREDITS:

John Sayles, dir., scr., ed.; Jan Foster, John Sloss, Maggie Reanzi, R. Paul Miller, pro.; Mason Daring, mus.; Stuart Dryburgh, cin.; Sayles, ed.; 2.35:1; C; Columbia/Castle Rock.

CAST:

Chris Cooper (*Sam*); Elizabeth Pena (*Pilar*); Stephen Mendillo (*Cliff*); Stephen J. Lang (*Mikey*); Kris Kristofferson (*Charley Wade*); Frances McDormand (*Bunny*); Matthew McConaughey (*Buddy Deeds*); Joe Morton (*Del*); Clifton James (*Hollis*); Miriam Colon *(Mercedes)*; Oni Faida Lampley (*Celie*); Joe Stevens *(Travis)*; Richard Coca (*Enrique*); Ron Canada (*Otis*); Jeff Monahan (*Yung Hollis*); Chandra Wilson (*Athena*); Damon Guy (*Shadow*); Tony Plana *(Ray)*.

One man, one movie, *auteurist* critics claimed back in the late 1960s. For a film to rate as art rather than merely entertainment, there must be a single person who provides the primary vision for the piece. Not to neglect all the other and many necessary collaborators without whom no motion picture could be completed. Still, the theory held that a single central consciousness must propel a work if it is to be viewed as something more than a mere product for mass consumption. However questioned, even dismissed that approach may now be in favor of newer, different angles of perception on cinema, certain filmmakers (beginning, perhaps, with D.W. Griffith) clearly do dominate the proceedings for any movie.

RADICAL REVISIONISM: The advertising poster for John Sayles 'Western' implies that this film's approach to the Texas Rangers will be more critical than celebratory.

During the past forty years, no one has more clearly offered an example of this concept than John Sayles (1950-), originally of Schenectady NY. Beginning his career as one more of the legions of young talents given their first shots (though little money) at moviemaking by the legendary exploitation-avatar Roger Corman, Sayles moved on from the scripting of such Drive-In fare as *Battle Beyond the Stars* (1980) to make his own marginal (in terms of Hollywood as a business, though not as to impact on a small but loyal following) indie pictures. Controlling every aspect of production, including the all-important final cut, Sayles has essayed a variety of fascinating subjects that mainstream moviemakers tend to overlook, including the middle-age existence of former Youth Movement radicals (*Return of the Secaucus Seven*, 1979), the dynamics of a labor strike (*Matewan*, 1987), and baseball's most infamous scandal (*Five Men Out*, 1988). Always, the narrative thrust remains purposefully subdued so a viewer's focus will remain on Sayles' characters, developed in depth, interrelating in odd but believable ways.

This holds true too for his only Western thus far, though that term feels inadequate to describe *Lone Star*. Part contemporary Oater, part mystery, part updated tragedy involving the sins within a single family and complicated relations of any father and son, Sayles introduces his tale in what seems to be the set-up for an intriguing genre thriller. The sheriff of an isolated area in rural Texas, ever attempting to live up to the lofty reputation of his deceased dad who once held this position, happens upon a long-overlooked crime. Out on the desert, a skeleton is discovered. Apparently, it has been there for forty years, if unnoticed until now. Naturally, he must do what he can to learn the identity of the victim as well as the predator, whether or not that culprit remains alive today. But any objective analysis as to a criminologist's profession gives way to a subjective inner journey. 'Sam' gradually realizes that this case, seemingly random though as he will discover anything but, will lead him closer to home than he considers comfortable. In time, the situation will force this young man to re-evaluate everything he has ever believed about his family's past and, as a result, himself in the present.

NORTH OF THE RIO GRANDE: Chris Cooper and Elizabeth Pena as star-crossed lovers in a vision of the American West that borrows from Greek tragedy; Matthew McConaughey as Young Gun 'Buddy Deeds.

Ostensibly the protagonist, Sam Deeds is more correctly perceived as the first among equals in a rich ensemble-piece that involves characters from various communities which populate the border. Indeed, the Rio Grande itself---as a geographical fact but also a symbolic connection/separator of the United States and Mexico---transforms into something of a character, present at least by implication in every confrontation. All involved must deal with illegal crossings, drug smuggling, and other daily trials and tribulations. Here is something of a rural neo-noir in the tradition that the Coen Bros. initiated with their own low-budget contemporary Western, *Blood Simple* (1984). The presence of multi-Oscar winner Frances Sternhagen (1930-), star of that film (and many other Coen brothers projects, including the modern Northern-Western *Fargo,* 1996), cinches that tenuous connection. Indeed, her past screen-iconography allows Sayles to reference like-minded on-the-edge filmmakers. The Meryl Streep of non-mainstream cinema, Sternhagen brings a unique poignancy to her difficult role as a San Antonio woman who, to borrow a line from Orson Welles' classic *Citizen Kane* (1941), "knows where all the bodies are buried."

Or, in this case, one left unburied, for reasons that become all too clear as the seductively strange story progresses.

If *Hell or High Water* rates as the greatest single movie ever made about West Texas, then *Lone Star* holds that status for the state's Southern tier. Here we artistically enter into a unique world composed of interlocking demi-mondes, or in popular terminology, 'communities': The Anglo, the Native American, The African American, the Latino, and several others as well; all dependent on one another as to the area's economy, yet fiercely independent in terms of self-definition and values, cultural as well as moral. Though Sayles may be perceived as a latter-day Welles, he likewise is clearly influenced by the master storyteller Alfred Hitchcock. For what initially appear to be three bits of 'evidence'---a Mason ring, a tarnished badge, and an ancient pistol bullet---transform intro a triple MacGuffin. This Capra-esque Mr. Deeds goes to Alamo town, where he discovers that any one among these odd objects depends on each of the others to unlock a story that perhaps might be better left untold . . . except that, as in *Oedipus Rex*, the truth must 'will out,' however horrible its implications. Paternal and/or fraternal. Criminally and sexually. As a series of sins weave generations together, including unintended but all too real incest, the vision of Greek tragedy---a discovery that our supposed choices in life are in fact

"SINS OF THE FATHER...": Generations of Texans, Anglo and Latin, find themselves caught in a virtual spiderweb of intrigue as complicated as the narrative of a Shakespearean play.

the workings out of a profound destiny-- remains terrifyingly alive, if certainly not well, in the world today.

51. MAN FROM DEL RIO (1956)
Rating: ****

CREDITS:

Harry Horner, dir.; Richard Carr, scr.; Robert L. Jacks, pro.; Fred Steiner, mus.; Stanley Cortez, cin.; Robert Golden, ed.; 1.85:1; B&W; 82 min.; United Artists.

CAST:

Anthony Quinn *(Dave Robles)*; Katy Jurado *(Estella)*; Peter Whitney *(Ed Bannister)*; Douglas (V.) Fowley (Doc Adams); John Larch *(Bill Dawson)*; Whit Bissell *('Breezy' Morgan)*; Douglas Spencer *(Sheriff Jack Tillman)*; Barry Atwater *(Dan Ritchy)*; Katherine DeMille *(Townwoman)*; Jack Hogan *(Westin)*; Adrienne Marden *(Mrs. Tillman)*; Guinn Williams *(Fred Jasper)*.

Man from Del Rio was shot on a tight enough budget that it has been labelled a "B" movie. Note, though: that term refers to financing, not quality. And, lest we forget, *High Noon* (1952) likewise rated as such in regarding its budget. While hardly an iconic Western on the order of that classic, this tight, economic Oater shares several qualities with the acknowledged masterwork. *Man . . .* was like that better known classic mostly shot at Melody Ranch in Newhall CA, a drab, unattractive frontier town in ironic contrast to its lighthearted name. The location had been used for singing cowboy films, many starring owner Gene Autry. Several of the iconic buildings, including *High Noon's* stark, isolated church down at the end of main street, are likewise on view here. Though *Man* does not *High Noon*-like hone to actual time, a clock notably appears near the end, cinching the connection.

FROM SCENE STEALER TO 'CHARACTER LEAD': Anthony Quinn portrayed numerous Latin-American and Native American characters in Westerns until *Man from Del Rio* allowed him to prove that he could 'open a picture' as an offbeat leading man.

Also important is the presence of Katy Jurado (1924-2002), *High Noon*'s female second lead. Once again, she is cast as a Spanish woman who refuses to be lowered to the level of a prostitute by Anglo men in power. In both films, Jurado's character insists on living out the American Dream: becoming a store owner in *High Noon*, nurse to the town doctor here. In the Fred Zinneman piece, however well-to-do she became, her business arrangements were necessarily carried out in private, White financiers who respect her refuse to so much as smile should they pass 'Helen Ramirez' on the street. Here Katy's iconic image takea a significant step further in depiction of integration into the American mainstream. When the citizenry converges for a social gathering, she is on the invitation list. Jurado would continue to play such strong women for decades, finally as the wife of Slim Pickens in Sam Peckinpah's *Pat Garrett and Billy the Kid* (1972).

THE LAST ANGRY WOMAN: Here, as in *High Noon*, Katy Jurado portrayed Latin ladies who fight – and succeed – in their desire to be considered 'respectable' in an Anglo controlled town.

Such magnanimity is not extended to the title character, a Mexican gunfighter played by Anthony Quinn (1915-2001). Hardly a stranger to Westerns, Quinn often portrayed Native Americans in such big pictures as Cecil B. DeMille's *The Plainsman* (1936) and Raoul Walsh's *They Died with Their Boots On* (1941). He won the lead in a small picture (again as an indigenous American) in *Black Gold* (1947), his wife Katherine (daughter of Cecil B) DeMille) cast as the female lead there, she playing a supporting part here. In one of the most complex social situations in Westerns, 'Dave Robles' is hired as a lawmen of a half-deserted cow-town after he kills a notorious gunman in a fair fight. This plot development exists in line with history: Actual shootists Ben Thompson and James "Wild Bill" Hickok won their stars owing to unsavory past reputations. The respectable townsfolk believed no one would dare menace their peaceful communities if a killer with a badge walked the streets.

Yet this film offers something different. Latino Dave is paid well to guard Mesa. Having arrived in rags, he now struts about in a fancy suit. But he is not welcome at social gatherings. This has nothing to do with ethnicity. Again, Jurado's identity as a Mexican-American hardly excludes her character from this outpost of civilization's 'polite' society. Rather, the film raises a class issue. The petty townsfolk require his fast gun for security but do not wish to mingle with someone who, at the opening, kills three men. The psychological burden this creates, leading to the anti-hero's alcoholism, qualifies *Man...* as an 'adult' Western. With this work, Quinn proved his ability to move from supporting character roles to an offbeat character lead. Shortly, he would co-headline such "A" Westerns as *Warlock* (1958) and *Last Train from Gun Hill* (1959).

Others in the cast were Western troopers. Peter Whitney (1916-1972), as the crime boss, would co-star with Kent Taylor and Jan Merlin on TV's *Rough Riders* (1958-1959). Douglas Fowley (1911-1998), playing 'Doc Adams' (an in-joke for fans of CBS's *Gunsmoke*), showed up on ABC's *The Life and Legend of Wyatt Earp* as *two* doctors, deadly gambler Doc Holliday and gruff, lovable, elderly Fabrique. Whit Bissell (1909-1996), as the town drunk (a parallel to James Griffith's character in *High Noon*), would portray Tombstone mayor John Clum in *Gunfight at the O.K. Corral* (1957). Douglas Spencer (1910-1960), as the previous sheriff, played the role of a gentle farmer in *Shane* (1953) as well as cold-blooded killer in *River of No Return* (1954) and *The Kentuckian* (1955). Guinn Williams (1899-1962), as a gunslinger, had starred

'BIG BOY': The 'star' of B (to be kind) Oaters during the 1940s emerged as a top character actor during the 1950s; he is perhaps best remembered today for his roles in the John Wayne epics *The Alamo* (1960) and *The Comancheros* (1961).

in the low-budget 'Big Boy' Westerns of the 1930s and would be cast by John Wayne as an appealingly overweight Texan in *The Alamo* (1960).

Though director Harry Horner (1910-1994) would not be associated with the genre again, writer Richard Carr (1929-1988) enjoyed a lucrative career scripting such well-remembered TV series as *Rawhide*, *High Chapparal*, *The Virginian*, and *Bonanza*. The greatest asset occurred when the production team landed cinematographer Stanley (1908-1996; brother of actor Ricardo) Cortez. The sharp, unsparing black and white imagery recalls the masterful visuals he created for Orson Welles' *The Magnificent Ambersons* (1942) and Charles Laughton's *The Night of the Hunter* (1955). A highly capable team allowed this little film to exert a big impact, including the surprise finale of an unfired pistol when we expect the dusty street to blaze with gunfire, which would also occur in *Showdown at Boot Hill*.

52. MAN WHO LOVED CAT DANCING, THE (1973)
Rating: **** ½

CREDITS:

Richard C. Sarafian, dir.; Eleanor Perry, William H. Norton, scr.; Perry, Martin Poll, T.W. Sewell, pro.; John Williams, mus.; Harry Stradling Jr., cin.; Tom Rolf, ed.; 2.35:1; C; 114 min.; Metro-Goldwyn-Mayer.

CAST:

Burt Reynolds (*Jay Grobart*); Sarah Miles (*Catherine Crocker*); Lee J. Cobb (*Harvey Lapchance*); Jack Warden (*Dawes*); George Hamilton (*Willard Crocker*); Bo Hopkins (*Billy Bowen*); Robert Donner (*Dub*); Sandy (*Kevin*); McPeak (*Ben*); Larry Littlebird (*Iron Knife*); Nancy Malone (*Sudie*); Jay Silverheels (*The Chief*); Jay Varela (*Charlie Bent*); Sutero Garcia Jr. (*Dream Speaker*).

If any actor of the 1970s ought to have rivalled Clint Eastwood and Charles Bronson as one of the era's leading Western stars, that person was Burt Reynolds (1936-2018). A college football player for Florida State, the charismatic man with the killer smile had had his first success playing supporting roles in TV series, *Riverboat* (1959-1960) with Darren McGavin, then alongside James Arness in *Gunsmoke* (1962-1965) as blacksmith/part-time deputy 'Quint Asper.' The latter role allowed Reynolds to connect with his Native American bloodline, embodying what was then still referred to as a 'half breed.' This would be continued in the short-lived modern police drama

They Went That-A-Way

OUTLAW ANTI-HERO, ARISTOCRATIC-ESTABLISHMENT VILLAIN:
Burt Reynolds and George Hamilton embody the polar opposites of what might be thematically described as 'the populist Western.'

Hawk (1966), followed by numerous "B" movies. Always, Burt felt himself drawn to the Western, even if in "B" movie form: *Navajo Joe* (1966) and *Sam Whiskey* (1969). Then a triad of events propelled Burt into the epicenter of popular culture: *Cosmopolitan*'s first (semi-) nude center-fold; a sudden celebrity-sensation owing to his glib humor on *The Tonight Show with Johnny Carson*; and a stand-out role in the major-league movie when Charlton Heston turned down *Deliverance* (1972).

At last able to pick and choose his parts, Reynolds suggested to producers a book he had read and admired, *The Man Who Loved Cat Dancing* (1972), a one-shot by Indiana housewife Marilyn Durham (1930-2015), reached bestseller status and received mostly rave reviews. Reynolds knew the role of 'Jay Grobart,' an outlaw with a guilty conscience and code of behaviour in spite of his seeming wildness, might provide the part that would at last set him on a Hollywood "A" Western trail. That was not to be. Afterwards, he opted to play cowboy-ish Southern good ol' Boys in films like *Smokey and the Bandit* (1977). The loss was ours. Also his in terms of a

LOVERS ON THE RUN: Sarah Miles (right) as the great lady of an immense ranch who falls in love with her roughewn kidnapper (Burt Reynolds).

possible legacy. As to this powerful, underrated Western, shot by director Sarafian (1930-2013) in the classic style of Anthony Mann Oaters including *The Man from Laramie* (1955), the star--free of the silly, overdone mannerisms in his comedic films---refused to speak of it after a belated and unceremonious release.

What went wrong? The cast and crew, residing at a motel in Gila Bend AZ, celebrated Burt Reynolds' birthday (born 2/11/36) late into the night. He allegedly spent considerable time in the company of co-star Sarah Miles (1941-). The British beauty had appeared in *Ryan's Daughter* (1970), written by her husband Robert Bolt, he not present on the current set. Accompanying her, however, was Sarah's business manager; they allegedly had engaged in a long-time love affair. Suspecting Miles likely would desert him for Reynolds, the jealous paramour assaulted her. Threatened and terrified, she spent the night with Reynolds in his room. The following day, the interloper was found dead of a drug overdose, foul play a possibility though never proven. The tabloid-headline-grabbing event left a cloud over all those involved as well as the film itself.

As to the movie, though . . . as a *movie*? Initially, the storyline seems simple enough: Even as Jay's gang stops and robs a train on an isolated stretch of prairie, 'Catherine' arrives on the scene. The well-dressed, elegant, sophisticated young woman has run away from her wealthy husband. She cannot tolerate his possessive attitude, despite the luxury surrounding this 'lady' who would prefer to belatedly discover herself as 'a woman.' Waiting for the train, she is kidnapped by a wild outlaw, 'Billy,' soon finding herself on the trail with a dangerous group of rough-necks. Rape by him or a rough older gang member, 'Dawes,' remains a threat. But Jay fights to stop such an outrage. Initially, Catherine believes this indicates a sensitive and moral element under the harsh surface. While this may, to a degree, be true, Jay has a more pressing, even insidious motivation. For as the two misfits fall in love, Catherine comes to grasp that the train robber was once happily married to another woman named Cat: a Shoshone named Cat Dancing, whose death remains clouded in mystery.

The project was overseen by writer-producer Eleanor Perry (1914-1981). What drew her to Durhan's manuscript was less the Western element than the then-budding feminist movement. Here, the female lead 'pulls a Nora' (referring to Henrik Ibsen's 1879 play *A Doll's House*) and walks out, slamming the door behind her. For Perry, *Cat Dancing* presented an opportunity

ONE MORE VARIATION ON 'BILLY THE KID': Bo Hopkins (left) embodied the quirky 'young gun' modelled on William H. Bonney in Sam Peckinpah's classic *The Wild Bunch* (1969) as well as this lesser know though high-quality Western.

to create an American version of that influential stage drama, even as upper-middleclass women, inspired by Betty Friedan's *The Feminine Mystique* (1963) and other feminist writings, questioned whether conventional marriage was indeed the be-all and end-all for a female. Every major female star expressed interest in playing Catherine, from Jane Fonda and Fay Dunaway to Julie Christie and Candace Bergen. Miles' intense if quirky acting and unconventional though potent sensuality won her the role.

One controversial aspect of the storyline (at least in retrospect) has to do with a sequence in which Catherine is (almost) raped by three Indians after they become drunk on White Man's Whiskey. At a time when Hollywood filmmakers were trying to re-invent our image of the Native American in films as diverse as *Soldier Blue*, *Little Big Man*, and *A Man Called Horse* (all 1970), the inclusion of such a scene caused many observers even then to raise high a collective eyebrow. Still, that questionable moment is offset by two others. While on the trail, Billy and Dawes attempt to force themselves on Catherine, the latter successfully. A certain sort of man, whatever his ethnicity, is prone to this crime, ethnicity aside. Also, when Durhan and Catherine arrive at the Shoshone camp, the Native people there prove more warm, friendly, and fair-minded (including the chief, portrayed by Jay Silverheels, of "Tonto" fame) than any Anglos on view.

Clearly, then, the film does not suggest that Indians 'by their very nature' (another offensive phrase that has hopefully been put to rest) are so inclined. As Fess Parker's wise scout noted in Disney's *The Light in the Forest*: "there's good and bad on both sides." By the mid-1970s, Hollywood films in general were belatedly sharing this truth with the mass audience.

53. MARSHAL'S DAUGHTER, THE (1953)
Rating, Mainstream B Western: NO STARS
Rating, Unique Cult/Camp Classic: ****

CREDITS:

William Berke, dir.; Bob Duncan, scr.; Ken Murray, Steven A. Harris, pro.; Darrell Calker, mus.; Ray Browne, ed.; 1.37:1; B&W; 71 min.; United Artists.

CAST:

Laurie Anders (*Laurie Dawson*); Hoot Gibson (*Marshal Ben Dawson*); Ken Murray (*'Smiling Bill' Murray*); Preston Foster, Johnny Mack Brown, Jimmy Wakeley, Buddy Baer (*Poker Players*); Harry Lauter (*Russ Mason*); Pamela Ann Murray (*'Baby' Laurie*); Tex Ritter (*Balladeer*); Francis Ford (*Gramps*); Walter Brennan (*Hanger-on*).

This film's narrative is basic, to say the least. Aging lawman 'Ben Dawson' always hoped his (now passed) wife would bear him a son to carry on the family's noble tradition. Instead, she delivered a daughter, 'Laurie,' a dainty little girl he adores. She however knows how frustrated dad is to be reaching the end of the trail without ever having had a pop/son marshal/deputy relationship. So late at night, donning a Zorro-like mask, the not-so-delicate beauty slips out into the wilderness to bring in those outlaws her well-intentioned pappy can no longer catch. While she primarily hopes to prove her worth to pop, Laurie inadvertently also reveals the equality of women to achieve anything a man might, if given the chance, qualifying this as a proto-feminist film, however unlikely it may be that this humble "B" (to be kind!) picture's creators had such a lofty ambition in mind.

ONCE WAS NOT ENOUGH!: Pretty Laurie Anders, top-billed in this grade Z (budget wise) Oater, projected enough strength and charm that viewers might well wish her career in motion pictures had continued.

Even more complex, fascinating, and unique is the story of how *Marshal's Daughter* went into production, if at a budget so low that the term *shoe-string* seems extravagant. It all began with Ken Murray (1903-1988), raised in a family of vaudevillians, much like the legendary George M. Cohan. Any similarity ends there, however. For if the latter proved something of a show business genius/legend, Murray was at best a figure of minor talent. Nonetheless, he did wrangle his way into the movie business, serving (modestly) in such varied capacities as actor, writer, producer, director, and editor. By the 1950, Murray's career appeared to be wrapping up. But TV, in its infancy, proved so desperate for product that anyone with even a minor name could land a series. *The Ken Murray Show* (1950-1953), which ran for a whopping 86 episodes, featured a montage of stand-up comedy, conversation, and music/dancing. Incredibly, such major figures as Kirk Douglas and Ronald Reagan appeared, more out of friendship than anything else. In addition, Murray assembled a continuing cast that included Darla Hood (formerly of the 'Our Gang' comedies) and 'Stooge' Curly Joe Besser. Also, like Johnny Carson's inclusion of Carol Wayne as the late-night movie co-host, Murray unveiled a pretty unknown from Casper, Wyoming, Laurie Anders (1922-1992)--not to be confused with Roger Corman protégée Luana Anders. During nine instalments, the perky cowgirl stared down the camera, stating in a provocative voice: "I love the wide-open spaces!"

When the show finally wound down, Murray became convinced this 'actress' (who physically resembled Gloria Winters, then playing the cute teenage daughter of Kirby Grant on *Sky King*) could become a movie star, with proper nurturing. As his funds were limited, Murray hired Bob Duncan (1904-1967), who had never before written a feature but did play bit parts in "B" Westerns like *Range Beyond the Blue* (1947). Uncertain as to where he ought to begin, Duncan settled in on a précis of Carl Foreman's brilliant Oscar nominated script for *High Noon* (1952). Noting the similarities between the two, Murray contacted Tex Ritter (1905-1974), former low-budget cowboy star, to sing a notably similar ballad: "there was a marshal's daughter, who did thinks that she

A PAIR OF ACES: Old-time Western star Hoot Gibson and the authentic Singin' Cowboy Tex Ritter joined the team of Ken Murray's makeshift Oater.

ain't oughta, helping her daddy keep the law . . ." The only director willing to sign on to so humble a project: William Berke (1903-1958), who in addition to several low-brow Oaters including *I Shot Billy the Kid* (1950), now eked out a living by doing the honors on such Flying 'A' Ranch series as *Range Rider* and *Annie Oakley*, both executive-produced by Gene Autry. During the shoot, everyone involved realized they could not say their lines with straight faces. Instead, the cast began to kid the script. The result is something of a mess, if an undeniably entertaining one. Worth noting: such an approach would prove to be the case with *Cat Ballou* a dozen years later, which in its original conception was supposed to be a conventional Western rather than a genre spoof.

Consciously or not, Murray initiated a pattern that would become basic to theatrical and TV Westerns a generation later by purposefully casting has-been cowboy stars in key roles. Edmund Richard 'Hoot' (short for 'Hoot Owl') Gibson (1892-1962), an authentic rodeo cowboy who had starred in Westerns since 1910 (his best: *Action*, 1921 for John Ford, one more variation on the 'Three Godfathers' legend), was brought out of retirement to play the pop. Several years later, Gibson's final role would be a grizzled sergeant in Ford's *The Horse Soldiers* (1959). Alabama's John(ny) Mack Brown (1904-1974), a

ONE GOOD TURN DESERVES ANOTHER: Producer Ken Murray cast John Ford's alcoholic older brother Francis as 'Gramps' when no one else in Hollywood would work with the onetime star/director; 'Pappy' returned the favor by casting Murray (standing, and wearing W.C. Fields' famous hat) in the majestic epic The Man Who Shot Liberty Valance (1962).

top college athlete who originally played lead roles in big Westerns like King Vidor's *Billy the Kid* (1930) before drifting into kiddie cowboy movies, was offered the role of a gambler, alongside singing cowboy Jimmy Wakeley (1914-1982). Three-time Oscar winner Walter Brennan (1894-1974) can be seen in ancient stock footage employed to pad out the saloon scenes. Even that originator of the theatrical Western, Francis Ford (1881-1953), received a role as beloved 'Gramps.' This would prove to be the final film for that alcoholic veteran. John Ford would repay Murray this favor by casting him as a W.C. Fields-style gin-drinking doctor in *The Man Who Shot Liberty Valance* (1962).

As for Laurie, she never received another role in movies or on TV. Yet this once lost, recently rediscovered piece attests to her charm and conviction onscreen. One more of those 'what might have been . . .' Hollywood fables that played out on the boulevard of broken dreams.

BETTIE PAGE? MOVE OVER!: Laurie in what was once referred to as a Cheesecake shot, though the costume never appears in the film per se.

54. MAVERICK QUEEN, THE (1956) Rating: *** ½

CREDITS:

Joseph (Joe) Kane, dir.; Kenneth Gamet, Devallon Scott, scr.; Kane, Herbert J. Yates, pro.; Victor Young, mus.; Jack A. Marta, cin.; Richard L. Van Enger, ed.; 2.35:1; C; 92 min.; Republic.

CAST:

Barbara Stanwyck (*Kit Banion*); Barry Sullivan *('Jeff Younger')*; Scott Brady *(The Sundance Kid)*; Mary Murphy (*Lucy Lee*); Howard Petrie ('Butch Cassidy'); Emile Meyer *(Leo Malone)*; Walter Sande *(Sheriff Wilson)*; George Keymas (*Muncie*); John Doucette (*Loudmouth*); Taylor Holmes (*Pete Callaher*); Al Bain, Chet Brandenburg, Russell Custer, Augie Gomez *(Barflies)*; Carol Brewster, Karen Scott (*Saloon Girls*); Tris(tram) Coffin (Card Player); Jack Harden (*Harvey Logan*); Cactus Mack (*Bad Hombre*).

In 1953, Republic studios boss Herbert J. Yates (1880-1966) faced a major crisis. His once profitable "B" pictures were losing money now that TV supplied much the same stuff every day for free. Bankruptcy loomed on the horizon. In hopes of avoiding that, Yates greenlighted a number of more expensive films. The first: *Johnny Guitar* (1954) starred Joan Crawford as a strong-minded Western woman. The film was directed by the well-regarded Nicholas Ray (*They Live By Night*). When the movie proved profitable, Yates starred that film's male lead, Sterling Hayden, in a big-budget (at $ 2 million, unheard of for Republic) epic about the Alamo, *The Last Command* (1955). But everyone had seen Walt Disney's *Davy Crockett* earlier that summer,

JOHNNY GUITAR REDUX: Like Joan Crawford in the earlier film, Barbara Stanwyck here dominates the West itself and every tough guy who rides into town.

before Yates' version could be released. Audiences took a 'just been there, done that' approach and the risky film fizzled. At a point of crisis, Yates decided to try and repeat the success of *Johnny Guitar* with a major (if fast-fading, box-office wise) female name again headlining, even a similar ballad performed by a lady vocalist (Peggy Lee for *J.G.*, Joni James in *Maverick Queen*). When it came time to pick a vehicle, a popular novel by the bestselling (if not best reviewed) of Western writers all but begged to be adapted to the screen.

The Maverick Queen was one of many bestselling Oaters penned by Pearl Zane Grey (alternately spelled 'Gray'; 1872-1939), an Ohio-born dentist turned author who had succeeded (commercially, that is) beyond his greatest dreams. Critics dismissed such books as *Maverick Queen* as the most vulgar sort of Westernized pulp fiction, filled with moral platitudes and exploitive violence. There were two exceptions: *Riders of the Purple Sage* (1912), a study of the after-effects of Utah's 'Mormon Massacre' of peaceful Christians passing by Salt Lake City, offered a serious social message; so did *The Vanishing American* (1922), a plea for better treatment of Indians confined to modern Reservations. Otherwise, the books (lapped up by fans, Dwight D. Eisenhower foremost among them) were criticized for, among other things, portraying Drug Store cowboy heroes in stories that mis-represented the past, both as to lifestyle and specific facts. *Maverick Queen* provided a case in point: A high-minded (and fictional) Pinkerton man passing himself off as gunslinger 'Jeff Younger' (not one of the historic Younger boys who rode with Frank and Jesse James) becomes involved in a three-way romantic struggle with (historical) outlaw Harry Longabaugh and a (fictional) mature woman with beauty and brains,' Kit Banion.' Here then would be a *Johnny Guitar* redux, with Scott Brady brought back from the earlier film in a similar role, morphing from The Dancing Kid to The Sundance Kid. Yates hoped (and possibly prayed) that lightning would strike twice. It didn't, though this did prove a minor success.

Par for the course for the person behind the camera. Joe/Joseph Kane (1894-1975) was one of the most (if not *the* most) prolific directors of Western films, turning out more than 100 for Republic. These included humble Singin' Cowboy pictures starring Gene Autry *(In Old Monterey*, 1939) and Roy

TORN BETWEEN TWO LOVERS: The title character finds herself torn between a Pinkerton agent (Barry Sullivan, seated) and a wanted outlaw (Scott Brady, standing).

Rogers (*Song of the Prairie*, 1942). And, in time, somewhat loftier productions that would appear in the 1950s (*Jubilee Trail*, *Rails into Laramie*, both 1954) once Gene and Roy left Republic to do their own television shows. If the greatest of all Western directors, John Ford, rated as a perfectionist who resembled a master chef preparing perfect meals for the discriminating gourmet, Kane might be described as the equivalent of a hash-house short-order cook, knocking out burgers, fried egg sandwiches, and hot coffee for whoever drifted into the greasy spoon diner from the cold outside, seeking a modicum of warmth and humble nourishment. Everyone agrees, at the very least, that Kane was unpretentious; while detractors like to label him a hack, defenders insist he did the best he possibly could with impossibly low budgets. Again, though, *Maverick Queen* offered a step up as to production values from much of what had gone before. The film was shot in Trucolor,

Republic's three- (originally two-) color process that tended to reduce everything onscreen to either blue-green or orange-red. Now, though, Yates went a step further, allowing Kane to shoot in Naturama, the fast-failing studio's response to the trend for widescreen initiated two years earlier by 'the majors.'

And, of course, there was Barbara Stanwyck (1907-1990), a leading star for Sam Goldwyn during the 1930s. Now, like Crawford, Bette Davis, and others of ther ilk, Stanwyck found herself scrounging for roles. Born

AUTHOR! AUTHOR! Pearl Zane Grey (aka Gray) created a body of work that still remains (with the possible exception only of Louis L'Amour's stories) the most famous and popular library of Western pulp fiction.

in Brooklyn, 'Babs' had proven her acting chops with serious social drama (*Golden Boy*, 1939), lighthearted sophisticated comedy (*The Lady Eve*, 1941), and film noir *(Double Indemnity,* 1944). No stranger to Westerns, she had starred in Cecil B. DeMille's enjoyable if over-the-top epic *Union Pacific* (1939) as one more sexy tomboy, and Anthony Mann's darker-than-noir *The Furies,* 1950) as an Electra-like father-obsessed ranch woman. More recently, Stanwyck had proven her abilities in the new subgenre of Strong but Still Attractive Aging Women Oaters with *Cattle Queen of Montana* (1954), opposite Ronald Reagan.

Maverick Queen is appealing in many ways, close attention to historicity not among them. As the legendary film *Butch Cassidy and the Sundance Kid* (1969) well illustrated, the so-called Wild Bunch had been an essentially non-violent outlaw gang more interested in robbing than killing. Here, they are reduced to the lowest level of Western trash, without moral compass. But Babs and the assorted other cast members grab hold of their roles and give it their all. She would win the lead in a TV Western, *The Big Valley* (1965-1969) a decade later. Here, for once, the color comes closer to what audiences expected from other studio's films, with some intriguing pastels highlighting the vast horizons. Barry Sullivan (1912-1994), an underrated actor and medium-level star, would reunite with B.S. in Sam Fuller's similar though superior project *40 Guns* (1957). He would play Sheriff Pat Garrett in TV's *The Tall Man* (1960-1962). Though certainly not a classic on the order of Ray's earlier proto-feminist Western, here is a worthy representation of yet another sub-genre of Western films that came into being during the 1950s. All the same, two years later, Republic Pictures went belly-up, unable to overcome the horrific losses that they suffered with their fascinating Alamo film, overshadowed in the eyes of mainstream moviegoers five years later by John Wayne's colossal version.

55. MISSING, THE (2003)
Rating: **** ½

CREDITS:

Ron Howard, dir.; Ken Kaufman, scr.; Howard, Brian Grazer, Daniel Ostroff, pro.; James Horner, mus.; Salvatore Totino, cin.; Daniel P. Hanley, Mike Hill, Ron Vignone, ed.; 2.39:1; C; 137 min. (theatrical), 154 (director's cut); Revolution/Imagine.

CAST:

Cate Blanchett (*Magdalena Gilkeson*); Tommy Lee Jones (*Samuel Jones*); Evan Rachel Wood (*Lilly*); Jena Boyd (*Dot*); Aaron Eckhart (*Brake Baldwin*); Val Kilmer (*Lt. Jim Ducharme*); Sergio Calderon (*Emiliano*); Eric Schweig (*Chidin*); Steve Reevis (*Two Stone*); Jay Tavare (*Kayitah*); Simon Baker (*Honesco*); Ray McKinnon (*Wittick*); Deborah Martinez (*Maria*); Clint Howard (*Purdy*); David Midthunder (*Scout*).

Shot on a budget that reached beyond $60 million, with an international return of less than $40 million, *The Missing* is perceived as a failure so far as Hollywood economics are concerned. Still, hardcore Western buffs consider this to be as impressive an example of the Indian War subgenre as Kevin Costner's *Open Range* (2003) was to the Trail Drive films. *Missing* boasted a fine pedigree as to its origins, beginning with a powerful novel by Thomas Eidson (1944-) titled *The Last Ride*. Like the movie Ron Howard (1954-) fashioned from it, Eidson's book was in part inspired by Alan Le May's *The Searchers* and John Ford's 1956 classic derived from that novel. The film's title suggests something of a reference, suggesting 'the searchers' as perceived from the Other side of the

MEAN AS HELL: In contemporary Westerns, Tommy Lee Jones has created some of the most menacing characters imaginable; 'Samuel Jones' may be the toughest of them all.

gun barrel. Here a teenage girl, 'Lilly Gilkeson,' is in 1885 New Mexico (*The Missing* was shot entirely on location), abducted by broncho Apaches intent on heading south toward the border, there selling Lilly and other abducted females to Mexican slave-traders. Pursuing them are 'Magdalena,' the girl's unrelenting mother; 'Dot,' a younger sister; and' Samuel Jones,' Magdalena's father. Decades ago, Jones deserted his Anglo family to live with Native Americans. Though Magdalena despises the man, she knows that his remarkable abilities as a tracker offer the only viable means of freeing her daughter. While Jones does wish to rescue his blood-granddaughter, he secretly hopes also to redeem himself, in Magdalena's eyes. And, perhaps, his own.

From the opening sequence, Ron Howard makes clear this will purposefully offer a bleak picture, and an anti-romantic one as well. The first shot is of Magdalena, seemingly in physical pain or mental distress. We may expect this to be the result of something exciting, such as a raid by outlaws. Then the camera reveals that Magdalena is in an outhouse, where she relieves herself on a horrifically hot day. Clearly, this film will not wax sentimental about its subject: The West, here rendered realistically rather than mythically. In the following shot, Magdalena heads for the farmhouse to help a Spanish woman suffering from a toothache. Not out of the goodness of M's heart, rather because she wants ... *demands!* ... coins in payment. Here then is a notably different vision of a pioneer woman from the ones offered by, say, Olive Carey and Vera Miles in Ford's *The Searchers*. Nonetheless, Magdalena will emerge as a worthy, even remarkable person owing to the heroic dimensions to which she rises as a result of family loyalty. And, more specifically,

STRAIGHT SHOOTERS: Continuing in the tradition of strong pioneer women, Cate Blanchette's 'Magdalena' takes her place fighting alongside the menfolks.

the mother/daughter bond that has defined so much of feminist discourse, whether set in the west or anywhere else.

In some regards, *The Missing* appears to have been conceived as a direct retort to Kevin Costner's vastly overrated *Dances with Wolves* (1990). It's important here to make a distinction between the indigenous people portrayed in each: Costner's characters were members of the northwest's Lakota Nation; here, we encounter southwestern Apaches. Despite the inherent differences in those distinct peoples, *Dances . . .* played to the falsehood that the Cheyenne specifically, Native Americans in general, were essentially a peaceful nation. In fact, their men all but lived for warfare. Costner's film succeeded at the box-office owing to its aura of political correctness, telling an audience of its era what they hoped to 'learn': A supposedly enlightened nouveau myth rather than any sort of historical truth about who the plains people in fact were.

However sympathetic Howard may be to causes involving the diversity of ethnicities, he like Eidson refused to offer an anachronistic illustration of contemporary values. The narrative's Apaches are frightfully violent, almost beyond belief that any current post-P.C. moviemaker would dare offer. Not only do they enjoy the thrill of battle but the long cruel process of torturing captives. Howard dares to have his female protagonist shout that "we ought to exterminate all of them." However horrible such a statement may strike mainstream moviegoers today, that was indeed the mindset of most Anglo women of that time; particularly those who, like the film's Magdalena, had personally suffered at the Indians' hands. Howard includes the line without suggesting that he agrees with it, rather to counter Costner's gorgeous but inaccurate glorification. Overall, the film offers a more expansive view than is expressed in M's words, not limited to her subjectivity.

We discover that these very Apaches had been quietly living on the San Carlos Reservation, learning the White Man's Way, sincerely making an attempt to integrate. Things exploded when a vainglorious, self-important army officer chose to hang one of their chiefs over a minor issue. Apaches revolted as any oppressed people might, would, perhaps *must* do when

ANOTHER SET OF 'SEARCHERS': Tommy Lee Jones and Cate Blanchette as an estranged father-and-daughter who agree on only one thing: Bring the abducted child back home.

confronted with the fact that the compromise between old and new ways turned out to be entirely one-sided. The intensity of such an event remains with us throughout. In the Contemporary Western, at least at its best, there are no 'good guys' or 'bad guys' as to Anglos or Indians, en masse . . . only a tragic conflict between differing societies attempting to co-exist in the unique 'world' that is America.

How appropriate, then, that signs of the future appear everywhere. The telegraph has just recently reached this far outpost of civilization. New-fangled toilets are brought in by the wagonload to replace rough wooden ones. A photographer (modelled on Edwin S. Curtis) is on hand to try and create a record of the Old West before it fades from actuality into history, then legend. Recall, in context, that before assuming the director's chair, actor Howard appeared in a pair of films that enshrined the myth: *The Spikes Gang* (1974, with Lee Marvin) and *The Shootist* (1976, John Wayne). Here, his own bent is to set aside any joyous falsities of Dime Novel heroics and reveal the way it was . . . or, at least, as close to actuality as anyone can possibly come today.

56. MONTE WALSH (1970)
Rating: *****

CREDITS:

William A. Fraker, dir.; Lukas Heller, David Zelag Goodman, scr.; Hal Landers, Bobby Roberts, pro.; John Barry, music. David M. Walsh, cin.; Richard Brockway, Ray Daniels, Gene Fowler Jr., ed.; 2.55:1; C 106 min.; Cinema Centers Films.

CAST:

Lee Marvin (*Monte Walsh*); Jeanne Moreau (*Martine Bernard*); Jack Palance (*Chet Rawlins*); Mitchell Ryan (*Shorty Austin*); Jim Davis *(Cal Brennan)*; G.D. Spradlin (*Hal Henderson*); John Hudkins (*Sonny Jacobs*); Michael Conrad (*Daily Johnson*); Raymond Guth (*Sunfish Perkins*); Tom Heaton (*Sugar Wyman*);Ted Gehring (*Skimpy Eagans*); Bo Hopkins *(Jumpin' Joe Joslin)*; John McLiam (*Fightin' Joe Hooker*); Allyn Ann McLerie (*Mary Eagle*); Matt Clark (*Rufus*); Billy Green Bush (*Powder Kent*); Richard Farnsworth (*Cowboy*) Roy Barcroft (*Townsman*).

"Nobody gets to be a cowboy forever."

Mid-way through this long-neglected masterpiece, the greatest film ever made about a hard-working cowboy with the possible exception only of the better-known *Will Penny* (1967) starring Charlton Heston in a similar role, one aging ranch hand whispers this to his best friend. The speaker: 'Chet Rawlins,' whose life has been dedicated to the profession (some might say 'art') of cowboying. Ever since the fierce blizzards of the mid-1880s wiped out entire ranches, large and small, freezing the cattle in their tracks, jobs have

THE LAST ANGRY MAN: Lee Marvin ought to have won a second Best Acting Oscar for his role as an authentic old-time cowboy who cannot comprehend that the way of life that he lived and loved is swiftly coming to an end, and there is nothing he can do to stop that.

been all but impossible to come by. Forcing such a person to make a choice: Go to town and take a job there . . . maybe a good wife as well . . . or perish somewhere out on the prairie, searching for a way of life that no longer exists. The listener: Fellow range rider 'Monte Walsh,' likewise broke and busted. Though Monte has an adoring woman, aging prostitute 'Martine,' working in a nearby village, he can't hang up his spurs. Like an old soldier, this old drover prefers to just fade away . . .

Bartending or work as a bouncer? Available, but not for him. He'll live or die a cowboy. When Chet insists the glory days of the trade are now gone, Monte replies in the only manner he can. "It ain't over. As long as there's *one* cowboy still out there, tending to *one* doggie, it *ain't over!*"

If the words are quixotic, Monte an anachronism, he is noble and tragic as well as sadly delusional. Lee Marvin (1924-1987) plays him with a conviction, gusto, integrity, and a three-dimensionality that allows this figure to come across as both a unique individual and an icon of a vanishing breed. Marvin's fans insist that here is the film for which he ought to have won a Best Actor Oscar, rather than the enjoyably goofy *Cat Ballou* (1965). Born to well-to-do New York parents, Lee managed to get himself tossed out of one private school after another. Joining the Marines at the outset of WWII, he was decorated for service in the South Pacific and wounded at the siege of Saipan. Kicking around after the war, he accepted an odd job as a janitor. While cleaning a decrepit theatre, Marvin was asked to do a walk-on for a no-show extra. Next stop, Hollywood. The craggy character actor played maniacal villains in two film classics, the police procedural/noir *The Big Heat* and the original biker flick, *The Wild One*, both 1953. Westerns seemed a natural, including a scene-stealing villain in the cult favorite *7 Men from Now* (1956). Lee played TV's toughest cop as 'Ballinger' on *M Squad* (1957-1960) and was considered as a replacement for Ward Bond on *Wagon Train* when that actor passed away. (The role went instead to kinder, gentler John McIntyre). L.M. embodied the worst villain in the West as the eponymous killer in John Ford's *The Man Who Shot Liberty Valance* (1962); it took two superheroes, John Wayne *and* James Stewart, to put him out of commission. With *The*

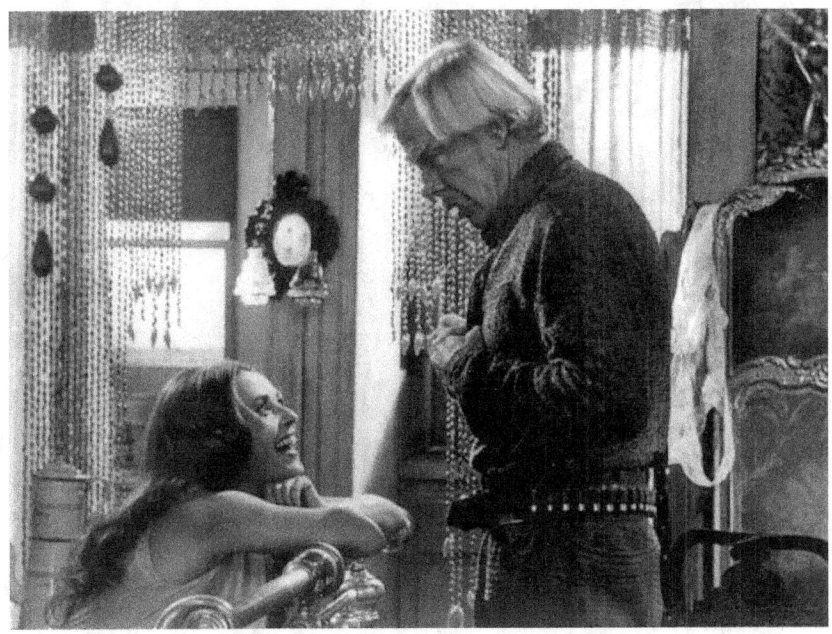

"I THOUGHT ALL YOU FOREIGN WOMEN WERE COUNTESSES OR SOMETHIN' LIKE THAT": In his own silent, sincere way, Monte is truly dedicated to the prostitute (Jeanne Moreau) he visits while 'in town.'

Professionals (1966) and *The Dirty Dozen* (1967), Marvin transformed into a top-billed action star. Sadly, he chose all the wrong roles after *Monte Walsh*, turning down one of the greatest Westerns: *The Wild Bunch*, yet appearing in one of the worst, *The Great Scout and Cathouse Thursday*.

Monte Walsh offers his greatest contribution to the genre. Key sequences stand out in the memory... leading his fellows on the most spectacular wild horse round-up ever filmed, trying to roll and light a cigarette while his lovely bed-mate attempts to win away his attention, playing a dirty trick on the

AT LONG LAST HE GOT TO PLAY A GOOD GUY!: (In)famous as the villain (opposite Alan Ladd) in *Shane*, (Walter) Jack Palance finally had the opportunity to reveal his sensitive side as 'Chet.'

cook and paying dearly for it, confronting a wild wolf that reminds him too much of himself to shoot, tracking down and ruthlessly killing the member of his group ('Shorty') who gave up The Cowboy Way, riding down a wild broncho that supposedly couldn't be tamed . . . Marvin's co-star was likewise no stranger to the genre. Jack Palance (1919-2006) created (as 'Walter Jack Palance') the demonic gunfighter 'Wilson' in *Shane* (1953). Though he effectively portrayed likable anti-heroes on TV's *Playhouse 90* ('Requiem for a Heavyweight' by Rod Serling) and the powerful anti-war mini-epic *Attack!*, both 1956, the public never did warm up to him as an offbeat lead. So on it was to villain after villain, including Attila the Hun in *Sign of the Pagan* (1954) and the kill crazy son of Genghis Khan in *The Mongols* (1963). At least his Mexican outlaw in *The Professionals* with Marvin had been a character worthy of sympathy; that proved true here with the fine and decent Chet as the two former bad men actors revealed that beyond their machismo images existed a potential for sentiment and goodness.

Monte was based on a book by Jack Schaefer (1907-1991), whose contributions to the genre included the novels *Shane*, *Tribute to a Bad Man* (1956), and *Trooper Hook* (1957). Director Fraker (1923-2010) won fame a first-rate cinematographer, 'shooting' such significant films as *Bullitt* and *Rosemary's Baby*, both 1968. Here, he got lucky with the perfect script and

THE GRANDEUR OF A PAINTING BY REMINGTON OR RUSSELL: The visions of the greatest artists of the American West comes alive in the wild horse round-up sequence.

once-in-a-lifetime cast, Fraker was required to do little but capture their memorable antics in Mescal AZ. When assigned to another Western, *The Legend of the Lone Ranger* (1981), he failed miserably and returned to cinematography, a craft at which he proved himself gifted. Yet he does deserve one shot wonder status for this unforgettable if largely unseen if masterful Oater.

BACK WHEN JACK PLAYED THE MAN IN BLACK: The better part of two decades before creating his lovable cowboy in *Monte Walsh*, (Walter) Jack Palance embodied evil incarnate as the gun-slighter 'Wilson' in *Shane*; Elisha Cook Jr. portrays the sad-faced victim while John Dierkes (far right) looks on.

57. MY NAME IS NOBODY (1973) Rating: **** ½

CREDITS:

Tonino Valerli, dir.; Sergio Leone, Fulvio Morsella, Ernesto Gastaldi, scr.; Leone, Claudio Mancini, Fulvio Morsella, pro.; Ennio Morricone, mus.; Armando Nannuzzi, Giuseppe Ruzzoinni, cin.; Nino Paragli, ed.; 2.39:1; C; 116 min.; Titanus.

CAST:

Terence Hill *(Nessuno)*; Henry Fonda *(Jack Beauregard)*; Jean Martin *(Sullivan)*; R.G. Armstrong *(Honest John)*; Karl Braun *(Jim)*; Leo (V.) Gordon *(Red)*; Steve Kanaly *(Fake Barber/Gunslinger)*; Geoffrey Lewis (*Wild Bunch Leader*); Neil Summers *(Squirrel)*; :Piero Lulli *(Sheriff)*; Mario Brega *(Pedro)*; Marc Mazza *(Don John)*; Benito Stefanelli *(Porteley)*; Aexander Allerson *(Rex)*; Rainer Peets *(Big Gun)*; Antoine Saint-John *(Scape)*; Tommy Polgar *(Juan)*; Antonio Palombi *(Dirty)*; Emil Feist *(Carnival Dwarf)*; Carla Mancini *(Mother)*; Angelo Novi *(The 'Real' Bartender)*; Rick Lester, Larry Melton *(Gunmen)*.

So: when is a Sergio Leone (1929-1989) Spaghetti Western *not* a Sergio Leone Spaghetti Western? Here's the film that inspired this question, produced after the release of the *Dollars* trilogy of the mid-1960s and the masterful epic follow-up, *Once Upon a Time in the West* (1968). How to top that classic? Impossible, even for Leone, at least within the realm of this genre. So on to *Once Upon a Time in America* (1984), in which the cinematic master cast his auteurial gaze at the Hollywood gangster film, lovingly reconsidering

JOHN FORD, MOVE OVER!: Henry Fonda, long associated with the Hollywood filmmaker known as 'Pappy,' eventually discovered the European genius Sergio Leone, collaborating together on *Once Upon a Time in the West* (seen here) and, several years later, *My Name Is Nobody*.

cliches and conventions from an intellectual angle. Yet his adoration for the Western had not diminished. Knowing that bigger is not always better, Leone intuited that he needed to scale back. The filmmaker would, as producer, offer a smaller film in terms of budget and scope though no less ambitious as to what had come before as to ideology, politics, and what some argue rates

MEET 'JOHNNY NOBODY': Terence Hill had already become something of a star in spaghetti Westerns thanks to his "Trinity" films when Leone picked him to play the title character here.

as philosophy. Sergio set about writing (and unofficially contributing to the direction, without credit) a cinematic footnote to his previous work in this genre. That meant hiring someone else to officially direct: Tonino Valerli (1934-2016), who had turned out two minor if noteworthy examples of the form, *Taste of Killing* (1966) and *Day of Anger* (1967), as well as adding elements to Ennio Morricone's distinctive music. In time, Quentin Tarantino included some of Valerli's special sounds to his own tribute to the Spaghetti Western, *Django Unchained* (2012).

Throughout the 1960s, Tonino Valeri idolized Leone, wanting to contribute to that master's work in any way he might; also hoping that someday, when Leone moved on, to emerge from his hero's shadow. Their real-life situation inspired Leone to come up with the fictional story we here encounter: Nessuno is the kid who has always admired and followed the career of top gunslinger Jack Beauregard, competing with him by entering into a succession of gunfights, dreaming that someday when J.B. retires, which the aging legend is indeed considering (he wears glasses, his sight failing), pick up where that professional left off. Despite a fantastical Western setting that owes as much to Luis Bunuel and Salvador Dali as it does to John Ford and Howard Hawks, here is a disguised dual autobiography for the filmmakers and their own relationship. In the final sequence, Jack travels from the American frontier (or a purposefully caricatured vision of it) to Europe, suggesting a reversal of Leone's heading off to New York City for his legacy project, allowing Valerli to assume control of what had gone before.

If Leone had in his own work offered the cinematic equivalent of jazz riffs on Tinseltown films, Valerli presents a predecessor to some rap artist's 'sampling' of previous music that the performer most admires. If Leone always limited himself as far as borrowed generic homages to Westerns and Asian Samurai pictures he admired, *Cinema Paradiso* style, while as a child growing up in Italy, Valerli stretches such inclusions further. This innovator incorporates the speeded-up motion of Mack Sennett's famous chase sequences from the silent era and anticipates the full-blown burlesque (rather than Leone's semi-spoofing quality) of Mel Brooks' beloved *Blazing Saddles*, still a year

THE SERGIO LEONE ICONIC MOMENT: The filmmaker recycled a well-remembered confrontation from the earlier *Once Upon a Time in the West* for the crucial pre-showdown image in *My Name Is Nobody*.

away on the cinematic horizon. There's a pie throwing sequence worthy of the Ritz Brothers and a gross slapping scene that will recall *The Three Stooges*. Obtuse references also occur: One of the graves in this crackerjack comedy Western's Boot Hill belongs to Sam Peckinpah. Individual moments recall warm memories of glorious movies that haunt our memories: The shooting-off of one another's hats by the leads reaches back through Leone's Clint Eastwood/Lee Van Cleef friendly enmity in *For a Few Dollars More* (1967) to Gary Cooper and Burt Lancaster in *Vera Cruz* (1954), Robert Aldrich there providing the inspiration for Leone's later redux and Valerli's variation on the theme. The final twist is borrowed directly from *The Fastest Gun Alive* (1956).

Names of minor characters belong to previous figures in Leone's work. Guest appearances by Leo (V.) Gordon, R.G. Armstrong, and Geoffrey Lewis have as much to do with their Western movie iconography as talent. That's of course true of Fonda as the aging marshal. In his much-cherished Western films Fonda played Wyatt Earp twice, once by name (*My Darling Clementine*, 1946), later by implication (*Warlock*, 1959). Likewise, Terence Hill (1939-); this film's title recalls the 'Trinity is Still My Name' films he earlier appeared in. And, of course, this movie's title offers a wonderful twist on its plot. After witnessing J.B. knock off three villains *High Noon* style in the opening sequence, a little boy turns to his father, asking if anyone is faster than this living legend.

"*Nobody* is faster," the dad replies.

Next shot in the film: Terrence Hill embodying a character whose name is, by implication, 'Johnny *Nobody*.'

WHAT A CHARACTER! The casting of R.G. Armstrong (1917-2012) had as much to do with the old-timer's iconic presence as his keen acting abilities; the grim stalwart appeared in such notable Sam Peckinpah films as *Ride the High Country* (1962), *The Wild Bunch* (1969), *The Ballad of Cable Hogue* (1970), and *Pat Garrett and Billy the Kid* (1973).

58. NAKED SPUR, THE (1953)
Rating: *****

CREDITS:

Anthony Mann, dir.; Sam Rolfe, Harold Jack Bloom, scr.; Bronislau Kaper, mus.; William (C.) Mellor, cin.; George White, ed.; 1.37:1; C; 91 min.; Universal.

CAST:

James Stewart (*Howard Kemp*); Janet Leigh (*Lina Patch*); Robert Ryan (*Ben Vandergroat*); Ralph Meeker (*Roy Anderson*); Millard Mitchell (*Jesse Tate*).

The concept here is notably intimate: Five diverse people, four motivated by an obsession with money, thrown together in close proximity while off in the middle of nowhere. That recalls John Huston's *(The) Treasure of the Sierra Madre* as to theme and situation. Also, the two movies have in common a striking horizon of high mountains, here the memorable natural towers overlooking Lone Pine CA. These provide a visual sense of irony, dwarfing the sad little human drama that unfolds below. Like ants viewed from afar, the principals scurry about, struggling to make something out of gorgeous if ungiving natural surroundings as fate stamps down on one after another. This sounds all but identical to the premises of other vivid features in a quintet which director Anthony Mann (1906-1967) directed during the 1950s: *Winchester '73* (1950), *Bend of the River* (1952), *The Far Country* (1954), *The Man from Laramie* (1955), and *Man of the West* (1959). In the first four, James Stewart (1908-1997)), Gary Cooper (in the last) plays a wanderer who initially appears strong, solid, and mostly silent, only to be revealed as a flesh-and-blood barrel

AN ANGEL AND A BADMAN: The ethereal warmth of Janet Leigh (right) contrasted perfectly with the hard-edged cruelty of her virtual owner (Robert Ryan, left) in the highest point of the high country.

of neuroses. In each case, that initial image turns out to be a self-conscious pose, adapted to provide a cover for deep insecurities. On the other hand, those others feature the sensibility of a mighty epic, an important moment in the history of the West as well as taut drama in the characters' lives. Not surprisingly, Borden Chase (1900-1971) had a hand in writing most, bringing to those projects a sense of larger-than-life adventure, as he had for *Red River* (Howard Hawks, 1948). What occurs here more resembles the premise of Luigi Pirandello's "Six Characters in Search of an Author" (1921); in this case, five. Now, though, each lost soul searches not for a scribe but a means of escape, all as trapped by geography and circumstances as the doomed trio in Jean Paul Sartre's "No Exit" (1944).

And, make no mistake about it, this piece's aura likewise rates as existential in nature.

Rather than an easy-going cowpoke who drifts into an intense narrative, here Stewart plays a bounty hunter, such self-serving gunslingers constituting the scum of the West. While not romanticizing 'Howard Kemp,' the movie does humanize him, penetrating the man's rough surface to discover primal

AN ALL-PURPOSE ACTOR/STAR: James Stewart managed the near-impossible task of moving back and forth between genres, from comedy to thrillers to Western roles.

weaknesses that have (as with Randolph Scott's similar anti-hero in *Ride Lonesome*) prohibited this torn man from experiencing a normal life. Initially, Kemp's motive hardly appears pure: Bring in wanted man 'Ben Vandergroat' so the law can hang him, while collecting the cash reward. He embarks on the search not, like a lawman, for moral purposes. Kemp's only motivation? Money.

Or so it initially seems...

While the surface drama concerns the near-impossible task of bringing the fugitive back, Kemp's inner journey gradually emerges. Is regeneration even possible? Not, certainly, for two of his companions. 'Lt. Roy Anderson' (Ralph Meeker, 1926-1988), a dishonorably discharged serviceman, cannot conceive of any possible reason to complete the job but a big payoff. Failed miner 'Jesse Tate' (Millard Mitchell, 1903-1953) views this as his last chance to strike it rich. "Simple arithmetic," they agree; a mighty $5,000 reward split two ways adds a greater profit margin than if divided between all three. Neither would mind it if Kemp were to die along the way. We return, then, to a key recurring theme of The Western. For these are raw capitalists, as obsessed with cold hard coins as the two sad people who stand off against one another in the merciless sun of Death Valley in Eric von Stroheim's iconic *Greed* (1924), each ready and willing to die to keep the other man from achieving the fortune. At which point a growing obsession morphs into virtual insanity.

That, however, is not how things work out. For a woman is present: The teenage vagabond 'Lina' (Janet Leigh, 1927-2004). A country girl without education or experience, she has been seized by the killer as an unofficial bondservant and, by implication, sex slave. Yet a radical innocence in her character exerts a power to inspire a man's redemption; if not for her master, then the potential liberator. To capture the purity of her soul, composer Bronislau Kaper (1902-1983) drew on Stephen Foster's 1864 composition "Beautiful Dreamer" (1864) for this character's theme. Romantic in a manner Mann otherwise avoids, such an approach works in context, particularly when the haunting ballad is juxtaposed with Leigh's ethereal beauty.

THE GOOD, THE BAD, THE BEAUTIFUL, AND THE UGLY: The supporting cast in this closet drama ironically shot in the great outdoors included some of the finest actors in the business: Millard Mitchell, Robert Ryan, Janet Leigh, and Ralph Meeker.

Lina is unconcerned with money. However naïve, she believes Ben is innocent of the crime he obviously did commit. She 'sticks with him,' as long as she can cling to this belief. When truth will out, she has already fallen in love with Kemp, sensing there is something more to him . . . and his reason for being here . . . than has yet surfaced. While Kemp is only half-conscious owing to an accident on the trail, he believes Lina to be his lost wife, Molly. Meanwhile, Lina's keen mind grasps that Kemp hides (again, like Scott six years later in *Ride Lonesome*) a deep secret, desperate and non-monetary reason for his relentless pursuit of this particular lawbreaker. In truth, what he truly wants is not a reward but a reckoning.

Life is about choices. Kemp can have both the girl and the gold, though he will forever lose his humanity. Or he might bury the evil man's body and, with it, his horrid past. That will allow Kemp and his High Country inamorata to head on to California, where the two may not only live but be reborn in the Biblical sense of discovering a second Eden. Up until the final, unforgettable shot, which no one who has ever seen this film can ever forget, we have no idea whether he will see the light and win a final act to his sad life or embrace the darkness, once more and (this being his final chance) forever.

BEAUTIFUL DREAMER: The ethereal loveliness of the young Janet Leigh, as well as her gentle ways, helps to redeem the lost soul of a hardened bounty hunter.

59. NED KELLY (2003)
Rating: ****

CREDITS:

Gregor Jordan, dir.; John Michael McDonagh, scr.; Lynda House, Nelson Woss, Tim Bevan, many others, pro.; Klaus Abdelt, Bernard Fanning, mus.; Oliver Stapeton, cin.; Jon Gregory, ed.; 2.35:1; C; 110 min.; The Woss Group/Working Title Films.

CAST:

Heath Ledger (*Ned Kelly*); Orlando Bloom (*Joseph Byrne*); Naomi Watts (*Julia Cook*); Geoffrey Rush (*Francis Hare*); Joel Edgerton (*Aaron Sherritt*); Laurence Kilan (*Dan Kelly*); Philip Baratini (*Steve Hart*); Kerry Condon (*Kate Kelly*); Kris McQuade (*Ellen*); Emily Browning (*Grace*); Kiri Paramore (*Constable Fitzpatrick*); Rachel Griffiths (*Susan Scott*); Geoff Morrell (*Robert*); Peter Phelps (*Lonigan*); Charles 'Bud' Tingwell (*Premier Graham Berry*); Saska Burnmeister (*Jane Jones*); Russell Dykstra (*Wild Wright*); Nick Farnell (*Lloyd*) Brooke Harman (*Maggie*); Anthony O'Neill, Paddy O'Neill, Steve Simmonds (*Musicians*) Jida Gulpllil (*Aboriginal Tracker*).

Ought the Australian (or 'Down Under') Western be considered a subgenre of The Western Movie as originated in America, or a genre unto itself? Might as well ask that question about Spaghetti, Paella, or for that matter Israeli Oaters. Do note, though: shot in far corners of the world, all take place in a land (more mythic than historic) that can be called 'the frontier' as it once existed in the United States. An Australian Western, however, is more likely to take place . . . well . . . 'Down Under.' In place of the wilderness, there exists

HELLO, YOUNG LOVERS: Though the film presents its title character (Heath Ledger) as an unassuming lad enjoying a lark with a pretty girl, history suggests he may have actually been a well-known juvenile delinquent as well as horse-thief.

the Outback. Instead of Indians, Aborigines. Prairie dogs give way to kangaroos though cattle remain essential to each. The Northern Carpetbaggers who pressed down upon post-Civil War Southerners, forcing dirt farmers to become outlaws, give way to uninvited British Coppers, imposing their will on humble Irish immigrants living there. Rough policeman Alan Pinkerton's natural counterpart, Francis Hare (1830-1892), determines to end the banditry with, if necessary, genocidal violence. Jesse James, the criminal often considered a Robin Hood by poor Missouri working folk, gives way for Ned Kelly (1854-1880). Of course, robbing from the poor is not a particularly smart decision, be it in the U.S.A. or anywhere in the world; how much (if anything) James or Kelly really gave away is debatable.

Like James' long riders, Kelly's 'bushrangers' are often perceived more as social bandits than common criminals; defenders of an ethnic underclass, turning to robbery and killing only as a last resort, pushed to the limit by Anglo invaders. Refusing to accept status as underlings, they eventually fight back, even as the peons of Mexico including Emiliano Zapata and Pancho Villa did against the French Aristocrats who had seized control that country. Significantly, though, that vision of such men is but one interpretation. One man's noble outlaw is another's hardened criminal. As for Kelly, he emerged as an international figure of outlawry before either Jesse James or William H. Bonney (Billy the Kid) were immortalized by American filmmakers, A 1906 motion picture (some film historians consider it the first true feature film) brought in audiences to Nickelodeons and early theatres. At least part of Kelly's unique appeal had to do with a curious if fascinating detail: during the siege of Glenrowan, during which his gang was wiped out, Kelly wore a suit of armour. Whereas New Mexico lawman Pat Garrett found himself to be widely condemned, rather than celebrated, for shooting down the Kid, already a local legend at the time of his (presumed) passing in 1881, so too did the dedicated policeman Hare face contempt for bringing back alive 'The Beloved Bandit.' While those in power determined Kelly to be a final force of chaos in a swiftly modernizing civilization, to the people of the Bush, he represented the other side of that coin: Freedom.

TARGET PRACTICE: Like the police who relentlessly pursue them, members of the Kelly gang dutifully learn to shoot straight and squarely while engaging in outlawry 'down under.'

One of the earliest sequences allows us to grasp the approach that director Jordan (1966-) and screenwriter McDonagh (1967-) will assume throughout this balladic piece. Note too that their film was not based on one of several existing historical works about Kelly but a 1991 novel, *Our Sunshine*, by Robert Drew. What we watch is cinematic fiction derived from literary fiction, drawn from a moment of history already told and retold to the point that whatever actually occurred at that time, in that place, becomes difficult (if not impossible) to determine. Here, young Kelly relaxes in a pastoral area of their wilderness. He spots two other living creatures: A gorgeous white horse, obviously a runaway, and a lovely girl, whom he would like to impress. So he captures the mount, then draws her up behind him; a nice, normal teenage fellow on a bit of a lark. But when Ned rides into the nearest town to drop her off and turn the horse over to local authorities, he's accosted (for no reason other than social class) by a mean-spirited British policeman who falsely accuses the appealing lad of horse-thievery. Then it's off to prison as the utter innocent is sentenced to three years behind bars. The effective filmmaking on view here, its perfectly controlled lighting and color combining to suggest a vivid sense of the past as it once was, will convince an audience this is the way it must have been. As always, there's another way of considering the situation. Hardly a gentle child-man, Kelly was widely thought to be something of a juvenile delinquent, known to have experienced earlier unpleasant encounters regarding authorities. There are those who insist the horse had indeed been stolen.

So: Which was it? As always, perception is reality for each and every observer.

Ultimately, this simplified (that is not intended as a criticism) umpteenth retelling of this tale will maintain a special place in the history of film owing to the standout performance by Heath Ledger (1979-2008). Something of a latter-day James Dean, his rebel image and early death enhances the charisma experienced by viewers every time such a person steps in front of a camera. Anger, bitterness, youthful confusion, and an outrage at a surrounding universe that cannot even begin to comprehend such an individual's inner

THE RETURN OF KNIGHTS IN ARMOR: For their last stand, members of the Kelly Gang dress up as men of iron like the ancient heroes they admired.

torment and hysterical reactions are all there ... and the image is too mesmerizing for anyone to ever look away.

60. OKLAHOMA KID, THE (1939) Rating: ****

CREDITS:

Lloyd Bacon, dir.; Warren Duff, Robert Bruckner, Edward E. Paramore Jr., scr.; Jack L. Warner, Hal B. Wallis, Samuel Bischoff; Max Steiner, mus.; James Wong Howe, cin.; Owen Marks, ed.; 1.37:1; B&W; 85 min.; Warner Bros.

CAST:

James Cagney (*Jim Kincaid*); Humphrey Bogart (*Whip McCord*); Rosemary Lane (*Jane Hardwick*); Donald Crisp (Judge Hardwick); Harvey Stephens (*Ned Kincaid*); Hugh Sothern (*John Kincaid*); Charles Middleton (*Alec Martin*); Edward Pawley (*Doolin*); Ward Bond (*Wes Handley*); Lew Harvey (*Curley*); Trevor Bardette (*Indian Jack Pasco*); John Milian (*Ringo*); Arthur Avelsworth (*Morgan*); Irving Bacon (*Hotel Clerk*); Joe Devlin (*Keely*); Wade Boteler (*Sheriff*); Clem Bevans (*Postman*); Tex Cooper, Jack Curtis (*Townsmen*).

While not a flop per se, *The Oklahoma Kid* was one of those films that no one at Warner's knew precisely how to market. The male stars were best known for their contemporary urban crime dramas. James Cagney (1899-1986) had embodied the arrogant punk following a classic, *The Public Enemy* (1931); Humphrey Bogart (1899-1957) while not yet the superstar he would become, played tight-lipped, sadistic thugs in strong Depression-era items like *The Petrified Forest* (1936). The two squared off in *The Roaring Twenties* (1939), which some film historians rate as the best of the black-and-white

DEEP IN THE HEART OF THE WEST...A STAR FROM OUT OF THE EAST: Long associated with New York or Chicago gangster type roles, James Cagney struck most viewers as an odd choice for a frontier anti-hero.

proto-noirs released by Warner Bros. While everyone rushed to see that picture, audiences proved a bit more standoffish as to this rematch.

Bogie and Cagney . . . in a *Western*?

Somehow, that seemed odd. When Bogart's unkind comment that, in his high-reaching hat, co-star Cagney resembled "a mushroom" went public, *Oklahoma Kid* came to be perceived as something of a joke/misfire. When cultural critic Susan Sontag framed the artistic politics of 'camp' in the mid-Sixties---old movies we love because they're so bad that they're great, in their own unique way---this film was revived along with over-the-top Carmen Miranda musicals and Jon Hall/Maria Montez florid costume flicks. Setting that vision of the film aside at last, perhaps now we may be able to appreciate *Kid* for the first-rate Western it is . . . and in truth always ways.

AND BOGIE AS THE BADGUY? Humphrey Bogart played the evil foil to Cagney in the memorable gangster epic *The Roaring Twenties*, but a black garbed villain

First, the piece takes as its subject the Oklahoma Land Rush of 1889, which inspired key sequences in two silent classics, William S. Hart's *Tumbleweeds* (1925) and John Ford's *3 Bad Men* (1926), as well as one of the rare Oscar Best Picture Winning Westerns, *Cimarron* (1931). The similar sequence here compares favorably with the spectacular stunt-work in such earlier movies, though by this time the once-exciting incident had grown a bit old hat for filmgoers. What distinguishes this film's depiction is the growing consciousness in America as to mistreatment of the Native American. In *Oklahoma Kid*, there are 'the good' and 'the bad' among incoming pioneers: The former, those honest, hard-working capitalists who play by the rules and set out to earn their fortunes, American Dream-style, through the hard work of farming, while building a decent outpost of civilization. The latter: 'Sooners' who slip across the starting line early as part of their ruggedly individualistic, self-serving attempts to gain power and cash by any means possible, however

WELCOME TO LONE PINES: The Northern California on location work lent a strikingly authentic appearance to the wide open spaces wherein Cagney and Bogie play cat and mouse games on horseback.

illegal and immoral. They shortly create a Ten Percent Ring that demands payment money from humble settlers, set up saloons and gambling palaces instead of schools and churches, and firmly stands against statehood for fear that federal intervention would put an end to their raw, corrupt form of getting rich quick.

In a sense, such characters---led by the big bad boss Whip McCord---represent the historical concept of organized crime on the frontier as an equivalent of the gangs/mobs that would emerge in the East. In a sense, then, *Kid* suggests that Westerns are indeed Gangster films set during an earlier period and different geographical location. This diminishes the notion that Cagney is grossly miscast (some would say 'ridiculously'); the film may alternately be defended as one of the rare Oaters that gets the situation 'right.' Though there was no single outlaw known by that nickname, this film's Kid appears all but identical to Billy the Kid, who was in fact a fugitive from the New York slums (SEE: *Dirty Little Billy*). With that in mind, how better a choice Cagney is than a Lone Star accented traditional cowboy like Audie Murphy. In the most famous photo taken of Billy Bonney during his lifetime, the kid appears like . . . well . . . a big mushroom!

Again, there is the forward-looking approach to Indians' rights. *T.O.K.* begins not in the West but Washington D.C., where the president and members of congress cynically agree to break their solemn treaties with Native People to exploit rich potential farmlands. Later, the title character notes the abject cynicism of how the deal was negotiated. True, our government did indeed 'pay' Indians for the lands taken away from them. However, they received less than ten percent of what the fertile plains were worth. Here, then, was a clear case of 'legal thievery' by the Anglos who ran America at the time. Notably, *T.O.K.* was the first film to make clear that beyond our myth of a wonderful Expansion, a despicable form of Imperialism existed as well.

Oklahoma Kid effectively forwards the tradition of so many other Westerns: Collapsing various aspects of frontier history, with no actual relationship to one another, into a single narrative for the purpose of creating a legendary epic. In addition to the Kid's adventures in New Mexico and the settlement of the Cimarron territories, there is a strong sense of the Wyatt Earp adventures in Tombstone. Wyatt's motivation for 'the vengeance ride' following the O.K. Corral was the assassination of brother Morgan by members of the Clanton/McLowery bunch. Here, the Kid's father is murdered by a lynch mob. Among the villains that the film's Kid pursues are ones named Curly, Ringo, and 'Indian Jack'; they stand in for Brocious, Ringgold, and 'Indian Charlie' in Arizona legends. The Kid does away with an assassin (played by Ward Bond) on a railway car; that's how Earp dispatched Frank Stillwell. With these elements in mind, *The Oklahoma Kid* emerges as a far more impressive (and less laughable) work than previously thought.

WHEN MEN WAS MEN AND WOMEN WAS WOMEN? This seemingly innocuous staged/PR image of Rosemary Lane and James Cagney actually reveals a profound truth about the historic West: Females were as likely to wear pants and carry guns as their male counterparts.

61. ONE EYED JACKS (1961)
Rating: **** ½

CREDITS:

Marlon Brando, dir.; Guy Trosper, Calder Willingham, scr.; George Glass, Frank P. Rosenberg, Walter Seltzer, pro.; Hugo Friedhofer, mus.; Charles Lang, cin.; 1.85:1; C; 121 min. (theatrical print); 607 min. (director's cut, now believed lost); Pennebaker Prods./Paramount.

CAST:

Marlon Brando (*Rio*); Karl Malden *('Dad' Longworth*); Katy Jurado (*Maria*); Ben Johnson (*Bob Amory*); Pina Pellicier (*Louisa*); Slim Pickens (*Lon Dedrick*); Larry Duran (*Chico*); Sam Gilman (*Harvey*); Timothy Carey *(Howard Tetley)*; Mirian Colon (*'Red'*); Elisha Cook Jr. (*Carvey*); Rudolfo Acosta (*Rurale*); Tom Webb (*Farm Boy*); John Dierkes (*Chet*); Philip Ahn (*Uncle*); Margarita Cordova (*Nika*); Hank Worden (*Doc*); Eric Alden, Mickey Finn (*The Blacksmith*).

The most prominent Method actor of the 1950s, Marlon Brando (1924-2004) happened upon an obscure if notable novel "The Authentic Death of Henry Jones" by Russian émigré Charles Neider, based on the Billy the Kid myth (Bonney's first name was 'Henry.') The penultimate episode, in which the Kid finds himself in a jail manned by a pair of deputies, one cruel and the other good-natured, is drawn from an incident in New Mexico history. The narrative inspired Brando to take on the task of transforming this intriguing volume into his own epic Western. The first cut (for Pennebaker indie productions) ran well over five hours. When co-producer Paramount balked at the thought of attempting to sell

THE SHAPE OF THINGS TO COME: In his only directorial venture, star Marlon Brando set the pace for such future Existential Westerns as *The Good, the Bad, and the Ugly.*

such a lengthy piece to the general public, Brando vowed to never again embark on a highly personal project. Yet this compromised, fascinating, flawed film has developed an ever-enlarging cult following thanks to Quentin Tarantino, the influential moviemaker, who picked *One Eyed Jacks* as one of his favorite Westerns.

Pursued by a Mexican posse, 'The Kid' and his key companion, nicknamed Dad, split up; the latter takes their only horse, promising to acquire fresh mounts and return. Once at a ranch, however, 'Dad' has second thoughts. With two bags of stolen gold, he heads north to create a new life above the Rio Grande Likely, Rio has been killed or escaped on his own. In fact, the youth was captured, spending five years in prison. Once he and another convict, 'Chico,' escape, the Kid has but one interest: Vengeance, that great motivation in so many iconic Westerns. Rio heads to the town where his betrayer is sheriff, feigning friendliness. In truth, he hopes to kill the man he once referred to as Dad ... adding an Oedipal sense to the story ... after first destroying the man's enviable life. To achieve this, Rio sets out to seduce Dad's virginal stepdaughter, even as Chico and two other gunslingers prepare to rob the local bank. What the Kid didn't count on: Falling in love with the gentle girl he has impregnated.

Early on, Sam Peckinpah contributed to the adaptation. Though he does not receive credit, the future writer-director's vision appears in embryo. A key

WHAT WOMEN WANT: Despite the considerable machismo displayed onscreen, Brando's Western pays particular attention to the desires and needs of the story's female characters (Katy Jurado, Pina Pellicier).

theme in *Ride the High Country* (1962), *Major Dundee* (1965), *The Wild Bunch* (1969) and (most notable in this context) *Pat Garrett and Billy the Kid* (1972) is the appearance of such tragic drama. As to *Wild Bunch*, 'Thornton' (Robert Ryan) deserted his friend in a brothel when *federales* closed in. Their conflict parallels the issue here: Does an outlaw have a right to save oneself, or should pardners go down fighting together, as in the non-Peckinpah *Butch Cassidy and the Sundance Kid?* Dad's unforgivable sin: Though he rode with Rio, he didn't stick with him. Also, Peckinpah can be credited with bringing onboard several actors who would become members of his own post-Fordian stock company. Slim Pickens (1919-1983) as a bullying lawman and Ben Johnson (1918-1996) in the role of a shady thief add to the verisimilitude, as does the magnificent Katy Jurado (1924-2002), eventually co-starring in *Pat Garrett...*, Peckinpah's variation on the same legend that inspired this film.

During the period that Peckinpah remained onboard, Stanley Kubrick was to direct. Lest we forget, he would hire Pickens to play the cowboy-ish airman who bull-rides an atomic bomb down to Russia in *Dr. Strangelove* (1964). Also present is another Kubrick favorite, Timothy Agoglia Carey (1929-1994), a hit man in *The Killing* (1956) and a doomed WWI French soldier in *Paths of Glory* (1958). The edgy scene-stealer here incarnates a stark raving mad drunk, providing the Brando character with an excuse to engage in an intriguingly staged gunfight. The quick (and unique) cutting between these opponents, designed by the director and his editor, attests to Brando's undeveloped potential as a total filmmaker. This is evident in his insistence on finding fresh settings for conventional situations. Instead of what we think of as The Wild West, Brando chose to shoot on California's coastline, primarily on the surf at Big Sur. Though the wearing of a serape by the Anglo anti-hero has a precedent in *The Wonderful Country* (1958), Rio here makes it iconic, influencing Sergio Leone's then in embryo Spaghetti Westerns starring Clint Eastwood. As for Brando, he would don this guise again in *The Appaloosa* (1966).

The theme of betrayal dominates. Before the conclusion, every character betrays at least one other. With the exception of humble Paco, an unconventional, positive portrait of a Mexican peasant who pays for his loyalty with

A HEIGHTENED LEVEL OF VIOLENCE: As the 1960s wore on, the level of brutality depicted onscreen (here, Karl Malden whips Brando) in Westerns would constantly increase, with *The Good, the Bad, and the Ugly* and *The Wild Bunch* 'taking it to the limit' near the decade's end.

his life. In Nouveau Westerns, no good deed here goes unpunished. Likewise, Brando deeply believed (as did the playwright Luigi Pirandello, whom Brando admired) that Aristotle's age-old dictum, "art is an imitation of life," might be reversed. If we accept the action of the movie as, while watching, life itself, note that every character plays a role for the others. Even the seemingly pure Louisa lies to her father at a key moment. In the World According to Marlon, real life is a form of improvised street theatre.

The film is compromised by a happy (perhaps more fairly 'bittersweet') ending. Though Rio and Louisa part, it is suggested they will reunite. Brando's original (tragic) ending: Louisa was hit by a bullet that dying Dad had intended for Rio. Certain they have escaped, the Kid reigns in to watch Louisa pass away in his arms, then rides off alone. More lonely even than before. He, the ultimate victim of his own nasty strategy.

62. 100 RIFLES (1969)
Rating: **** ½

CREDITS:

Tom Gries, dir.; Gries, Clair Huffaker, scr.; Marvin Schwartz, pro.; Jerry Goldsmith, mus.; Cecilio Paniagua, cin.; Robert (L.) Simpson, ed.; 1.85:1; C; 110 min.; 20th Century-Fox.

CAST:

Raquel Welch (*Sarita*); Jim Brown (*Lyedecker*); Burt Reynolds (*Yaqui Joe*); Fernando Lamas (*Verdugo*); Dan O'Herlihy (*Grimes*); Hans Gudegast, aka Eric Braeden (*Von Klemme*); Michael Forest (*Humara*); Aldo Sambrell (*Sgt. Paletes*); Soledad Miranda (*Girl in Hotel Room*); Charly Bravo (*Lopez*); Alberto Dalbes (*Franciscan Padre*); John Manuel Martin (*Sarita's Father*); Akim Tamiroff (*Gen. Romero*); Lorenzo Lamas *(Indian Boy)*.

On January 1, 1959, even as the United States remained in the final days of the Eisenhower Era and simultaneous Cold War, guerrilla/revolutionary Fidel Castro succeeded in his five-year struggle to overtake Cuba from tyrant Fulgencio Batista. At once, a sense of unease consumed America's business and military interests. Were the Soviets about to build atomic missile sites close to the tip of Florida? Would economic interests, ranging from major corporations to Mafia gambling houses, be shut down? Hollywood, always eager to reflect contemporary world situations in timely films, was stymied as to whether their product should exalt or dismiss the people's movement toward freedom. How then to address the pressing reality without inciting controversy? By doing what artists have done for ages: Seize upon some

SEX SELLS!: The reigning screen beauty of her time, Raquel Welch refused to appear nude in films but willingly posed for provocative images that amply displayed her remarkable physique.

aspect of history, then create a period-piece which by implication allows for a commentary on modern times. The Mexican Revolution of 1912 offered a rich possibility. Producers had been focusing on that Civil War throughout the 1950s with such features as *The Americano* and *The Treasure of Pancho Villa* (both 1955) and *Bandido!* (1956), these B+ features green-lighted even as Castro's underground army made headlines. In them, Western stars Rory Calhoun, Glenn Ford, and Robert Mitchum portrayed Anglo heroes who drift south of the border to make their fortunes only to find themselves drawn into the great cause owing to a beautiful woman of enlightened political conscience.

That occurs here as a Federal Deputy Marshal, 'Lyedecker,' crosses the Rio Grande in pursuit of an outlaw who robbed a bank in Arizona. That is 'Yaqui Joe,' initially shaping up as yet another retro-vision of the 'half breed' (in modern P.C. terms, a person of mixed racial background): a drunken,

A WOMAN TO REMEMBER: Raquel Welch can hold her own even against macho men Burt Reynolds and Jim Brown.

selfish, misogynistic ne'er do well. Like earlier incarnations of such figures, Joe displays such behaviour during Act One. Then comes a key turning point: we discover that he did not rob the money to provide for himself, rather to pay for a cache of arms. The guns will be distributed to the Native Americans, oppressed for four centuries by aristocratic Spanish landowners. These near-fascistic forces of oppression are led in Senora by the heartless, strutting martinet 'Verdugo.' The oppressor does not stand alone. On a military level, Germany's 'Von Klemm'; has arrived to serve as an 'advisor'; what he hopes for is an alliance with Mexico's European-born tyrants for his homeland. Also tugging on Verdugo's shirtsleeves: A capitalist from the U.S., 'Grimes,' who represents the railroad interests back home and their financial investments here. Though initially Grimes sides with those in power, he amorally changes positions the moment that the rebels seize the upper hand. The leftists' Joan of Arc figure is 'Sarita,' a hero of the people who not only nurses wounded men but raises a rifle high, symbolizing strong women favored by feminists even then making their values known when *Rifles* was released.

Latina star Raquel Welch (1940-) would often turn to Westerns, the genre in which her limited acting abilities allowed the beauty to emerge as a latter-day Jane Russell-style rugged-woman. Other roles in the genre include *Bandolero!* (1968), *Hannie Calder* (1971), and *The Legend of Walks Far Woman* (1980), a TV Movie salute to Native American women which she herself produced. *The 100 Rifles* screenplay by Clair Huffaker (1926-1990), known for such earlier Westerns as *Flaming Star* (1960), downplays Brown's character's color, at the heart of *Rio Conchos* a mere five years earlier. By taking such a nouveau approach, the filmmakers were able to emphasizes his identity as a typical American Everyman. Like Humphrey Bogart as 'Richard Blaine' in *Casablanca* (1943), initially an anti-hero, Lyedecker must do the right thing by arcing from self-serving rugged individualist to righteous supporter of the community; a true old-fashioned hero even as Bogie emerged as such in that more famous film's warmly-remembered final shot. Also, we can trace the success of the Civil Rights Movement in America during this decade by focusing on Brown's Westerns. If in 1964

They Went That-A-Way

BREAKING DOWN OLD BARRIERS: Hard as it may be to believe today, *100 Rifles* proved controversial in its time for daring to depict a black man and white (though in truth Raquel was ethnic, a Latina) in love ... and in each other's arms.

his blackness (in *Rio Conchos*) had to be considered a key element in the drama, by decade's end, The Good Fight had advanced considerably. Here, his race is casually mentioned in passing. Two years later, in *El Condor*, Brown will play a similar hero in a narrative that never raises the issue of ethnicity, suggesting that as a nation we had (hopefully!) progressed. He is presented as a person in an adventure tale, precisely as a white performer would be.

Here we also experience another example of Hollywood's oldest conventions: The Romantic Triangle, two fascinating men in love with the same remarkable woman as in Stanley Kramer's *The Pride and the Passion* (1957), set during the Napoleonic Wars. There, sophisticated Cary Grant and rough-hewn peasant Frank Sinatra became wary co-conspirators owing to each hero's obsession with lovely revolutionary Sophia Loren. Important too is that at the end of *100 Rifles*, similar that film from a dozen years earlier, the messianic woman does indeed die for the good cause . . . The People. Leaving the male heroes to, in the final sequence, to conclude the Hawksian 'love story between men.' Implying that *100 Rifles*, like macho movies reaching back at least to *Red River* (1948) with John Wayne and Montgomery Clift, as well as *Butch Cassidy and the Sundance Kid* the same year as this less known film, is more often than not what the Western---whatever other changes occur to its form---is all about.

THE 'LATIN LOVER' INCARNATE: When not busy romancing such stars as Lana Turner and Esther Williams onscreen, Fernando Lamas often 'went west' as a hero or, in the case of *100 Rifles*, villain.

63. PALEFACE, THE (1948)
Rating: ****

CREDITS:

Norman Z. McLeod, dir.; Edmund (L.) Hartman, Frank Tashlin, Jack Rose, Mel Shavelson, many others, scr.; Robert L. Welch, pro.; Victor Young, mus.; Ray Rennahan, cin.; Ellsworth Hoagland, ed.; 1.37:1; C; 91 min.; Paramount.

CAST:

Bob Hope *('Painless' Peter Potter)*; Jane Russell *(Calamity Jane)*; Robert Armstrong *(Terris)*; Idris Adrian *(Pepper)*; Bobby Watson *(Toby)*; Jackie Searl *(Jasper)*; Joseph Vitale *(The Scout)*; Charles Trowbridge *(Gov. Johnson)*; Clem Bevans *(Hank Billngs)*; Jeff York *(Big Joe)*; Stanley Andrews *(Commissioner Emerson)*; Wade Crosby *(Jeb)*; Chief Yowlachie *(Yellow Feather)*; Iron Eyes Cody *(Iron Eyes)*; John Maxwell *(Village Gossip)*; Tom Kennedy *(Bartender)*; Henry Brandon *(Wapato)*; Trevor Bardette *(Rider)*; Lane Chandler, Kermit Maynard *(Cowboys)*.

"A joke," nihilist philosopher Friedrich Nietzsche once claimed, "is an epitaph on an emotion." Here, screenwriter (and sometimes zany animator) Frank Tashlin (1913-1972) had such a concept in mind for the film that would become 'The Paleface.' Initially he imagined the iconic/seminal Western *The Virginian* done once again, only this time played as broad comedy, spoofing not only that well-known work but the genre in its entirety up until that point in time. Had that film come into being, it would have been the *Blazing Saddles* of its time. Once in the hands of Paramount producer Robert L. Welch (1910-1964), the concept altered/evolved into a star

BEFORE *BLAZING SADDLES*, THERE WAS . . . : Remarkably popular in its time, surprisingly forgotten today, *Paleface* remains one of the great spoofs of the Oater, though only if one can manage to deal with the extraordinarily offensive portrayal of Native Americans in the context of retro-Hollywood ethnic stereotyping.

project for Bob Hope (1903-2003), that studio's most popular comedy star. A round-up of other writers, some with a little experience as to Westerns but admired for their gag-writing talents, took the project far from a burlesque of Owen Wister's classic tale. In fact, only one sequence . . . in which the inept would-be hero 'Painless' stalks (and is simultaneously stalked by) murderous/treacherous 'Big Jo' on a deserted street . . recalls Wister's conclusion. Here, in a reversal of the original, good man and bad peer down the wrong alleys, each unaware that his adversary is literally standing back-to-back with him, such tired clichés now open to parody.

If there is a direct predecessor to *Paleface*, it's *Destry Rides Again*. Not the 1930 novel by Max Brand, a pulp fiction tale of serious vengeance, but the 1939 movie starring James Stewart as a seemingly inept sheriff, mistaken for a coward, eventually proving himself braver than any other range rider. Here, that paradigm is turned inside out. Dentist Painless Peter Potter is indeed a coward, though circumstances cause him to be hailed as a bold Indian fighter. When push comes to shove, will he rise to the occasion? Here's a role tailor made for Hope, associated with such parts in WWII comedies and his delightful Road extravaganzas with Bing Crosby. *Paleface* might be viewed less as a comedy Oater than a standard Bob Hope vehicle set, this time around, in the West. The supremely cynical star here worked with director Norm McCleod (1895-1964), an old and sure hand at humor who guided The Marx Bros. through *Monkey Business* (1931) and *Horse Feathers* (1932).

The tale plays out on a frontier where the inevitable wagon train must pass through Indian country. That Native Americans were often the butt of crude/

"HOW'D YOU LIKE TO TUSSLE WITH RUSSELL?": However offensive to the feminist sensibility, that was the phrase employed by Howard Hughes to publicize his controversial 'sex Western,' The Outlaw; that film's popularity led to the actress being regularly cast in Westerns throughout her career.

cruel jokes in old Hollywood movies more or less goes without saying. Yet *Paleface* appears to go out of its way to (from our present perspective) offend. At one point, a chief imbibes some of the dentist's laughing gas, leading to frantic sight gags that elicited laughter way back then but will shock even the least P.C. person today. If there is indeed a line of defense, it must be this: The sequence is hysterical, every bit as much as when Hope himself is previously and later portrayed with much unsparing ridicule. If the Native shares such comedy antics with an Anglo, can the filmmakers truly by attacked for caricaturing an ethnic people when they likewise make just as much fun of the Whites? The point is, everyone on view is made to appear silly.

Perhaps that numbs the pain a bit. Perhaps . . .

One complaint that can't be levelled against this piece is sexism. The female lead, a legendary rather than realistic take on Calamity Jane, is played by Jane Russell (1921-2011). A major sex star long before she ever appeared on the screen, this 'discovery' of entrepreneur Howard Hughes. Russell first

"MY NAME NOW TWO-JAW CROW!" Best remembered today as the assistant cook to Walter Brennan in Howard Hawks' *Red River*, Chief Yowlachie appears in Paleface playing an extreme caricature that will shock modern viewers.

starred in *The Outlaw* (1943), a once notorious Sex Western most theatre-owners were too nervous to book until three years after its completion, when censorship loosened up considerably during the new morality of the postwar era. Here she played, to say the least, a new kind of female Westerner . . . not the meek schoolmarm from the East who questions her rugged man's employment of gun violence to achieve his ends (*The Virginian*) or a bad girl (half-Indian, half-Mexican at that) who coldly seduces him (*In Old Arizona*). Rather, an equal, as bad to the bone as he (Billy the Kid in that film) and, in movies to come (*Paleface* included) superior at what previously had been considered macho behavior. The Tough Girl incarnate (and initiator of those rough women who inhabit the super-women of today's fantastical films), Russell at one point allows a terrified Hope to leap into her arms, carrying

"NOW, THIS IS GOING TO HURT YOU MORE THAN IT DOES ME . . ." As a frontier dentist nicknamed 'Painless,' Bob Hope had ample opportunity to employ his comedic skills, at times appearing to be a living cartoon on the order of those created by animator Frank Tashlin.

him to safety: A reverse of the old Male Rescue Myth that feminists detest. Russell would play another such role, again opposite Hope, in *Son of Paleface* (1953), which also features Roy Rogers and Trigger. In that film, she gets to sing the pop hit song "Buttons, Bangles, and Beads," introduced here.

That same year, J.R. would incarnate Belle Starr in *Montana Belle*. Future Oaters included an "A" feature *The Tall Men* (1955) opposite Clark Gable and Robert Ryan. Eventually, there would be bottom of the barrel "B's such a *Johnny Reno* (1966). *The Paleface* remains her best showcase in defining the future for women . . . ever stronger women in Hollywood Westerns to come.

A TRUE CRACKER BARREL CHARACTER ACTOR: One of the old-timers in this film is played by the much beloved Clem Bevins, seen here with Fess Parker (left) in *Disney's Davy Crockett and the River Pirates*.

64. PILLARS OF THE SKY (1956)
Rating: ****

CREDITS:

George Marshall, dir.; Sam Rolfe, scr.; Robert Arthur, pro.; William Lava, Heinz Roemheld, mus.; Harold Lipstein, cin.; Milton Carruth, ed.; 2.35:1; C; 95 min.; Universal- International.

CAST:

Jeff Chandler (*Sgt. Emmett Bell*); Dorothy Malone (*Calla Gaxton*); Ward Bond (*Dr. Joseph Holden*); Keith Andes (*Capt. Tom Gaxton*); Lee Marvin (*Sgt. Lloyd Carracart*); Sydney Chaplin (*Timothy*); Willis Bouchey (*Col. Edson Stedlow*); Michael Ansara (*Kamiakin*); Olive Carey (*Mrs. Anne Avery*); Charles Horvath (*Dutch Williams*); Orlando Rodriguez (*Malachi*); Glen Kramer (*Lt. Winston*); Floyd Simmons (*Hammond*); Pat Hogan (*Jacob*); Martin Milner (*Waco*); Walter Coy (*Maj. Donahue*); Terry Wilson (*Capt. Fanning*); Beulah Archuletta (*Native American Woman*).

Most Westerns that address the issue of cavalry vs. Indian conflict focus on events in mid-1870s Montana involving Chief Sitting Bull and Crazy Horse or those in 1880s Arizona, placing an emphasis on Gernoimo and Cochise. Shamefully neglected: The equally important situation in Oregon several years following the Civil War. Based on a book by Heck Allen (1912-1991), who wrote Westerns under the pen name 'Will Henry,' this upscale program-picture offers as perceptive a portrait of life at an isolated cavalry outpost as John Ford's classic *Fort Apache*, if with considerably less sentimental rough-housing.

A SOAP OPERA ON THE PURPLISH SAGE: One more romantic triangle involving a furious husband (Keith Andes, left) discovering his wife (Dorothy Malone, right) in the arms of another man (Jeff Chandler, middle).

Here, the Chief in question is Kamiakin (1800-1977), of the Yakama. Between 1855-1858, he led his people and recruits from nearby nations in a spirited if doomed war against hordes of oncoming Anglos. In the film, as in reality, the source of an outbreak of violence derived from our government in Washington's creating a peace treaty which allowed indigenous people to live on their traditional lands, though purposefully failing to fully explain small print and tricky clauses. In this case, that included the right to create a trail that crossed territory which the Native people held sacred. Also, the creation of a fort halfway along the winding way that would be manned by soldiers. Though there had been no 'Indian trouble' (to borrow a now-dated phrase from 1950s films) until troops rode across the Snake River, the indigenous people were outraged (morally as well as geographically) that this could happen. As the bluecoats (on D.C.'s orders) completed a bridge and began the trek, all hell literally broke loose.

A 'history is written by the winners' approach is softened here by having the lead, an individualistic sergeant called 'Emmet Bell,' complain to his commanding officers that what they're doing is, simply, wrong. The answer, as expected: "Were only following orders." Like Ford's cavalry trilogy, *Pillars* offers a plethora of facts, many little known, about the frontier army. The manner in which a top sergeant runs the company is well illustrated. Also, a vivid depiction of the process by which a sergeant, promoted to brevet-officer during Civil War combat, must afterwards adjust to a lower rank. The issue of alcohol addiction, providing comedy relief in Ford's *She Wore a Yellow Ribbon* and *Fort Apache*, here receives a darker (and more realistic) treatment. Not only among members of the rank and file; our focal anti-hero has become a hardcase owing to constant pressures of fort life, as well as his sense of inferiority owing to alteration of his rank and status. As was often the case, we watch as young boys are brought out West and sent into combat without any

AN ALLEGORICAL OATER: The very title of this film suggests the emphasis on religion throughout the narrative.

training. However unlikely that may seem, the notion of soldiers who don't know how to handle firearms, much less ride a horse, ordered into the thick of things is completely accurate, based on the now inconceivable notion that they will best learn by actual experience.

The same sense of authenticity holds true for portrayals of Native People. Here, each tribe is specified as to a unique approach for Anglo observers. If the Palouse are stand-offish, the Spokane willingly accommodate to the

THE ALL-PURPOSE CHARACTER ACTOR: Equally at home in nasty roles (*Johnny Guitar*) and as a lovable best friend to the hero (*Rio Bravo*), Ward Band appears in *Pillars* as a decent minded, no-nonsense crusader for Indians' Rights of the type he would play on TV's *Wagon Train* (seen here).

new order of things. Here, one key issue of Westerns from the 1950s is more prominent than usual. Then, mainstream audiences easily accepted that 'good' Indians were those who adopted themselves to current realities, while the 'bad' refused, among other things, Christianity. Today, characters like the well-meaning reverend and teacher played by Ward Bond would not necessarily be portrayed as enlightened, the situation when this film was made. His means of 'helping' the Natives is to make Red White Men out of them, killing their culture, religion, values, and ways to 'save the people' by destroying their nation. The character's humanitarianism aside, a modern sensibility rejects his approach as much as that of the Anglos who hate all Indians. Today, most Americans perceive such an old film, embedded with values that went unquestioned back in the Eisenhower era, from a polar perspective. As a result, ethnic identity, and its maintenance despite pressures to conform, cause this Oater's once-liberal values to be questioned from our own different notion of what Civil Rights for ethnic Americans should and does mean.

Of interest too is the lead actor. Brooklyn-born (as Ira Grossel) Jeff Chandler (1918-1961) achieved fame by playing 'good' Indian' Cochise in three sturdy Westerns: *Broken Arrow* (1950), its prequel *Battle of Apache Pass* (1952), and in an opening cameo in their sequel *Taza, Son of Cochise* (starring Rock Hudson; 1954). Universal next cast Chandler as a tough but fair commander in the cavalry Western *War Arrow* (1953). In this, as in other period pictures, he played the ramrod-straight equivalent of B+ features in which Charlton Heston appeared over at Columbia. The latter actor moved on to full superstardom thanks to *The Ten Commandments* (1956) and *Ben-Hur* (1959). Chandler was considered for both roles. Had he achieved them, he might have become a superstar rather than, like Sterling Hayden, an also ran, at least while their careers were active. Each in time did win cult appreciation. Here, Chandler effectively embodies the bad boy icon, attractive to the female lead (Dorothy Malone, 1924-2018) in large part because, unlike her servile husband (Keith Andes, 1920-2005), he is casual with her and unattainable if not as a lover than a spouse. Chandler's career would be cut short when, after suffering a slipped disc while shooting the WWII drama *Merrill's Marauders* for maverick moviemaker Sam Fuller, the actor died in the hospital. *Marauders* was released posthumously in 1962, leading to an *Esquire* magazine piece entitled: "Don't Die, Jeff Chandler!" In it, fans watch one of his old movies at a Drive-In and weep at the thought that the man himself is now gone.

"VEIN OF IRON": The invisible source of strength with America's pioneer women, as described by novelist Ellen Glasgow, has always been best embodied by Olive (wife of Harry, mother of Harry Jr.) Carey, in *Pillars of the Sky* and, seen here, *The Searchers:* from left to right, John Qualen, Vera Miles, Carey.

65. RAMONA (1936)
Rating: **** ½

CREDITS:

Henry King, dir.; Lamar Trotti, many others, scr.; Darryl F. Zanuck, pro.; Sol M. Wurtzel, pro.; Alfred Newman, mus.; William V. Skall (cin.; Alfred DeGaetano, ed.; 1.37:1; C; 84 min.; 20th Century-Fox.

CAST:

Loretta Young (*Ramona*); Don Ameche (*Alessandro*); Kent Taylor (*Felipe Moreno*); Pauline Frederick *(Senora Moreno)*; Jane Darwell (*Aunt Ri Hyar*); Katherine DeMille (Margarita); Victor Kilian (*Father Gaspara*); John Carradine (*Jim Farrar*); J. Carrol Naish (*Juan Can*); Pedro de Cordoba (Father Salvierderra); Charles Wandron (*Dr. Weaver*); Russell Simpson (*Scroons*); Bill Benedict (*Joseph*); Chief Thundercloud (*Pablo*); Delores Reyes *(Dancer)*.

The legend of Ramona took shape in the creative imagination of writer Helen Hunt Jackson (1830-1885). Born into an upscale family in Amherst MA, young Hunt grew up in a liberal, intellectual home environment. Her greatest passion, after listening to Chief Standing Bear of the Ponca people of the southwest speak in public, would always be for Indians' rights. Shortly, she too wrote and delivered fervent speeches. Eventually, Hunt Jackson realized that few everyday citizens wish to be preached to/at. But, she knew, women in her own privileged small circle of friends loved to read romances, particularly doomed/tragic ones. The way to coax armchair suffragists to support her cause, then, was to create an irresistible story that sharply criticized our official Indian policy. Her experiment worked beyond anyone's wildest

AN AMERICAN MYTH: A popular bestseller became the source of a franchise that included stage productions and feature films, this early color feature perhaps the greatest incarnation.

expectations. An immediate bestseller, the book has since gone through more than 300 printings. Stage versions appeared, as well as silent films in 1910, 1916, and 1928. A popular song based on what soon became an American myth played constantly on the radio. Tourists who had read her piece traveled by train and, in time, automobile to visit the Southern California locations where the drama takes place. To accommodate such crowds with a fitting reward, in 1923 her 1884 novel was transformed into a live annual pageant that continues to this day. How surprising, then, that over the years the very idea of 'Ramona' slipped out of the mainstream myth pool. Most people today have never heard of the book or seen any of the films versions that still exist.

For this impressive version, Fox studio-head Daryl F. Zanuck (1902-1979) personally assembled an "A" list of talent. Director King (1886-1982) had a reputation for spectacular projects (*State Fair*, 1933), and would go on to create the classic Western *The Gunfighter* (1950). Lamar Trotti (1900-1952) had established a reputation as a fine writer of Americana with John Ford's *Steamboat Round the Bend* (1935) and would later adapt *The Ox Bow Incident* (1943). Actress Loretta Young (1913-2000) was even then in the process of being groomed for superstardom. Sealing the package, Zanuck made the then-risky decision to shoot in the still-emergent multi-color process, filming on locations in Utah. Like Jackson's novel, *Ramona* focuses on a person of mixed race . . . as such, the female equivalent of the 'half-breed' (to again cite that dated term, purposefully presented here in quotation marks) in many early Westerns. This *woman* of two races (Native and Scottish) is portrayed as, if anything, *superior* to those around her: Aristocratic Spanish, lower working-class Mexicans, Native Americans, and incoming Whites, the latter depicted in a notoriously negative manner. Pure-blood people from Spain, however, who own a vast ranchero (smaller than it once was, since the arrival of U.S. citizens following the Mexican American war) do not come off much better. Essential to the drama: 'Senora Moreno' has 'taken in' (but not adopted) Ramona only because she promised the girl's dying mother not to let the child flounder. Here, then, is a dramatically complex set-up. While

STAR-CROSSED LOVERS: Like Shakespeare's Romeo and Juliet, the young people played here by Loretta Young and Don Ameche are tragic victims of an insensitive society surrounding them.

Ramona enjoys the luxuries of this great estate, she is never allowed to forget that she is not a true/full family member.

This leads to a unique, and refreshingly non-conventional, romantic triangle. The handsome son of the Morenos, 'Felipe,' has always loved Ramona and wishes to marry her. His status-conscious mother will have none of it!

Felipe must find a 'suitable' bride among available daughters of high-born neighbors. This doesn't disturb Ramona, who loves kind-hearted Felipe like a brother. Then, a group of Christianized Indians arrive for sheep-shearing. Among them is the handsome 'Allesandro.' He falls in love at first sight; Ramona returns his affections. But Senora Moreno argues against this union as, in her mind, Ramona's identity as half-white dictates she ought not to

THE CONSUMMATE VILLAIN: John Carradine, who would in time replace Bela Lugosi n the role of "Dracula" for the Universal horror franchise, here plays the most insensitive of Anglo immigrants to the American southwest.

marry below herself, to a 'lowly' Indian. Not that Allesandro's tribesmen are keen on a pure blood Native marrying a half Anglo girl. As the piece rightly notes, prejudice is, however tragically, known to all races of the world. Though critics often dismiss *Ramona* as a simple soap opera, the attitude toward racial prejudice is fascinatingly complex. Whereas some novelists simplify, suggesting that racism is a 'white problem,' this more richly-textured piece makes clear that it is a human issue. Bloodlines are, simply, essential to any ethnicity's vision of itself as a community, despise individual emotions of a member of the group.

In the second half, critical attention turns to the abuse of Native Americans by Anglo arrivals during the 1850s. Jackson hoped to incur the wrath of liberal-minded thinkers even as Harriet Beecher Stowe would write her own equally sentimental, often hokey novel *Uncle Tom's Cabin* (1852) to raise the consciousness of all right-minded Americans against slavery. "So you are the little woman who wrote the book that started this big war?" President Lincoln said to that lady upon meeting her. However primitive (some might argue sub-literary) Stowe's or Jackson's writing styles may have been, particularly as to creating characters who often do not qualify as three-dimensional, each book deeply touched the middle-American citizenry and led to long overdue changes in our country's vision of race. That proved true for this gorgeously realized film as well. The sequences of Native People being forced off their lands by the worst sort of redneck whites, and sometimes subjected to cold-blooded killings, remains as upsettingly powerful today as when this sadly forgotten film was first released.

66. RANCHO NOTORIOUS (1952)
Rating: **** ½

CREDITS:

Fritz Lang, dir.; Daniel Taradash, Silvia Richard, scr.; Howard Welsch, pro.; Emil Newman, Arthur Lange, Hugo Friedhofer, mus.; Hal Mohr, cin.; Otto Ludgwig, ed.; 1.37:1; C 89 min.; Fidelity Pictures/RKO Releasing.

CAST:

Marlene Dietrich (*Altar Keane*); Arthur Kennedy (*Vern Haskell*); Mel Ferrer (*Frenchy Fairmont*); Gloria Henry (*Beth Forbes*); William Frawley (*Baldy Gunder*); Lisa Ferraday (*Maxine*); John Raven (*Saloon Dealer*); Jack Elam (*Mort Geary*); George Reeves (*Wilson*); Frank Ferguson (*Preacher*); Francis McDonald (*Harbin*); Dan Seymour (*Comanche Paul*); John Kellogg (*Jeff Factor*); Rodd Redwing *(Rio)*; Roger Anderson (*Red*); Lane Chandler *(Sheriff Hardy)*; Charlita (*Mexican Barfly*); John Doucette (*Whitey*); Dick Elliott *('The Storyteller')*.

By the early 1950s, several long-time conventions of the Western had been so overused that they now seemed silly when presented at face value. One was the personal vengeance motif for the hero's motivation, included in Raoul Walsh's spectacular *The Big Trail* (1930) with John Wayne, continuing through many of the ultra-low-budget quickies Duke appeared in for Lone Star during the next decade. And, with Wayne's return to the big-time, in John Ford's *Stagecoach* (1939): Another: the fact-based notion of a secret retreat for outlaws, a land of lost souls where doomed men might find refuge from the

DESTRY RIDES AGAIN … AND AGAIN … AND … : The classic comedy Western starring James Stewart and Marlene Dietrich allowed the actress a new lease on her career as a star of musical Westerns; her presence would be spoofed in the Mel Brooks burlesque *Blazing Saddles*.

law for a price. Perhaps the best later incarnation of this appears in *Last of the Fast Guns* (1958) starring stuntman turned "B" movie star Jock Mahoney. Last but hardly least among the tired cliches: The chorus line of gorgeous girls performing the Can-Can, a staple in cinematic saloons in films ranging from *Dodge City* (1939) with Errol Flynn to *Destry Rides Again* (1939), the comedy-Oater that re-introduced boy-next-door James Stewart as a Western star.

There, the dream girl star/singer was played by Marlene Dietrich (1901-1992), typecast as such shady ladies ever since Josef von Sternberg picked her to play 'Lola Lola' in the early German sound-classic, *The Blue Angel* (1930). When the two migrated to Hollywood, her Svengali-like maestro would wrap Marlene in feathers and furs for exotic singing-dancing roles in films such as *Blonde Venus* (1932). Then came George Marshall's *Destry*, which posited such a sultry and seemingly cold-hearted vamp in the Wild West. The concept

"LOVE STORIES BETWEEN MEN . . .": Though the characters played by Arthur Kennedy and Mel Ferrer spend most of the movie competing with one another for Marlene Dietrich, gradually they come to realie that their own relationship takes precedence.

clicked: Marlene would play precisely 'that sort of woman' in *The Spoilers* (1942) opposite two shooting stars, Wayne and Randolph Scott, then again here. Indeed, the icon became so solidified that when short-lived super-producer Mike Todd required such a hostess for his Barbary Coast sequence in *Around the World in Eighty Days* (1956), he would consider no one but Marlene.

Here, she runs Chuck-a-Luck, a remote outpost where guns on the run gather, paying her ten percent of their ill-gotten gains for the privilege of hiding out here. Complications arise when two disparate fellows ride in together. One is 'Frenchy,' her duded-up former lover and the fastest gun alive, returning to reclaim his lost love. The other: 'Vern Haskell,' formerly an Everyman-type cowboy working the range in hopes of buying a small spread, then settling down with his sweet fiancée. But when she is raped and murdered during a hold-up, Vern becomes obsessed with vengeance. Giving up any chance for a normal life, he tracks the predator across the West, with but a single hope of locating that man: A beautiful broach (here serving as a Hitchcock-like MacGuffin) which the villain stole during his crime. Hearing that this outlaw may be hiding out in Chuck-a-Luck, Vern heads there, only to discover that magnetic 'Altar Keane' wears it whenever she sheds her blue jeans for an elegant basic black gown. Soon, the saddle-pals find themselves in conflict over the most beautiful woman in the West.

If the material sounds clichéd, that's putting it mildly. This might have turned out to be one more convention-ridden B+ color Western if not for the influence of Fritz Lang (1890-1976), the inspired, temperamental genius who had all but invented 'sound noir' with the German classic *M* (1930). Like Dietrich, Lang abandoned his homeland to escape Hitler. In Hollywood, he specialized in dark crime dramas such as the classic *Fury* (1936) starring Spencer Tracy. His first two color Westerns, *The Return of Frank James* (1940) and *Western Union* (1941), did not allow for the unique if peculiar style that has come to be associated with Lang's work to shine through, each a relatively routine studio program picture. Then came *Rancho* which, with its outlandish piano-playing female dominatrix, set the pace for Joan Crawford in Nicholas Ray's *Johnny Guitar* (1954). Though that follow-up has earned a reputation as a quirky classic, this less remembered item has similar 'camp' appeal for fans of the self-consciously overdone Tinseltown entertainments of yore. While there is a typical Western style ballad, accompanied by narration, here it seems so arch that at times the film has more in common with an outright farce such as *Paleface* than any serious Oater. The color scheme is as otherworldly as the one on view for the Emerald City in *The Wizard of Oz* (1939): lavender skies atop urine-yellow horizons caused *Rancho* to become a *cause-celebre* among fans of Tiffany lampshades, neon bar shades, and old super-hero comic books.

THE SCENE-STEALER SUPREME: Jack Elam's rough and tumble appearance added 'texture' to this and more than two dozen other Western movies and TV shows, including the unforgettable opening sequence in Sergio Leone's Once Upon a Time In the West.

That carries over to the storyline. Though the heroes appear headed for a collision course over the fiercely independently lady, we sense early on that this is one more of what Howard Hawks described as "love stories between men." That director's *Red River* concluded not (as might have been expected) with either John Wayne or Montgomery Clift embracing Joanne Dru, rather the two men together in the penultimate shot. So too does *Rancho* close as the pair rides off, side by side, the tragic Altar having expired. However intense either of the male character's feelings for the great beauty may be, the film is in truth as much about their relationship as would be the case in *Brokeback Mountain* (2005), if here (as in all Golden Age Hollywood movies) by implication.

"I'M SO TIRED!": In Mel Brooks' *Blazing Saddles*, Madeleine Kahn spoofs Marlene Dietrich in *Rancho Notorious* . . . though in all truth that actress had there spoofed her own earlier roles including *Destry Rides Again*.

67. REPRISAL! (1956)
Rating: ****

CREDITS:

George Sherman, dir.; David P. Horner, Raphael Hayes, David Dortort, scr.; Lewis J. Rchmil, Helen Ainsworth, Guy Madison, pro.; Mischa Bakeleinkoff, mus.; Henry Freulich, cin.; Jerome Thoms, ed.; 1.85:1; C; 74 min.; Romson Prods.

CAST:

Guy Madison (*Frank Madden/Neola*); Felicia Farr (*Catherine Cantrell*); Kathryn Grant (*Taini*); Michael Pate *(Bert Shipley)*; Otto Hulett *(Sheriff Jim Dixon)*; Wayne Mallory (*Tom Shipley*); Edward Platt (*Neil*); Robert Burton (*Jeb Cantrell*); Ralph Moody *(Matara)*; Frank DeKova (*Charlie Washackle*); Fred Aldrich *(Lyncher)*; Malcolm Atterbury *(Luther Creel)*; Philip Breedlove (*Takola*); Patrick R. Brown, Bruce Cameron, Slim Gaunt *(Citizens)*; Herman Hack (*The Blacksmith*); Eva McVeagh (*Nora Shipley*); John Zaremba *(Mr. Willard)*; Donnelly Rhodes (*Buck*).

Not since William Wellman's classic *The Ox Bow Incident* (1943), from the rightly famous 1940 novel by Walter Von Tilburg Clark, had lynching in the Old West in general, the concept of a hanging tree in particular, been so prominent as this darkly symbolic object would become in films of the mid-to-late 1950s--*Ride Lonesome*, *The Hanging Tree*, and the little-known *Reprisal!* among them. Each contained in its advertising one-sheets (as would prove true as well for the upcoming *Ride (in) the Whirlwind*) a vivid, terrifying image of such a gnarled natural object. The question that begs to be asked:

ONE MORE 1950s' ADULT WESTERN, ONE MORE HANGING TREE: This B+ Oater may have appeared conventional and generic in terms of its cast and setting, yet the script rates alongside such classics as *High Noon* as to ambitiousness of theme.

Could this have been coincidence, or was there some reason numerous filmmakers were all at once drawn to such a gruesome concept?

In *Reprisal!* we view the object immediately, via a shot that will be duplicated in the 1959 Delmer Daves vehicle for aging superstar Gary Cooper. This "B" picture opens on a considerably lesser-known TV actor: Guy Madison (1922-1996), featured in the *Wild Bill Hickock* kiddie-oriented TV series of the mid-1950s. Here he's cast as a loner who rides across the grim landscape, a look of sheer determination in his eyes. A predecessor to Cooper's anti-hero, Frank happens upon a hideous, ghostly tree, employed for hangings . . . in truth, *lynchings* . . . on the edge of the very land he intends to purchase. Once in town, Frank realizes that owing to his contract for the property, he will become in some vague notion connected to what took place, even though

CIVIL RIGHTS CINEMA: Inter-racial love, a key issue of the 1950s American scene, may have been too controversial for mainstream Hollywood to yet deal with in black and white contemporary terms, though the Western genre offered an attempt to make such statements within the setting of a long-gone historical situation; here, Guy Madison 'romances' Felicia Farr.

he was nowhere around at the time. In the West, and in The Western, legal ownership brings with it a sense of personal responsibility.

'Frank Madden' walks the streets of this unpleasant town (recalling the Hadleyville of *High Noon*) only to discover a trial in session. Such a narrative device links this film to *Good Day for a Hanging* and *The Young Land*, both studies of 'the law' in relationship to 'human justice.' Two Native Americans were lynched on that tree, one a woman. There is little doubt as to who committed this atrocity: 'The Shipley Brothers,' white-trash ranchers who own considerable land hereabouts. Officials of the government----a noble judge, a right-minded sheriff, and a dedicated prosecuting attorney---desperately hope for a conviction. Ultimately, such a decision is up to the jury, all white men. Collectively, they insist—despite the presence of 'Taini,' a Native American woman who bore witness to the deaths—on a not guilty verdict. These 'good citizens' employ their power as land-owners to continue a White Supremacist policy. Since Indians are here considered to be less than human, it's impossible for any Anglo to go to jail after murdering an indigenous American.

Among those angered by this recurring situation is 'Catherine,' a genteel Anglo woman who represents the mean little town's liberal faction. The

RACIAL IDENTITY IN AMERICA: Guy Madison (far right) plays a Native American who attempts to 'pass' in white society, only to discover that his greatest need is to accept the reality of his ethnicity.

lynched woman had long been her close friend, with no concern as to ethnicity. Catherine attempts to convince the handsome newcomer (with whom she falls in love) to join this righteous minority. Intriguingly, Frank is sympathetic to their cause yet standoffish. At mid-movie, a turning point will explain his inability to commit. A greater surprise, however, awaits when Catherine comes to believe Frank is secretly sleeping with Taini. Momentarily, we assume her outrage is the norm for a woman scorned. Then comes the bombshell: "If it had been any woman in town ... other than that ... *Squaw*!" Now, what appeared to be one more "B" Western, if with a Civil Rights theme, dares introduce a sense of thematic complexity. Even the proto-feminist/supposed anti-racist/ good liberal reveals an Anglo bias when under pressure. She can be right-minded in theory but wrong-headed in expression, a duality we don't necessarily expect to experience in what appears to be a humble program picture.

Similarly, the older Shipley brother 'Neil' is horrified to learn that his younger brother Bert, though married to an Anglo, sneaks off to visit 'Indian town' a mile away to satiate his lust for women of color, then beats the females to assuage his guilt. Though the film suggests that just outside every settlement, a separate/non-equal Indian Town existed, this was not the case. Indians were reservated far from pioneer villages. Note, then: the book on which *Reprisal!* is based did not take place in the Old West but the 20th Century South, specifically Georgia. There were indeed African American neighborhoods close to White areas. The book directly addressed racially-motivated lynchings in then-contemporary America. While books, read by a precious few, have a liberty to dramatize controversial themes, commercial movies must reach a large mainstream audience to break even. That includes potential audiences the South. Unfortunately, no studio in town would touch the original and worthy project owing to fear of financial loss; the era of powerful Civil Rights movies *(The Defiant Ones*, 1958; *A Raisin in the Sun,* 1961) remained several years in the future. But by altering the place and period, an anti-lynching message for 'today' could be expressed by re-envisioning the event in a distant past.

68. RETURN OF A MAN CALLED HORSE, THE (1976)
Rating: **** ½

CREDITS:

Irvin Kershner, dir.; Jack DeWitt, scr.; Terry Morse Jr., Richard Harris, Sandy Howard, Theodore R. Parvin, pro.; Laurence Roenthal, mus.; Owen Rollzman, cin.; Michael Kahn, mus.; 2.39:1; C; 129 min.; United Artists.

CAST:

Richard Harris (*John Morgan*); Gale Sondergaard (*Elk Woman*); Geoffrey Lewis (*Zenas*); William Lucking (*Tom Gryce*); Jorge Luke (*Running Bull*); Enrique Lucero (*Raven*); Claudio Brook(e) (*Chemin De Fer*); Regino Herrera (*Lame Wolf*); Pedro Damian (*Standing Bear*); Humberto Lopez (*Thin Dog*); Alberto Mariscal (*Red Cloud*); Eugenia Dolores (*Brown Dove*); Ana de Sade (*Moon Star*).

Social observers of the American scene were quick to note that the so-called Hippie (or Youth) Movement that began in the mid-Sixties embraced elements of Native American culture. This led literary critic Leslie A. Fiedler to pen *The Return of the Vanishing American* (1968), in which he recalled an old Native legend: Even as the original Americans were on the verge of extinction, ghosts of ancient warriors would rise again and inhabit the bodies of the Whites' children, turning them against those basic values of their parents that had led to an Indian dystopia. When the book proved to be an Underground bestseller, Hollywood took note. Eager to speak to the emergent Youth Audience, old Studios attempted to create New Westerns. Not that the films

THE GREAT WHITE HOPE: Richard Harris (left) returns from England to rally his Native American friends against white-trash capitalists conquering their land; however much the film may have been intended as a pro-Indian statement in its time, today the notion that Lakota could not, or would not, defend themselves without a 'golden warrior' appearing proves controversial . . . and, for that matter, historically inaccurate.

were entirely successful: The Critical and box-office bombs *FLAP* and *Soldier Blue* preceded a true classic, *Little Big Man*, in 1970.

In between, *A Man Called Horse* premiered. The movie did well commercially and received mixed-to-positive reviews. One person not satisfied with results was screenwriter Jack DeWitt (1900-1981). Decades earlier, he penned "B" Westerns--*Battles of Chief Pontiac* (1952), *Sitting Bull* (1954), *Oregon Passage* (1957)--which at least attempted to present a more enlightened vision of indigenous Americans. For *Horse*, he seized on a superb short story by Dorothy M. Johnson, who also penned "The Man Who Shot Liberty Valance." Her original concerns a young Bostonian who, captured by Crow, gradually wins their respect, becoming a full member of the nation. But these were the late 1960s. As the British Invasion, heralded by the arrival of the

Beatles in 1964, remained in effect, not only as to music but movies (*Georgy Girl*, *Alfie*, *Morgan!*, etc.), DeWitt had re-imagined the eponymous hero in hopes this might make his script more saleable.

Also, the scribe felt the need to come up with a spectacular central sequence. He chose a ritual that long fascinated him: The Sun Dance, in which Native Americans pierce their chests, place a rawhide string through the two puncture holes, and create self-inflicted pain by stretching against the knotted cord. Here, the problems began. First, the Crow did not practice this ritual. Second, DeWitt studied a painting by the great George Catlin depicting the Mandan Sun Dance, always performed within their lodge-houses. As these were farming people, the Mandan would not be appropriate for an action-oriented film. Thus, DeWitt changed the identity to the Sioux, in his script referred to as Yellow Hands. Their Sun Dance was performed in

OLD HABITS ARE HARD TO BREAK: As in the 1950s, when beautiful Latin women were cast as Native Americans, this purportedly 'enlightened' film featured Mexican actress Ana de Sade as one of the Native women attached by white rednecks who invade the far west.

the open air, Lakota people living in tee-pees for their migratory lifestyle. As DeWitt included several incidents from Johnson's piece that accurately depicted The Crow Way, what audiences saw (and took as The Truth) turned out to be a misleading hodge-podge: Natives who behave according to Crow customs but inhabit a temporary Sioux village which unaccountably has a semi-permanent Mandan dwelling at its epicenter.

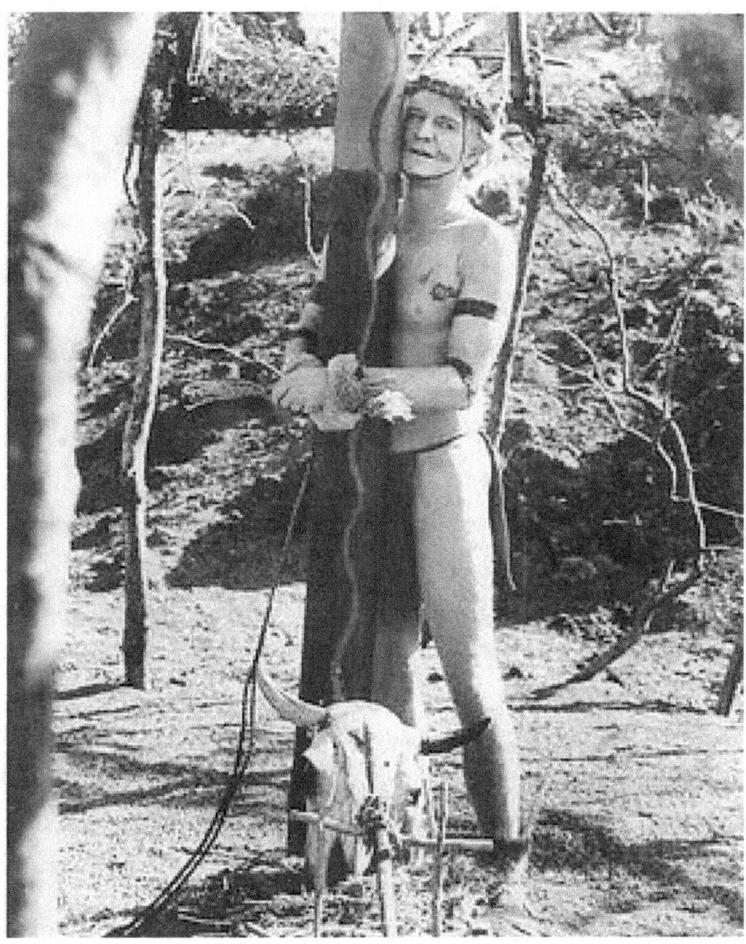

GETTING IT RIGHT, THE SECOND TIME AROUND: One major problem with the first 'Horse' film had been the unrealistic depiction of a Sund Dance; here, the religious (not machismo) ritual is accurately portrayed,

Entertainment value aside, a movie that also set out to educate the mainstream as to the 'reality' of Native people did precisely the opposite, even as *Dances with Wolves* would some twenty years later. 'John Morgan' (Richard Harris, 1930-2002) undergoes the ritual to prove his masculinity. Neither Mandan nor Lakota employed the Sun Dance as a machismo performance. A tribal member might choose (never pressured) to embark on a Vision Quest, a religious rite. Director Elliot Silverstein took a broad burlesque approach not unlike the one he had for the popular comedy *Cat Ballou* (1965), presenting the film's Sun Dance as if it were a sadistic psychedelic happening. Harris' body spins in circles, this never a part of the Lakota or Mandan Sun Dance.

Receiving considerable criticism from Indian and Anglo historians alike, DeWitt set out to create a sequel that would offer a corrective to his own earlier project. Here, Morgan (who has been living an unsatisfying life in 'civilized' Britain) longs for the romance of the West. He returns, only to find his old friends scattered. White trappers (mountain men) have entered the area and, forming a bond with the Rikkies (Arakawa), now control the territory. To become one with his people again, Morgan undergoes the Sun Dance for a second time. Here, though, the ceremony is portrayed with great precision as to the Lakota sense of spirituality. Others in the tribe dance with him; the Sun Dance had always been a communal, not individualistic, ritual. Appreciated too: A superior director, Irvin Kershner 1923-2010), best known today for the second *Star Wars* film, told the story in purely visual terms, taking a low-key, sophisticated, almost arthouse approach to the considerably more solemn proceedings.

Though primary Lakota characters are once again played by Latin actors, the vast majority of extras are indeed Native Americans, not the Fiji Islanders employed for the first film. Language is handled marvelously: Lakota speak their own authentic tongue with subtitles. Best of all is The Buffalo Hunt, the finest ever onscreen. (And we're not forgetting *Dances With Wolves* here) Still, several flaws keep *Return . . .* from rating as *the* classic Native American film. The idea that Lakota would grow psychologically depressed when forced from their burial grounds is inaccurate. After all, they were nomadic people, seldom remaining in one place for long. The notion of Morgan becoming their messiah offers another example of The (faux) Great White Hope myth. Such limitations, however, do not take away from the majestic visuals and vast improvement over the original. If clearly another Anglo conception of the plains people, here is one that comes closer to the truth.

GETTING IT RIGHT... THE SECOND TIME AROUND: screenwriter Jack De Witt and director Irvin Kershner labored to create a more authentic verisimilitude of Native American life in this little known sequel, as an assortment of the studio's publicity stills reveal.

"YOU GONNA TALK? TALK. YOU GONNA SHOOT? SHOOT!" Eli Wallach says that before blowing away an opponent while relaxing in a bubble bath in The Good, The Bad, and the Ugly; *The stars of My Name Is Nobody* live out that Leone legend.

ONCE UPON A TIME...IN A REVOLTION: During the late 1960s, such socially conscious Westerns as 100 Rifles employed Mexico's past revolutions to comment on current ones worldwide.

69. RIDE (IN) THE WHIRLWIND (1965/66)
Rating: ****

CREDITS:

Monte Hellman, dir.; Jack Nicholson, scr.; Nicholson, Hellman, Roger Corman, John Herman Shaner, pro.; Robert Drasnin, mus.; Gregory Sandor, cin.; Hellman, ed.; 1.85:1; C; 82 min.; Proteus Films/Santa Clara Prods.

CAST:

Jack Nicholson (*Wes*); Millie Perkins (*Abiga*l); Cameron Mitchell (*Vern*); George Mitchell *(Evan)*; Katherine Squire (*Catherine*); Harry Dean Stanton (*Blind Dick*); John Hackett (*Winslow*); Tom Filer *(Otis)*; B.J. Merholz *(Edgar)*; Brandon Carroll (*Quint)*; Peter Cannon (*Hagerman*); William A. Keller (*Roy*); Neil Summer(s) (*Ward*); Charles Eastman (*Drummer*); James Campbell, Walter Phelps, Gary Kent (*Westerners*).

The release of *How the West Was Won* (1962) had a major impact on Hollywood Westerns. The mega-epic (in Cinerama) boasted an all-star cast (Wayne, Stewart, Fonda, etc.), a trio of top genre directors (John Ford included), while combining every major frontier tale (mountain men, wagon trains, Indian raiders, the coming of the railroads, bold lawmen) into a single work. The result? A virtual apotheosis of the traditional Western. Box office returns were phenomenal. That was the good news. The Bad? Tinseltown's once potent 'A' cowboy movies now had nowhere to go, all future attempts to make more (*The Sons of Katie Elder*, 1965; *Alvarez Kelly*, 1966; *The Way West*, 1967) falling flat owing to a sense of familiarity that led if not to contempt

A PAIR OF MAVERICKS: Then struggling actors Jack Nicholson and (Harry) Dean Stanton would, in the decades to follow, would respectively become a superstar and a heralded character actor.

than at least disinterest. Meanwhile, the B theatrical studio Western had all but disappeared owing to television's popular Oaters. So: Was the Western dead? Hardly. In Germany, Teutonic features starring American expatriate actors like Stewart Granger tapped into Europe's continuing interest in the genre. With the birth of Spaghetti and Paella Westerns in Italy and Spain, the great tradition continued, if in a notably altered state. Like a Phoenix, the Western had crashed only to fly again, perhaps more gloriously than ever.

Back in the U.S.A., several aspiring filmmakers also sensed that this viable staple had to be re-assessed. During the 1950s, Roger Corman (1926-) churned out low budget Westerns, horror movies, sci-fi flicks and the like for an emergent Youth Audience. Not surprisingly, he hired youthful wannabes, unable to break into the mainstream movie business, willing to work cheap for the experience. Among them: Monte Hellman (1932-2021), previously employed in summer stock theatre productions, and Jack Nicholson (1937-), a triple-threat with ambitions to write, direct, and act. As the new decade began, the former head of production at A.I.P., now producing his own more ambitious films (in color; with higher production values), allowed such maturing mavericks to come up with their own projects. When Hellman and Nicholson approached Corman with a script for an existential Western, 'The Shooting,' he agreed to finance … but only if they would create two films back-to-back, with the same crews and casts, turning out a pair of pictures for little more than the price of one. Nicholson sat down and penned a second

"LA BELLE DAME SANS MERCI": Millie Perkins, best known for her earlier role as the innocent Anne Frank, here portrays a dangerous woman with complex motivations.

script in a matter of days. While *Ride*... has never achieved the cult status that *The Shooting* acquired, in its own low-key manner the piece rates as an important, if overlooked, step in the modernization of our oldest and still enduring film genre.

Consciously intended or not, *Ride*... captures the sense of despair that Americans found themselves unable to shake in the days, months, then years following the Kennedy assassination. The film opens as three out-of-work cowboys, hoping to join a cattle drive, come upon a corpse hanging from a misshapen tree. Such an image referenced the previous decade's darker Westerns such as *Ride Lonesome* and *The Hanging Tree*. 'Vern,' 'Wes,' and 'Otis'. . . randomly, or by a trick played on them by (as Walter Huston says in *(The) Treasure of the Sierra Madre* (1948): "God, or nature, or whatever you choose to call it," take refuge in a forlorn building. Inside are killers, pursued by an out-for-blood posse. When that group arrives, our innocent heroes realize they will be perceived as part of the monstrous group . . . and that, if these bad men are summarily lynched, likely they will be as well. Here, as in *Treasure* . . .., life does not make sense. Instead, to again quote Walter Huston's old-timer in that classic, "it's a great joke" . . . if a cruel and cynical one. The cosmos has become absurd. Or, worse still, malevolent.

Here is a noir Western from the late 1940s (*Pursued, Blood on the Moon*) taken to new and extreme limits. If the setting is bleak, then any sense of character is ambiguous, and purposefully so. Products of The Beat Generation, Hellman and Nicholson inebriated themselves in the writings of Jean-Paul Sartre, Albert Camus, and other Paris Left Bank intellectuals who no longer believed the human personality is fixed, rather fluid, altering like a chameleon to survive. Here then is a work that paves the way for the quasi-Western *Bonnie and Clyde* (1967) and Peckinpah's revolutionary *The Wild Bunch* (1969). A journey turns out to be as essential here as it was, say, to *Along the Great Divide*. There, however, the end-point always remained definite, if difficult to reach; the woman, knowable. Here, there is no solid sense of space or place, no desperately wished for finishing point. 'Abigail' is as impossible to comprehend for her male companions as Jeanne Moreau was to the title

"THEY WENT THATAWAY...." Like so many classic Westerns from Hollywood's golden age, Monte Hellman relies on the recurring motif of a great and perilous journey... though now the destination remains unknown in a way that it had not been in earlier Oaters.

characters in Francois Truffaut's New Wave classic *Julies and Jim* some three years earlier. Youthful Vern mourns for a golden age that has passed before he had a chance to 'seize the day.'

As Nicholson would emerge as a modern Everyman in the 1970s, we might take his role here as a period-piece version of then contemporary teenagers about to drop out owing to the shattered dream of an America new frontier. Following the debacle in Dallas, a new sort of genre film was required: One in which things did not make sense; a Western world as George Orwell and Lewis Carroll might have jointly imagined it. Here, that sort of film was introduced. The paradigm would be continued indefinitely.

70. RIDE LONESOME (1959)
Rating: **** ½

CREDITS:

Budd Boetticher, dir.; Burt Kennedy, scr.; Boetticher, Harry Joe Brown, Randolph Scott, pro.; Heinz Roemheld, mus.; Charles Lawton Jr., cin.; Jerome Thoms, ed.; 2.35:1: C; 73 min.; Ranown/Columbia.

CAST:

Randolph Scott (*Ben Brigade*); Karen Steele (*Mrs. Carrie Lane*); Pernell Roberts (*Sam Boone*); James Best (*Billy John*); Lee Van Cleef *(Frank)*; James Coburn (*Whit*); Bennie E. Dobbins, Roy Jenson, Boyd 'Red' Morgan (*Outlaws)*; Dyke Johnson (*Charlie*); Boyd Stockman (*Apache*).

"Funny, isn't it?" outlaw 'Sam Boon' (Pernell Roberts, 1928-2010) chuckles at this film's conclusion. "How a thing can seem one way, then turn out altogether else?"

This Westerner speaks of the strange situation he and his younger partner, 'Whit' (James Coburn, 1928-2002) have witnessed. For the past week, they've traveled in the company of three other riders of the wastelands, each lonesome within this grim, merciless, ironically beautiful desert. There's a remarkable woman, 'Carrie, whose fool of a husband managed to get himself killed by Apaches. A cold-blooded killer, 'Billy John'; this grinning maniac shot down a man and must be taken back for trial. And, finally, the subject of Boone's comment: 'Ben Brigade,' a seemingly callow bounty hunter who plans to bring Billy in, dead or alive. Even if it means shooting down Boone and Whit, who know that if *they* turn in the crazy boy, they'll be granted full amnesty for past misdeeds.

"YOU'D DO IT FOR . . . " That line in Mel Brooks *Blazing Saddles* revived interest in the career of one of the most successful of B Western stars, Randolph Scott.

"I don't know how much they're payin' you to bring me in," Billy John taunts Brigade, even as B.J.'s brother 'Frank' and other gang members close in, "it ain't enough. Not *nearly* enough!"

That's when Brigade mumbles something to the cuffed convict no one else hears: "I'd hunt you *free*."

Though Billy does not possess the rational logic or emotional sensitivity to grasp Brigade's meaning, the statement hangs in the audience's mind,

THE NEXT GENERATION OF WESTERN STARS: James Coburn would portray frontiersmen in such films as Sam Peckinpah's *Major Dundee*; Pernell Roberts would be among the original ensemble of TV's fabulously popular *Bonanza*.

helping us grasp there's more to this man, also more at stake here than money, in this beyond-the-main B+ feature.

"You just don't seem the kind that would hunt a man for *money*," perceptive Carrie tells Brigade when the two stand apart from the others at night.

"I am," he insists.

But this is a Boetticher/Kennedy project. As such, onscreen people (including the anti-heroes) don't necessarily speak the truth . . . at least until the time is right. Bountyman or no, Brigade has something else on his mind other than the cash he'll earn once they reach Santa Cruz. His desperate and disparate companions on this western Argonautica eventually sense their Jason is not trying to outdistance Frank and his cohorts. In fact, Brigade clearly hopes the criminals will catch up.

And not just anywhere.

For what seemed a random series of events has all been part of an elaborate chess game, Brigade the master player. Unwilling to allow forces, above and beyond, to control his destiny, the man with steely eyes steadily moves toward a fate forming in his head since the journey began. Indeed, long before that. Even as a previous film by the director, writer, producers and star had taken 'The Tall T ' as its symbolic title, here this idea becomes physical . . . in

THE BURNING CROSS: In this allegorical Western, such a sight proves as symbolic as it is in another Randolph Scott Western titled "The Tall T."

the form of one more of those hanging trees that came to dominate Westerns during this particular decade ... a gnarled natural object that appears to have been patiently waiting for all to arrive the entire time.

STRONG MEN, STRONGER WOMEN: The Western film has always offered an assortment of female leads (here, Karen Steele) who prove themselves as self-empowered as they are beautiful.

The narrative's resolution turns out to be a true reckoning, in the most profound sense. Helping us understand something else previously said: "There are some things a man just can't ride around." Here is The Cowboy Way illustrated; the Code of the West incarnate. Only one trail allows any rider of the sage, purple or otherwise, to cut through the isolation each feels and fears, whether he reveals the latter or not. Friendship, in the full and trusting sense of the term, is necessary for not merely physical but spiritual survival in this red-hot, seemingly God-abandoned territory. Love, if you will, though such diehards would . . . well . . . *die* before speaking that word openly, owing to their rugged senses of self.

Unconditional love at that. Which is, of course, the only sort that ever matters.

In life, as in Western movies of the highest order.

Here, as in all seven of the magnificent Westerns films this team turned out, a central idea cuts across myriad plots that Burt Kennedy (1922-2001) and other scribes prepared for producer Harry Brown (1890-1972) to ride herd over; Boetticher (1922-2001) providing the inspired dramatization. Again, the whole turns out to be more than the sum of its parts. However fine any individual film may be, taken as a collective, this body of work conveys a greater meaning, in which the very idea of The West (beyond the stunning Lone Pine settings) as America's ultimate arena for meaningful action is distilled from a philosophic point of view into an aesthetic of visual splendor that only a wide-open-spaces Western film can offer.

Initially, Randolph Scott (1898-1987) served as an all-purpose actor, including occasional Westerns. During the late 1940s, he made the career decision to appear exclusively in this genre. Movies Randy and Bud did together: *7 Men from Now* (1956), *The Tall T* and *Decision at Sundown* (both 1957), *Buchanan Rides Alone* and *Westbound* (both 1958), *R.L.* and *Comanche Station* (1960) provide a set of narratives in which a singular man---always Scott, usually in black garb---sets out on a mission, deeply meaningful to him though no one else can comprehend, at least initially. Always, the final point: Money was not his motive, even if he purposefully (and to a degree perversely) chooses to allow others to perceive things that way.

Why? It served his purpose. And satisfied an odd, embittered humor deep inside that tall Man of the West cliche icon which he carefully cultivates and self-consciously projects to go on living until the time is right to reveal . . . well . . . the truth.

BEST OF THE WEST: James Best was the guy whose face, voice, and manner you will of course recall from countless Oaters on the big or small screen, even if you can't recall his name.

71. RIO CONCHOS (1964)
Rating: *** ½

CREDITS:

Gordon Douglas, dir.; Jason London, Clair Huffaker, scr.; David Weisbart, pro.; Jerry Goldsmith, mus.; Joseph MacDonald, cin.; Joseph Silver, ed.; 2.35:1; C; 107 min.; 20th Century- Fox.

CAST:

Richard Boone (*Lassiter*) Stuart Whitman (*Capt. Haven*); Anthony Franciosa (*Rodriguez*); Wende Wagner (*Sally*); Jim Brown (*Sgt. Franklyn*); Rodolfo Acosta (*Bloodshirt*); Edmond O'Brien (*Pardee*); Vito Scotti (*Bandit*); Warner Anderson (*Col. Wagner*); House Peters Jr. (*Pardee's Officer*); Kevin Hagen (*Blondebears*); Timothy Agoglia Carey (*Chino*); Mickey Simpson (*Bartender*).

Released the same year as the Western comedy *Cat Ballou*, this more conventional project serves as a vivid foil for that burlesque. The traditionalism inherent in *Rio Conchos*'s conception: All such elements are taken with total seriousness, qualifying this as one of the final B+ Hollywood Oaters in the style of those that flourished back in the 1950s. Many featured Richard Boone (1917-1981) as a hard-edged villain, the meanest man west this side of Lee Marvin. These include *City of Bad Men*, 1953; opposite Dale Robertson); *Siege at Red River*, 1954; Van Johnson; *Robbers Roost*, 1955; George Montgomery; *Ten Wanted Men*, 1955; Randolph Scott; *Man Without a Star*, 1955; Kirk Douglas. When Boone did a TV series, he brought the Man in Black image with him to the ground-breaking role of 'Paladin' in *Have Gun, Will Travel* (1957-1963). Eventually, Boone would return to villainous roles opposite

PALADIN, THIS WESTERNER IS NOT! Forsaking 'the last knight' image of his TV hero on *Have Gun, Will Travel*, Richard Boone portrays an Indian hating racist similar to those portrayed by John Wayne in *The Searchers* and Robert Taylor in *The Last Hunt*.

Paul Newman in *Hombre* (1967). Here he plays as bloodthirsty a bad man as Jack Palance in *Shane*; the character has a heroic name: Lassiter, the tall in the saddle righteous-gunfighter in Zane Grey's *Riders of the Purple Sage* (1912).

Additionally, the film's retro-element is clear in the choice of location: Monument Valley, with its immediate salute to the great John Ford films shot there, if in this movie they are less obviously on view than in the past. Likewise, the script derives from a novel by Utah's Clair Huffaker (1926-1990), whose *Seven Ways from Sundown* had been adapted into an Audie Murphy vehicle in 1960. Huffaker's *Badman* would become *The War Wagon* in 1967, with John Wayne and Kirk Douglas kidding their stock roles as solemn gunfighter and slick con-man to adapt to the post-*Cat Ballou* climate for such fare.

Nowhere though is *Rio's* ties to the past so evident in the choice of director. Gordon Douglas (1907-1993) had long been considered a studio dependable, one of those professional no-nonsense journeymen who

THE ISSUE OF RACE IN WESTERNS; Once more, the Native American woman is portrayed by an Anglo actress (Wende Wagner); now, though, the African American Western hero comes into his own thanks to the heroic presence of Jim Brown.

brought a work in on time, on budget, and with precisely what the public hoped for from a program picture. *Rio Conchos'* concept draws on an old, reliable plot that would never go away: The dependable hero who must turn a group of dangerous men into a heroic unit to get a job done for the general good. In Westerns, this can be traced back at least to Guy Madison rounding up The Jailhouse Brigade in *The Charge at Feather River* (1954), likewise a film by Gordon Douglas; and before long transferred to a World War II setting for Lee Marvin (now an edgy hero) in *The Dirty Dozen* (1968).

For this film's solemn commanding officer, Stuart Whitman (1928-2020) was chosen. He is assisted by a beautiful Native American woman who, at mid-movie, sheds her ethnic loyalties to aid in the Anglo establishment hoping to achieve peace for all. In reference to works from the previous decade, young Wende Wagner (1941-1997) embodies a type played by Joan Taylor in *War Paint* (1953) with Robert Stack in the Anglo good-guy role. Boone's Indian-hating racist (his wife and child were killed by Native Americans) is a separated-at birth-twin for John Wayne in *The Searchers* and Robert Taylor in *The Last Hunt* (both 1956).

Yet another recurring element: Edmond O'Brien (1915-1985) as the megalomaniac who builds a secret army below the border in hopes of eventually taking over the U.S. is reminiscent of Nehemiah Persoff in Michael Curtiz' *The Comancheros* two years earlier, also featuring Whitman. O'Brien's character recalls those "it ain't over 'til it's over!" former Confederate officers (modelled on William Clark Quantrill) as played by Brian Donlevy in *Kansas Raiders* (1950) *The Woman They Almost Lynched* (1953) and, earlier still, Walter Pidgeon in *The Dark Command* (1940).

A REGRETTABLE RETRO CLICHÉ: If *Rio Conchos* offered an enlightened image of an African American Westerner, the film sadly fell back on the despised 'greaser' cliché for a scurvy Latin character, totally amoral and with no redeeming qualities whatsoever, played by Tony Franciosa.

But if in many regards *Rio Concho* appears to be an apotheosis of a type of Western then about to bite the dust, so too does it offer elements of the genre's new horizons. Jim Brown's (1936-) heroic African American (the football star here making his film debut) is hardly the first noble Buffalo Soldier to appear in a Western: Leroy 'Sachel' Paige embodied such a bold figure in a supporting role in *The Wonderful Country*; Woody Strode portrayed the title figure in Ford's classic *Sergeant Rutledge* (1960). Continuing with the then-emergent nouveau-Western, Brown set the pace for anti-racist Westerns such as *The Professionals* (1966) featuring Strode, as well as films the former gridiron great would star in during the next decade, including *El Condor* (1970).

Less satisfying in this search for the stolen rifles that must be kept from the Indians (a motif that had been employed dozens of times though here is given a notably exciting context) is Tony Franciosa (1928-2006). He portrays one more of the stereotypical sleazy Latin Americans in old Hollywood Westerns as a dishonest, sex obsessed figure. Played numerous times in the 1950s by Gilbert Roland and/or Fernando Lamas, this would (thankfully) be one of the final projects in which such a figure would embody every ugly cliché of Mexican Americans that can be traced back to *Broncho Billy and the Greaser* (1914). In the future, more often than not the complex Latin character previously played by Quinn in *Man from Del Rio* would provide a model for more positive portrayals.

72. RIO LOBO (1970)
RATING: *** ½

CREDITS:

Howard Hawks, dir.; Barton Wohl, dir.; Hawks, Paul A. Hemick, pro.; Jerry Goldsmith, mus.; William H. Clothier, cin.; John Woodcock, ed.; 1.85:1; C; 114 min.; Cinema Center Films.

CAST:

John Wayne (*Col. Cord McNally*); Jorge Rivero (*Capt. Pierre Cordona*); Jennifer O'Neill (*Shasta Delaney*); Jack Elam (*Phillips*); Christopher Mitchum (*Sgt. Tuscarora Phillips*); Victor French (*Ketcham*); Susana Dosmantes (*Maria Carmen*); Sherry Lansing (*Amelita*); David Huddleston (*Doc*); Mike Henry (*Sheriff Hendricks*); Bill Williams (*Pat Cronin*); Jim Davis (*Riley*); George Plimpton (*Gunfighter*); Don(ald) Barry (*Feeny*); Chuck Roberson (*Trainman*); Bob Steele (*Deputy*); Hank Worden (*Hank*).

An old Hollywood legend (if this one isn't true, it *ought* to be!) goes this way ... one day during the late 1960s, Howard Hawks (1896-1977) called John Wayne (1907-1979) on the phone and offered him the lead in an upcoming Western. When the Duke confirmed that he'd be interested, Hawks said he'd send the script for *Rio Lobo* over. "Why bother?" the Duke chuckled. "I've already done it twice." He referred to two of the three previous movies they had done together. Setting aside the Fordian-style epic *Red River* (1948), *Rio Bravo* (1959) and *El Dorado* (1966) were essentially variations on a single theme. A small band of rugged individuals transforms into a true community while forted up in a jail, surrounded by badguys. These American

END OF AN ERA: Following *Red River* (1948), *Rio Bravo* (1959), and *El Dorado* (1966), *Rio Lobo* would mark the end of the John Wayne/Howard Hawks Western.

equivalents of the ancient world's bold Spartans are surrounded by low-lives, following orders of a raw capitalist who has assumed near total power over the title town. Here, though, the heroes somehow win against all odds and appear to be having a crackling good time doing so.

In his review of *Rio Lobo*, Pulitzer-prize winning critic Roger Ebert noted that much of the third film's appeal derived from its ritualistic sensibility, familiarity here not breeding contempt, rather proffering pleasure for genre fans. Yet we do see a progression both for Hawks and Wayne when the three movies are considered as an ongoing project, each named after a Western town, all shot on the same Old Tucson streets and nearby prairie. *Rio Bravo* is about early middle-age, Wayne's hero 'John Chance' reaching fifty, much like the star. In *El Dorado*, 'Cole Thornton' encounters more trouble than had previously been the case. The aging hero relies more on the kindness of strangers to get the job done and, in the final shot, is seen stumbling along on crutches (beside his best friend, played by Robert Mitchum). *Rio Lobo* has 'Cord McNally' getting the job done one final time, though (and for the

AIN'T NO FUN GETTIN' OLD!: John Wayne's once vibrant hero realizes that a beautiful young woman chooses to sleep beside him not owing to attractiveness on his part, rather because he is not perceived as a potential threat, as are the younger men nearby.

first time) without a romantic lead. One young beauty, the impossibly named 'Shasta Delaney', curls up under a blanket with him on a chilly night, rather than a sexually aggressive younger man a few feet away, knowing that the old-timer will be "comfortable" (safe). At movie's end, a wounded Cord stumbles away from the inevitable gunfight with the help of yet another young woman, 'Amelita.' "Just don't tell me I'm comfortable," he quips in the film's final line, obviously aware the good ol' days are now gone.

In many regards, this might be thought of as the belated final entry in a form of Western even then disappearing. The audience of 1970 proved notably different from that of a decade earlier, back when family fun was offered at any local bijou. Such nouveau Westerns as *The Wild Bunch* and *Butch Cassidy and the Sundance Kid* (both 1969) had attracted a youth-target audience that recently responded to such Outlaw Cinema experiments as *Bonnie and Clyde* (1967) and *Easy Rider* (1969). Older, onetime movie lovers mostly stayed home and watched their favorite earlier Oaters on TV. Understandably, then, *Rio Lobo* would be the first Hawks/Wayne collaboration to fail to earn a profit, bringing in $4 million on a $5 million budget. It ain't over till it's over? Well, here indeed this Western subgenre reached the end of its trail.

Yet for the diehard Hawks/Wayne fan, *Rio Lobo*—admittedly, less exciting than either of its predecessors—offers several rewards. The director brings together such a wide assortment of bygone players that *R.L.* serves as an unofficial apotheosis not only of his Western work but the Old Hollywood Oater. Hank Worden (1901-1992) appeared with Wayne in Hawks' *Red River* and Ford's *The Searchers*, as well as Wayne's most personal project, *The Alamo* (1960). Rugged Chuck Roberson (1918-1988) had been featured in that tale of old-time Texas. Don Barry (1912-1980) starred in the popular 'Red Ryder' "B" movies, while Bill Williams (1915-1992) and Jim Davis (1909-1981) enjoyed TV stardom in the 1950s with *The Adventures of Kit Carson* and *Stories of the Century*. Once the top-billed star of ultra-low-budget pictures (not unlike Wayne in his early days), Bob Steele (1907-1988) had become a permanent fixture for virtually every traditional Hollywood Western. The key departure from such nostalgia was the jaunty soundtrack by Jerry Goldsmith.

WELCOME TO THE OLD TIMERS' CLUB: Along with many other veterans of film and TV Westerns, Hank Worden (here seen relaxing in his beloved 'chair' from *The Searchers*) brought a rich sense of verisimilitude to *Rio Lobo*.

Gone if not forgotten? The epic sounds Dmitri Tiomkin once provided for such fare, notably *The Alamo* and so many other bygone classics.

Another key element: What has been called 'the Hawksian woman,' a staple of his films that earned respect from many feminists during the 1970s. Whereas Ford's women tended to be old-fashioned and reserved, Hawks' were ultra-modern and highly independent: Joanne Dru in *Red River*, Angie Dickinson in *Rio Bravo*, a succession of women young, middle-aged, and older in *El Dorado*. Each talks back to would-be patriarchal men; joins in the good fight as equals rather than cringing in a corner in hopes of protection; and offers a giddy, kittenish sense of sensuality that leaves the menfolk standing around like clowns, trying to get their bearings in a bold new world of self-sufficient females. While *Rio Lobo* hardly rates as required viewing, the piece does provide many sentimental rewards for a Western movie buff, particularly Hawks and/or Wayne completists.

A WINNING TEAM: Director Howard Hawks and star John Wayne clicked perfectly as collaborators for a series of rough and tumble action films with an undercurrent of smart humor; here, they chat during a lull of shooting on *Hatari!* (1962).

73. ROCKY MOUNTAIN, aka ROCKY MOUNTAIN TRAIL, aka GHOST MOUNTAIN (1950)
Rating: ****

CREDITS:

William Keighley, dir.; Winston Miller, Alan Le May, scr.; William Jacobs, pro.; Max Steiner, mus.; Ted D. McCord, cin.; Rudi Fehr, ed.; 1.37:1; B&W; 93 min.; Warner Bros.

CAST:

Errol Flynn (*Capt. Lafe Barstow*); Patrice Wymore (*Johanna Carter*); Scott Forbes (*Lt. Rickey*); Guinn 'Big Boy' Williams (*Pap Dennison*); Dickie Jones (*Jim 'Buck' Wheat*); Howard Petrie (*Cole Smith*); Slim Pickens (*Plank*); Chubby Johnson (*Craigie*); Robert 'Buzz' Henry (*Kip Waterson*); Sheb Wooley (*Kay Rawlins*); Peter Coe (*Pierre Duchesne*); Yakima Canutt (*Outrider*).

While many Westerns are set during the Civil War, such a premise transformed into a virtual sub-genre during the 1950s. Examples include *The Last Outpost* (1951, with Ronald Reagan), *Escape from Fort Bravo* (1953; William Holden), (*The*) *Siege at Red River* (1954; Van Johnson), and on a considerably larger scale *The Horse Soldiers* (1959; Holden, John Wayne). First and foremost, this film, originally to have been titled "Ghost Mountain" (owing to a historical setting in north-eastern California), that altered at the last moment owing to the studio's fear people would arrive expecting a horror flick. As a prologue points out, the narrative is (loosely!) based on an actual incident. On

THE AMERICAN INDIAN AS 'THE OTHER': This shot featuring Errol Flynn and an extra portraying a Native American reveals the dated sensibility of so many Old Hollywood Westerns; though the white man is the invader, encroaching on the homeland of indigenous people, an Anglo orientation suggests that the defender of one's longtime place of living the true villain of the piece; most modern Oaters (including *Hostiles*, featured in this volume, take a notably different and more enlightened approach.

March 26, 1865, a small coterie of Confederates infiltrated the Big Bear State in hopes of saving the southern cause by creating a second front. Instead, they found themselves surrounded by hostile Shoshones. From this footnote, author Alan Le May (1899-1964) created a tense screenplay containing several similarities to his best-known novels, *The Searchers* and *The Unforgiven*, each featuring a Civil War underpinning. Here, the Southern leader, 'Lafe Barstow,' originally perceives a blue-coated officer, 'Rickey,' as an enemy who must die if the secret mission is to succeed. But as Lafe develops warm feelings for one of his hostages,' Johanna Carter,' the two become allies in assuring that she is not taken by Indians. Once again, Native Americans are 'The Other,' a savage enemy to be exterminated if Anglos are ever to reunite and create a lasting civilization. Such a theme, once idealized as an element of Manifest Destiny, has long since been questioned and re-assessed, now considered to be imperialist White Supremacy.

If such a motif is essential to virtually all Old Hollywood Oaters, the Civil War subgenre raises yet another issue. Most such movies present the North and South as equally admirable opponents, villains likely to be portrayed as raw capitalist men in suits eager to exploit the war, or deadly gangs such as Quantrill's Raiders. Most such films end with a theme initiated in D.W. Griffith's *The Birth of a Nation* (1915). Its title refers to North and South reunited as the fighting comes to an end, the characters grasping that their "Aryan birthright" (Griffith's term, *not* the author of this book!) must unite them once more if the country is to survive. Less aggressively, perhaps, *Rocky Mountain* features just such a conclusion. When Flynn's magnificent seven give their lives to protect the White Woman, the Yankee leader orders his men to hoist the Stars and Bars high on the title mountain as "Dixie" plays. In the first two decades of the 21st century, when long-standing statues of such famed Southerners as Robert E. Lee are dismantled from town squares in the South and the Confederate flag no longer hangs over public buildings, *Rocky Mountain*'s supposedly sentimental closing shot may be perceived in a disturbing manner, communicating more about the decade during which the movie was made than the historical era in which it is set.

THE BLUE AND THE GRAY: Southerner Errol Flynn (right), initially in conflict with a northern officer (Scott Forbes, who would play the lead on ABC TV's *The Adventures of Jim Bowie*), finds himself siding with that lieutenant when menaced by the local ethnic people; such a situation, presented without protest seventy years ago, now raises the issue of widespread if mostly unconscious racism in the genre.

As to the star, Australia's Errol Flynn (1909-1959) is best known for period pieces, playing noble pirates and social outlaws in such epics as *The Adventures of Robin Hood* (1938) for William Keighley (1889-1984), a solid studio hand also assigned to helm this project. Though not a noir-Western per se, *Rocky Mountain* does feature a bleak aura of imposing visuals in its stark black-and white-imagery. Here is a notable contrast to Flynn's more glamorous 1940s Westerns, *Dodge City* (1939), *Virginia City* (1940), and *San Antonio* (1945). The contrast between them and this (his last Oater) is extreme. The glory days of WWII had given way to our murky conflict in Korea as part of the larger Cold War. Here was a different sort of Western film for a swiftly altering American audience. One fascinating aspect of *Rocky Mountain* is the showcase that it provides, within the context of a B+ theatrical project, of those TV Westerns even then coming into existence. Lone Star native Dickie Jones (1927-2014), a child rodeo performer, would become a protégée of producer Gene Autry, who co-starred him as 'Dick West' in the Jack Mahoney vehicle *The Range Rider* (1955-1956), then featured Jones in the fanciful *Buffalo Bill, Jr.* (1956-1957). Today, Dickie is best remembered as the voice and model for the title character in Disney's *Pinocchio* (1940). England's Scott Forbes (1920-1997) would play the eponymous hero on Desilu's *The Adventures of Jim Bowie* (1956-1958). A Gabby Hayes of the small screen, Slim Pickens (1919-1983) appeared as the rangy sidekicks on Disney's mini-series "The Saga of Andy Burnett" (1957-1958), *(The) Outlaws* (1961-1962), *(The) Wide Country* (1962-1963), *Custer* (1967-1968) and *How the West Was Won* (1978). Always though he'll be best remembered by Western fans for

THE FACE OF A (REAL AS WELL AS 'REEL') COWBOY: Despite his authentic portrayals of cowboys in this and numerous films (as well as TV's *Rawhide*), Sheb Wooley's place in American popular culture will always be the hit .45 R.P.M. "The Purple People Eater," which in a goofy mood he composed and performed.

his incarnation of the dumbest cowboy ever in *Blazing Saddles* (Mel Brooks, 1974) and, previously, the atomic bomb riding buckaroo in Stanley Kubrick's *Dr. Strangelove* (1964). Oklahoma's authentic cowboy Sheb Woolley (1921-2003) appeared in *High Noon* (1952) and *Johnny Guitar* (1954) before winning the third lead in *Rawhide* (1958-1965) as scout 'Pete Nolan.'

Rocky Mountain would itself have a second life during the early days of TV's adult Westerns. Premiering in the fall of 1955, *Cheyenne* would become one of the most memorable of all televised Oaters. *Rocky Mountain* would be retooled as the pilot episode, "Mountain Fortress" (9/29/1955), with star Clint Walker substituting for Flynn in the new medium- and close-shots; the spectacular panoramic images are all stock footage from this Warner's feature film.

AND FEATURING, AS 'THE OUTRIDER'...: Native-American actor, stuntman, and second-unit-director (he, not William Wyler, staged and shot the chariot race for *Ben Hur*) Yakima Canutt starred opposite John Wayne in *The Star Packer* (1934) and other B Oaters, also doubling as The Duke's stunt man; *Rocky Mountain* is one of many big budget features in which he appears.

74. ROUGHSHOD (1949)
Rating: **** ½

CREDITS:

Mark Robson, dir.; Peter Viertel, Hugo Butler, Daniel Mainwaring, Hugo Butler, scr.; Richard H. Berger, Jack L. Gross, pro; Roy Webb, Paul Sawtell, mus.; Joseph F. Biroc, cin.; Marston Fay, ed.; 1.37:1; B&W; 88 min.; R.K.O.

CAST:

Robert Sterling (*Clay*); Gloria Grahame (*Mary*); Claude Jarman Jr. (*Steve*); John Ireland (*Lednoy*); Jeff Donnell (*Elaine*); Myrna Dell (*Helen*); Martha Hyer (*Marcia*); George Cooper (*Jim Clayton*); Jeff Corey (*Jed Graham*); Sara Haden (*Mrs. Wyatt*); James Bell (*Pa Wyatt*); Sean (McClory) McGlory (*Fowler*); Robert B. Williams (*McCall*); Steve Savage (*Peters*); Ed(ward) Cassidy (*Sheriff*); Stanley Andrews (*Sam Ellis*); Chuck Roberson (*Deputy*); Paul E. Burns (*Hayes*); Richard M. Norman, Michael Wallace (*Posse*).

With Jacques Tourneur's *Out of the Past* (1947)--arguably the definitive post-war crime film--at the top of R.K.O.'s list of triumphs, it can be claimed that this studio set the pace for film noir; post-war tales of the mean streets in our asphalt jungles and the wounded, lonely men and gorgeous, two-faced women who meet there after midnight. Likewise, their producers updated the Western by blending old conventions with the new aesthetic. Joel McCrea starred in *Ramrod* (1947; Andre de Toth) and *Colorado Territory* (1949, Raoul Walsh); Robert Mitchum in *Pursued* (1947; Walsh) and *Blood on the Moon* (1948; Robert Wise), all box-office hits. Perhaps the commercial failure of *Roughshod* has to do with the absence of such a star; possibly its lack

THE RETURN OF THAT SAD-EYED BOY FROM *THE YEARLING*:
Claude Jarman, Jr. once again portrays a rural youth in this sadly forgotten noir-Western.

of notoriety derives from the meandering narrative and low-key approach. Whatever! Here was the only RKO noir Western to lose money. Yet in its haunting quietude and eerily slow moving (*not* a criticism) pace, the film stands apart from the emergent noir-Western subgenre, providing a one-of-a-kind movie experience, worthy of close study owing to the refusal of all involved to hone to either Western *or* noir conventions.

In an intense montage of opening shots, the cold-blooded killer 'Lednoy' and two companions escape an isolated prison. Though the others would prefer to disappear from the area, Lednoy is motivated by obsessive vengeance: He will not run for freedom until he visits Sonora and murders a decent horse breeder, 'Clay,' who once did him what the hardcase sees as a bad turn. Easygoing Clay and his younger, naive brother Steve, meanwhile drive a small herd of horses to their home. On the way, they encounter several 'fallen' women ... saloon girls 'Mary', 'Elaine,' and 'Helen,' forced out of a nasty little town (recalling Bret Hart's short story "The Outcasts of Poker Flat," 1869) attempting to 'turn respectable.' His hands full, Steve must constantly keep an eye on the far mountains, having been forewarned that a force of abject evil is steadily moving in his direction.

THE WOMEN OF 'ROUGHSHOD': From left to right, Jeff Donnell, Martha Hyer, Myrna Dell, and Gloria Grahame; Bret Harte's Poker Flat was not the only Western community that hoped to turn respectable by exorcising itself of hardworking prostitutes.

The film begins with the murder of three innocent range riders by the convicts, which in its sudden, unexpected, harsh presentation pushes beyond anything presented onscreen in Western films of that era. This sets the pace for and initiates a brutal sensibility that would come to dominate the genre during the next decade. A near-nihilistic aura may remind modern viewers of such 21st century neo-noir-Westerns as the Coen Bros.' *No Country for Old Men* (2007). Shortly thereafter, the outlaws dress in the deceased wranglers' clothing. As they ride toward their destination, we are treated to a startling preview of *High Noon*'s rightfully famous prologue; and perhaps wonder if any of the collaborators in the creation of that classic may have seen, and been influenced, by this obscure item.

Pretty much everything on view might have easily been presented as a cliché: The nice cowboys, evil villains, 'fancy' ladies, posse members, simple farm family met along the way, a goofy prospector. Other than the baddies, however, no one is what we expect. Despite the striking images of California's rugged terrain, we might almost forget at various points along the way that this is indeed a Western--more an analytic study of human nature that just happens to be set more a hundred and fifty years ago. If the women initially appear carbon copies of similarly situated females in many moves before and after this, they turn out to be anything but. One in particular presents a great problem for the nominal hero: Overcoming entrenched prejudice against women of experience and coming to see Mary as a human being, worthy owing to her positive personality rather than of dismissal owing to the hard times she, like the others, have fallen on. Eventually, we are less intrigued by the issue of whether Steve will cease being 'a man' in the machismo sense, and finally transform into one in the mature, enlightened meaning of that term. As to the ultimate gunfight, when this does occur, in rocky terrain with bullets bouncing off stones which magnify their sound, we are treated to a preview of that unforgettable confrontation between James Stewart and Stephen McNally at the finale of Anthony Mann's *Winchester '73* the following year.

The production team merits attention. Key writer Peter Viertel (1920-2007), a refugee from Hitler's Germany who served in the U.S. military,

IS THIS THE MEANEST MAN ALIVE? John Ireland (seen here as 'Cherry Valance' in Red River) portrayed an even more ruthless gunslinger is this Western noir.

had been hired during the war to pen Alfred Hitchcock's combination of patriotism and thrills, *Saboteur* (1942). He would work on such classics as John Huston's *The African Queen* (1951), eventually penning a novel about the making of that legendary film. That book would serve as the basis for one of Clint Eastwood's quirkiest projects, *White Hunter, Black Heart* (1990). Canadian-born director Mark Robson (1913-1978) began his career as a member of Val Lewton's team of low-budget filmmakers who redefined the horror movie. Robson directed three of the best: *The Seventh Victim* (1943), *Isle of the Dead* (1945), and *Bedlam* (1946). He moved on to helm one of the 'serious' dramas about boxing, *Champion*, and racism in the military, *Home of the Brave*, both 1949. Sadly, his reputation would be tarnished when, nearing career's end, he turned out three of the worst movies ever made: *Valley of the Dolls* (1967), *Happy Birthday, Wanda June* (1971), and what may be the most awful WWII adventure film, *Avalanche Express* (1979). Lee Marvin and Robert Shaw were (sadly) at last co-starred, much to the disappointment of each tough-guy's fans. If that caused Robson's legacy to falter, *Roughshod* ought to serve as a footnote to the golden era of his career.

A WOMAN TO REMEMBER: Gloria Grahame's unique beauty, suggesting a world of past experiences and not all (or even most) of them good, qualified her for edgy film noirs and dark postwar Westerns.

75. SEA OF GRASS, THE (1947)
Rating: **** ½

CREDITS:

Elia Kazan, dir.; Marguerite Roberts, Vincent Lawrence, Edward E. Paramore Jr., scr.; Pandro S. Berman, pro.; Herbert Stothart, mus.; Harry Stradling Sr., cin.; Robert Kern, ed.; 1.37:1; B&W; 123 min.; Metro-Goldwyn-Mayer.

CAST:

Katharine Hepburn (*Lutie Cameron Brewton*); Spencer Tracy (*Col. James B. Brewton*); Robert Walker (*Brock*); Phyllis Thaxter (*Sara Beth*); Melvyn Douglas (*Brice Chamberlain*); Harry Carey (*Doc. J. Reid*); Ruth Nelson (*Selina Hall*); William 'Bill' Phillips (*Banty, a Cowboy*); Robert Armstrong (*Floyd McCurtin*); James Bell (*Sam Hall*); Robert Barrat (*Judge Seth White*); Charles Trowbridge (*Cameron*); Russell Hicks (*Maj. Dell Harney*); Trevor Bardette (*Boggs*); Morris Ankrum (*A.J. Crane*); Eddie Acuff (*Cattlemen*); Douglas F. Fowley (*Gamblin' Man*); Stanley Andrews (*Sheriff Bill*); Whit Bissell *(Ted)*; Jimmy Hawkins *(Young Brock)*; Carol Nugent (*Young Sara Beth*); Glenn Strange (*Roach*).

Approximately 22 minutes into Sergio Leone's *Once Upon a Time in the West*, a train roars into a small frontier town. Passengers disembark; people hurry to meet them. Then, a lone woman from the East (Claudia Cardinale), dressed in finery and holding her head high, steps down from the passenger car. She glances about, looking for her ranch owner fiancée, he nowhere in sight. Briefly, she stands stock still, as tides of people and animals drift by on either side. Several women and men glance toward her with curiosity in their

WHEN A WOMAN FROM THE EAST MEETS A MAN OF THE WEST:
Katharine Hepburn and Spencer Tracy as the mismatched couple, their opposing liberal and conservative values destroying any initial sense of romantic love.

eyes, though most citizens are oblivious to the elegantly dressed lady's plight. Refusing to be so abandoned, this singular female empowers herself, boldly marching down the dusty street filled with everything from serious minded business people to dangerous miscreants, insistent on discovering what went wrong ... and why.

Like virtually every image in *Once Upon a Time* . . . , here is an homage/reference to a key moment in some previous Western, most well-known. Leone's opening portrayal of a gunfight combines elements of *Johnny Guitar* and *High Noon*. Here, though, the genre genius recalls a moment from a movie that rarely comes to mind when aficionados of Westerns discuss their all-time favorites. Though set on the New Mexico frontier, *Sea of Grass* (like the 1936 Conrad Richter novel that inspired it) is perceived less as a Western, in any generic sense, more a sweeping melodrama for those who admire the piece, a sentimental soap opera to those who do not. Either way, the narrative is indeed set in the 19th century's second half, in a kingdom within the greater nation of America that can vaguely be defined as The West..

The fourth of nine films starring real-life lovers Spencer Tracy (1900-1967) and Katharine Hepburn (1907-2003), *Sea* . . . like so many thoughtful fables about the frontier, from *Drums Along the Mohawk* to *The Virginian* . . . opens in the East. At least, in comparison to the many southwest settings to follow: St. Louis, perceived as middle-America in *Meet Me in* . . . (1944); here (by way of contrast to the film's key setting) a civilized world where gentility reigns. Like the heroine of Edna Ferber's famous stories *Cimarron* and *Giant*, a well-bred, well raised, if headstrong young woman determines to marry a

HOMAGE: Katharine Hepburn's female lead disembarks a train to find herself all alone in an unfriendly town; Twenty years later, Sergio Leone revived that iconic image for his epic *Once Upon a Time in the West*, starring Claudia Cardinale.

rugged rancher with whom she fell in love 'at first sight,' as the cliché goes. But the reality of 'Jim,' and the world he not only inhabits but is virtually married to, will provide 'Lutie' with culture shock. Like cattle baron 'Ryker' in *Shane*, her husband is determined to drive all sodbusters away and maintain open range, essential for watering his cattle. If he is a rugged individualist, a social conservative, and a civil libertarian, his enemies form a community of liberal-minded folks dedicated to bringing civilization, by way of schools, churches, and law and order, to tame the land. Their spokesman: 'Bruce,' a sophisticated lawyer of Lutie's class. In her naïveté, she once turned down such suitors in favor of pursuing romance and adventure in what momentarily seemed a bold new world; after living on the edge of a vast wilderness, harsh experience educates her to the West's harsh realities. Lutie finds herself drawn to what she once believed was too 'soft' a man, growing ever more uncomfortable with Jim's social Darwinism: Survival of the fittest, no prisoners taken; not even women and children spared.

If Jim serves as a three-dimensional portrait of Ryker, portrayed with considerable empathy as a torn person though never sympathy for his views, he also resembles Lionel Barrymore in *Duel in the Sun*. In fact, at the midpoint in each movie, the rough cattle baron organizes a virtual army of cowboys to attack the advance of progress. In that film, the oncoming railroad and, here, a caravan of settlers. As the separated-at-birth twins turn out to be, when push comes to shove, men of conscience, neither can bring himself to give the order to fire. At that moment, the tide changes. Though Jim in *Sea of Grass* does ride away, licking his emotional wounds, the man is virtually dead. His way of life, gone. The future has arrived and *Sea*... even more specifically than *Duel*... makes clear that there is both good and bad as to the new order of things. If much has been gained, certainly something has been lost in transition from a frontier outpost to a thriving city. As in *Cimarron*, the town we here perceive is more than a mere backdrop. As step by step the area becomes modernized, we witness the advances of civilization set against the losses of a stark beauty to be found in virgin land. *Sea*'s story is bittersweet, no surprise as it was written by Richter, whose *(The) Light in the Forest* likewise depicted the

"WHY, IS THAT 'SAM,' THE BARTENDER FROM *GUNSMOKE*?": Massive Glenn Strange, who came across as a combination of Boris Karloff and Lon Chaney Jr., had one of his first roles in a major Western as a rugged cowboy in *Sea of Grass*.

complexities of personal relationships in a country perceived in the process of inventing itself. Something essential in the interaction of humans creates a ritual that repeats itself, again and again. In the world, and in our literary and cinematic arts that distill, crystalize, and reflect reality.

Sadly, *Sea* . . . misses full greatness. Though Elia Kazan (1909-2003) wanted to film entirely on-location for a full verisimilitude of nature and society conjoined, MGM insisted that he and his team complete most of the shooting on their backlot and on soundstages for financial reasons. Only in rare shots, done by the second unit director far from Tinseltown, do we perceive the full sweep of people and places that, if only *Sea of Grass* had been created entirely on location---from the ground up, so to speak---this thematically worthy if aesthetically flawed film might have conveyed.

WHERE HAVE I SEEN THAT 'SHOT' BEFORE?: Fans of *Once Upon a Time in the West* will recall, on discovering *Sea of Grass*, that great moment when Claudia Cardinale and a driver pass through the vastness of the frontier.

76. SHEEPMAN, THE, aka STRANGER WITH A GUN (1958)
Rating: ****

CREDITS:

George Marshall, dir.; William Bowers, James Edward Grant, William Roberts, scr.; Edmund Grainger, pro.; Jeff Alexander, mus.; Ralph E. Winters, ed.; 2.35:1; C; 85 min.; Metro-Goldwyn-Mayer.

CAST:

Glenn Ford *(Jason Sweet)*; Shirley MacLaine *(Dell Payton)*; Leslie Nielsen *(Col. Stephen Bedford)*; Mickey Shaughnessy *('Jumbo' McCall)*; Edgar Buchanan *(Milt Masters)*; Willis Bouchey *(Frank Payton)*; Pernell Roberts *(Chocktaw Neal)*; Slim Pickens *(The Marshal)*; Robert 'Buzz' Henry *(Red)*; Pedro Gonzalez-Gonzales *(Angelo)*; Leon Alton, Richard Alexander, Eile Avery, Walter Bacon, Sam Bagley *(Citizens)* Irene Barton *(Mme. Fifi)*; Roscoe Ates *(The Town Loafer)*; Lane Bradford *(Cowboy)*; Lorraine Carol *(Amy)*; Harry Harvey *(Storeowner)*.

An under-discussed subgenre of the traditional cowboy film is the 'light-hearted Western,' not to be confused with burlesques of the genre such as *Cat Ballou* or *Blazing Saddles*. Rather, an easy-going Oater in which a charmingly genial tone is taken toward recurring themes and motifs. Perhaps the most beloved examples are *Destry Rides Again* (1939) starring James Stewart and *Destry* (1954/55) with Audie Murphy. In each, warmth and wit carry the

A DIFFERENT SORT OF 'OATER': Shirley Maclaine brought the elfin charm that would be most effectively displayed in Billy Wilder's *The Apartment* to a roughewn Western starring Glenn Ford.

day ... until the shooting starts. Both versions were directed by the same old Hollywood hand: George Marshall (1891-1975), who revealed elements of his unique approach in such early projects as *When the Daltons Rode* (1940). Marshall would eventually join various other directors to assemble *How the West Was Won* (1962). For *The Sheepman* , he was fortunate enough to collaborate with James Edward Grant (1905-1966). John Wayne's preferred scribe, this screenwriter had already revealed his abilities to extend comic relief as far as possible with the Duke's independently produced *Angel and the Badman* (1947). In the near future, he would do the same for *The Alamo* (1960) and *McLintock* (1964).

Here, the star is Canadian-born Glenn Ford (1916-2006), who in his own boy-next-door-now-grown-up lackadaisical manner easily shifted between Hollywood genres. As comfortable in classic film noir (*Gilda*, 1946;

GABBY HAYES, MOVE OVER! Beginning in the early 1950s, Slim Pickens gave that beloved old timer mighty competition as the greatest comic sidekick ever.

The Big Heat, 1953) as in service comedies (*Don't Go Near the Water*, 1957; *Imitation General*, 1958), Ford balanced such popular fare with a succession of high-quality Westerns. *Texas* (1941), *The Desperadoes* (1943), *The Man from Colorado* (1948), *3:10 to Yuma* and *The Fastest Gun Alive* (both 1957) are but a handful of upscale prairie dramas that showcased him in a variety of guises; shy hero, cold-blooded killer, hard-driven avenger, or simple townsman. Here, he plays a fast-talking con-artist who may remind movie lovers of Robert Preston in *The Music Man* (1962). In *Sheepman*, the 'trouble' is not pool but the title animal. 'Jason Sweet' arrives by train and announces to folks living in cattle country they will have to accept that he's bringing in The Woollies. As a former fast gun, he'll back up any opposition with hot lead. His brash appeal causes the local ranch woman 'Dell Payton' to break off her longstanding engagement to the cruel territorial boss known as 'The Colonel.' A gifted comedienne who would shortly deliver her greatest single performance opposite Jack Lemmon in Billy Wilder's classic *The Apartment* (1960), Shirley MacLaine here conveys the elfin appeal that transformed this talented actress into a superstar.

She also embodies a stock character in Westerns, The Tomboy, delivering what may be the definitive portrait of such a type. Previous examples include Barbara Stanwyck in *Annie Oakley* (1935), Claire Trevor in *Alleghany Uprising* (1939), Jean Arthur in *Arizona* (1940), and Ella Raines in *Ride the Man Down* (1952); future incarnations will be offered by Debbie Reynolds (*The Second Time Around*, 1961) and Doris Day (*The Ballad of Josie* (1965). Here is a third continuing role for women in Westerns along with the knowing yet vulnerable saloon singer and the demure, virginal, educated young woman from the East. Hard as nails but with a heart of gold, The Tomboy may wear masculine garb while on the trail, but she's eager to switch from pistols to petticoats when the right man ... one truly worthy of her ... comes along.

Two other stock characters on view here prove considerably less acceptable in retrospect. One is our hero's faithful sidekick, Angelo. He is played by Texas-born Pedro Gonzales-Gonzales (1925-2006), a flesh and blood incarnation of the Mexican caricature that Pat Boone once sang about in a then popular, now embarrassing 1950s comedy recording, "Speedy Gonzales." Here is a virtual embodiment of the slow-moving, weak-minded Latin male, a self-styled equivalent of Stepin Fetchit among African American supporting players. If there is any possible defense from our perspective as to such a gross caricature, it's that he is also lovable, loyal, and generous, as he would be the following year in the classic *Rio Bravo* with John Wayne. At the very least, this is not a reinforcement of negative iconography that once limited to Latin male characters as shifty, lazy, and more likely than not criminal.

The other, every bit (perhaps more so) unpleasant caricature is the unstated but obvious half Breed cliché, in which a man of mixed races is presented as abject evil. Though no one in the film ever does speak of the character's lineage, Choctaw draws on a despicable convention of the part-Indian desperado that reaches back to such figures in silent movies, long before Cecil B. DeMille challenged the negative cliché with his various versions of *The*

CLOWNING ON THE SET: Mickey Shaughnessy attempts to wrestle the director's job away from George Marshall.

Squaw Man. The difficulty with *Sheepman* is that there is no reason for the character played by Pernell Roberts (later of *Bonanza* fame), to be so identified; otherwise, issues which might have addressed race/ethnicity are not present. With a different moniker, this "bad man's bad man" figure would be no more offensive than Jack Palance in *Shane*, Lee Marvin in *The Man Who Shot Liberty Valance*, or Charles Bronson in *4 For Texas*. Not that anyone involved in this mostly likeable film intended an insult, however glaring today. What we encounter is simply another example of Westerns, like all movies, containing those once-unquestioned prejudices of the era during which they were produced and released.

HERE COME 'THE WOOLIES!: The hatred of cattlemen for sheep was not born out of any unfounded prejudice; unlike cattle, sheep rip foliage up out of the ground roots included, which means that the vegetation will not restore itself next year, a disaster for the ranchers.

77. SHOWDOWN AT BOOT HILL (1958)
Rating: ****

CREDITS:

Gene Fowler Jr., dir.; Louis Vittes, scr.; Harold E. Knox, pro.; Albert Harris, mus.; John M. Nickolaus Jr., cin.; Frank Sullivan, ed.; 2.35:1; B&W; 71 min.; Regalscope/20th Century-Fox.

CAST:

Charles Bronson (*Luke Walsh*); Robert Hutton *(Sloane)*; John Carradine (*Doc Webber*); Carole Matthews *(Jill Crane)*; Fintan Meyler (*Sally Crane*); Paul Maxey (*Judge Wallen*); Thomas Brown Henry (Con Mayer); William Stevens (*Corky*); Martin Smith (*Tex*); Joe McGuinn (*Mr. Creavy*); George Douglas (*Charles Maynor*); Mike Mason (Les Patton); George Penbroke (*Sheriff Hinkle*); Argentina Brunetti (*Mrs. Bonaventura*); Ed Wright (*Brent)*; Stacey Marshall (*Saloon Girl*); Shirley Haven (*Townswoman*); Tony Douglas (Will); Jose Gonzales-Gonzales (*Mexican Man*); Barbara Wooddell (*Mrs. Maynor*).

If nothing else, this little (to put it mildly) Western deserves a footnote in film history as the first Oater in which Charles Bronson (1921-2003) received top-billing. Born 'Bunchinsky' in a rough Pennsylvania coal mining town to poor Lithuanian immigrants, his service during WWII earned the future tough guy star an opportunity to pursue art studies under the G.I. Bill. Bronson's stark, chiselled, stoic aura caused Hollywood producers to cast him as thugs, villains, and half-human monsters. One early Creeper role: 'Igor,' the mad Vincent Price's partner in crime in the greatest color/3-D horror

BALLAD OF A SMALL MAN: Charles Bronson received his first lead in a theatrical Oater via this low-budget, big impact piece about a short fellow who proves that the Colt .45 was indeed "the great equalizer."

movie ever made, *House of Wax* (1953). Shortly, Bronson portrayed deadly gunmen (Robert Aldrich's *Vera Cruz*) and noble savages (Sam Fuller's *Run of the Arrow*) in those rugged postwar Westerns then redefining the genre. Charlie could have had 'The Man with No Name' role in Sergio Leone's *Dollars Trilogy* but turned that opportunity down, allowing Clint Eastwood to swiftly achieve superstardom. Still, the powerful performer had acquired a fan base in Third World countries, where humble people who did not even know his name lined up to see 'Il Brutto' at local Rialtos. When Eastwood eventually turned down Leone for 'The Man with a Harmonica' role in *Once Upon a Time in the West* (1968), Bronson belatedly came on board. Sadly, the superstar afterwards squandered his possibilities. Instead of like Clint opting for mainstream work, he instead appeared in third-rate hack projects helmed by fourth-rate directors. Yet the legend far outweighs the work: however mediocre his later films may be, the weather-beaten, squint-eyed, so-ugly-he's-handsome face transformed into a Western icon.

Here was where that all began. Shot in the low-key, noir-influenced, unsparingly unromantic style set in place by *High Noon*, the narrative obeys

A WOMAN IN THE WEST: Carole Matthews effectively brings to life a young female whose experiences on the frontier have caused her to become frigid in this *very* adult Western.

ancient-world unities of time and place. The plot unfolds in an unknown shabby outpost of civilization, takes place over a brief period of time, and continues the theme of a threatened individual standing against an entire community, refusing to compromise his values even if this costs him his life. Intriguingly, though, the script by Louis Vittes (1911-1969) reverses the situation of 'Will Kane' in Hadleyburg, turning everything upside down, inside out, and virtually backwards. Whereas that classic film's paradigm posited a decent man of the people up against craven raw capitalists, here we encounter the inverse. Like *High Noon*'s bad men, 'the Miller gang,' Luke is an outsider who heads into town and, so far as the locals are concerned, brings four invisible horsemen of the Apocalypse along with him. A bounty hunter, he arrives to pick up a well-to-do citizen, 'Maynor,' dead or alive, then head off to a large city where he can collect the reward. But Luke cannot leave without written proof that he did indeed kill this specific wanted man. Meanwhile, the body must be buried at once owing to extreme summer heat. But no witnesses will sign the necessary death certificate, standing up to Luke's cold-hearted raw capitalism. The only way he can possibly prove that he did indeed bring down the wanted man is to arrive for an early morning funeral at Boot Hill, where burial will necessitate admission of the dead man's name. Here, though, instead of cowering in their homes, the citizens of this little burg head out to

RETURN OF THE SCENE STEALER: John Carradine (right) is the town barber who provides a Jiminy Cricket like conscience to a wild west Pinocchio Charles Bronson, left).

meet him and do whatever may be necessary to make certain no profit will be garnered this time around.

However different the two narratives may be, this movie's concept, and the anti-hero's arc, recalls that of James Stewart in the considerably loftier studio Western *The Naked Spur*. Once again, it is an angel of mercy,' Jill' (this, fascinatingly, the first name of Bronson's real-life future wife, J. Ireland). The girl's back story is utterly unique from anything experienced in a Western film; big-scale or, like this, an indie. Jill's mother is the well-liked town prostitute 'Sally.' The older woman's comfort with casual sexuality has caused daughter Jill to become frigid, paralyzed when surrounded by machismo town boys who have easy access to Jill's mother. Luke has his own cross to bear. Short as to physical stature, he's never been able to properly respond to women for fear they will laugh at him. Indeed, his killings (as we gradually discover) may have more to do with a bitterness against his birthright as 'a little man' than any desire for profit. Luke is out to prove that he's tall, in every sense but physical height. Gradually, the two social misfits come together, each healing the other's psychological problems through a convincing development of love as well as need. The question, though, remains: What will happen when Luke makes the gunman's walk to ...

Better known as a top Tinseltown editor (including the upcoming Western *Monte Walsh*), Gene Fowler Jr. occasionally had an opportunity to direct. His two youth-oriented monster movies (*I Was a Teenage Werewolf*, 1957; *I Married a Monster from Outer Space*, 1958) rank alongside *The Blob* (1958) as memorable classics of what was otherwise a *declasse* subgenre of horror. Here, Fowler's directorial choices are precise, economic, convincing. Though hardly in a class with *High Noon*, this stark, mood-drenched, atmospheric piece comes closer in quality to that masterwork than most other mid-1950s examples of the 'adult' Western form.

"PLAY IT AGAIN, SAM!": Some fifteen years following the initial release of *Showdown*, someone had the bright idea of sending it around once again to Third World markets, where Bronson had become a superstar; note that the imagery suggests a contemporary spaghetti Western rather than the most 'adult oater' that the film in fact is.

78. SLOW WEST (2015)
Rating: ****

CREDITS:

John Maclean, dir.; Maclean, scr.; Iain Canning, Rachel Gardner, Conor McCaughan, Emile Sherman, Michael Fassbinder, pro.; Jed Kurzel, mus.; Robbie Ryan, cin.; Roland Gallois, Jon Gregory, ed.; 1.66:1; C; 84 min.; Film4/British Film Institute.

CAST:

Kodi Smit-McPhee (*Jay Cavendish*); Caren Pistorius (*Rose Russ*); Michael Fassbender (*Silas Selleck*); David T. Lim (*The Tattooed Man*); Bryan Michael Mills (*Minstrel*); Aorere Paki (*Young Native American*); Jeffrey Thomas (*A Union Officer*); Joseph Pasi, Sam Manzana, Tawanda Manvimo (*Congolese Singers*); Eddie Campbell (*Skelly*); Ben Mendelsohn (*Payne*); Jon Cummings (*Gull*); Michael Whalley (*'The Kid'*); Karl Willetts (*Johan*); Rory McCann (*John Ross*); Brooke Williams (*Maria*); Evie Simon, George Simon (*The Swedish Children*); Ken Blackburn (*McKenzie*); Tony Croft (*Angus*).

If Spaghetti Westerns were shot in Italy, Paella Oaters in Spain, and the Teutonics in Germany, what will be the nickname for films that take place on the American frontier but are shot in New Zealand? If *Slow West* turns out to be the first in a succession of such projects, then international audiences will have cause to consider a subgenre term. This film was conceived by John McLean, something of a man of mystery since (at this writing) he has not released the official date of his birth. Scottish as to ethnicity, Edinburgh educated, McLean (who shares the last name of but is not believed to be related

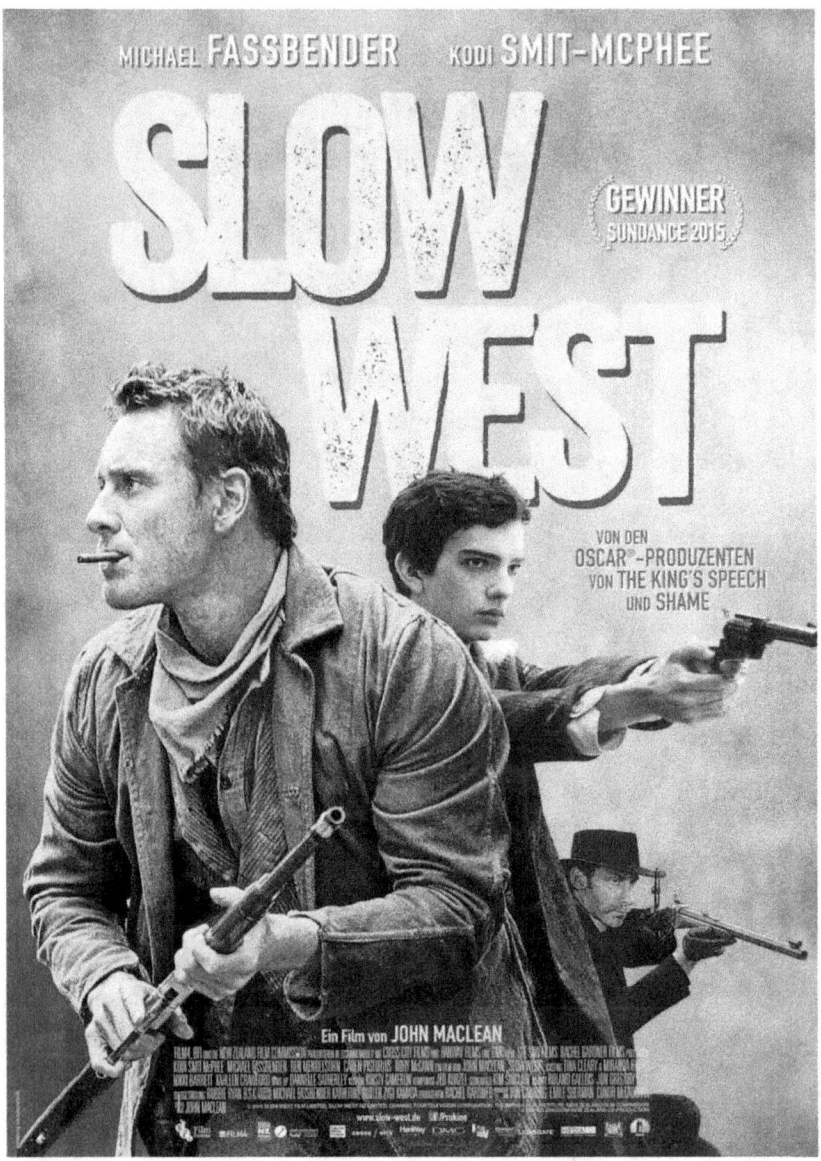

THE 21st CENTURY OATER: Some old cliches are abandoned while others remain in this New Zealand filmed Western that adds a modern sensibility to the period-piece tale.

to the original Marlboro Man, David) turned from edgy musician to eccentric filmmaker with several acclaimed shorts and this, his first feature. An award winner on the festival circuit, the aptly named *Slow West* reconsiders several key elements of the conventional Western, eliminates others, and visualizes the wide-open spaces from a unique, curious, and highly original perspective. If any previous film comes to mind in terms of pacing and sensibility, it's *Bad Company*, with a similar dreamlike aura of ordinary people who, while making the long hard journey, come into contact with various non-generic folks. They too are off on their own individual odysseys, along the brutal pathway to that amalgam of place, idea, and symbol known as the West. Some of these meetings will prove significant. Others, as in life, nothing more than land-locked ships which pass in the symbolic night. Diverse experiences--some horrific, others bleakly comedic--initially appear random; until, at the end, characters and story elements merge together in a notably cynical, contemporary variation of ancient-world fate.

The focal character is 'Jay,' a high-born 16-year-old Scotch lad who has left his homeland in search of the great lost love of his life. That is 'Rose Russ,' a girl of humble origins with whom Jay became involved back home. When his father attempted to end the relationship by storming into the Russ family's rural home, something untoward happened. As a result, Rose and her own father fled, booking passage to America. Somehow, in some way (like most other elements in the narrative, this is purposefully left ambiguous, at least until the conclusion), Jay has managed to determine the location where these fugitives hide, deep in the looming, threatening, omnipresent wilderness. Such a vagueness, which at times can prove unsettling and confusing for the viewer, adds something of a surreal sense to a work that otherwise hones to abject realism in terms of people and places. During a confrontation with a crazed military officer hoping to kill off the Indians one by one, Jay happens to meet and throw in with a rugged, experienced frontiersman, 'Silas Selleck.' He offers to guide Jay to the youth's destination for a price. But as Selleck provides the voiceover narration, we soon discover what Jay remains oblivious to. Though the older man may seem to be nothing more than a seasoned

THE UN-KNOWABLE FEMALE: Caren Pristorius as the woman our hero pursues across America . . . only to realize that the lady he so loves may not be precisely what he thought so long ago.

scout making a decent living by hiring out to help confused immigrants, he is in fact a bounty hunter. Deep in Silas' pocket, a wanted poster names and pictures Rose and her father at a price of $2,000. Selleck's plan: Deliver Jay to his destination, as promised; then take the two back to civilization for justice, dead or alive.

Confounding matters further . . . a professional killer with his long-range rifle as well as a scurvy group of rawhiders hoping to claim that considerable fortune.

Bounty hunters are, of course, nothing new to Westerns. On the other hand, most other familiar elements are missing. We see no towns or forts. The only Indians these 'searchers' pass appear to be living in a world all their own, casually squatting in an open-air camp, barely noticing as the leads happen by. Here is cinematic solipsism: Each of us inhabits an invisible country of our own making, existing only in an individual's own mind. At one point, a desperate Swedish family--driven to outlawry owing to the poverty that settles in on those foolish enough to believe the myth that they might 'live off the land,' which proves frightfully ungiving, at times seemingly hostile--cause Jay to finally come to terms with an existential brand of violence. And, as a result, at last know himself . . . his own true nature, previously a mystery. As a result, and in a strange sort of way, this might be thought of as a coming-of-age tale, also related to such Existential tales of self-discovery as Albert Camus' *The Stranger*.

Always, too, there is the question of his dream girl, supposedly waiting at the end of this little odyssey. She may be something else entirely from the idealized female who exists only in Jay's mind. (Is it mere coincidence that, like Scott Fitzgerald's most famous creation 'Gatsby,' this melancholy romantic remains true to a beautiful female who proves herself unworthy of his devotion?) Otherwise, there is no sense of the grand adventure to be found here. If anything, *Slow West* appears to have been designed to make a mockery of the Western myth. This uncompromising piece constantly brings up the issue of survival in place of any fabled Code of the West. Who will and who won't still be standing after the final shot is fired? If initially Mclean suggests this is a matter of being at the wrong place at the right time, or vice-versa, eventually

ONE MORE MAN IN BLACK: Like Jack Palance in Shane or Lee Van Cleef in *The Good, the Bad, the Ugly*, the icon of the cold-blooded killer returns in this odd, intriguing Oater.

the filmmaker implies that all along, a dark, odd, compelling, cruel, sense of destiny hangs over all that happens, even out in the middle of nowhere: The West.

Or at least this film's unique incarnation of that time, that place, that American construct.

MEN WITHOUT WOMEN: Westerns of today such as *Slow West* bring the once closeted theme of 'love stories between' men to the public at large following the impact of that contemporary classic, *Brokeback Mountain*.

79. SON-OF-A-GUN, (THE) (1916, filming; 1919, release date) RATING: ***

CREDITS:

Gilbert M. Anderson, Jean Robbins, dir./scr./pro.; 1.33:1; B&W; 65 min.; Golden West Photoplay Company.

CAST:

Gilbert M. Anderson (*Broncho Billy*); Joy Lewis (*May Brown*); Fred Church (*Buck Saunders*); Frank Whitson (*Double Deck Harry*); A.E. W(h)itting (*W.L. 'Old Man' Brown*); Mattie W(h)itting (*Mother Brown*); Paul Willis (*Buddy Brown*); Harry Todd (*Sheriff*).

The first Western movie star was born Maxwell H. Aronson (1880-1971), a son of Jewish immigrants who eventually settled in rural Arkansas. Feeling vaguely out of place from his early years, fascinated by stories about the (supposedly) Good Ol' Days in the Big Apple as spun by his father, the future filmmaker left home once he reached age 18. In 1900, Aronson Anglicized his last name to better assimilate with the evolving American mainstream. When jobs proved difficult to find in Manhattan, he fortuitously learned that across the river in Orange, New Jersey, a company owned by Thomas A. Edison shot flickers for the new entertainment craze, Nickelodeons: those raised boxes that allowed people to peer inside and watch silent flickers. Anderson met with the production manager, Edwin S. Porter. The abundant enthusiasm that characterized this tall, gawky fellow won him bit roles in pictures.

WHERE IT ALL BEGAN: Gilbert M. Anderson, aka "Broncho Billy": the first onscreen cowboy star.

Shortly, Edison and Porter determined to tell stories on film. One of the earliest was *The Great Train Robbery* (1903). Anderson played three roles: A tenderfoot forced to 'dance' by rough cowhands aiming pistols at his feet; a duded-up train passenger shot in the back during a robbery by the Wild Bunch; a gang member who falls from his horse during an attempted getaway.

The fall, incidentally, had not existed in the brief script, Anderson the worst rider in the crew. Yet he felt inspired by the very *idea* of a Western, a form of drama that had its roots in ancient world tales of adventurers and outlaws, now specifically American-ized even as had been the case with himself. Spurning offers to stick around the Black Maria, Anderson thanked his mentors but struck out to make his own pictures. These would depict the lives of cowboys on a fast-fading frontier, even then passing out of a regional history if simultaneously emerging the great national myth via popular culture: prairie songs, now being recorded on discs, pulp paperbacks, and perhaps most essential, The Movies. Hoping to position himself central in this process, Anderson moved to Chicago, where those restrictive copyrights that Edison held on various aspects of moviemaking might ,not have legal jurisdiction to restrain others, himself included.

AN EMPHASIS ON REALISM: Anderson insisted that his Western towns, and the saloons therein, appear as accurately primitive as possible; this led to a tradition of such Oaters that included those starring William S. Hart and Harry Carey Sr. in the Silent Era.

Again, Anderson's guileless excitement overwhelmed others. Borrowing money, he was able to open the Essanay Film Company, a pioneer endeavor in the filmmaking business that would all but corner the market until the settlement of Hollywood-land some ten years later. As to that, Anderson played a key role in such expansion. Whereas Edison and Porter were content to shoot near to the Atlantic, Billy travelled by train to the far west. In all truth, the concept of shooting on actual locations was born of his desire to share the most authentic visualization possible of such spectacular vistas with theatregoers all over the country and, in time, the world.

Though Anderson had already completed nearly a dozen shorts, his *Resurrection of Broncho Billy* (1910) initiated a 150-entry series of short films about a Westerner with a horsey moniker. Crude as the piece was, the 'flicker' included a key theme that would become essential to the genre.

BIRTH OF THE HOLLYWOOD WESTERN: Anderson was responsible for moving 'on-location' work from the wilds of New Jersey to the actual west for the sake of an accurate landscape.

That still emergent genius of the Western, John Ford, would in numerous upscale Oaters reject the idea of a pure hero, good in thought and action from birth to the grave. In films ranging from *Three Bad Men* through *Stagecoach* (1939) to *The Searchers* (1956), that avatar of Americana told tales of 'damaged goods' types, people who have (often through alcohol abuse) fallen from their heights. The Western has often featured such a Redemption tale. If the man known as 'Pappy' perfected such a narrative paradigm, Anderson all but invented it. Broncho Billy's humble legacy: He may have not 'got there' with the most, though he did get there first.

The better part of a decade later, Anderson would film the final instalment in the "Broncho Billy" saga. Fittingly, *Son-of-a-Gun* is one more tale of a man's redemption, inspired by a pure woman. Here, Billy plays an upstanding cowhand hoping to court and marry the lovely, respectable 'May Brown.' But as a man torn by all his years of desperate survival between civilization and the wilderness (as Teddy Roosevelt would frame our country's situation in his 12-volume *The Winning of the West*, 1900), Billy succumbs to his animalistic instincts and spoils a polite fiesta. Scorned by the girl's family, this outcast wanders the wastelands, eventually showing up in a meaner town. There, in a low-level saloon, he notices several con men, gambling at a table and taking a poor youth for all he's worth. Emerging as a hero (without quite realizing that's what's happening), B.B. draws his guns and forces them to return the swindled money. As it turns out, the boy was supposed to spend it on medicine for his ill mother. In what may strike a modern viewer as overly contrived plotting, she happens to be May's mother. Seasoned cowboy and young sidekick head home, where both are embraced and forgiven, leading to happy domestication for all. Many more sophisticated Western movies of the future would elaborate on such a primitive yarn.

So what brought the swift and sudden end to Anderson's short if intense career? Perhaps he overexposed himself with numerous Westerns, many shot on the cheap and barely satisfying, rather than leave his fans wishing for more on rarer encounters. Truth be told, though while he was indeed the original Western star, Billy never emerged as a strong actor. So long as there was no (or little) competition, he owned the cinematic open range. Then, more striking, gifted, and powerful performers--Tom Mix, William S. Hart, Harry Carey Sr.---appeared on the Hollywood horizon. Like an old soldier, Anderson faded away, eventually returning to the Western with a cameo in a star-studded old-timers' reunion, *The Bounty Killer* (1965). He may not have been the greatest Western star, or even close. But you've got to give Broncho Billy this: He was the original!

"WELL, YOUNG FELLA, HERE'S HOW WE DONE IT IN THE OLD DAYS!" In his final years, Anderson greeted one after another ambitious hopeful who hoped to learn from 'the original' how to play a gunslinger in the movies.

80. SPOILERS, THE (1914)
Ratings:
Contemporary Viewing Appeal: ** ½
History of the Western Value: *****

CREDITS:

Colin Campbell, dir.; Lanier Bartlett, scr.; William Nicholas Selig, pro.; Robert Stronach, mus. (original); Harry W. Gerstad, Alvin Wyckoff, cin .; 1.33:1; B&W; 110 min.; Polyscope.

CAST:

William Farnum (*Roy Glenister*); Kathlyn Williams (*Cherry Malotte*); Tom Santschi (*Alex McNamara*); Bessie Eyton (*Helen Cester*); Frank (M.) Clark (*Dextry*); Jack McDonald (*Slap Jack*); Wheeler Oakman (*Drury/The Broncho Kid*); William Ryno (*Struve*); Marshall Farnum (*Lawyer Wheatin*); Cleo Ridgely, Jules White (*Alaskans*).

Sex and violence: The two great obsessions of humankind since the origin of our species and, more specifically, Americans once the founding fathers set foot on these shores. From the moment motion pictures came into existence at fin-de-siecle, that has been the case too with this modern medium of entertainment and art. The latter first appeared in (*The*) *Execution of Mary, Queen of Scots* (1895), allowing audiences to believe (via a trick shot and invisible editing) that they witnessed the monarch suffer such a bloody fate. The former? A year later in Edison's *The Kiss*, in which stage stars John Rice and May Irwin--in devastating close-up--publicly smooched, then an illegal act

THE 'NORTHERN': Rex Beach's bestselling novel and the films derived from it stretched our frontier values up to the Klondike.

in New York City. Typical of a nation forged in Puritanism, still existing in the final days of Victorianism, outrage on the citizenry's part was directed more at *The Kiss* than *The Execution*. As actor/star Jack Nicholson observed in the 1970s, once the Ratings System allowed for an 'anything goes' approach: "Cut off a woman's tit and they give you a PG; kiss it, and you're branded with an X."

A bit of an exaggeration, to be sure. But certainly to the point. As to The Western film, sex (though not chaste romance) would long remain a taboo. Violence? Another matter entirely.

During the first decade and a half of The Movies' existence, flickers were frequented almost exclusively by urban society's lower-classes. Immigrants pouring off boats hungered for cheap distractions, discovering in the Nickelodeons a language without words. The Movies would not achieve full respectability until the release of D.W. Griffith's *The Birth of a Nation* (1915) which in its drama and spectacle justified films deemed worthy of the more polite middleclass. One year earlier, this emergent medium was still written off as fit only for what playwright Edward Bulwer-Lytton labeled 'The Great American Unwashed.' Another notable favorite of the least educated

WORTHY OPPONENTS: The great tradition of rough hero and slick villain began here, with William Farnum and Tom Santschi embodying archetypes that would reappear often.

among our citizenry: Boxing. Pugilism remained, in the early 1900s, a form of brutal gladiatorialism, outlawed in many cities, certainly not regarded as an acceptable sport like baseball. Boxing would become respectable in 1919, when on July 4, clean-cut young Jack Dempsey defeated giant Jess Willard in a championship bout fought not in a back alley but deep in the American heartlands. Previously? Oh, how the underclass loved it . . . even as they did those uncensored early movies.

None of this was lost on William Nicholas Selig (1864-1948), a Chicago-born entrepreneur bitten by the movie bug while watching Edison's *The Great Train Robbery* (1903). During the following decade, he turned out several dozen short subjects a year, including at least one early Oater, *Cupid in the Cow Camp* (1913). Hoping to draw in seismic-sized crowds by combining the twin appeals of boxing and movies, Selig combined the two in an unforgettable manner. Also, he was aware that something called 'the feature film' had just then come into being. Running more than an hour, Australia's budding industry had turned out *The Story of the Kelly Gang* (1906), about their own home-grown Jesse James. In England, a full-length version of *Richard III* (1911) brought a touch of Shakespearean drama to The Flickers. Closer to home, Frank Lloyd announced his intentions to push the length further still in his adaptation of Victor Hugo's *Les Miserables* (1917). And of course Griffith was hard at work on *The Birth of a Nation*. Selig needed an already existent story; hopefully, occurring in a frontier setting and including a fight sequence that would set everyone to talking.

He found his heart's (and mind's) desire in a bestselling novel (written off by most critics as sub-literary) by Rex Beach (1877-1949), an athlete and adventurer who had turned his own escapades into a primitive form of writing which emphasized the 'he-man' pulp adventure stories featured in male-oriented magazines. Beach cleverly combined such elements with soap-opera-ish situations, then the basis of popular women's fiction. In *The Spoilers* (1906), the author had created a melodrama set during the last great Gold Rush (1897-1899). With the closing of our continental frontier, the wilds of Alaska were perceived as the next potent land of risk, romance, and a potential to earn the American Dream through luck, pluck, and a determined refusal to fail. Beach included a triangular love story between rugged, honest prospector 'Glenister' and slick, shallow mine-thief 'McNamara' over Nome's most gorgeous saloon-girl, daringly named 'Cherry.' This also allowed for a patina of social commentary that would haunt the Western (including its northern variety) all the way through to Henry Hathaway's *North to Alaska* (1960): the essential conflict between raw and enlightened capitalists, the latter righteously winning in the end. In drama, if not necessarily so in actuality.

But what brought in the crowds was the ultimate fistfight. Director Campbell (1859-1928), who had been knocking out ten-minute shorts, dared extend the confrontation beyond what Beach had imagined. The duel begins in a barroom, where mortal enemies argue. Shortly, the action turns horrific, for others in the saloon and theatregoers as well. Every punch is duly recorded; we watch as the men literally rip one another's shirts off, blood flowing, bruises appearing on their chests and faces. The fight continues out into the muddy streets, an inspiration for the aforementioned Wayne/Hathaway Alaska film still far off in the future as well as the 1944 version of *The Spoilers* in which Wayne's hero goes up against Randolph Scott's villain in conflict over Marlene Dietrich, one of five theatrical versions of *The Spoilers*. All other screen fistfights, including those in non-Westerns---*The Quiet Man* (1952) with Wayne and Victor McLaglen; *From Russia, With Love* (1963) as Sean Connery and Robert Shaw duke it out on a train---are measured against this one.

Afterwards, Santschi (1878-1931) and Farnum (1876-1953) would find plentiful work in generic Westerns, as would William's brother Dustin. The Western (including Northerns) would become a key genre (contemporary crime films another) in which our fascination with violence would be most effectively expressed, for better or worse.

Sex? That would prove to be a more prickly issue . . . no pun intended, of course!

ALL FOR THE LOVE OF A GIRL: Though land-grabbing and mine-robbing are issues, Santschi and Farnum mostly fight for the hand of 'Cherry" (Kathlyn Williams, far right).

81. SQUAW MAN, THE (1931)
Rating: ****

CREDITS:

Cecil Be De Mille (aka DeMille), dir.; Lucien Hubbard, Lenore J. Coffee, Elise Janis, scr.; De Mille, pro.; Herbert Stothart, mus.; Harold Rasson, cin.; Anne Bauchens, ed.; 1.37:1; B&W; 107 min.; MGM.

CAST:

Warner Baxter (*Jim Wingate/Jim Carston*); Lupe Velez (*Naturich*); Eleanor Boardman (*Lady Diana Kerhill*); Charles Bickford (*Cash Hawkins*); Roland Young (*Sir John Applegate*); Paul Cavanagh (*Henry, Earl of Kerhill*); Raymond Hatton (*Shorty*); Julia Faye (*Mrs. Chichester Jones*); DeWitt Jennings (*Sheriff Bud Hardy*); J. Farrell MacDonald (*Big Bill*); Mitchell Lewis (*Tabywana*); Dick Moore (*Little Hal*); Victor Potel (*Andy*).

By 21st century standards, everything about this early sound era film is politically incorrect, beginning with its title. The term 'squaw,' however present (and prescient) during the westward migration, has long since come to be perceived as a negative racial/sexist epithet. Indeed, the designation of 'squaw man,' when applied on the frontier to an Anglo who married an Indian, suggested a state of degeneracy: Someone who had given in to forbidden instincts and 'slipped back' on the evolutionary scale. Yet when viewed in the context of the time-period during which it was produced, *Squaw Man* emerges as a bold attempt to redeem that phrase from deep-seated negativity. The film's Native American woman is portrayed in a far more positive light than had previously been the case, while the eponymous hero emerges as a figure of

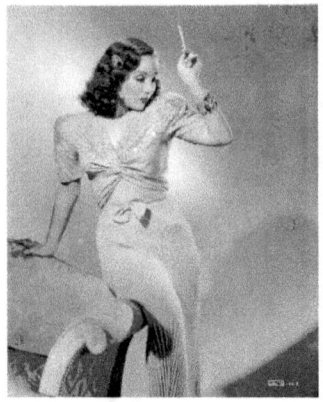 

RE-VAMPING THE VAMP: Early in her career, Lupe Valez played heartless seductresses of Anglo men; as The Movies matured and more enlightened images of women of color appeared onscreen, she here portrayed a fine and decent person who nurtures a white man back to physical and mental health, thus providing a new image for audiences to appreciate.

tragic nobility. The original intent here: Oppose bigotry as to a couple in a then-damned multicultural marriage; treat the couple, and their multi-racial offspring, with dignity.

Perhaps surprisingly, considering the cinematic sweep of the piece, the project originated as a 1905 stage play by Edwin Milton Royle (1862-1942). Though little is known about that forgotten scribe today, descendants insist he was an avid reader of socially/culturally significant novels. It's unlikely then that he would have missed *Heart of Darkness* (1899) by the Polish/English author Joseph Conrad. It too opens in London as several civilized Anglos cruise along the Thames, discussing one of their kind, 'Kurtz,' who disappeared into an unknown stretch of jungle adjacent to an offshoot of Africa's Congo. The much lauded man had travelled there to raise up the natives from their 'primitive' state. The opposite occurred, intellectual Kurtz sucked down into the primordial bog. 'One of them' now, he lived with a native woman in a hut. Conrad's reaction (by way of his author's spokesman 'Marlowe') to such a situation? "The horror! The horror!" Arriving as it did at the tail end of the Victorian century, *Heart of*

Darkness apotheosized a tradition of literature that offered up numerous such cautionary fables.

But a different literary light was about to emerge. A.E. Hudson's *Green Mansions* (1904) offered a self-conscious corrective, as its contrary bright-sounding title suggests. Here, a fugitive from the world of men disappears into southwestern Venezuela. He, like Kurtz, takes a native woman as his lover. 'Rima,' the bird girl, offers a sense of innocence that has less to do with the moral ignorance suggested in *Heart*... and instead comes across as romantic enlightenment. Close to nature, she embodies the notion of true spirituality found not in a church but The Green World: Religious "Splendour" in the grass, the "Glory" (of God) in the flower, as poet William Wordsworth dared to claim almost a century earlier. Shortly thereafter, in America, such Transcendental poets of the mid-to-late 19th century as Henry David Thoreau encouraged readers to return to nature by heading into the forest and discover a Second Eden at places like Walden Pond.

"LIGHTS! CAMERA! ACTION!" Cecil B. DeMille sets up a shot for *The Squaw Man*.

Likewise, G.M., Royle's *Squaw Man* set the pace for a re-evaluation. In this film version, Warner Baxter plays the male lead, originally performed on stage by early Western star William S. Hart.' Jim,' a leading member of the British aristocracy, is an upstanding gentleman deeply in love with Lady Diana, unhappy wife of Jim's 'rotter' of a brother. That wastrel has stolen money from charity to pay off debt owing to his gambling addiction. In the same lofty tradition of 'Beau Geste,' our noble hero takes the blame upon himself, in this case so Diana will not be publicly humiliated. On, then, *not* to the French Foreign Legion this time around but the vast American southwest. There, Jim recreates himself as 'a Westerner': rancher and honest entrepreneur who opposes a local bully, land-grabber, and raw capitalist, appropriately named 'Cash.' An ambushed Jim is saved by a Native woman who fell in love with him, aware he alone treats her people with respect. They marry,

A NEW VISION OF INTERRACIAL LOVE: If D. W. Griffith's *The Birth of a Nation* had warned that nothing good can ever come from the mixing of bloodlines, Cecil B. DeMille here insisted that the results can lead to a better future.

much to the chagrin of white trash neighbors who believe Jim has 'fallen.' But as in *Green Mansions*, the woman (significantly named 'Naturich') symbolizes everything that is finest, if simplest, in this vast land. Soon they share a child, whose love for the ways of cowboys *and* Indians is portrayed as a good thing. Everything changes, though, when Diana arrives unannounced. Her horrible husband died during a fox hunt. She has come to bring her beloved back home, only to discover ... and attempt to reckon with ... his situation.

What might have been a soap opera reaches tragic dimensions owing to De Mille's (1881-1959) unsparing portrait of an individual who only wishes to perform a Plato-like Good for everyone but inadvertently creates a no-win situation. Then there are the women, not presented as foils in the usual manner during the early 1900s--the dark lady as dangerous and seductive, the blonde as source of salvation--but as equally fine people, each in her own way. Mexican actress Lupe Valez (Maria Guadalupe Villalobos Valez, 1908-1944) here is presented in stark opposition to her more (in)famous 'Mexican Spitfire' image, emotionally hysterical, casually sexual. If the icon of a monosyllabic 'primitive' appears discomforting today, the better part of a century ago this offered a breakthrough. A noble savage cliché? True. Yet Naturich presents, in her goodness and simplicity, a great leap forward from the bloodthirsty savages cliché which Indians were all too often portrayed as then. How heartbreaking to observe her alongside Eleanor Boardman (1898-1991) as an Anglo woman every bit as sincere and strong as she is sophisticated. Women of color and white women must be seen as equally worthy; any judgement ought to be based on the individual person. Here is popular melodrama presented as what critic Kenneth Burke would hail as "equipment for living"; mainstream entertainment that does not play to the masses' prejudices but attempts to raise the communal consciousness of the public while watching.

Here then was a revolutionary message at the time. However retro *The Squaw Man* may seem today, when viewed in context---social, political, cultural, moral---of its initial appearance, the first significant step on a long journey toward anti-racist ideology in popular movies. And, hopefully, the citizenry that flocks to films.

82. STAGECOACH (1986)
Rating: ****

CREDITS:

Ted Post, dir.; James Lee Barrett, scr.; Jack Thompson, Hal W. Polaire, Willie Nelson, pro.; David Allan Coe, Willie Nelson, mus.; Gary Graver, cin.; Geoffrey Rowland, ed.; 1.85:1; C; Original air date: 5/18/1986; CBS; 100 min.; Heritage Entertainment.

CAST:

Kris Kristofferson (*Bill Williams*, aka '*The Ringo Kid*'); Johnny Cash (*Marshal Curly Wilcox*); Willie Nelson (*Doctor John H. Holiday*); Waylon Jennings (*Hatfield*); Elizabeth Ashley (*Dallas*); John Schneider (*Buck*); Anthony Newley (*Trevor Peacock*); Tony Franciosa (*Henry* Gatewood); Merritt Butrick (*Lt. Blanchard*); June Carter Cash (*Mrs. Pickett*); Jessi/Jesse Colter (*Martha*); Alex Cubick (*Luke Plummer*); David Allan Coe (*Ike Plummer*).

In art and entertainment as in ordinary life, everything exists in terms of contrasts. Take the case of this made-for-TV feature, originally to have been a major undertaking, with a pair of new Western towns built for the opening and concluding sequences. At the last minute, such plans were scaled back for a less prestigious TV Oater shot in and around Old Tucson. As co-producer, star, and provider of much of the film's music, raspy-voiced Willie Nelson (1933-) expressed disappointment that the piece would not be 'something special' as he had hoped for. Yet rather than merely one more routine small-screen Western, this version of *Stagecoach* played more effectively than Willie himself might have guessed possible.

They Went That-A-Way

THE KINGS OF 'OUTLAW COUNTRY' MUSIC: Members of The Highwaymen united to create an above-average made-for-TV Western movie: Back row, from left to right: Johnny Cash, Willie Nelson, Waylon Jennings; front, kneeling: Kris Kristofferson.

As to that promised comparison? If this *Stagecoach* fades in comparison to John Ford's 1939 classic, a Western on the level of artistry and importance of Orson Welles' *Citizen Kane* a year and a half later, a more immediate predecessor to Nelson's film is the expensive but empty 1966 widescreen/color theatrical release. Directed by the ordinarily reliable Gordon Douglas (*Rio Conchos*), featuring a cast of young hopefuls and old has-beens (from Ann-Margret to Bing Crosby), the piece looked like a particularly bad episode of TV's *The Hollywood Squares* set on the last frontier. Worst of all: Alex Cord, a lackluster/wooden actor cast in what had been the John Wayne role. 'The Ringo Kid' joins a wide-ranging troupe of pioneers traveling to Lourdsbourg. There, Ringo hopes to avenge the death of his brother, murdered by the wicked Plummer brothers.

Initially, Nelson had hoped to cast close friend/fellow Country/Western singer Waylon Jennings (1937-2002) as Ringo. Unfortunately, the recording stars both realized early on that, without previous acting experience, the

They Went That-A-Way

A HARD ACT TO FOLLOW!: The filmmaking crew for this 'new' *Stagecoach* (top) well knew the lofty reputation of the original (bottom).

part would prove too demanding. Instead, Jennings plays a mysterious gambler, the great John Carradine in the original, TV actor Mike Connors in in 1966. The lead went to Kris Kristofferson (1936-), who had risen to fame as a country/rock singer/songwriter during the 1970s. Kris had, owing to his considerable charisma, gone on to become a movie star: *Pat Garrett and Billy the Kid*, Michael Cimino's *Heaven's Gate* (1980). Willie cast himself as Doc, significantly altering Thomas Mitchell's Oscar winning (for Best Supporting Actor) 'Doc Boone' to the historical Doctor John H. Holliday, dentist, gambler, and deadly gunfighter.

This creates an original dramatic paradigm when 'Mrs. Mallory,' wife of a cavalry officer, gives birth in the middle of nowhere. The question is not whether a drunken doctor can redeem himself (a key Ford theme also present in *My Darling Clementine*, 1946) but whether a man who has not been trained for such a specific task can pull it off. In the post-feminist environment in which this piece was written, the great responsibility is not his but hers. As the prostitute Dallas notes, "It's the *woman* who does most of the work!" Both Dallas and Mrs. Mallory are portrayed less as the whore with a heart of gold and classy woman from the East stereotypes, rather more complex human beings, beyond attitudes based on class or gender.

Another motivation for Nelson's involvement was his dedication to Native American issues. His version of Doc serves as a spokesperson for what had then recently come to be referred to as Indians' Rights. Though an Anglo, he points out that Apaches led by Geronimo are not killing without motivation, rather in a last-ditch effort to hang on to the land that they believe to be theirs. However fine such sentiments may sound, the old problem inherent in both earlier versions again arises: When the attack occurs, we are induced to side with the Anglo heroes as they desperately defend themselves, in what can only be referred to as 'white solidarity.'

In truth, the pursuit of the coach appears paltry compared to the Ford version, there staged by stunt coordinator Yakima Canutt. On the other hand, the final gunfight with The Plummers is effectively re-imagined. Ford staged

A MAN WITH A VISION: Star/co-producer Willie Nelson made certain that in addition to exciting action and human drama, his *Stagecoach* would include a worthy message about America's mistreatment of our indigenous people.

this as an example of rugged individualism, Wayne's Ringo marching alone to the final reckoning. Here, marshal 'Curly' (Johnny Cash, 1932-2003) and the gamblers walk alongside him, much like Doc and the Earps in an O.K. Corral gunfight scene, based on solidarity and community. Here is an appropriate way to conclude a film which not only stars four musical performers but an already existing musical group. The quartet, who often played in pairs or trios, officially came together in 1985 as The Highwaymen. Annoyed by a then-recent shift toward mainstream 'gentrification,' they set out to bring back the golden age of raw, raunchy 'outlaw' country-folk performance.

Notably, then, Ringo is not in fact the male lead this time around. The focus shifts back and forth from him to the other three, each given a powerful backstory and allowed to emerge as a fully developed character for a true ensemble. The music completes the sense of community as all four contribute. If Ford's film had embodied one aspect of the Western … the lone hero/anti-hero who marches to a different beat and solves the situation alone … here we encounter that other aspect of The Gunfighter Trope: The community that, as in *Rio Bravo* (1959) or *The Magnificent Seven* (1960), must come together to get the job done.

83. STALKING MOON, THE (1968)
Rating: ****

CREDITS:

Robert Mulligan, dir.; Alvin Sargent, Wendell Mayes, scr.; Alan (J.) Pakula, pro.; Fred Karlin, mus.; Charles Lang, cin.; Aaron Stell, ed.; 2.39:1; C; 109 min.; National General Pictures.

CAST:

Gregory Peck (*Sam Varner*); Eva Marie Saint (*Sarah Carver*); Robert Forster *(Nick Tana)*; Nolan Clay (*The Child)*; Russell Thorson *(Ned)*; Frank Silvera (*The Major*); Lonny Chapman (*Purdue*); Lou Friz(z)ell (*The Stationmaster*); Henry Beckman (*Sgt. Rudabaugh*); Charles Tyner (*Dace*); Richard Bull (*Doc*); Sandy Brown Wyeth (*Rachel*); Joaquin Martinez (*Julio*); Boyd 'Red' Morgan (*Shelby, the Stage Driver*); Richard Farnsworth (*A Westerner*); James Olson (*Cavalry Officer*); Nathaniel Narcisco (*Salvaie*).

1968 turned out to be a fascinating year for American films in general, the Western particularly. Old-fashioned epics like *The Big Country* starring Gregory Peck or *The Unforgiven* with Burt Lancaster were all at once a thing of the past. The form had become more realistic during the decade, when *Duel in Diablo* (however incompetent as a genre piece, retro or nouveau, owing to the talentless director Ralph Nelson) focused with graphic intensity on the difficult status of women who had been captured, married to Native American men, then attempt to return to their homes. The Spaghetti Western

A MAN OF GOOD WILL: Like his previous role as a conscientious citizen in his Oscar winning project To Kill a *Mockingbird*, Gregory Peck here embodies the same sort of stalwart person of righteous conviction that has been basic to the Western genre from Harry Carey Sr. to Gary Cooper and beyond.

simultaneously introduced the notion of a 'whistling soundtrack' as musical accompaniment to vivid, colorful images, adding a haunting sense of nostalgia to quirky tales from the past. Only a year later, even as the Ratings System appeared in the wake of *Bonnie and Clyde* and *The Graduate* (1967), the already strained Hollywood studios fell apart at their seams. Then *Mackenna's Gold* with Peck headlining an all-star cast flopped while the bloodthirsty *The Wild Bunch* and kinder, gentler *Butch Cassidy and the Sundance Kid* scored with audiences and critics.

One year before the release of those big pictures, this intimate piece appeared, fascinating the rare diehard Western fans who sought it out, sadly ignored by most moviegoers who had at least temporarily lost interest in the genre. The story bears a striking similarity to a "B" Western of a decade earlier, Charles Marquis Warren's *Trooper Hook*, in which cavalryman Joel McCrea found himself saddled with a woman (Barbara Stanwyck) rescued from Indians, as well as her child with a warrior. The trio is pursued by a relentless and vengeful Native American husband/father who wants his son back and will kill anyone who stands in his way. As a Western of the 1950s, it isn't surprising that there the tale was told entirely from the Anglo point of view. Though movies like *Broken Arrow* had depicted the Apache in more human (and humane) terms than ever before, Warren had been the sole holdout. His *Arrowhead* featured Jack Palance as a Geronimo-like warrior who kills not only to hold on to his land and his nation but for the sheer love of doing so. Likewise, *Trooper Hook* (by the same filmmaker) offered no sense of dimensionality to the pursuing Native American. He might be something out of a monster movie, a malevolent force determined to keep the child from joining the Anglo majority where his son is scheduled to be 'saved' in a now-questioned manner: Stripped of his Native culture if not the bloodline.

A decade later, America had---socially, culturally, politically and morally---transformed into an entirely other world. Though the Civil Rights Movement focused on issues in the Deep South as to clear inequities between white and black citizens, many activists had also taken up the cause of the Native American. Shortly, films---great *(Little Big Man)*, mediocre (*A Man Called Horse*), and horrible (*Soldier Blue,* not surprisingly directed by Nelson)---would bring the necessity of a new, more enlightened vision of the Indian to the mainstream. How strange, then, at least from today's perspective, to

A CONTRAST IN CHARACTERIZATiONS: Though the pureblood Native American is here once again portrayed as a deadly symbol of abject brutality by Nathaniel Narcisco, the man of mixed blood and complex heritage receives a much-welcomed sense of enlightenment as here embodied by Robert Forster.

discover a film from that era which presents a Native American as something of a predecessor to the shark in *Jaws*--an inhumane agent of death and torture, if certainly not without a hint of sympathy. Notably (perhaps ironically), *Stalking Moon* was created by the same producing team (and with the same star) that had released *To Kill a Mockingbird* a mere five years.

That said, on the level of a thriller Western, *Stalking Moon* rates as a near-perfect adventure, with gorgeous shooting in out of the way areas of Arizona, a slow-building tension that reaches an intense crescendo as the antagonists go at one another with the fury of Achilles and Hector outside the walls of Ilium. A sly sense of humor (most notably at a quiet mealtime in which Peck's scout attempt to strike up a conversation with insistently silent observers) during the film's first half (before the long duel begins) carries an open-minded audience through purposefully slow (though never tedious) sections. The wait proves worth it, setting up one of the greatest mano-e-mano fights since *The Spoilers*. If today we may cringe at the film's dehumanization of the Apache, so far as sensitivity to ethnic minorities takes us, the discriminating viewer may appreciate that the Avenger is glimpsed only at the far edges of the frame, less a flesh-and-blood Apache than a ghost warrior. As a result, this might be thought of as a horror film set in the old West rather than a generic Western, per se.

THE PLIGHT OF A WOMAN: An Anglo female who cherishes her son by a Native American male, previously embodied by Barbara Stanwyck in the high-quality B picture *Trooper Hook*, is here embodied by Oscar-winner Eva Marie Saint.

In another sense, though, *The Stalking Moon* does reveal a heightened sensitivity toward racial issues. Perhaps no more despised element in studio movies was the portrayal of people of mixed race as displaying the worst of both worlds. Here, that bias is challenged. No matter how sympathetic Peck's frontiersman may be, we become more emotionally involved with his loyal pal 'Nick Tana.' Other characters regularly refer to him as 'The Breed.' However deplorable the use of that term strikes us as today today, that was the word in use at the time of this narrative. Happily, Nick's character reverses the stereotype in context. The underappreciated actor Robert Forster (1941-2019) closely resembles Charles Bronson in similar roles: Brave, smart, sympathetic, dedicated to his true friends, with a strong moral compass. *The Stalking Moon* offers, for those who revisit it, a memorable if difficult antique from an era when Hollywood, and the Western, were seriously searching to find a new, progressive voice for an old, traditionalist genre.

THE OFT-TOLD TALE: Some ten years earlier, *Trooper Hook* offered a similar narrative to the one featured in *The Stalking Moon*

84. STATION WEST (1948)
Rating: ****

CREDITS:

Sidney Lanfield, dir.; Frank Fenton, Winston Smith, scr.; Dore Schary, Robert Sparks, pro.; Heinz Roemheld, mus.; Harry J. Wild, cin.; Frederic Knudson, ed.; 1.37:1; B&W; RKO Radio Pictures.

CAST:

Dick Powell (*Haven*); Jane Greer (*Charlie*); Burl Ives (*Balladeer/ Hotel Clerk*); Agnes Moorehead (*Mrs. Carlson*); Tom Powers (*Capt. Iles*); Gordon Oliver (*Prince*); Steve Brodie (*Stellman*); Guinn Williams (*Mick*); Regis Toomey (*Goddard*); Michael Steele (*Jerry*); Olin Howland (*Cook*); John Berkes (*Pianist*); John Doucette (*Bartender*); Dan White (*Pete*); John Kellogg (*Ben*); Charles Middleton (*Sheriff*): Suzi Crandall, Marie Thomas (*Girls*).

If not before then certainly after 1945, every studio turned out noirs, none with such success as R.K.O. Indeed, the small company veered in this direction before the war ended with odd, shadow-strewn horror items such as *Cat People* (1942) and the hardboiled detective tale *Murder, My Sweet* (1944). The latter opened a new niche (and second act in a rich Hollywood career) for Dick Powell (1904-1963). Previously written off as a light leading man in such appealingly over-the-top Warners' musicals as *Footlight Parade* (1932) and *Dames* (1934), he now embodied a brash anti-hero/lone wolf—Raymond Chandler's 'Philip Marlowe'—in a glib, suave, nonchalant manner that compares well with Humphrey Bogart's interpretation in *The Big Sleep* (1946).

WHERE 'FILM NOIR' INTERSECTS WITH 'THE OATER': 'The City of Fear,' as *Station West* was known in several foreign markets, offered a contemporary crime movie title for a story sent in a Western setting.

RKO also turned out what many consider to be the most perfect example of the emergent genre with *Out of the Past* (1947), featuring the nouveau femme fatale. Earlier, such figures were mainly Spiderwomen and/or Dragon Ladies, often seen in sharp contrast to pure, virginal heroines. Now, Jane Greer (1924-2001) provided what fans consider to be the perfect/definitive genre woman: soft as a kitten when it serves her purposes, without pity when

THE BALLADEER: Burl Ives' dual careers as a folksinger and an actor qualified him to offer a combination of the two in *Station West*.

push comes to shove. Additionally, R.K.O.--realizing that the old-fashioned Western would not be tenable in a brave new nuclear world--experimented with Western Noir, Oaters shot in their usual locations though now presented in a murky form of black and white cinematography that characterized those modern mysteries set in our asphalt jungles.

In the Western noirs—*Pursued* (1947), *Blood on the Moon* (1948), both starring modern-day noir favorite Robert Mitchum—any old notions as to The Good Guys vs. The Bad Guys dissipated. Here instead were flawed people, scrambling desperately to succeed at their ambitions and obsessions or, at least, survive. The forgotten classic of this nouveau Western is *Station West*, with Powell all but reincarnating his Philip Marlowe icon: one more brazen, self-assured 'investigator' (rather than the traditional 'marshal' or 'sheriff' of conventional Westerns) opposite Greer as a period piece version of the heartbreaker/maneater she had already perfected. Here though the situation is shifted to a drab, menacing version of a frontier town that's fallen under the spell of a virtual ganglord. In this case, a gorgeous female with a man's 'handle': 'Charlie,' as powerful (if vulnerable when the right man finally comes along) as Joan Crawford in her then-contemporary crime films *A Woman's Face* (1941) and *Possessed* (1947). Close observers of the Western note a direct line running from Greer's Charlie to Joan's 'Vienna' in *Johnny Guitar* (1954), if that color-noir Western has a notably less tragic conclusion that what we experience here. Toss Marlene Dietrich in *Rancho Notorious* into the mix, and we have the top triad of this type--at least until Barbara Stanwyck joined the group and, in a succession of films, blew all other contenders out of the water.

The snappy dialogue provided for the anti-hero by writers by Frank Fenton 1903-1971) and Winston Miller (1910-1994) was not new to movies, essential to the classics *Double Indemnity* (1944) and *(The) Lady from Shanghai* (1947). What allowed such brisk talk to come across as fresh, unexpected, even mildly shocking was their appearance not in a snappy Bogart-and-Bacall confrontation but a cowboyish setting. Everything about Dick Powell defied conventions of the Western hero. Hardly Tall in the Saddle like

John Wayne in the film of that title, here was a pugnacious little tough guy of the sort James Cagney (*The Roaring Twenties*, 1939) had effectively portrayed in contemporary Mean Street situations. In many ways, this film also set the pace for what would become known as the adult Western that shortly developed during the 1950s. Though *The Gunfighter* (1950) and *High Noon* (1952) are recalled as early examples of neo-Westerns that forsook the visual glory of our wide-open spaces and magnificent Monument Valley natural spires to focus intensely on small, self-contained citified settings, *Station West* was the original work to set such an approach into place ... and motion.

More telling, it's the film too that predates *High Noon* with a ballad which sums up the central theme in a way that recalls an ancient Greek Chorus. Here, it's performed by folksinger Burl Ives, also onscreen as the wise, witty hotel clerk, presaging an unseen Tex Ritter in *High Noon*. Again, those who consider themselves aficionados of this form love to debate whether producer

THE COWBOY AND THE LADY: Jane Greer and Dick Powell brought their ulta-modern images to this dark tale of the old West.

Stanley Kramer would have thought to add such a musical accompaniment to his classic had he not previously seen this unappreciated but impactful film.

This was the first Western for director Sidney Lanfield (1898-1972), who as a result of his success with later medium budget Oaters would soon be hired to helm episodes of TV's adult Westerns including *Wagon Train*. Even the supporting cast suggests a desire to mix and match elements of the Western with others from noir. Representing the former is Guinn Williams (1899-1962), who played similar supporting roles in such big-scale Oaters as *Santa Fe Trail* (1940) and *Billy the Kid* (1941). Contrasting with him is Steve Brodie (1919-1992), already associated with the contemporary crime film thanks to *Out of the Past* and *Crossfire*, both 1947. Seeing the two together as a silent bodyguard and overeager young lieutenant adds to the complex mixing and matching of genres. Do note: The film is based on a pulp novel by Luke Short. No relation to the actual gambler-gunfighter of that name, the Illinois-born scribe was born Frederick D. Glidden, assuming that pen name in order to add a sense of authenticity to his many so-called border tales.

THE MAN WHO WOULD BECOME PERRY MASON: Long before achieving good-guy status in the most popular lawyer TV show ever, Raymond Burr was cast as slick, sleazy villains in numerous Westerns including *Station West*.

85. STRAIGHT STORY, THE (1999)
Rating: *****

CREDITS:

David Lynch, dir.; John Roach, Mary Sweeney, scr.; Sweeney, Neal & Pierre Edelman, pro.; Angelo Badalamenti, mus.; Freddie Francis, cin.; Mary Sweeney, ed.; 2.39:1; C; 112 min./ Assymmetrical Prods./Channel Four Films/Walt Disney Films.

CAST:

Richard Farnsworth (*Alvin Straight*); Sissy Spacek (*Rose*); Anastasia Webb (*Crystal*); Matt Guidry (*Steve*); Jane Galloway Heitz (*Dorothy*); Donald Wiegert *(Sig)*; Joseph A. Carpenter (*Bud*); Jennifer Edwards-Hughes (*Brenda*); Tracey Maloney (*Nurse*); Ed Grennan (*Pete*); Jack Walsh (*Apple*); Everett McGill *(Tom the John Deere Dealer)*; James Cada (*Danny Riordan*); Sally Wingert (*Darla Rioardan*); Barbara Kingsley *(Janet)*; Jim Haun (*Johnny*); Wiley Harker (*Verlyn Heller*); John Lordan (*The Priest*); Russ Reed (*Bartender)*; Ralph Fneldhacker (*Farmer*); Harry Dean Stanton *(Lyle)*.

"Walt Disney Pictures Presents a Film by David Lynch."

'I wouldn't have believed it if I hadn't see it with my own eyes,' more than one theatregoer marvelled when that credit appeared as a prelude to one of the most oddly original yet appealingly mellow movies ever set in the American West. Walt Disney (1901-1966) had been no stranger to positive tales about families surviving in the West. Beginning with the *Davy Crockett* TV shows and feature film version (1954-1955), Disney Westerns offered

THE LAST COWBOY: Doomed old-time Western actor Richard Farnsworth took on the role of an equally challenged real life contemporary folk-hero in this mellow, deeply moving film.

inspired family films set on the wild frontier. David Lynch (1946-), on the other hand, more recalls a hipster/intellectual/maverick on the order of New York's infamous Andy Warhol. Such Lynch classics as *Eraserhead* (1977), *Blue Velvet* (1986), and *Mulholland Drive* (2001) offer surreal and violent (emotional as well as physical) caricatures of the very sort of small-town life that Disney aggrandized in such films as *Summer Magic* (1963), as well as the Main Street U.S.A. that awaits visitors to Disney parks.

Then again, we might recall that one of Lynch's most revered films-- also his breakthrough from the arthouse to the mainstream, *The Elephant Man* (1980), about deformed genius John Merrick--recalls such early Disney shorts as Walt's two versions of *The Ugly Duckling* (1931; 1939) as well *Dumbo*. Also, we might note that, despite Lunch's aura of sophistication, he was born and raised in Missoula MT: cowboy country. Also, that the story of Richard Straight might have been developed by Uncle Walt as a live-action piece back in the early 1960s, if the tale had occurred then. Strikingly, the concept contains all the key Disney elements: an iconoclastic character who insists on doing things *his* way; a supportive daughter who, her impairments aside, maintains a spiritual faith that her daddy can overcome all obstacles; and an optimistic belief that, whatever feuds separate us, a bittersweet reunion is always possible if one only recalls the old expression . . . blood of my blood.

In 1994, aging and partly disabled World War II vet 'Richard Straight' (1920-1996) learned that his estranged brother 'Lyle' recently suffered a stroke. The two had years earlier parted on less than congenial terms, the reasons somewhat vague in real-life and purposefully (also effectively) left unexplained in the film version. Determined to reunite with his sibling before either went to visit what Westerners like to refer to as the Sky Boss, Straight determined to travel from Laurens, Iowa to Blue Run, Wisconsin, a distance of approximately 243 miles. As a result of his physical issues, the elderly fellow could not drive; nor could his daughter Rosie, despite her dedication to the man, owing to her having been labelled as 'slow.' With no money for flying and no real desire to travel by such a modern means, Straight purchased a 30-year-old John Deere 110 lawnmower, hitched a trailer to the back, and set out at five miles per hour.

This was not illegal, as a driver's license isn't required for such a vehicle. Endless problems with the tired machinery, and constant episodes along the way (the journey consumed six months), led to a dual sense of being born

CAPTURING THE PLIGHT OF 'THE CHALLENGED': Oscar winner Sissy Spacek (*Coal Miner's Daughter*) here portrayed a woman with only simple and basic mental abilities in a notably enlightened manner.

again, in a non-parochial notion of that spiritual concept. For while learning from people as varied as a young pregnant runaway and a generous priest, Straight (at least in the Disney/Lynch version) experienced the getting, as well as giving, of wisdom. Without having made their acquaintances, could his eventual reunion with brother Lyle have concluded as successfully as it does?

The casting of Richard Farnsworth (1920-2000) proved a perfect choice. Born the same year as the character he portrays, Farnsworth had early-on developed capacities as a broncho tamer and horse whisperer. This led to him heading up the remuda for such big pictures as *Gone with the Wind*. Naturally, he was drawn to Westerns, varying in quality from Howard Hughes' camp classic *The Outlaw* (1943) to Howard Hawks' towering epic *Red River* (1948), at which point Farnsworth also became a bit player. In time, he rose to the status of supporting actor in *Monte Walsh* and *The Cowboys*. When director Alan Pakula needed someone to perform as (or, more correctly, embody) the last of the old timers in *Comes a Horseman* (1978), he passed over Oscar-winner Lee Marvin and chose Farnsworth as the more authentic candidate. A best supporting actor Oscar nomination led to the lead in an excellent Canadian Western, *The Grey Fox*, 1982, as real-life bandit Bill Miner. In a

AN INAUSPICIOUS SEND-OFF: Few of Alvin Straight's friends and supporters actually believed he might be able to complete the personal odyssey, though he 'refused to fail.'

terrible irony, and like Straight himself, Farnsworth learned while filming this deeply moving work that his own days were numbered. Following completion of the project, he chose to Hemingway-like take his own life.

And how appropriate that Harry Dean Stanton (1926-1917) was persuaded to play the brief but significant part of Lyle. Like Farnsworth, this superb professional achieved a cult following for his diverse roles, including parts in Oaters: *Ride (in) the Whirlwind* (analyzed in this volume) and episodes of *Gunsmoke, The Adventures of Tin-Tin-Tin, The Virginian,* and *Daniel Boone*. Stanton's own penultimate film, *Lucky* (2017), handsomely stands alongside *The Straight Story* as a legacy to this sad-mournful performer, as well as the equally mournful Farnsworth.

RETURNING TO HIS ROOTS: Sophisticate and surrealist David Lynch offered a surprisingly tender vision of the heartland in which he had been born and raised in this Disney release.

86. SUGARLAND EXPRESS, THE (1974)
Rating: **** ½

CREDITS:

Steven Spielberg, dir.; Spielberg, Hal Robbins, Matthew Barwood, scr.; David Brown, Richard D. Zanuck; John Williams, mus.; Vilmos Zsigmond, cin.; Edward M. Abroms, Verna Fields, 2.39:1; C; 110 min; Universal.

CAST:

Goldie Hawn *(Lou Jean Clovis)*; Ben Johnson *(Captain Tanner)*; Michael Sacks *(Slide)*; William Atherton *(Clovis)*; Gregory Walcott *(Mashburn)*; Steve Kanaly *(Officer Ernie Jessup)*; Louise Latham *(Mrs. Looby)*; Harrison Zanuck *(Baby Langston)*; A.L. Camp *(Alvin T. Nocker)*; Jessie Lee Fulton (Mrs. Nocker); Dean Smith *(Russ Berry)*; Ted Grossman *(Dietz)*; Bill Thurman *(Hunter)*; Buster Daniels/Danials (A Drunk); Frank Steggall *(Logan Waters)*; James N. Harrell *(Fenno)*; Roger Ernest, Guich Koock *(Hot Jocks)*.

This film, the first theatrical release for Steven Spielberg (1946-), is based on a true story; the plot features a throwback to the old days of a lawman out to capture a pair of young people whose values he cannot grasp. 'Lou Jean' and 'Clovis' are sweet-spirited young marrieds; the lawman after them, 'Capt. Tanner,' is an outwardly rugged, inwardly gentle person who has never been responsible for anyone's death and hoped (until now) he might retire with that proud record intact. Along for the ride: 'Officer Slide,' whom Lou Jean and Clovis inadvertently kidnap even as she helps her husband escape from a minimum-security prison for non-violent types. Their baby daughter has

A KINDER, GENTLER PRELUDE TO *NO COUNTRY FOR OLD MEN:* Oscar winner Ben Johnson (*The Last Picture Show*) embodied the essence of a decent law officer who hopes only to retire without taking the life of another human being.

been seized by authorities owing to a perception of the two as unfit parents. Though Clovis could bide his time and shortly walk out a free man, he is too much in love with Lou Jean to risk her abandoning him. So begins an odd journey as these gentle outlaws come ever closer to a fate of the sort that awaited Bonnie Parker and Clyde Barrow, true killers.

Stylistically, Spielberg distances himself from other auteurs of contemporary Westerns. Their bleak visions and understated narratives, such as Terrence Malick's classic *Badlands* of one year earlier starring Martin Sheen and Sissy Spacek, resemble an oblique/highbrow arthouse item by Ingmar Bergman. Instead, we here encounter a movie as emotionally engaging as anything but John Ford or Walt Disney, they the greatest influences on Spielberg, at least during his early years. First, note that in addition to several impressive directorial efforts for such high-quality TV series as *The Name of the Game* and *Columbo* (both 1971), Spielberg also helmed what many believe to be the most impressive made-for-TV movie of all time. *Duel* (1971), likewise featuring a southwestern setting, also qualifying as a Road Movie. There, a traveling salesman found himself in a one-on-one battle to the death with an angry trucker determined to force this isolated Everyman (Dennis Weaver) off the road. Such a setting proved a natural for this genius-in-embryo. Though born

A NON-VIOLENT 'BONNIE AND CLYDE': Clovis and Lou Jean take officer Slide captive, but never harm him in any way in Steven Spielberg's variation on the rural young outlaws on the run film.

in Ohio and raised in New Jersey, Spielberg had travelled to Arizona with his mother following his parents' breakup. Rather than a stranger in a strange land, he felt curiously at home with redneck locals, certainly more so than when the family moved again to Northern California. There, S.S. was bullied by upscale well-to-do Anglo boys. At this point, the great American southwest (which he'd also been viewing in Western movies, most notably *The Searchers*) took on a magical presence in memory: Spielberg's great love for the land and lifestyle, and the joy of being a Boy Scout, would be immortalized in the opening sequence of *Indiana Jones and the Last Crusade* (1989). From a distance, the uniformed kids initially appear to be members of John Ford's cavalry. Merging Spielberg's personal memories with his favorite movies. Hs classic Flying Saucer picture, *Close Encounters of the Third Kind* (1977), also takes place in such wide-open places.

That film also concerns a devoted mother, desperate to find her little boy, swept away (in that film's case, by non-violent invaders from the stars). Spielberg also produced *Poltergeist* (1982), featuring a similar mom who crawls deep into the land of the dead to rescue her child when the well-intentioned but hapless husband proves unable to function. The best males, however inferior to strong women, are those who try their best to return absconded children to their mothers. This theme links an imaginative-fantasy picture like *Jurassic Park* to the Holocaust drama *Schindler's List* (both 1993). Film historians coined a phrase, 'The Steven Spielberg Narrative,' to describe such diverse variations on a continuing theme.

Sugarland, then, rates not only as his first technical job as a director, but a surefire provider of initial proof that here was a true artist, however entertaining for a mass audience the movies are in initial encounters.

While the entire cast is convincing, the presence of Goldie Hawn (1945-) ought to be considered noteworthy. For here Goldie received an early opportunity to prove that she could excel in intense drama as well as light comedy. Equally significant as to casting: Ben Johnson (1918-1996), a long-time cowboy actor (and an authentic Westerner, from Oklahoma) who had supporting roles in "A" pictures including *Shane*, and such legendary Ford

WHERE IT ALL BEGAN: Steven Spielberg (left) made his theatrical premiere with Sugarland, here directing William Atherton as the hapless young ant-hero

films as *She Wore a Yellow Ribbon*. As well as *The Last Picture Show* (1971), for which the old-timer won a Best Supporting Actor Oscar playing . . . an old-timer. In large part, Spielberg chose Johnson for his film owing to that actor's gracious, humble sense of personal integrity, such qualities long since associated with the Ben Johnson image. Here he provides a predecessor to many such characters to come, perhaps most notably the world-weary, melancholic aging ranger played by Tommy Lee Jones in the Coen Bros.' *No Country for Old Men*. But this is a Spielberg film, so the adversary is not a calculated killing machine but a pair of harmless kids. This throwback of a lawman cannot grasp the way people 'out there' perceive the world in comparison to his own generation; that allows *Sugarland* to function as a Generation Gap fable, so significant in the early 1970s.

THE SHAPE OF THINGS TO COME: In addition to yet another southwestern youth-oriented Road movie, Steven Spielberg transcended the genre to offer the first of his many studies of motherhood, and such a woman's desire to recover her lost child at any cost.

87. SUPPORT YOUR LOCAL SHERIFF (1969)
Rating: ****

CREDITS:

Burt Kennedy, dir.; Walter Bowers, scr.; William Bowers, Bill Finnegan, James Garner, pro.; Jeff Alexander, mus.; Harry Stradling Jr., cin.; George W. Brooks, ed.; Cherokee Prods./Three Pictures/United Artists.

CAST:

James Garner (*Jason*); Joan Hackett *(Prudy)*; Walter Brennan (*Pa Danby*); Harry Morgan *(Olly Perkins)*; Jack Elam (*Jake*); Bruce Dern (*Joe Danby*); Walter Burke (*Fred Johnson*); Dick Peabody (Luke); Gene Evans (*Tom Danby*); Chubby Johnson (*Brady*); Dick Haynes, (*Bartender*); Kathleen Freeman *(Mrs. Danvers)*; Bill Borzage, Danny Borzage (*Townsmen*); Tom Reese (*Gunfighter*).

The very title, seemingly innocuous today, was the source of controversy more than half a century ago. For this was the year when straights and hippies found themselves locked in a culture war that split America in two. On the one hand, there were longhairs, openly hostile over issues including the nation's involvement in Vietnam and Civil Rights. On the other, a Silent Majority; Middle Americans no longer willing to remain quiet as cherished institutions became targets of violent rage, calling for law and order. Ronald Reagan, who had starred in a 1953 film of that name, became a political icon with their help. This movie managed to gently kid the 'Support Your Local Police' mentality in the 'safe' context of a period comedy/Western.

'MAVERICK' REDUX: Following ten years of movie stardom playing diverse roles in various genres, James Garner returned to an easygoing, cynical character who very much resembled 'Bret' on the popular TV show from the late 1950s and early 1960s.

The casting of James Garner (J. Scott Bumgarner of Norman OK; 1928-2014) allowed for a greenlight. After reading the script and sensing it was written with himself in mind, he not only agreed to star (for considerably less than his then-asking price), but co-produce as well. One of many virtual unknowns recruited to play leads in Western TV series during the 1950s, Garner had the good luck to land in Warner Bros.' most innovative Oater: *Maverick*. The lighthearted series, produced by Roy Huggins, offered a goofy sensibility in sharp contrast to *Cheyenne, Bronco, Colt. 45, Lawman*, and other examples of ABC's Western fare. Gambler 'Bret,' a fun-loving, female- seducing, living on the edge of respectability cardsharp wore a *black* hat. Though Maverick drew the line at killing anyone who didn't absolutely deserve it, he took the world around him with a caustic grin and casual shrug of those broad shoulders. Audiences followed the show until its star left for the greener pastures of feature films. When he deserted, they did too, accepting Big Jim as a key movie star for the new decade

In between Doris Day romantic comedies (*The Thrill of It All*, 1963), serious social dramas (*The Children's Hour*, 1961), and (with Steve McQueen) the World War II action classic, *The Great Escape* (1963), Garner appeared in two

THE RETURN OF 'OLD MAN CLANTON': More often than not cast as lovable old codgers in films like *Red River* and *Rio Bravo*, as well as TV's *The Real McCoys*, three-time Oscar winner Walter Brennan here brought back the kind of mean redneck family patriarch he had played in John Ford's *My Darling Clementine*.

big Westerns: The deplorable *Duel at Diablo* (1966) and the excellent *Hour of the Gun* (as Wyatt Earp, 1967). But as the 1960s came to an end, so too did Old Hollywood. In the post-*Easy Rider* (1969) era, Garner and others of his ilk returned to their TV origins. In *The Rockford Files* (1974-1980), he played a contemporary variation of his earlier Western hero. Eventually, he would return to that role in *Bret Maverick*. (1980-1981). First, though, came *Support* ... in which he brought Bret back if with a different name.

The premise:' Jason,' a no-account wanderer, is talked into taking over as lawman in a wild town by the 'respectable' citizens and assigned to make it safe for 'the right kind of people.' Yet the suited businessmen are so corrupt that they put the area's outlaws to shame. Still, Jason arrests dumb as an ox 'Joe Danby,' who has just shot a man down in cold blood. Shortly, 'Old Man Danby' and his other sons, as well as an army of hardened cowboys, ride into town, demanding Joe's release. This premise is identical to that featured in *Rio Bravo* ten years earlier. But if that Howard Hawks film boasted a sly sense of humor, here we encounter full blown satire . . . in part on that picture, also the entire Western genre. *Support* . . . appeared halfway between *Cat Ballou* (1965) and *Blazing Saddles* (1974), serving as a watershed moment for the Western genre as all the old serious conventions came to seem silly.

In addition to *Rio Bravo*, the film's plot references many other earlier Westerns. The lawman who prefers not to use a gun provided the premise for both *Destry Rides Again* (1939) with James Stewart and *Destry* (1954-55) starring Audie Murphy. The sweet, respectable heroine resembles Cathy Downs in Ford's *My Darling Clementine* (1946), here re-envisioned in what might be thought of as a predecessor to post-modernist humor. Initially, 'Prudy' seems the perfect catch for our hero. Step by step she is revealed to be a bimbo, beautiful but incompetent at pretty much everything from cooking to kissing. Luckily, the filmmakers were able to land an actress worthy of the role. Joan Hackett (1934-1983), had proven perfect opposite Charlton

A FORGOTTEN STAR TO REMEMBER: The late Joan Hackett brought her remarkable gifts for comedy to this 'fun' Western; three years earlier, she had revealed her dramatic chops opposite Charlton Heston in the classic *Will Penny*.

Heston in the classic cowboy drama *Will Penny* (1967) There and again here, she revealed a Carol Lombard-like ability to suggest elegance and class even while performing rough physical comedy of a sort that recalls the much-loved Keystone Cops of silent days.

Speaking of *Clementine*, three-time Oscar winner Walter Brennan (1894-1974) effectively spoofs his vicious patriarch in Ford's film. As an upright but uptight citizen, Harry Morgan (1915-2011) revives the very sort of stuffed shirt he played in *High Noon*. Gene Evans (1922-1998) starred in TV's *My Friend Flicka* before moving on to character roles in two dozen Oaters. Long-time villain and Popeye lookalike Jack Elam (1920-2007), here cast as a wary deputy, had earlier that year spoofed his own deadly image in Sergio Leone's *Once Upon a Time in the West*. Bruce Dern (1936-) offers a dry-run for his 'Man with Long Hair' who shoots down John Wayne in *The Cowboys*. As to the collaborators, Bowers (1916-1987) had written the short story that inspired a classic, *The Gunfighter* (1950). Burt Kennedy (1922-2001) first made his mark by writing four of the seminal Randolph Scott-starring/Budd Boetticher-directed films before moving on to direct *The War Wagon* and *The Train Robbers*, both starring Wayne. Here is his legacy movie, as charming a surprise today for first time viewers as it was way back when.

MEANEST MAN IN THE WEST: In John Ford's classic *My Darling Clementine*, Walter Brennan incarnated the historic scourge of Tombstone AZ; nearly a quarter century later, he effectively spoofed that role in this post-*Cat Ballou* comedy Oater.

88. SUSANNA PASS (1949)
Rating: *** ½

CREDITS:

William Witney, dir.; Sloan Nibley, John K. Butler, scr.; Edward J. White, pro.; R. Dale Butts, Nathan Scott, Stanley Wilson, mus.; Reggie Lanning, cin.; Tony Martinelli, ed.; C; 67 min.; Republic Pictures.

CAST:

Roy Rogers (*Roy Rogers*); Trigger (*Himself*); Dale Evans (*Dr. Kay Parker*); Estelita Rodriguez (*Rita*); Martin Garralaga (*Carlos*); Robert Emmett Keane (*Martin Masters*): Lucien Littlefield (*Russell*); Douglas (V.) Fowley (*Roberts/Walter P. Johnson*); David Sharpe (*Vince*) Robert Bice *(Bob Oliver)*; Foy Willing (*Guitaris*t); Riders of the Purple Sage (*Forest Rangers*); Peter Brocco (*Carter*); Bullet (*The Dog*); Jimmy the Crow (*The Black Bird*); Shug Fisher, Ken Cooper (*Jailbirds*): Johnny Paul (*Johnny*).

As the 1950s approached, issues that hadn't been attended to during the dark days of the Depression or our Crusades in Europe and the Pacific came to a head. As onetime candidate for the presidency Michael S. Dukakis would write in retrospect: "we began to recognize the limits of our ability to exploit our environment for private gain, thus creating environmental awareness and ultimately a political movement." This would culminate in *Silent Spring*, Rachel Carson's three-part series in the *New Yorker* magazine, published in book form during the early 1960s. In fact, for nearly a decade and a half, the government had worked at legally protecting our natural resources with legislation aimed at the

KING OF THE COWBOYS, QUEEN OF THE WEST: Though Roy Rogers and Dale Evans headlined many B budget musical Oaters from Republic, Susannah Pass is the one that still speaks to environmentally minded audiences of today.

preservation of forests, fields, and clean water. As early as June 30, 1948, The Federal Water Pollution Control Act came into being. As always, Hollywood (even Poverty Row studios) rushed to support the latest good cause.

A FORGOTTEN LATIN LADY TO REMEMBER: Estrelita Rodriguez portrayed Spanish and Mexican women in an overly simplistic but always positive manner in B Westerns like Susannah Pass and such A films as Rio Bravo; here, co-star Ricky Nelson serenades her on the set of that Howard Hawks classic.

They Went That-A-Way

In this film, Singin' Cowboy 'Roy Rogers' (born Leonard Sly; 1911-1998) sets out to make certain that a beautiful lake and privately owned fish hatchery operating on its shore in Southern California's Simi area will not be polluted by scoundrels who plan to dynamite the pristine area while searching for oil down below. The Rhinestone Cowboy delivers a notably didactic speech composed by the film's head writer, Sloan Nibley (1908-1990): "Work done by hatcheries like this doesn't just mean restocking lakes and streams, it means that sportsmen and the youth of America will have a chance to get away from crowded cities and their troubles, go fishin', and enjoy the privileges our forefathers had." Once again, here is a case of moviemakers with an eye on contemporary social progress as well as their necessary profits at the box office reflecting, and hoping to further, a valuable ideology. "So," Roy concludes, "good luck to ya, Doc!"

The 'Doc' in question is 'Kay Parker,' played by Roy's wife Dale Evans (1912-2001). Only four years earlier, in the best of their mini-musicals (and possibly the greatest Singin' Cowboy movie ever made, thanks in large part to Cole Porter's memorable title tune), *Don't Fence Me In*, she enacted a snoopy Lois Lane like reporter. That go-getter cared not a whit for the lives that her 'personal interest stories' destroyed. She gleefully performed as an erotic dancer to earn her considerable pay from a sleazy scandal-sheet. No such sexy (today, some might argue 'sexist') costumes appear in this film. Kay embodies the new (and then still emergent) post-war woman in all her guises. She wears the non-descript official garb of an educated inspector--heavy rubber boots and cap, fatigue-like non-gender clothing--while working in the woodlands. Later, the simple white outfit of a doctor while perusing scientific findings in the laboratory. She's completely at home in tomboy jeans and flannel shirt that the fellas all wear while relaxing once her professional tasks are done. Thereafter, she classes up her act with big city couture as party time arrives. However much a proto-feminist (as a former U.S. Marine, she employs judo on men foolish enough to think her easy prey) icon, Doc has not lost touch with her feminine side. Now, though, it's but one aspect of her complex personality.

DUAL ROLES: The remarkable character actor Douglas Fowley plays two very different characters here; a decade later, he would likewise portray deadly Doc Holliday and gruff but warmhearted Doc Fabrique on ABC-TV's *The Life and Legend of Wyatt Earp*.

The film's other female will prove more problematic to 21st century viewers. Cuban-born Estrelita Rodriguez (1928-1966), added by studio head Herbert J. Yates (1880-1966) to 'spice up' the Rogers Westerns, comes across as something of a Latin clown: As overtly sexual as Lupe Valez, the (in) famous Mexican Spitfire of early sound-era films; and over-the-top caricature Carmen Miranda, the original fruit-embellished camp queen. Estelita appears in this story strictly for gross comic relief, though in her (and the filmmakers') defense, 'Rita' is a positive character. Allied with the good guys (and girl), she gives her all for the preservation of nature. As such, Rita qualifies as one more positive attempt (at least in context of the film's era of production) to veer away from the nasty image of South of the Border women as wicked and shallow that dominated Hollywood pre-WWII. The chief villain (in fact, something of a dual role) is played by Douglas V. Fowley (1911-1988), one of the most durable scene-stealers in Hollywood history. Initially, he appears as a brutal, ruthless prison escapee who kills without conscience. At mid-movie, the criminal passes himself off as a slick entrepreneur from the East and proves equally believable in each role.

One interesting note: Here, Roy's backup singers are the Riders of the Purple Sage (more often appearing in Gene Autry's parallel films) rather than the Sons of the Pioneers, of which he had once been a member. On a sad note, be aware: some cheap DVD versions of *Suzannah Pass,* released by unscrupulous dealers, are minus the sweet-spirited songs. The above rating applies only to the complete theatrical release. The original cut, achieving a delicate balance between sentimental singing sequences and pro-environmental drama, remains a valuable artifact in tracing our contemporary issues in the 21st century to their initial post war roots.

89. TAKE A HARD RIDE (1976)
Rating: ****

CREDITS:

Antonio Margheriti, aka 'Anthony Dawson,' dir.; Eric Bercovici, Jerry Ludwig, scr.; Harry Bernsen, Maria Luisa Alcaraz, Leon Chooluck, pro.; Jerry Goldsmith, mus.; Riccardo Pallattoni, cin.; Stanford C. Allen, ed; 1.85:1; C; 103 min.; 20th Century-Fox..

CAST:

Jim Brown (*Pike*); Fred Williamson (*Tyree*); Jim Kelly (*Kashtok*); Catherine Spaak (*Catherine*); Lee Van Cleef (*Kiefer*); Barry Sullivan (*Kane*); Dana Andrews (*Morgan*); Robert Donner (*Skave*); Charles McGregor (*Cloyd*); Leonard Smith (*Cangey*); Ronald Howard (*Halsey*); Ricardo Palacios (*Calvera*); Robin Levitt (*Chico*); Buddy Joe Hackett (*Angel*); Hal Needham (*Garmes*).

The success of *Butch Cassidy and the Sundance Kid* (1969) inspired a rash of Buddy-Buddy Westerns during the following decade. Simultaneously, martial arts movies became a staple of every downtown's urban theatres following the popularity of *Enter the Dragon* (1973). As did the so-called Black Exploitation Flicks, in which African American heroes (often played by James Brown) took on The Man and The Mob in low-budget crime flicks including *Slaughter* (1972). *Hard Ride* successfully combines elements of all three, ranking as the best film from Antonio Margheriti (1930-2002), as he moved up the ladder from Sergio Leone's F/X expert to full authorship. Clearly, the distinct style of Margheriti's overpowering mentor was imitated here.

NEW RIDERS OF THE PURPLE SAGE: By the mid-1970s, Westerns had matured enough that mainstream audiences were (however belatedly) able to accept a pair of African American actors (Fred Williamson and Jim Brown) as a Butch and Sundance type team.

Diverse characters and storylines are held together by a single central narrative: Trail boss 'Pike' has given his word to the dying rancher, 'Morgan,' for whom he has completed a final long drive. Somehow, Pike will bring the payroll back to their southern Texas ranch so everyone there might be paid a fair share. The strong, solid, and often silent hero's name recalls 'Pike' (William Holden), the leader in Peckinpah's *The Wild Bunch* (1969). This film's Pike's uneasy travelling companion is 'Tyree,' a slick, charming professional gambler who, as a foil to Pike's Gary Cooper-ish silent type, can't keep his mouth shut. Tyree strikes a devil's bargain with the hero: He'll ride with Pike, helping him combat low lives hoping to steal the stash of greenbacks. But when they reach their destination, the two will fight it out . . . to the death, if necessary. Here, they recall such Oater uneasy-ally odd couples as Gary Cooper and Burt Lancaster in *Vera Cruz* (1954), another unappreciated forerunner of Westerns to come.

However belatedly, the polar leads are played by Black actors, both former football greats. F.W. (1938-) and J.B. (1936-) had become major 'names' in

BAND OF OUTSIDERS: Martial arts expert Jim Kelley and Gallic beauty Catherine Spaak play a pair of lost souls in this international co-production.

violent contemporary action-mini-epics. The former had notably appeared in *That Man Bolt* (1973). With them here is African American martial arts expert Jim Kelly (1946-2013), who rose to worldwide fame in support of Bruce Lee in *Enter* . . . All three had appeared a modern tale, *Three the Hard Way* (1974). The film also draws on earlier traditions of the four additional cast members. Barry Sullivan had played 'Pat Garrett' in TV's The *Tall Man* and appeared opposite Barbara Stanwyck in *The Maverick Queen* and *Forty Guns*, his character here named after Gary Cooper's in *High Noon*. Dana Andrews (1909-1992) headlined well-mounted studio Westerns (*Smoke Signal*, 1955; *Comanche*, 1956) in his prime, lesser Oaters (*Town Tamer*, 1965; *Johnny Reno*,

1966) during the next decade. Harry Carey Jr. appeared in more Westerns---big, medium, and small---in his career than any other character actor, even receiving billing in one (Howard Hawks' *Rio Bravo*, 1959) in which he doesn't appear. Tying that package together in a Western ribbon: Lee Van Cleef, cast as outlaws beginning with his first, *High Noon*, later The Man in Black opposite Eastwood for Leone.

Adding to the mix is Catherine Spaak (1945-) as a mystery woman whom the focal duo rescues from rape by white rednecks. Her role might have been merely ornamental (The Blonde, desired by all), yet stretches further than that thanks to a smart script. Spaak's character, owing to her desperate attempt to survive while whacked around by the winds of the wasteland, has lost the will to live. In a subplot that enriches the piece, we watch as she undergoes an inner (as well as the more obvious outward) journey toward reclaiming her soul and sense of self, if at a terrible price. Indeed, each character has an intriguing back story, enriching what at first seemed like nothing more than stock figures, allowing them emotional depth and range.

Most fascinating of all is the issue of race, and the manner in which it played out at this precise moment in the history of popular movies. Williamson had appeared in *The Soul of N***** Charley* (1973) and *Boss ***** * (1974), both of which were virulently anti-White, all Anglo characters cast as The Enemy. *Hard Ride* reverses that. Rancher Morgan does not exploit Pike but loves him as a son, ethnicity aside. Likewise, Pike embraces the dying man as a father figure. "I gave my word," he explains when Tyree suggests that the 'promise' doesn't hold water owing to the deceased's race. "To a white man," Tyree laughs. "I gave my word," Pike counters, "to . . . a *man*!" Moreover, Tyree comes to realize that the other fellow, not he, is correct. Healing time is at hand, in the film and in society at the precise juncture when this feature was released.

The movie's flaws are minor yet noteworthy. Despite Carey's playing a character named 'Dumper,' did we really have to watch as he takes one? And to the tune of "My Darling Clementine," no less! The producers might have searched to find a more appropriate actor to play the William Clark Quantrill

EVERYTHING OLD IS NEW AGAIN: In *Red River*, Howard Hawks entertained audiences with a fist fight between Montgomery Clift and John Wayne in which the two anti-heroes brutally beat each other but no one actually gets hurt seriously; that much loved convention would be revived by the stars of *Take a Hard Ride*.

Bible-spouting outlaw/cult leader than dull Ronald Howard. John Anderson, Royal Dano, and John Carradine all come to mind. Likewise, having the Mexican child 'Chico' portrayed by a whiter-than-white little boy appears odd! Otherwise, this superbly paced, richly visual (images of hard-riding recall paintings by Frederick Remington), a medium-level commercial hit in its time, deserving of revival today.

A FORGOTTEN WESTERN STAR TO REMEMBER: Barry Sullivan, who portrayed 'Pat Garrett' on NBC's *The Tall Man*, here offered one of his final screen performances; he returned to the New Mexico range war playing John Chisum in *Pat Garrett and Billy the Kid* but his fine performance landed on the cutting room floor.

90. THREE BAD MEN (1925)
Rating: *****

CREDITS:

John Ford, dir.; Ford, John Stone, Ralph Spence, Malcolm Stuart Baylor, scr.; Ford, William Fox, pro.; George Schneiderman, cin.; 1.33:1; B&W; 92 min.; Fox Film Corp.

CAST:

George O'Brien (*Dan O'Malley*); Olive Borden *(Lee Carleton)*; Lou Tellegen (*Layne Hunter*); Tom Santschi *('Bull' Stanley)*; J. Farrell MacDonald *(Mike Costigan)*; Frank Campeau *('Spade' Allen)*; Priscilla Bonner (*Millie*); Otis Harlan (*Zach Little*); Phyllis Haver (*Lily)*; George Harris *(Joe Minsk)*; Alec B Francis *(Rev. Benson)*; Jay Hunt *(Nat Lucas)*; Grace Gordon (*Millie's Pal*); George Irving (*Gen. Neville*).

In 1935, as The Great Depression caused cash-strapped companies to merge for the sake of survival, the 20th Century studio combined with a previous competitor controlled by William Fox (1870-1952). This Hungarian-born, New York City businessman, adoring The Flickers, opened Nickelodeons all around the town, drawing in Easterners fascinated by brief images of the geographic place and American ideology then coming to be known as the West. When he moved to Hollywood and established a Dream Factory, Fox initially turned out Tom Mix Rhinestone Cowboy Oaters. No sooner did Fox meet John (Feeney) Ford (1894-1973) than the former came to understand his favorite genre's full potential. Their memorable *The Iron Horse* (1924) may not have been the first epic Western (that was the inferior/uneven *The Covered*

MYTH AND HISTORY: As in all John Ford films, the director presents a legendary image of his characters, then sets that aside to focus on brutal reality.

Wagon, 1923) but by far the best silent incarnation of that form. Rather than attempt to top himself (wisely sensing bigger is not always better), Ford convinced Fox that their next offering ought to be a more intimate character study, if with some spectacular sequences.

The script is drawn from the novel *Over the Border* by Herman Whittaker (1867-1919). Three hardened men stumble upon a desolate girl whose father has died on the trail. Moved to compassion for the first time in their lives by her innocence, the outlaws swear to watch over her while alive; and, after their death, as loving ghosts. It's not surprising that Ford, an Irish Catholic, was drawn to the redemption saga, which would prove basic to such future classics as *Stagecoach* (1939), *Fort Apache* (1948), and *The Searchers* (1956). Here, 'the Bordens' were in 1876 on their way to Custer City in the Dakotas, hoping to mine for gold. Our government removes indigenous people, then establishes

COWBOY CHEESECAKE: Olive Borden brought precisely the right combination of radical innocence and unconscious sensuality to this early version of 'the Fordian woman.'

a Land Rush in which these American Dreamers are allowed to line their horses, wagons, even bicycles along a flat horizon. And—at the sound of a cavalryman firing the all-important shot—rush forward to reach and mark off stretches of land as their own. Olive and her protectors are present, along with a happy-go-lucky Southerner, 'Dan O'Malley,' he as eager to claim Olive for his bride as he is to strike it rich. The fly in this buttermilk: 'Layne Hunter,' a suited villain willing to cheat to get his hands on the golden ore just beneath the earth's surface. And, eventually, the golden girl.

Serving as Hunter's foil, there is a Reverend in town. He and his church symbolize the forces of Goodness even as the two do in William S. Hart's more puritanical *Hell's Hinges*. Ford, however, makes certain that many minorities are positively played. A likeable Jewish resident hails the reverend as 'Rabbi'; Catholics like the Irish 'O'Malley' openly mix with descendants

QUIET ON THE SET; GENIUS AT WORK: "Pappy" casually watches as his team sets up a scene; often without speaking a word, he inspired those around him to achieve iconic moments in films that emerged as America's origination fable during the 20th century.

of Anglicans who have arrived from Virginia. Ford's frontier embodies that melting pot myth of Eastern cities, shifted to the west. Even 'Lily,' a once-good-girl gone wrong owing to the villain's seduction, can set her dark deeds aside and return to 'the light.' While this may not be a West that ever existed, historically speaking, we are persuaded that this is the way such a small town (representing America itself) *ought* to operate--a model for a kinder, gentler America that might indeed come into being if only we allow ourselves to not only be entertained by this film but learn from it. As such, an answer (or corrective) to Hart's less forgiving vision of such a place.

While Ford accurately recreates the precise details of history (costuming, the weaponry and saddlery, construction of buildings, etc.), his presentation can only be described as legendary. To provide an origination myth for our nation, the filmmaker who would come to be called 'Pappy' feels free to add, subtract, and rearrange diverse events for the sake of creating an abiding vision of America, as set in the symbolic West of our post-'Buffalo Bill show' collective imagination. This land rush, so vividly portrayed, never took place. For his model, Ford seized on the 1899 Oklahoma incident, in which 50,000 pioneers raced to claim choice pieces of farmland. The idea of a rush to seize a territory containing gold is, when closely considered, absurd. Individual miners necessarily spent months searching the mountains (*not* flatlands!) for a trace of valuable minerals. The film actually admits this by having the Reverend insist that "grain" is the true gold, and that the truly righteous should return to farming. Getting if not rich then at least 'solid' and doing so slowly.

By combining the 1874-76 Black Hills incident in which individuals invaded Indian territory with the totally separate Oklahoma settlement (depicted in the 1931 and 1960 versions of Edna Ferber's 1929 novel *Cimarron*), Ford sets the pace for such anachronism in his later films. At the opening of *She Wore a Yellow Ribbon* (1949), riders of the Pony Express carry news of the Custer massacre to isolated army posts along the frontier. In fact, the Pony Express went bust more than ten years before the battle of the Little Big Horn. Deceptive on Ford's part? Perhaps. Explaining why, though, during his twilight years, the filmmaker (in *The Man Who Shot Liberty Valance*,

They Went That-A-Way

THE FORDIAN APPROACH: Borrowing from the earlier work of D.W. Griffith, Pappy juxtaposed spectacular long shots for an epic sweep with telling close-ups that play on an audience's most intense emotions.

1962) had an auteur's spokesperson proclaim: "When the legend becomes a fact, print the legend." He firmly believed that every nation ought to have its origination myth, and happily provided that in one of America's contributions of an original art form (jazz, followed by rock 'n' roll, the other): The Hollywood Western Film.

The Cinema of John Ford, as established here, combines the sweep of Shakespeare's history plays (likewise more fiction than fact); the folk wisdom of Benjamin Franklin's "Poor Richard"; the sentimental strains of Gaelic ballads that the Feeney clan sang together in their homeland and then again as immigrants; anecdotes from the 'Crockett Almanacs' published during the 1840s; Ned Buntline's pulp-ish Dime Novels a generation later; the morality inherent in 19th Century novels; action-filled splendor as presented in Col. Cody's Wild West show; and, visually, the realistic details heightened by a sense of romanticized majesty in the paintings of Frederick Remington. To a degree, Ford reflected our past. More significantly, he invented it, presenting incidents from history in a mythological manner that allowed a country still in the process evolution to see themselves, and the entire American Adventure, in a positive light.

For better, as some still claim. Or for worse, as others insist today. Which is it, then? As the Bard himself once put it: "Noting's either good nor bad; thinking makes it so."

91. TOMBSTONE, THE TOWN TOO TOUGH TO DIE (1942)
Rating: ****

CREDITS:

William C. McGann, dir.; Albert S. LeVino, Edward E. Panama, scr.; Harry Sherman, pro.; Gerald Carbonara, mus.; Russell Harlan, cin.; Carroll Lewis, Sherman A. Rose, ed.; 1.37:1; B&W; 79 min.; Paramount.

CAST:

Richard Dix (*Wyatt Earp*); Francis Gifford (*Ruth Grant*); Edgar Buchanan (*Curly Bill Brocious*); Don Castle (*Johnny Duane*); Kent Taylor (*Doc Holliday*); Clem Bevans (*Tadpole Fisher*); Victor Jory *(Ike Clanton)*; Rex Ball (*Virgil Earp*); Harvey Stephens (*Morgan Earp*); Wallis Clark (*Ed Schieffelin*); Chris-Pin Martin (*Chris*); Donald Curtis (*Phineas Clanton*); Dick Curtis (*Frank McLowery*); Paul Sutton (*Tom McLowery*); Charles Middleton (*Original Mayor*); Charles Halton (*Mayor Dan Crane*); Charlie Stevens (*Indian Charley*); Roy Barcroft (*Piano Man*); James Ferrara (*Billy Clanton*); Emmett Vogan (*Editor John Clum*); Jimmie Dodd (*Type-setter for the* Tombstone Epitaph).

Other than the abhorrent *Doc* (1971), this may be the least remembered among films that focus on Wyatt Earp (1848-1929) and the events in Tombstone, AZ. involving the (in)famous Gunfight at the O.K. Corral (10/26/1881). Most notable, perhaps, is the inclusion of that shoot-out as the film's midpoint rather than, as is so often the case, a grand finale. This would not be repeated until the popular *Tombstone* (1993) half a century later, also in *Wyatt Earp* (1994). Worth mentioning in context is John Sturges' *Hour of*

THE STREETS OF TOMBSTONE: Despite several dramatic concessions, this long-forgotten mini-epic offered the most accurate account of 'the town too tough to die' up until the much-loved *Tombstone*.

the Gun 1967), a belated follow-up to his *Gunfight at the O.K. Corral* (1957). Sturges' latter film begins with the legendary duel, then covers the dark days of the so-called Vengeance Ride. Here Earp appears less a true hero than a killer with a badge, as his detractors often describe Wyatt.

Other than the early talkie classic *Law and Order* and the now apparently lost film *Frontier Marshal* (1934), also its remake (1939), this was the fourth movie to present 'the town too tough to die.' Like *My Darling Clementine* yet to come, the two versions of *Frontier Marshal* were based on Stuart N. Lake's 1931 biography (now questioned as to validity, even dismissed in some quarters) titled *Wyatt Earp, Frontier Marshal*. That, notably, would *not* be the case here. As the credits reveal, this is taken from an earlier and, according to Earp aficionados, more accurate depiction of what went down. For his own book *Tombstone* (1927), subtitled "an Iliad of the Southwest," Walter Noble Burns researched the subject at length, gathering reports from numerous witnesses rather than allowing a single person to dictate how the tale would be told, that the situation with Lake and Earp. As had been the case with Burns' book, this film attempts to raise the events to the level of a heroic myth . . . an American variation on the Siege of Troy, thereby suggesting to its audience that our own still evolving homeland boasted the same sort of brutal greatness that occurred in ancient times. Or at least the literary legends that immortalize what more than likely is a romanticized version of whatever actually occurred.

To achieve this effect, the screenwriters (working from a detailed outline by brothers Dean and Charlie Reisner) included a prologue. This tells (from the perspective of a God-like being that identifies itself as The Voice of the Past) the tale of prospector Ed Schieffelin (1847-1897). Ridiculed as a fool for setting off into the Chiricahua Mountains in search of silver. Warned that all he would discover would be his tombstone, Old Ed purposefully named his rich mine in an ironic tribute to those 'nay' sayers. Here, as always, the three Earp brothers happen upon the corrupted town and (with the help of gambler Doc Holliday) clean it up. Most movies depict Wyatt as the new marshal, though he and Morgan were deputies to older Virgil. Instead, Wyatt is here appointed 'sheriff,' which is quite impossible, as that was an elected position.

REAL AND 'REEL': Wyatt Berry Earp and Richard Dix, the underrated Western star who brought the lawman to life in this seek-it-out-at-all-costs little gem.

Factually, Wyatt did covet that position and ran (but lost) in an election against arch enemy John Behan. (*Doc*, for all its faults, is noteworthy as the only film to dramatize such a political aspect.) Necessarily, then, Behan is eliminated from this *Tombstone*. Added is a long sequence in which, as sheriff, Wyatt sets out to collect unpaid taxes from hillbillies and other rednecks scattered throughout Cochise County. He involves the deadly if charming Curly Bill to help him accomplish this. The incident itself is accurately portrayed, though it was not Wyatt but one of Behan's deputies, William Clairbourne, who dared to take on this mission and succeeded. Here again, we experience the self-conscious collapsing of diverse occurrences into a larger-than-life legend.

The film's crowning jewel is the depiction of the titular gunfight. Onscreen, it lasts between 26-27 seconds, precisely the case in real life. The number of bullets fired and particular people wounded and/or killed on either side is, for once, precisely as it went down way back when. Here then is one more

THE BALLAD OF CURLY BILL: *Tombstone* was the first film to emphasize the significance of William Brocious in the complicated situation that developed in rural Arizona; Edgar Buchanan (left) as the noted gunman, Victor Jory as Ike Clanton, and bit player.

example (directly comparable to *(The) Woman of the Town)* of the manner in which any Hollywood film can play fast and loose with certain facts while remaining accurate to others. Noteworthy is that the Wyatt/Doc relationship, ordinarily an essential aspect of any rendering, is here played not as the love-hate story seen in Sturges' two films or Ford's *Clementine*, instead as a relatively casual friendship. Rather, the main drama involves Wyatt and young Johnny Ringo (here re-named 'Johnny Duane'). At issue: whether the young gunslick will be mentored by Earp or fall in with the Clanton/McLoury outlaw bunch.

For reasons left unexplained, John P. Clum is broken down into two characters, the new mayor and the newspaper editor. He was both. Richard Dix (1893-1949), in his prime years, won the leads in such high-profile Oaters as *The Vanishing America* (1925) and *Cimarron* (1931). Though shot on a "B" budget, this rates as a noteworthy contribution to the evolution of the Earp myth, and a must-see for those Western fans fascinated by the most immortal of all frontier gunfights.

COTTAGE INDUSTRY FOR A FAUX NATIVE-AMERICAN: Charlie Stevens (1893-1964) played the historic 'Indian Joe' in this and three other Westerns: *The Plainsman* (1936), *Frontier Marshal* (1939), and *My Darling Clementine* (1946); though claiming to be a pureblood Mescalero whose grandfather had been Geronimo (a recurring role for C.S. on TV's *Rin-Tin-Tin*), his parents were in fact an Anglo male and a Latin woman.

92. UNFORGIVEN, THE (1960)
Rating: *** ½

CREDITS:

John Huston, dir. JP Miller, Ben Maddow, scr.; James Hill, Burt Lancaster, pro.; Dimitri Tiomkin, mus.; Frnz Planer, Russell Lloyd, ed.; 2.35:1; C; 125 min.; United Artists.

CAST:

Burt Lancaster *(Ben Zachary)*; Audrey Hepburn (Rachel Zachary); Audie Murphy *(Cash)*; John Saxon *(Johnny Portugal)*; Charles Bickford *(Zeb Rawlins)*; Lillian Gish *(Mattilda)*; Albert Salmi *(Charles Rawlins)*; Joseph Wiseman *(Abe Kelsey)*; June Walker *(Hagar)*; Kipp Hamilton *(Georgia)*; Arnold Merritt *(Jude Rawlins)*; Doug McClure *(Andy)*; Carlos Rivas *(Lost Bird)*.

Too many cooks spoil the broth ... one more of those old sayings that never go away because they are, in essence, accurate. Rarely in the history of Hollywood Westerns has that phrase been so vividly illustrated than by this epic tale of post-Civil War Texas. Based on a novel by Alan Le May (1899-1964), *The Unforgiven* has several similarities to a previous book and film derived from this first-rate author of non-generic Westerns. Four years before this movie from the indie company Hecht, Hill, and Lancaster, which optioned projects specifically as a vehicle for superstar Burt, Le May's *The Searchers* had been brought to the screen by John Ford. That story involves a five-year trek by several trail hardened cowboys to locate, free, and return a white girl abducted by Kiowa/Comanch. In *The Unforgiven*, Le May offered

A SELF-CONSCIOUS EPIC: An artist's rendering of this tale of old-time Texas, employed for the huge publicity campaign surrounding *The Unforgiven*.

an inverse of that situation. Here, lovely 'Rachel' lives a happy if modest life on an isolated ranch with her adopted family: Puritanical mother 'Matilda,' dominating big brother 'Ben,' quick-tempered 'Cash,' and naïve, innocent 'Andy'. Rachel is courted by a cowboy, 'Charlie,' whose parents (like her own) have always assumed these two would marry. Then, a series of unexpected events interrupt this pastoral of the prairie. Charlie is shot dead by Indians, surprising as they had been peaceful enough in recent months. Previously, a strange, ghostly man appeared on a nearby hill. 'Abe Kelsey' terrifies Rachel, insisting that she is not whom she believes herself to be.

From that moment on, an aura of impending tragedy replaces the simple, humble, hard but rewarding life of these isolated pioneers. Something out of the past, a terrible occurrence that only one person ... the distressed mother ... may be able to explain. Frantic, Matilda refuses to do so. Yet in this southwestern variation on a theme by Sophocles, truth will out. Long ago sins within a family are about to erupt, with a potential to destroy the living as, in the Greek tragedy of Oedipus Rex, crimes of the fathers (or mother) are visited upon a son (or daughter).

As a novel, *The Unforgiven* rates as the equal (some might suggest superior) to *The Searchers*. Not so, sadly, regarding the movie. Ford's 1956 film

OF GENDER AND ETHNICITY: A mixed race vaquero (John Saxon) senses a forbidden desire to touch the seemingly Anglo American beauty (Audrey Hepburn); sadly, this subplot, so basic to the novel's appeal, was all but excised in order to create a more generic A budget Oater.

reached the screen as a near-perfect work owing to the talent and efforts of one man. 'Pappy' drew from the Le May manuscript precisely what he needed to make 'a John Ford film.' One man, one movie. *The Searchers*, as a film, pre-existed in the mind of this artist, who without any resistance realized his vision, completely and without compromise. The cast (including superstar Wayne) and all other collaborators, from cinematographer to gofers, were true believers in the primary artist's vision. One can agree with, or argue against, the vision of Race in America as it unfolds in *The Searchers*. No question, though, that the work and its themes appear before us with Ford's integrity of insight intact; open for acceptance, condemnation, or debate as to its difficult implications as to the mixing of bloodlines.

If one Hollywood director equals Ford as just such a 'serious' filmmaker, it is John Huston (1906-1987). Though his involvement with the Western has been sparse--writer on *Law and Order*, co-writer and director of *(The) Treasure of the Sierra Madre)*, director of *The Misfits*, 1961)--his great films leave little doubt that here is something other than a journeyman, however talented, plying his craft. *The Maltese Falcon* (1941), *The Asphalt Jungle* (1950), *The African Queen* and *The Red Badge of Courage* (both 1951), *Moulin Rouge* (1952), and the underappreciated *Moby Dick* (1956) reveal that, despite the diversity of genres and subjects, a *personal* vision . . . the hallmark of a true artist rather than a mere entertainer, however gifted . . . runs through the individual pieces. Eventually, the films together constitute a body of work in which each individual project serves as a specific piece in the great celluloid jigsaw puzzle that the French refer to as a director's *oeuvre*. *The Unforgiven* might have offered Huston's own vision of the West, told from the perspective of the 1950s Civil Rights Movement as to issues of ethnicity inn America, even as *The Searchers* did Ford's.

Here, that was not to be. For Huston did not discover the material, embrace it, and fight to get the film made as precisely the sort of vision he pre-envisioned while first reading the book. Rather, he was brought on board as a hired hand by Lancaster after at least one director for hire attempted but

THE COMING OF CIVILIZATION: As in so many other Western films, novels, and paintings, a piano symbolizes the advent of Eastern society into the Western wastelands.

failed to get a handle on what *Burt* wanted . . . a screen vehicle to further his personal (and personally shaped) screen iconography. As in the book, this film's narrative inexorably moves to a foregone conclusion: Rachel is not the Anglo survivor of a wagon train massacre, as reported, but a Native American woman, stolen away from the Kiowa as a child by lonely Matthilda after her own daughter died. The greatness of Le May's novel stems from his critique not only of racism per se but the complex concept of racial identity: Should Rachel consider herself an Indian owing to ancestry or Anglo by environment and upbringing? Is she a woman without a country, doomed to always search for an elusive sense of self?

In Le May's piece, 'Johnny Portugal' (a mostly Spanish, part Indian ranch hand) by his very presence causes Rachel to sense a stirring of previously unknown emotions and ideas. A major character in the book, Portugal is reduced to a virtual bit so that Lancaster could get the girl at the end. Popular cowboy star Audie Murphy did not care whether his character lived or died, insisting only that he ride in shooting at the conclusion and save everybody. Indecision as to how they might wrap up the tale to satisfy all involved (with little loyalty to either director or novelist) led to angry confrontations and a finale that satisfied no one.

And, in fact, makes no logical sense.

The tragedy of this is heightened by the film's considerable qualities. The symphonic music, settings and costumes, a palpable sense of the historic Panhandle come to life can only be described by a single word: breathtaking! Individual scenes (particularly those between mother and daughter, as when they celebrate the arrival of civilization by a way of a piano from back East), when removed from context, ring with truth and beauty. The performances are mostly exquisite, particularly Gish in what might be thought of as a continuation of her *The Wind* character into old age. Yet there is a gnawing sense that, in the final shot, any intended plea for Native American equality is dissipated by a visual incarnation of White Supremacy, however unintended this may have been at the time.

93. WALK THE PROUD LAND (1956)
Rating: **** ½

CREDITS:

Jesse Hibbs, dir.; Jack Sher, Gil Doud, scr.; Aaron Rosenberg, pro.; William Lava, Hans J. Salter, mus.; Harold Lipstein, cin.; Sherman Todd, ed.; 2.35:1; C; 88 min.; Universal-International.

CAST:

Audie Murphy (*John Philip Clum*); Anne Bancroft (*Tianay*); Pat Crowley (*Mary Dennison*); Charles Drake (*Tom Sweeney*); Tommy Rall (*Taglito*); Robert Warwick (*Chief Eskiminzin*); Jay Silverheels (*Geronimo*); Eugene Mazzola (*Tono*); Anthony Caruso (*Disalin*); Victor Milian (*Santos*); Ainslie Pryor (*Capt. Larsen*); Eugene Iglesias (*Chato*); Morris Ankrum (*Gen. Wade*); Addison Richards (*Gov. Safford*); Maurice Jara (*Alchise*); Beulah Archuletta (*An Apache Woman*); John Pickard (*Tucson Sheriff*).

Between 1950 and 1960, Congressional Medal of Honor winner Audie L. Murphy (1925-1971) starred in nearly two dozen films for Universal-International, mostly B+ Westerns. Following his spectacular appearance as himself in *To Hell and Back* (1955), studio executives wondered if perhaps they might upscale his career by maintaining the frontier settings while providing more ambitious scripts. Though the serious-minded, thought-provoking *Walk . . .* did not prove as profitable at rural Drive-Ins as Audie's more action-oriented projects, this little-known gem allowed him to stretch as an actor. For here, Murphy plays not one more itinerant cowhand but an educated

"IT TAKES A HERO TO PLAY A HERO!" Audie Murphy, World War II's most decorated American serviceman, brings his special sense of dignity to the role of John Clum, one of the few 'honest' Indian agents.

RIDE TO THE SOUND OF THE GUNS: Though *Walk the Proud Land* does include an action sequence involving an endangered wagon train and the U.S. cavalry riding to the rescue, most of the film's running time is spent chronicling the trials and tribulations of reservation life.

WOMEN OF THE WEST: In addition to the relationship between John Clum and Geronimo, this remarkable film also portrays a meeting of the minds for a Native American and Anglo woman who love the same man.

and articulate man: John P. Clum (1851-1932), one of the few honest Indian agents in his youth, later the mayor of Tombstone AZ and editor of its pro-Wyatt Earp newspaper, the *Epitaph*.

Here is another entry in a sub-genre of the Western that 20th Century-Fox had initiated with *Broken Arrow* (1950): the pro-Indian in general, pro-Apache in particular Civil Rights Oater.

Broken Arrow also kicked off the dubious paradigm of 'good-vs.-bad Indian,' the latter embodied by Jay Silverheels as the Mescalaro warrior Geronimo (1829-1909), a freedom fighter to his people, terrorist to Anglo settlers. Here, Silverheels again was cast in a role that would become almost as associated with him as 'Tonto' in *The Lone Ranger*. Most such films were told from the point of view of an enlightened white hero, including *Chief Crazy Horse* and *White Feather* (both 1955), each with its sympathetic if fictional Anglo storyteller. For *Walk* . . . it was unnecessary to invent one. Clum's son Woodrow (1878-1946) had written a book detailing all of what happened, as told to him in his youth by his father: History funneled through nostalgia.

Murphy's convincing representation of Clum serves as the centerpiece for a work that relies more on words that the usual excitement found in most films shot at the Old Tucson Studio. While we are treated to a brief saloon fistfight, as well as an abbreviated wagon train attack, this is an engaging drama about people of varied ethnicities attempting to forge positive relationships while caught in the vise of an untenable social/cultural/political bind. Providing the Apache at San Carlos reservation with Bibles rather than booze and, in comparison to the most corrupt whites who illegally/secretly sold guns to the Apache, Clum convinced the government and military to provide 'his Indians' with weapons. This would allow them to hunt within their land boundaries and also police themselves . . . integrating into a still emergent America without being forced to entirely assimilate by giving up the old ways.

Like another honest Indian agent, Tom Jeffords (played by James Stewart in *Broken Arrow*, 1950), Clum brought a radical new theory to the reservation concept. In the past, strict military discipline had been imposed by the omnipresent army, reducing Apaches to virtual prisoners on their homelands. Now, Eastern Christian organizations hoped to move in, employing schools and churches to indoctrinate Native people to the 'civilized' way, essentially by "beating the Indian out of the Indian," killing their old national identity to 'save' the flesh and blood people. Only Clum fully understood such total repression of traditions would prove as poisonous to such a proud race as the other extreme, genocide. He hoped to achieve a delicate balance to secure a workable future in which Apaches would be encouraged to maintain elements of their heritage including religious ceremonies and dances. Though they must now eat the white man's cattle rather than wild bison (nearly gone anyway), Clum believed that Apaches should be allowed to kill the beasts with rifles from horseback. Rather than soldiers policing the reservation, the most trusted among the Indians would become a self-contained police force, an historic event detailed more fully in *Taza, Son of Cochise* (1954), starring

THE SURRENDER OF GERONIMO: Apache 'police' replace the regular army and the warrior chief surrenders to Clum, for better or worse.

Rock Hudson. Apaches would farm and construct houses and be paid for their work. They could spend the money on anything but whiskey at their trading post.

Clum succeeded whereas many others had failed by thinking outside of the existing box, so to speak. He achieved what no other Anglo, military or civilian, had been able to do: 'Persuading' Geronimo to surrender after capturing the chief *sans* violence. The movie sensitively handles a largely fictional romantic triangle between Clum's wife 'Mary' and a Native American woman. Though she is played (as had been the case with Debra Paget in *Broken Arrow*) by a non-Native, the role did go to Anne Bancroft (1931-2005), a topflight talent and eventual Academy Award winner for *The Miracle Worker* six years later. Her role here is, happily, unexpectedly three-dimensional. Those sequences involving Murphy's appealing depiction of Clum and her young, bright Indian son are heartwarming. Sadly, the film cops out at the conclusion. Tired of endless government/military interference, Clum is about to quit when both women convince him to remain. For the sake of a happy ending, the film suggests that Clum changed his mind, continuing at San Carlos.

In actuality, he and Mary moved to Tombstone. There, he ran the pro-Republican liberal newspaper, also running for and winning the position of mayor. Becoming a close friend of the Earp brothers, Clum and his Citizens Committee backed the lawmen in their ongoing feud with the Clanton/McClaurey bunch. Years later, following the death of Mary as well as his first child, Clum accompanied Wyatt to Alaska in search of new adventures. Sadly, no one has ever made a film about their last great adventure together.

94. WAY OF A GAUCHO (1952)
Rating: **** ½

CREDITS:

Jacques Tourneur, dir.; Philip Dunne, scr.; Dunne, Joseph C. Behm, pro.; Sol Kaplan, mus.; Harry Jackson, cin.; Robert Fitch, ed.; 1.37:1; C; 87 min.; 20th Century-Fox.

CAST:

Rory Calhoun (*Martin Penalosa*); Gene Tierney (*Teresa Chavez*); Richard Boone (*Salinas*); Hugh Marlowe (*Don Miguel Aleondo*); Everett Sloane (*Falcon*); Enrique Chaico (*Father Fernandez*); Jorge Villoldo (*Valverde*); Ronald Dumas (*Julio*); Teresa Acosta *(Dancer)*; Raoul Astor (*Huerta*); Linda Campos *(Tia Maria)*; Hugo Mancini, Nestor Yoan (*Soldiers*).

What The Cowboy has always represented to the U.S.A., and the Vaquero to those living in Mexico, The Gaucho symbolizes in South America: An icon of rugged individualism if, ironically, almost always existing as part of a community of like-minded men, eking out a living on the Argentinian prairie. Or, as far-stretching areas of wilderness are known in that land, The Pampa(s). Such a hero's moniker, drawn from Spanish and Portuguese languages, identifies a fierce silent type, defined by his skills at riding *tropilla,* an equivalent of the trusted cowpony. Often penniless, a Gaucho crosses seemingly endless ranges in search of jobs serving *padrones* (landowners) who hire such skilled men of the saddle to care for wide-roaming cattle herds. Also like the Cowboy or Vaquero, a Gaucho worships the open spaces (a geographical symbol of the freedom he so cherishes) as

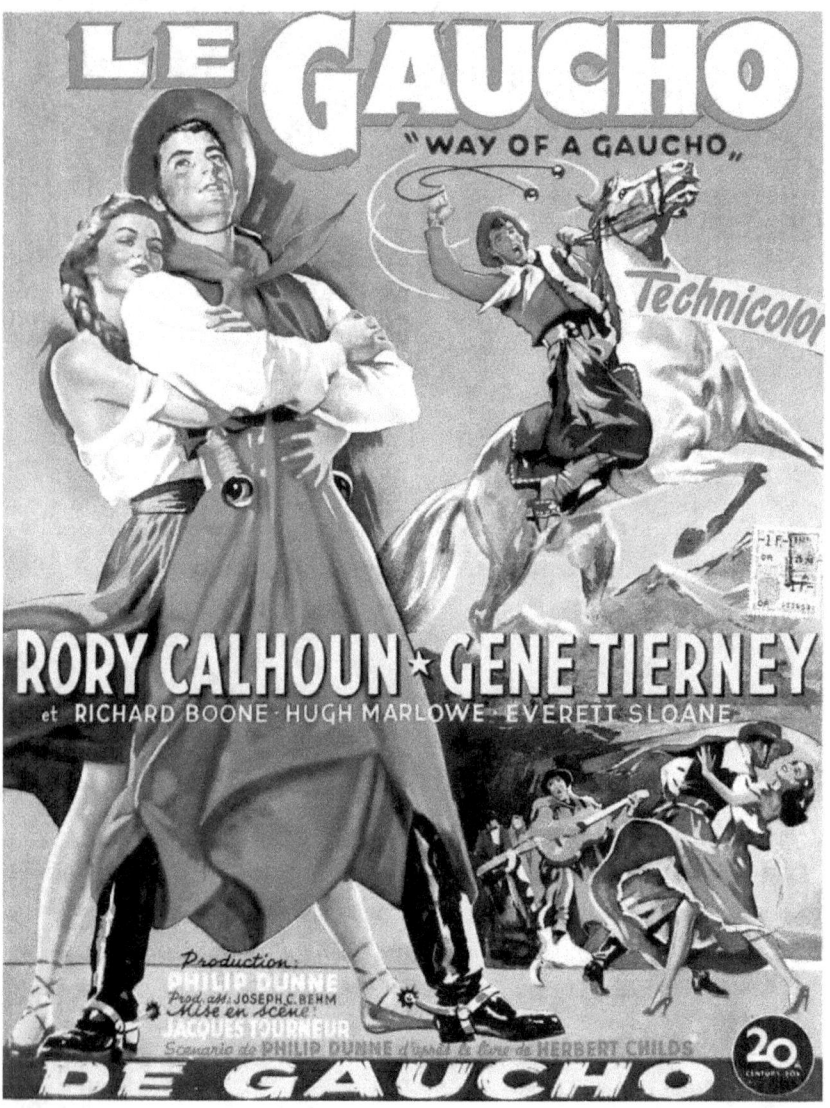

SALUTE TO A SPECIAL SUBCULTURE: Way is one of the rare films to depict the unique lifestyle of this 'Argentinian cowboy.'

much as he despises change, however invaluable to the surrounding society such progress may be.

On a less romantic, more dangerous plane: The Gaucho, in his defiance and arrogance of anything that has to do with civilization, may without warning turn violent. If he was, in his own golden age, feared by more conventional folk, as his era of significance closed owing to what others call progress as the 20th century approaches, he---again like the cowboy north of the Rio Grande--transformed into a figure of myth.

Though at least a thousand Cowboy Movies and TV episodes exist, only a few rare films have attempted to accurately present The Gaucho. The best is *La Guerra Gauch(o)* (1942), sadly little-known outside of Argentina. Hollywood offered only one "A" movie on the subject, a silent called *The Gaucho* (1927), yet another spectacular melodrama for charismatic/acrobatic swashbuckler Douglas Fairbanks Sr. of 'Robin Hood' fame. Only once during the sound era has a studio approached this most fascinating subject in what was at the time marketed as a colorful B+ Western. In all truth, there's nothing conventional about *Way*....A minor masterpiece, here is the title subject preserved under glass, a cinematic paean to a unique, misunderstood subculture. Originally, the film was scheduled to be produced as a major offering from Fox to star A lister Tyrone Power and be directed by Henry King. Studio chief Daryl F. Zanuck had happened upon Herbert Childs' historically accurate novel, believing this could become an epic. Though scaled down during the development process for Fox's "B" unit, the budget remained at nearly 2 ½ million, previously unheard of for 'second features' that ran under 90 mins with only a nominal star.

Born Frances Timothy McCown in California, Rory Calhoun (1922-1999) played the role of a tough, surly loner so well in part because he had, previous to Hollywood's beckoning, lived a life on the open road. To eat, Rory accepted odd jobs as a boxer, cowhand, truck driver, and high-timber lumberjack. By chance, star Alan Ladd noticed the dark, intense actor-in-embryo and arranged for a screen test. Hired as a contract player, Calhoun found himself cast in varied studio projects, mostly in supporting roles. Then

GOOD TIMES, BAD TIMES: The outlaw couple (Rory Calhoun, Gene Tierney) enjoy a brief sense of romantic escape similar to Launcelot riding out of Camelot with Guenivere behind him; all too soon, their 'adventure' turns into an *Elvira Madigan* type tragedy.

his villainous turn in the high-profile Western *River of No Return* (1954), opposite Robert Mitchum and Marilyn Monroe, convinced casting directors that this was Calhoun's proper venue. Leads in such solid projects as *Five Guns to the Border* (1954), *The Treasure of Pancho Villa* (1955), and *Red Sundown* (1956) culminated in Calhoun's winning the lead in TV's *The Texan* (1958-1960). In it, he portrayed a glorified version of real-life gunman/convict Bill Longley. Aiming for something far more complex here, Paris-born Tourneur (1904-1977) effectively toned down the often-exaggerated aspect of Calhoun's performance for a more ambitious work in terms of scope, character, and theme.

Way of a Gaucho plays like a regional legend, effectively opened up so as to reach international audiences. In a rage, 'Penalosa' kills a man, is assigned to the army rather than prison, deserting when bullied by a martinet officer, 'Salinas.' In what expands into a *Les Miserables*-like social epic, the loner is obsessively pursued by that agent of the law. Like Calhoun, A-lister Gene Tierney (1920-1991) likewise appears more subdued, even nuanced, than usual as an aristocratic woman who chooses to ride the outlaw trail with the appealing bad boy rather than marry his non-biological brother' Aleondro,' a respected don. The ever more desperate romance between the seemingly doomed lovers grows as foreboding as that in the better-known European

Elvira Madigan (1967). In a surprisingly mature plot twist for that era, 'Teresa' becomes pregnant out of wedlock, with no aspersions cast on her character by the filmmakers despite the still powerful Hays/Breen censorship office. Here, though, such full tragedy is avoided in favor of a bittersweet finale, a bit of a pulled punch in comparison to the original novel's bleaker view.

The director's 'signature' in horror films (*Cat People*) and noirs (*Out of the Past*) consists of his ability to allow for a dream-like aura that overshadows realistically written sequences. While watching, we do not bear witness to an event as it supposedly happened (as in most Tinseltown products), rather the central character's nocturnal recalling of remembrances of what may have been, drawn from vague, haunting memories. True here as well. Happily, we leave with the impression that what we have just experienced is not the usual reduction of a difficult-to- comprehend Way but, as the title insists, an honest

LES MISERABLES ON THE PAMPAS: Richard Boone (left) offers a remarkable performance as the Jaubert-type police officer who relentlessly tracks Argentina's 'Bonnie and Clyde.'

vision of the Gaucho as those in his native land recall him. Long hours of careful research proved rewarding, resulting in a rich backdrop of sight and sound. Costuming, weaponry, music, and local music and dance all merge to offer a vivid distillation of a singular Gaucho who, beyond that, defines his entire breed.

A UNIQUE LIFESTYLE, PRESERVED IF UNDER GLASS: Though originally released on a double-bill as one more B Western, this ambitious film tells a singular story that also immortalizes a unique way of life.

95. WHEN THE LEGENDS DIE (1972)
Rating: **** ½

CREDITS:

Stuart Millar, dir.; Robert Dozier, scr.; Miller, Gene Lasko, pro.; Glenn Paxton, mus.; Richard H. Kline, cin.; Louis San Andres, ed.; 1.85:1; C; 117 min.; Sagaponack Films/20th Century-Fox.

CAST:

Frederick Forrest (*Tom Black Bull*); Richard Widmark (*Red Dillon*); Luana Anders *(Mary)*; Vito Scotti *(Meo)*; Herbert Nelson (*Dr. Wilson*); John War Eagle *(Blue Elk)*; John Gruber *(Clyde 'Tex' Walker)*; Garry Walberg (*School Superintendent*); Jack Mullaney (*Gas Station Attendant*); Malcolm Curley (*Benny Grayback*); Roy Engel (*Sam Turner*); Mel Gallacher (*A Cowboy*); Rex Holman (*Neil Swenson*); Tillmn Box (*Young Black Bull*); Sondra Pratt (*Angie*); Verne Muehlstedt *(Harold)*; Evan Stevens *(George)*; John Renforth *(Elderly Man)*; Rhonda Stevens (*Mrs. Devon*); Mel Flock (*Car Salesman*); Joyce Davis (Mom).; Bennett Thompson (*Albert Left Hand*).

The Nouveaux Western of the early 1970s, more often than not focusing on Native American issues, brought back two all but forgotten sub-genres of the Oater. One was The Reservation Western, which can be traced back at least to *The Vanishing American* (1925). These dealt with the plight of Indians attempting to survive on an Anglo-controlled stretch of land. Too often, though, the latest examples (*FLAP*, or 'What Do You do With a Drunken Indian?'; 1970) flopped (pun intended) critically and commercially. This owed

"NATURAL MAN IS THE BEST MAN!" Jean-Jacques Rousseau's famous statement from the Romantic Revolution in Europe is vividly illustrated by this film's vision of a happy youth living in the wilds ... until civilization arrives to supposedly 'better' him.

to the filmmakers' failure to present the characters as human beings in general, Native Americans (and of specific tribes) particularly. Another was The Rodeo Film, with such classics as *The Lusty Men* (1952) as milestones. All at once, the concept ... with an emphasis on machismo, male vs. beast, in its rawest state ... re-emerged. Cliff Robertson brought to fruition his long planned *J.W. Coop* (1971); James Coburn appeared in *The Honkers* (1972); McQueen offered one of his finest performances in Sam Peckinpah's *Junior Bonner*, contained herein.

One film stands out for its integrity and authenticity while merging the two subgenres. *When the Legends Die* is one of the few films directed by Stuart Millar (1929-2006), better known as a producer of serious-minded projects including *Little Big Man* (1970), the most successful pro-Indian film of the era. Always hoping to emerge as the primary artist behind an important project, Millar chose the powerful, poetic 1963 novel *When the Legends Die* by Hal Borland (1900-1978). A reporter for such prestigious newspapers as the *New York Times*, Borland also wrote poetry, short stories, and book-length fiction based on early experiences as a boy in Colorado, where his parents once homesteaded. In this tale, Borland shared his first-hand knowledge of the reservation and rodeo circuit by employing a representative figure of a young Native American who attempts to escape the one by means of the other, with tragic results.

Millar's film version opens with a series of images that draw from the European Romantic tradition of philosophy and poetry as well as American transcendentalism: Nature is good, the big city (i.e., civilization) bad. The child 'Black Bull' has been living alone in the wilderness other than his 'brother,' a bear. But if he has seemingly succeeded in making what Hemingway would have called a separate peace, society will not allow such pastoral tranquillity to continue. Members of his tribe, as well as Anglos who believe it's their solemn duty to integrate the child, bring him to society where the youth (now called Tom) must attend school and learn the White Man's Way. Shortly, Tom Black Bull exists as a man without a country. Even when he attempts to conform, no one will meet him halfway. Tom adores horses and would love to work as a wrangler but "do-gooders' have other (supposedly 'better') careers in store for him. Eventually, he sets off with 'Red Dillon,' an old-time rodeo hand who becomes Tom's self-appointed manager. Yet if The Circuit initially offers the youth an acceptable compromise that will allow this unique individual to be moderately satisfied, even that small gifft is denied him. For Red turns out to be less a likeable mentor than an alcohol-fuelled exploiter. He manipulates Tom, persuading the youth to ride in in fixed races, earning fast money while corrupting the very sport/profession that might have provided Tom's salvation.

Honest and unsentimental as a rodeo-Western, *When . . .* is, among other things, the most authentic movie ever made about the Utes. Originally living in The Great Basin (Utah, Colorado) and divided into twelve distinct bands,

THE KIND OF A BOY YOU ARE, THE KIND OF A MAN YOU WILL BE:
Abraham Lincoln may well have been speaking about 'Tom Black Bull,' dragged as
a child back to a reservation but, even as a young man (Frederick Forrest), never able
to forget the purity he once knew in the wilds.

each with its own identity and lifestyle within the greater community, these warrior people (excellent horsemen after acquiring mounts from the Spanish) preferred to dwell in single family habitations rather than within those villages more prevalent among other indigenous people. This qualified them, in history and today as well, as a unique mini-nation among our indigenous people. Everything possible was done to allow the viewer a true, unsparing vision of their current---and horrifying---existence at the hands of Anglos representing our government. The clothing and language displayed via sight and sound does not (and this is a rarity) reduce the people to generalized Hollywood Indians but depicts their unique identities as an American community. Better still, there is no simplistic anti-white diatribe to be found here. However exploitive Anglos like Red may be, Tom Black Bear is initially betrayed by a seemingly paternal tribesman, 'Blue Elk.'

People are people, for better or worse. And, as we learned long ago from Walt Disney's *(The) Light in the Forest*, there are good and bad on both sides.

Frederick Forrest (1936-) brought considerable charisma as well as acting ability to the role. Today, a complaint might be registered in retrospect that here again is a non-Indian actor in a part that might have been played by

A FAGIN OF THE LAST FRONTIER: Richard Widmark (left) plays the youth's 'mentor' though, like that memorable character from Charles Dickens' Oliver Twist, he hardly does so out of simple goodness, always interested in making a quick buck off the trusting innocent.

one of the then-rare Native performers in the movie business. Yet we ought to recall that this film is a product of its time; that worthy contemporary practice as to casting Indians as Indians was not yet in place. Noteworthy too is Widmark (1914-2008), one of the old-timers along with Kirk Douglas, Robert Mitchum, and Sterling Hayden who not only brought their talents but also career-long associations with past Oaters to such a latter-day work. With roles in *Backlash* (included here), *The Last Wagon* (1956), *The Law and Jack Wade* (1958), *The Alamo* (1960), and *How the West Was Won* (1962) to his credit, Widmark might well have been blessed with a Best Supporting Actor Oscar (even as fellow cowboy star Ben Johnson had been the previous year for his acting and presence as 'Sam the Lion' in *The Last Picture Show)* for this final go-around in theatrical films as the sneering hardcase no other actor played so effectively, with the possible exception only of Dan Duryea (SEE: *Along Came Jones*, also in this volume).

A FILMMAKER WITH A STRONG SOCIAL CONSCIENCE: Though *When the Legends Die* was the first film directed by Stuart Millar, previously he had played a pivotal role in bringing *Little Big Man* (1970) with Dustin Hoffman and Chief Dan George to the big screen.

96. WIND, THE (1928)
Rating: *****

CREDITS:

Victor Sjostrom, dir.; Frances Marian, scr.; Louis B. Mayer, pro.; John Arnold, cin.; Conrad A. Nervig, ed.; 1.33:1`; B&W; 95 min.; Metro-Goldwyn-Mayer.

CAST:

Lillian Gish *(Letty)*; Lars Hanson *(Lige)*; Montagu Love *(Roddy)*; Dorothy Cumming *(Cora)*; Edward Earle *(Beverly)*; William Orlamond *(Sourdough)*; Carmencita Johnson, Leon Janney, Billy Kent Snyder *(Cora's Children)*; Sam Appel *(A Vaquero)*; Si Jenks *(The Dancin' Fool)*; Cullen Johnson, Seesel Anne Johnson *(Children)*; Gus Leonard *(Old Timer)*

With the possible exception of *Greed* (Eric von Stroheim, (1924), *The Wind* rates as the greatest non-generic Western of the Silent Era. Perhaps the absence of cowboy conventions has to do with the centrality of a single (and singular) woman as to the project's history. Lillian Gish (1983-1993) abandoned her alcoholic father in childhood and, with sister Dororthy, entered Broadway's newly respectable live-theatre to earn a living. Success came swiftly for both; by 1900, they reigned as the beautiful/talented princesses of the midtown New York stage scene. By happenstance or fortuity, when the sisters likewise joined the budding East Coast film industry, they had the good fortune to meet and work with D.W. Griffith. A technical/aesthetic genius, here was the first great director/producer and avatar of the 'visual vocabulary' of this emergent medium of expression. Gish starred for Griffith in his superspectacular (if highly controversial) *The Birth of a Nation* (1915)

Douglas Brode

BiRTH OF THE PSYCHOLOGICAL WESTERN: Forsaking genre conventions, this film's avatar Lillian Gish set out to make the most honest Oater ever about a woman's actual existence on the prairie.

and, a year later, his catastrophic box-office disaster *Intolerance*, now considered a classic. Continuing to occasionally work with her mentor in such successful projects as *Broken Blossoms* (1919) and *Way Down East* (1920), Gish (like her close friend Mary Pickford) eventually struck out on her own. She became to the final decade of Silent Cinema what Bette Davis would proffer during the early sound era and, following that, Meryl Streep in modern movies: A great actress as well as box office draw. As such, Miss Lillian could dictate to such patriarchal figures as Louis B. Mayer, self-styled emperor at leading studio MGM, which projects she would appear in.

Meanwhile, Mayer (like other movie moguls) began to import foreign talent to class up his studio's product. Among the émigrés: Victor Sjostrom (1879-1960), the Swedish genius who had crafted one of the earliest phantasmagoric films to catch the world's attention, *The Phantom Carriage* (1921).

Aware of his splendid work, Gish picked Sjostrom to helm an important, imaginative 1926 version of Nathaniel Hawthorne's definitive American novel *The Scarlet Letter*. When the picture received critical accolades and audience appreciation, the team of Gish and Sjostrom were in a position to choose whatever they desired to do next. An avid reader, Gish had become fascinated with Dorothy Scarborough's portrait of a well-bred Virginia woman who travels to Texas. Naively believing in the myth of grand ranches and marvelous men, she instead finds herself trapped in a lonely Dust Bowl, populated by old sourdoughs and cynical ne-er-do-wells. Marrying the best of a bad lot (a likeable lout, nothing less or more), she exists all alone each day in a pathetic cabin while he's out on the prairie, farming. Worse still is the wind, which has been known to drive locals ... particularly women ... stark raving mad.

For the screenplay, Gish insisted on Frances Marion (1888-1973), one of those self-empowered women who had established herself as a top writer in Hollywood. Pre-production began in 1925, the same year that the fabled Scopes Monkey Trial brought the writings of Charles Darwin to the American public's attention. His theory of the evolution of our species owing to natural selection rather than spiritual conception shocked the world. One impact was to bring into question the Romantic vision that had developed during the 19th century: William Wordsworth and other poet/philosophers had insisted that nature was a good garden, where citified people could cast off their learned sophistication and come back in touch with the simpler life, finding "glory in the flower" and "splendor in the grass." Owing to a reluctant but inescapable acceptance of Darwinism, such transcendent thinking gave way to the darkness of Naturalism: The world around us is a jungle or, as Joseph Conrad put it, the heart of darkness. Nature does not allow civilized people to be reborn as beautiful creatures but turns them into hairy apes, as Eugene O'Neill wrote, succumbing to animal instincts. This had been the basis for Frank Norris' muckraking novel *McTeague* and the aforementioned von Stroheim film *Greed*, devised from it. Both book and film conclude with two men, who had hoped to achieve a higher level of life for themselves, dueling to death like a pair of doomed bugs in the hell on earth that is Death Valley.

The Wind, Gish sensed, provided the perfect female equivalent to such a work. A Victorian woman---embodying all the virtues of society, particularly her closely guarded virginity---is dragged down ever further into the muck, finally succumbing to rape by a monstrous neighbor. Most modern feminists do look back on the piece as ahead-of-its-time, for here (as compared to in Griffith's *Way Down East)* the female fights back, righteously killing the intruder. In this context, the Western ballad "bury me not, on the lone prairie!!" takes on a far more ominous tone than when accompanying the burial of Harry Carey Jr.'s sweet cowhand in *Red River* two decades later.

Here then is a Western-situated realistic horror film, allowing Sjostrom to pendulum-like swerve back and forth from depressing documentary-like imagery to symbolist visions of a Phantom Horse. The latter serves as a virtual incarnation of the endless wind as the Native People perceive it. Only one compromise interfered with the actress/auteur's concept: For the sake of box-office, the novel's ending (Letty, at wit's end, wanders off to die) was scrapped

FROM ROMANTIC ILLUSION TO STARK REALITY: The pioneer woman (Lillian Gish) rides behind her tall, dark and handsome man into the West; not long after, she finds herself attacked by a brute and, after killing him in self-defense, desperately attempting to bury the body.

to allow for a bittersweet reunion with her returning (now more enlightened) husband. While this destroys the essence of the intended Naturalist theme (for that, we ought to see Letty pass to dust in the same sort of situation McTeague did, overcome by the cruel wasteland), it in fact increases the degree to which modern (post-feminist) women are able to respond to the work. For Letty *survives*; the implication (intentional or not, if certainly implicit) then is that women are not the weaker sex, after all. Though for a full-blown feminist statement, she ought to (like 'Nora' in Henrik Ibsen's A Doll's House) walk away on her own rather than returning to her husband. All the same, even partial victories ought to be hailed during the emergence of a popular cinema that both reflected and altered the surrounding society.

A WOMAN OF SUBSTANCE: Lillian Gish was the first, and perhaps greatest of all time, actress (as well as 'star') in the history not only of Westerns ... but The Movies!

97. WOMAN OF THE TOWN, (THE) (1943)
Rating: ****

CREDITS:

George Archainbaud, dir.; Norm Houston, Aeneas MacKenzie, scr.; Lewis J Rachmill, Harry Sherman, pro.; Miklos Rozsa, mus.; Russell Harlan, cin.; Carroll Lewis, ed.; 1.37:1; B&W; 90 min.; United Artists.

Claire Trevor (*Dora Hand*); Albert Dekker *(Bat Masterson)*; Barry Sullivan (*King Kennedy*); Henry Hull (*Inky Wilkinson*); Marion Martin (*Daisy Davenport*); Porter Hall (*Mayor James* 'Dog' Kennedy); Percy Kilbride (*Rev. Samuel Small*); Beryl Wallace (*Louella O. Parsons*); Arthur Hohl (*Robert Wright*); Clem Bevans (*Buffalo Burns*); Teddi Sherman (*Fanny*); George Cleveland (*Jack Blackburn*); Russell Hicks (*Publisher*); Herbert Rawlinson *(Doc Sears)*; Marlene Mains (*Annie*); Dorothy Granger *(Belle)*;Charlie Foy (*Eddie Foy Sr.*); Hank Worden (*Barber*).

On the evening of October 4, 1878, Mayor James H. Kelly of Dodge City, KS learned that a young punk named William Kennedy was gunning for him. The spoiled brat son of a wealthy Texas rancher, Kennedy had met the most popular of Dodge's saloon girls, Dora Hand (1844-1878). A possible progenitor of that chestnut of a term "the whore with a heart of gold," Dora was known to attend church every Sunday, whatever her activities during the previous week. Kelly, previously a saloon owner (The Lady Gay), had fallen under her spell and asked for Dora's hand in marriage. Kennedy, outraged when Dora spurned his advances, threatened to shoot Kelly on sight. Town

THE FEMALE AS FOCAL CHARACTER: Though 'Dora Hand' appears in many movies and television shows about the taming of Dodge City, here is the only one in which she is not 'the female lead' opposite Bat Masterson or Wyatt Earp but the central figure in this fact-based story.

Deputy Marshall Wyatt Earp put Kelly under protective custody in the jail. Unaware of this, a drunken Kennedy slipped close to the window of Kelly's house at midnight. Spotting a shadowy figure inside, he fired, killing Dora Hand, she patiently waiting for her fiancée's return.

Within an hour, what may be the greatest single posse in the history of the West came together. Ford County Sheriff Bat Masterson (1853-1921) deputized Earp along with Big Bill Tilghman and Charles Bassett, the four eventually to become legendary as The Dodge City Peace Commission. When Kennedy attempted to flee, Masterson wounded him with a single shot from a Winchester. Learning from his captors that it was Dora Kennedy had killed, he fell to his knees and wept. Though tried for murder, Kennedy's lawyer (paid for by his wealthy father) managed to get the youth off on a technicality. As it had been Kelly whom Kennedy hoped to kill, and the lesser charge of manslaughter had not been entered as a possible verdict, Kennedy walked free.

Those are the bare facts. Like many tales from The Queen of the Cowtowns, the ballad of Dora Hand has been told several times by Hollywood. The first, and by far most impressive, is this virtually forgotten picture, put together by veterans of the Hopalong Cassidy kiddie-films. Producer Sherman,

QUICK ON THE DRAW: Albert Dekker, in a rare heroic role, gets the drop on a young squirt (Barry Sullivan, right) while Claire Trevor looks on.

wondering if the team might stretch their talents and come up with a piece that would appeal to a larger, broader audience, settled on this curious yarn, attempting a delicate balance between fact and fiction. While most elements of a generic Western are present (gunfights, saloon brawls, hard riding, etc.), likewise present are key elements, however true to the history of the Wild West, that are sadly overlooked in most traditional Oaters.

Notably, this is the only film that depicts Masterson's later career as a New York newspaperman. In the opening, an elderly Bat is seen in his office circa 1919, as (then)-young gossip columnist Louella Parsons stops by to chat with the sportswriter. That much is true. Then, in a moment created by Sherman's writers, Parsons wonders why Bat no longer has his gun 'from the old days.' Melancholy, he cannot answer. The film then flashes back to relate the full story. To tell the tale within tight limitations of time and budget, Earp is mentioned once but never seen. Rather than duly elected county sheriff, Masterson here has what was in fact Earp's job. Conforming to the dictates of Hollywood romance, it is Masterson, not Kelly, who falls for Dora. Also, she is collapsed into another historical figure, Molly Brennan, while Kennedy is combined with Sergeant King. Several years earlier, in Sweetwater TX, young Masterson wooed saloon girl Molly, she involved with the brutish King, who came looking for Bat. Fortunately, Earp had earlier mentored his younger friend on gunfighting. Masterson managed to kill King while taking a slug in the leg that caused him to walk with a cane afterwards. Molly, caught in the crossfire, died.

Whether Bat was in love with her or merely enjoying that woman's company is not known. But the notion of him tossing his gun in the grave with Molly (much less Dora's, whom he knew only by way of Kelly), is pure fiction. Still, by merging the separate incidents in Masterson's life, the writers (one a direct descendant of Texas' Sam Houston) transformed history into the realm of legend. Other key elements set *Woman* . . . apart from generic conventions of the time. While most feature only dancing girls in saloons, here we witness a comedy performance by the dapper Eddie Foy (1956-1928), a favorite on the Western show biz circuit. He is played by one of Foy's now grown

REAL AND 'REEL': William Bartley Masterson in the flesh; Albert Dekker as the pistolero.

children; in two previous films, *Frontier Marshal* (1939) and *Lillian Russell* (1940), Senior had been portrayed by another son, Eddie Foy Jr. Dekker (1905-1968), more a character actor than a leading man, proved a fine choice for Bat. No question, though, that the spotlight is on the female lead. Claire Trevor (1910-2000) had appeared opposite John Wayne in *Stagecoach* and the under-appreciated Eastern-Western *Alleghany Uprising* (both 1939). Eventually, she would win the Best Supporting Actress Oscar for her memorable work in the John Huston gangster classic *Key Largo* (1948), opposite Humphrey Bogart and Edward G. Robinson. In truth, Trevor might well have received a Best Actress statuette for her memorable performance in this impressive overlooked Oater.

98. WONDERFUL COUNTRY, THE (1959)
Rating: ****

CREDITS:

Robert Parrish, dir.; Robert Ardrey, scr.; Robert Mitchum, Chester Erskine, pro.; Alex North, mus.; Floyd Crosby, cin.; Michael Luciano, ed.; 1.66:1; C; C; 98 min.; United Artists.

CAST:

Robert Mitchum (*Martin Brady*); Julie London (*Helen Colton*); Gary Merrill (*Maj. Stark Colton*); Pedro Armanderiz (*Governor Castro*); Albert Dekker *(Capt. Rucker, Texas Rangers)*; Jack Oakie (*Travis Hyte*); Charles McGraw (*Dr. Herbert J. Stovall*); Leroy 'Satchel' Paige *(Sgt. Tobe Sutton)*: Anthony Caruso (*Santiago Santos*); Mike Kellin (*Pancho Gil*); Victor Manuel Mendoza *(Gen. Marcos Castro)*; Jay Novello (*Diego*); John Banner *(Ben Sterner)*; Max Slaten (*Chico*); Tom Lea (*Mr. Peebles*).

The film's anti-hero,' Martin Brady,' is an outcast: Uncertain whether his loyalties are to the country in which he lives (Mexico) as a hired gun, or the one (the U.S.) where he was born. However long Brady has put off a necessary resolution, he finds himself drawn into a situation that will determine who and what he truly is, once and for all. Brady travels northward on his only meaningful possession, a magnificent horse, on orders from the governor of a south of the border province. His mission: Secure a shipload of rifles that will prove invaluable as the area is torn apart by revolutions, leading to virtual brother-vs.-brother hostilities. Once in Texas, however, Brady

BIRTH OF THE NOUVEAUX WESTERN: Robert Mitchum here set the pace for Clint Eastwood and other serape-wearing Anglos who move back and forth between the west's various ethnicities.

is approached by army officer 'Colton' and Texas Ranger 'Rucker' to betray his long-term mentor. As an Anglo who fluently speaks Spanish, Brady is their perfect choice to discover whether a difficult alliance may be established between the two hostile governments, allowing Mexico and the U.S. to 'eliminate' Apaches raiding both sides of the Rio Grande.

The company of troopers stationed nearby is the 9th Cavalry; aka, The Buffalo Soldiers, their presence in the narrative allowing this period-piece to address contemporary issues. The 1950s witnessed a mainstreaming of our Civil Rights Movement in everyday discourse and our films, Westerns included. A year later, John Ford released *Sergeant Rutledge* (1960) with Woody Strode as an African American trooper. A parallel role is played here by 'The Great' Satchel (Leroy) Paige (1906-1982), lauded Olympian athlete. Significant too: Robert Mitchum (1917-1997) took a cue from his former (*Out of the Past*) and future (*The Way West*) co-star Kirk Douglas (who had established his own development company, Bryna) by creating P.R.M. Prods. Texas-born Tom Lea's novel deeply touched Mitchum, the macho man with melancholy eyes, who wanted his film to look, feel, and play differently from any previous or contemporary Western. Here, then, we experience Texas and Mexico as two unique worlds, separated by a long if not wide body of water, the two lands so near geographically yet so far apart culturally.

Locations in Durango and Guanajuato, Mexico, rarely employed before *Wonderful Country*, allowed for a visual sense of historicity, even if the focal story is fictional. These are not the scaled down permanent set buildings employed by studios to represent specific locales but the originals. Here is one of several American-financed films (another is Robert Aldrich's *Vera Cruz*, 1954) which set the pace for a new breed of Western that would emerge during the following decade, beginning with John Sturges' *The Magnificent Seven* (1960). Thereafter, Sergio Leone's famous Spaghetti Westerns would follow suit. Mitchum's character, iconically remote, offers a predecessor of Clint Eastwood and Charles Bronson in *The Good, The Bad, and the Ugly* and *Once Upon a Time in the West*. Brady even dons a serape

TORN BETWEEN TWO CULTURES: Robert Mitchum's anti-hero is seduced by a variety of Anglos (from left, Gary Merrill, Julie London, Albert Dekker) to abandon his South of the Border lifestyle and once again integrate into their Texas society.

during the film's final sequence, as would Marlon Brando in the upcoming *One Eyed Jacks* (1961).

Director Robert Parrish (1916-1995) did not have a significant history with the genre. However, he had helmed a World War II adventure film, *The Purple Plain* (1954), with Gregory Peck as a downed World War II pilot searching for some sign of civilization. That realistic thriller was shot in a then innovative aesthetic featuring low-key pastels rather than the ultra-bright and heightened colors so popular at the time. Mitchum sensed this to be precisely what he required if his project were to project a dream-like aura. Despite the notable authenticity of the Mexican lifestyle seen on the sidelines of the primary story (including dances and celebrations by survivors of the country's Native population, an approach Sturges would borrow for *Seven* the following year), a hint of other-worldliness settles in during the first sequences and continues throughout. Thereafter, the tale bounces back and forth across the border, each nation different from the other, conveying an 'apart-from-everyday-life' appearance.

HOLLYWOOD'S FIRST BUFFALO SOLDIER: A year and a half before Woody Strode embodied the title character in John Ford's *Sergeant Rutledge*, Leroi 'Sachel' Paige paved the way for more inclusionary images of African Americans in Western movies.

Important, too, is that Mitchum and Parrish had a history: the latter assumed direction of the contemporary Western *The Lusty Men* (1952) starring Mitchum when assigned director Nicholas Ray proved unable to work. Mitchum had also been impressed by Parrish's only other Western, *Saddle the Wind*, the previous year. That movie's psychological approach taken toward characters was precisely what the actor/avatar required. For Brady, however stoic and self-reliant he may appear, suffers from an identity crisis of the type that haunted so many leading characters in the psychological dramas, whether set in modern terms or various eras of history, prevalent during the 1950s.

Which will win out? Brady's Anglo heredity or, as we say today, DNA? Perhaps the Latin environment that shaped him? This can only be determined by a final decision as to which side of the Rio Grande he will choose to walk for the remainder of his life. If Brady decides to head north, he must abandon all associations with Latin culture---his sombrero and serape, his unique gun, even his beloved black stallion---to re-embrace a long-lost vision of himself. In the final moments, Brady's fate is determined for him by forces beyond his, or any man's, ability to control. As in Greek tragedy, any efforts to determine his own fate dissolve as a destiny that appears reserved especially for him takes its unexpected but, as we grasp, necessary course.

A BOLD FIGURE ALWAYS: Whether playing good or bad guys, or more complex parts (including Pancho Villa himself in several Mexican lensed features), Pedro Armendariz created onscreen characters who demand attention and respect.

99. YELLOWSTONE KELLY (1959)
Rating: ****

CREDITS:

Gordon Douglas, dir.; Burt Kennedy, scr.; Jack Warner, pro.; Howard Jackson, mus.; Carl E. Guthrie, cin.; William H. Zeigler, ed.; 1.37:1; C; 91 min.; Warner Bros.

CAST:

Clint Walker (*Luther Kelly*); Edd (Edward) Byrnes (*Anse Harper*); John Russell (*Gall*); Ray Danton (*Savapi*); Andra Martin (*Wahleeah*); Claude Akins (*Sergeant*); Rhodes Reason (*Maj. Towns*); Gary Vinson (*The Lieutenant*); Warren Oates (*The Corporal*); George American Horse, Chris Willow Bird, Raven Grey Eagle (*Lakota Warriors*); David Armstrong (*Cavalryman*); Chief Yowlachie (*Medicine Man).*

    Previous to the Oscar winning Leonardo DiCaprio vehicle *The Revenant* (2015), films about mountain men were few and far between. Exceptions include *Across the Wide Missouri* (1952), *The Last Frontier* (1955), "The Saga of Andy Burnett" on ABC's *Disneyland* (1957-58), *Jeremiah Johnson* (1972), *The Life and Times of Grizzly Adams* (1977), and *The Mountain Men* (1980). Otherwise, the Rockies' "Hivernant," as he was known on the frontier, would more often be portrayed as a sidekick to a conventional clean-cut (and idealized) hero. That was the case with grizzled Ward Bond and handsome Jon Hall in *Kit Carson* (1940). But this above-average Oater from Warner's (originally to have been directed by John Ford, starring John Wayne) captures

REAL AND 'REEL': Luther Kelly, the last mountain man; Clint "Cheyenne" Walker portraying that frontiersman in a superior B+ Western.

several key elements of the trapper's generalized lifestyle, and a few poignant elements from the reality of Luther Kelly (1849-1928). Though he had been born long after the Golden Age of the Mountain Man (1825-1840), missing out on the great annual Rendezvous that others like Jim Bridger and Bill Williams had experienced, Kelly did effectively represent the last of his breed--the lone individual who continued to bring back beaver skins to isolated forts, eking out a living at a once financially rewarding trade.

In Burt Kennedy's (1922-2001) script, the seasoned frontiersman (Clint Walker, 1927-2018) reluctantly agrees to take a greenhorn, 'Anse Harper,' along as handyman and cook. Little trapping is actually portrayed; mostly, the drama takes place in the cabin where the two care for (while each falls in love with) a Shoshone princess. The perfect beauty (this is Hollywood, not history!) escaped from the Sioux and hopes to return to her people. Here is popular fiction, then, drawn from Missouri author Clay Fisher's (Heck Allen, 1891-1912) paperback novel. Though Warner's marketed this as an action-oriented Western for fans of Walker's popular TV show *Cheyenne* (1955-63), the impressively staged big battle between cavalrymen and Lakota takes a backseat to a highly erotic tale of two men and a female stuck in a frozen-over cabin. Indeed, before the arrival of 'Wahleeah,' Gordon Douglas' camera angles suggest a sense of homoerotic attraction between the male bunkmates. This carries on a tradition that can be traced back to *The Outlaw* (1943), *Red River* (1948), *The Big Sky* (1952), and shortly *Ride the High Country* (1962) before *Brokeback Mountain* (2005) brought such possibilities out of the celluloid closet.

Several elements of the latter mountain man lifestyle are accurately portrayed. When the fur companies found it no longer economical to have their representatives meet the trappers at some halfway point between the wilderness and civilization (such a weeklong rendezvous is beautifully staged in *Across the Wide Missouri* and the second and third episodes of TV's *Centennial* (1978-79), the abject loneliness of a latter-day mountain man's existence is strikingly communicated. It's necessary to head down to some fort and trade beaver skins for food, weapons, alcohol, and tobacco. Also, Luther here takes up scouting for the army (the film takes place several months after 1876's Battle of the Little Big Horn) as did many others when the demand for fur

THE NATIVE AMERICAN WOMAN AS SEX SYMBOL: Andra Martin was one of many gorgeous non-Indian Hollywood starlets who at the very least picked up where Cecil B. DeMille's *The Squaw Man* had left off, this and other films insisting on the healthiness of inter-racial marriage.

gradually diminished owing to the new popularity of silk fashions in the east. Also, the notion of a revenant enjoying a long-lasting understanding with a Native American nation that allowed him to trap in their lands, whereas other Anglos who drifted in might be killed, is indeed historical as to the mountain man/Native American relationship.

Though Walker would never become the next Wayne, as many predicted at the time, he did appear in several Westerns (*Fort Dobbs*, 1958; *Night of the Grizzly*, 1966; *More Dead than Alive,* 1969). When the conventional Hollywood "B" Western all but disappeared, Walker attempted a return to TV with *Kodiak* (1974); unfortunately, the show was not a hit. Today, he's best remembered for the role of Native American 'Posey' in *The Dirty Dozen*. Co-star John Russell (1921-1991), here cast as the historical chief Gaul, had

HERE'S TO THE 'HIVERNANTS': Clint Walker and Edd 'Kookie' Byrnes (of TV's 77 *Sunset Strip*) as a pair of mountain men spending a long winter in the Rocky Mountains; rumors persist that early on in production, John Wayne and Elvis Presley were approached to play these parts.

performed in diverse Westerns including *Yellow Sky* (1948) and *The Jubilee Trail* (1954), the latter for Herbert J. Yates at Republic. Also, as a factual character, Almeron Dickinson, in that producer's big budget Alamo epic *The Last Command* (1955). Like Walker, he would enjoy TV stardom as the lead in the WB Western *Lawman*, playing a Wyatt Earp-type no-nonsense character, 'Dan Troop.' His most famous film roles were as memorable villains in *Rio Bravo* (1979) and *Pale Rider* (1985). The latter brought him belated critical attention as a striking and charismatic performer. Far too late, though, to usher in the considerably loftier film career he ought to have enjoyed.

Claude Akins (1926-1994) would often play in Westerns including *Joe Dakota* and *The Lonely Man*, both 1957; in *Return of the Seven* (1966), he and his co-star here, Warren Oates, would be reunited as saddle pals. Ray Danton (1931-1992) had previously played an evil Lakota who goes up against the eponymous hero (Victor Mature) in *Chief Crazy Horse* (1955). He too would appear on a WB Western (make that 'Northern'), *The Alaskans* (1959-1960). Director Douglas (1907-1993), a reliable journeyman, turned out such solid genre pieces as *The Great Missouri Raid* (1951) and *The Big Land* (1957). With *Yellowstone Kelly*, Douglas outdid himself, the film's majestic sweep recalling classics by John Ford. Ultimately, though, the director hit an all-time low with his poorly conceived remake of one of Ford's classics, the dismal 1966 version of *Stagecoach*.

THE B+ WESTERN MEETS THE SEXUAL REVOLUTION: Even as America prepared to enter the Swingin' Sixties, old-time Oaters were infused with a strong dose of eroticism.

100. YOUNG LAND, THE (1957/1959)
Rating: **** ½

CREDITS:

Ted Tetzloff, dir.; Norman S. Hall, John Reese, scr.; Pat Ford, Lowell J. Farrell, pro.; Dimitri Tiomkin, mus.; Henry Sharp, Winton C. Hoch; C; 89 min.; C.V. Whitney Prods/Columbia Pictures.

CAST:

Patrick Wayne (*Sheriff Jim Ellison*); Yvonne Craig (*Elena de la Madrid*); Dennis Hopper *(Hatfield Carnes)*; Dan O'Herlihy (*Judge Millard Isham*); Roberto De La Madrid (*Don Roberto de la Madrid*); Cliff Ketchum (*Marshal Ben Stroud*); Pedro Gonzales-Gonzales (*Santiago*); Ed Sweeney (*Sully*); John Quijada (*Lead Vaquero*); Tom Tiner (*Court Clerk Charlie Higgins*); Miguel Camacho (*Miguel*); Carlos Romero (*Francisco Quiroga*); Richard Alexander (*Lead Juror*); Eddie Juarequi (*A Drifter*); The Mariachis Los Reyes De Chapala (*Mariachis*).

After sitting on the shelf for nearly two years, *Young Land* was briefly, belatedly released to second-string theatres on a double bill with a minor monster movie late in 1959. C.V Whitney (1899-1992) had hoped to interest Walt Disney in releasing the medium-budget film. When negotiations broke down, Whitney (this one of only three films produced by his company, the first being John Ford's *The Searchers* a year earlier) went instead with Columbia. That company unceremoniously tossed *Young Land* onto the marketplace as if it were one more of run of the mill Oater. Kids who headed for the local Rialto considered it disappointing (with but two brief shootouts and one half-hearted fistfight) in comparison to more conventional popcorn Westerns. In retrospect, what seemed to be the work's weakness is the essence of this meaningful movie's considerable worth.

Based (albeit loosely) on an actual incident, the tale takes place in a small, isolated California community in 1848, a decisive moment in history. The Mexican American War had only recently ended. Though statehood appeared as a hope on the horizon, California remained a U.S. territory. Its citizenry included the Native People (Quechon, Yuman, Miwok, Yurok, and Modoc), Mestizos (a mixed race of varied Indian nations and poor Spanish settlers), pureblood Spanish (holders of land grants), and Anglo Americans of all classes who poured into the pre-Gold Rush lands, including everything from cowboys and business-people to loafers and drunkards. One of the latter, here called 'Hanfield Carnes,' purposefully picked a fight with an off-duty Vaquero

HOLLYWOOD DISCOVERS THE YOUTH MARKET: Teenagers were the target audience for this unappreciated Oater featuring Pat(rick) (son of The Duke) Wayne and Yvonne Craig, who would embody Batgirl on ABC TV in the late-1960s; here was one more Civil Rights Western that came out in favor of inter-racial marriage as the true American 'melting pot' way.

in a cantina, bullying the Mexican-American into drawing first. Carnes' initial bullet wounded the hapless victim. If the incident had ended there, Carnes would likely have been cleared on the highly questionable grounds of self-defense. But the lout fired two more shots, the second killing his victim. A federal judge and territorial marshal were called in to conduct the trial and hopefully insure that the results were fair. The United States government had, in the Treaty of Guadalupe Hidalgo, guaranteed that all people of Spanish descent in California must be treated as 'equal under the law.' Arriving to relieve a young, inexperienced sheriff (Jim), judge and Lawman instructed the jury that it must take into account the concept of malice aforethought. Could the third/fatal shot possibly be justified?

A jury composed of seven Anglos and five Latinos found themselves under pressure. If the Anglo gunslinger were to be turned free, the Latin population, aware that America's "promise" of equality carried no weight, would likely riot in the streets. But if this teenage killer---played by Dennis Hopper (1936-2010), who had portrayed 'Billy Bonney' on TV's *Sugarfoot* and 'Billy Clanton' in *Gunfight at the O.K. Corral*, both 1957)--were to be declared guilty and hang, his redneck saddle pals might storm the jail. Not only the verdict, then, but the precise sentencing had explosive consequences for the future of Anglo/Latin relationships.

Clearly, this 'little' film was ahead of its time in dealing with issues that still haunt us today. The production team was strictly second-string. Cinematographer turned director Ted Tetzloff (1903-1985) had mostly been associated with minor league entertainments such as *Son of Sinbad* (1955). Also, there are limitations to the social consciousness on view here. Notably, the role of 'Santiago,' a goofy Mexican deputy unable to count beyond the number of fingers on his hands. He's played by Pedro Gonzales-Gonzales (1925-2006), who fashioned a career out of such caricatures in more famous films including *Rio Bravo* (1959). Despite the embodiment of such a now maddening cliché, Santiago is devoted to the general cause of peaceful coexistence via law and order. All other people of color on view here are, happily, portrayed as more sophisticated and enlightened than the local Whites on view.

SELL IT WITH SEX: Dennis Hopper, in one more of his juvenile delinquent roles, attacks Yvonne Craig while Pat Wayne hurries to the rescue: however titillating, nothing even remotely like this occurs in *The Young Land.*

Also ahead of its time is the movie's anti-gun message. Pat Wayne's young sheriff does not wear a handgun at any time in the film. Like many historical local peace officers, he prefers to go the British Bobbie route. If he carries no weapon, then no one in his right mind would dare shoot him for fear of being charged with cold-blooded murder. Such an actual preference for avoiding gunplay as to local lawmakers is likewise on view in two key 'Wyatt Earp Westerns,' Ford's *My Darling Clementine* with Henry Fonda and John Sturges' *Gunfight at the O.K. Corral* starring Burt Lancaster. However much the convention of the two-gun sheriff may dominate the genre, rare films like *The Young Land* come closer to the truth. Here, when the jailed gun-slick sarcastically makes fun of the hero for going unarmed, Wayne's (1939-) character retorts: "If *you* hadn't carried one, you wouldn't be *here* now," referring to the murder charge.

At the end, our young hero does indeed shoot it out with the killer, though only after retiring to the office where he picks up a weapon after receiving a death threat from the crazed kid. Also admirable: as the Anglo lawman becomes engaged to the daughter of a local Spanish landowner, the film ends with a positive portrayal of inter-racial marriage. Once more, a tale set in the past is presented in the temporal 'now' to offer an anti-racist message.

THE CLICHE THAT WOULD NOT GO AWAY: Despite the overall sense of modern enlightenment to this film, the stereotype of a Mexican-American as comically dimwitted does reappear; other than that lapse, however, he (and other Latins) are all portrayed in a positive manner.

101. ZORRO'S BLACK WHIP (1944)
Rating: *** ½

CREDITS:

Spencer Gordon Bennett, Wallace Grissett, dir.; Basil Dickey, Jesse Duffy, Grant Nelson, Joseph F. Poland, scr.; Ronald Davidson, pro.; Joseph Dubin, mus.; Bud Thackery, cin.; Cliff Bell (Sr.), Harold Minter, ed.; 1.37:1; B&W; 211 min./12 chapters; Republic Pictures.

CAST:

Linda Sterling (aka 'Sterling') (*Barbara Meredith*); George J. Lewis (*Vic Gordon*); Lucien Littlefield (*Tenpoint Jackson*); Francis McDonald (*Dan Hammond*); Hal Taliaferro (*Baxter*); John Merton (*Ed Harris*); John Hamilton (*Mr. Walsh*); Tom Chatterton (*Crescent City Councilman*); Jack Kirk (*Marshal Wetherby*); Jay Kirby (*Randolph Meredith*); Si Jenks (*Zeke Hayden*); Stanley Price (*Hedges*); Tom Steele (*Ed*); Duke Green (*Evans*); Dale Van Sickel (*Karl*); Roy Brent (*Wagner*); Robert J. Wilke (*Outlaw*).

When nostalgia buffs consider the long, rich history of the movie serial, they conclude that the focus is more often than not on adventure tales of bold men. These chapter plays were released during the Great Depression for kiddie audiences that attended early Saturday morning screenings. Most were Westerns or Science Fiction adventures including *Flash Gordon* and *The Phantom Empire* (1935) starring Gene Autry. As to womenfolk, they were either damsels in distress or double-dealing outlaw queens.

WHO SAYS "IT'S A MAN'S WORLD?" Queen of the Cliffhangers, Linda Sterling proved herself equally capable as an Amazonian woman of the lost jungle and, here, as a no-nonsense avenger in ... Idaho?

Reach back further, though, to note that the first silent serials focused on bold New Woman protoptypes: *What Happened to Mary (1912)* with Mary Fuller, *The Hazards of Helen* (1914; Helen Holmes) and, most popular of all, *The Perils of Pauline* (1914; Pearl White). Lest we forget, commercial films premiered in 1901, the year of Queen Victoria's death. Passing with her was the 19th century's traditionalist/conservative notion of women's roles in society. Suffragists made an impression, and even before Hollywood emerged as a geographical center for films circa 1915, East Coast moviemakers were playing to female viewers (the target audience for matinees) with strong ladies in leading roles. If such an emphasis disappeared when the daring Roaring Twenties gave way to the depressing Dust Bowl era, women depicted again as wives and mothers, the pendulum would swing once more during the post-war years. Then, American women once more asserted themselves ... in real life, and in the movies that influence and reflect our attitudes during any single period.

At this point, the crowning title of 'Queen of the Cliffhangers' went to Linda Sterling (1921-1997). Trained in dance and serious acting technique in Long Beach CA, she found work modelling fashions live and in magazines. Executives at Republic signed the beauty to a long-term contract in 1944. Though Sterling initially played demure leading ladies in that company's "B" Westerns (*Sheriff of Sundown* and *Santa Fe Saddlemates*, both 1944), her most memorable roles feature her as a seemingly demure lady who slips off to round up those bad guys the good men can't handle. Sterling's first such outing had her pursuing bad Anglo killers of elephants (for their tusks) in *(The) Tiger Woman* (1944). The following year, she brought such a superhero to the old west in *Zorro's Black Whip*.

The title aside, Linda's character is never referred to by that name. Johnston McCauley's (1883-1958) fictional male avenger of old Los Angeles had been a popular culture mainstay since his first appearance in pulp literature in a 1919 short story. In 1940, 20th Century-Fox gambled on an "A" film, *The Mark of Zorro* starring superstar Tyrone Power. When this clicked with audiences, Poverty Row film companies set out to exploit the phenomenon. Owing to the peculiarities of copyright law, the 'Zorro' moniker could not be applied to a character within the film that did not have McCauley's blessing but was acceptable for a title. This stunt-laden female Zorro adventure features a woman who wears the famous black outfit and wields not only fast gun but a mean whip.

To further distance themselves from anything that might incur a lawsuit, the storyline was shifted from pre-Anglo California to, of all places, Idaho. This led to an interesting (and indeed historical) situation. In the year 1889, that territory had the possibility of becoming a state. While the common men and women dearly hope for this, particularly military protection, economic assurances, and advanced educational possibilities that come with such status, statehood was vehemently opposed by rugged individualists who had for decades all but owned the territory. Knowing that the area's joining the union would bring in U.S. Marshals, their era of power based on the rawest form of capitalism swiftly concluding, they banded together to try and squash

TWO SIDES OF A FEMALE HERO: When not tangling with the badguys, this "Lady Zorro" enjoys a night of quiet romance.

such an arrangement. When the heroine's brother tries to oppose their plans, he is killed. At that point, elegant 'Barbara' determines to live a double life.

However much this may have been intended as a mere plot device, the narrative (however inadvertently) creates a feminist fable. One reason Barbara is not captured or even suspected owes to longstanding male prejudices. As one of the bad-guys says: "The Black Whip's *got* to be a man! He's outshot outrode us, and outfought us, stopped us at every turn!" Never underestimate the powers of a woman. Or, for that matter, her ruthlessness. At one point, this Zorro facsimile forces a pair of bad men to the end of a cliff by brutly wielding her black leather whip. Each throws up his hands in gestures of surrender, hoping to be taken alive. No way! Barbara snaps her weapon at the s of one, then the other, forcing them to fall to their deaths. *No mercy.* A from the look in Sterling's eyes, her character appears to enjoy taking live long as they are among the no-account outlawry. It's often said that ma am culture is simply pop culture plus time. Though no good girl would per ch acts during the 1940s, a decade later Donna Reed would carry a wh *lash* while Joan Crawford donned a similar black outfit in *Johnny Guitar* Here is the original junk movie (that meant in a non-judgmental manner) h paved the way.

A NEW TWIST ON THE OLD 'RESCUE MYTH': Whereas in most cliffhangers a male hero must save the girl in bondage, here 'Barbara' appears to accomplish the freedom as her own alter ego!

About The Author

DOUGLAS BRODE is widely recognized as one of the world's leading experts on the Hollywood Western. His previous books on this subject include *The 100 Greatest Western Movies of All Time, Dream West: Politics and Religion in Cowboy Movies, Shooting Stars of the Small Screen: Encyclopedia of TV Western Actors, 1946-Present, John Wayne's Way: Life Lessons from the Duke*, and *The Twenty-First-Century Western: New Riders of the Cinematic Stage*. Brode has contributed articles to such publications as *True West, Cineaste, American Cowboy*, and *Wild West*, and lectured on The Western at numerous venues including the Buffalo Bill History Center in Cody, Wyoming. Brode also authored two acclaimed graphic novels with Western themes, *Yellow Rose of Texas: The Myth of Emily Morgan* and *Sand*. Brode's 50-something other books include novels as well as in-depth studies of cinema history. In 2016, Brode joined Turner Classic Movies' Ben Mankiewicz and writer/director Seth MacFarland (*A Million Ways to Die in the West*) as co-host of *The Cowboy*, a two-part TV documentary that continues to play. Over the years, Brode has been employed as a screenwriter, playwright, radio announcer, film and theatre critic, TV talk show host, multi-award-winning college and university professor, and multi-award-winning journalist.

www.ingramcontent.com/pod-product-compliance
Lightning Source LLC
Chambersburg PA
CBHW060748230426
43667CB00010B/1479